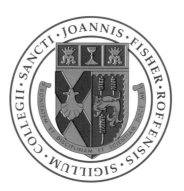

MARKETING HERITAGE

MARKETING HERITAGE

Archaeology and the
Consumption of the Past

EDITED BY
YORKE ROWAN & UZI BARAM

ALTAMIRA PRESS
A Division of Rowman & Littlefield Publishers, Inc.
Walnut Creek • Lanham • New York • Toronto • Oxford

ALTAMIRA PRESS
A division of Rowman & Littlefield Publishers, Inc.
1630 North Main Street, #367
Walnut Creek, California 94596
www.altamirapress.com

Rowman & Littlefield Publishers, Inc.
A wholly owned subsidary of The Rowman & Littlefield Publishing Group, Inc.
4501 Forbes Boulevard, Suite 200
Lanham, Maryland 20706

PO Box 317
Oxford
OX2 9RU, UK

British Library Cataloguing in Publication Information Available

Library of Congress Cataloging-in-Publication Data

Marketing heritage : archaeology and the consumption of the past / edited
by Yorke Rowan and Uzi Baram.
     p. cm.
Includes bibliographical references and index.
     ISBN 0-7591-0341-0 (hardcover : alk.paper) — ISBN 0-7591-0342-9
(pbk. : alk. paper)
     1. Cultural property—Protection. 2. Heritage tourism. 3. Excavations
(Archaeology)—Interpretive programs. 4. Archaeology—Economic aspects.
5. Historic preservation. I. Rowan, Yorke M. II. Baram, Uzi, 1964–

     CC135.M325 2004
     338.4'791—dc22   2003018553

Printed in the United States of America

♾™ The paper used in this publication meets the minimum requirements of American
National Standard for Information Sciences—Permanence of Paper for Printed Library
Materials, ANSI/NISO Z39.48-1992.

CONTENTS

Part III: The Past as Commodity

Part IV: Archaeology in the Global Age

Part V: Representing the Past

Preface

EIGHTEEN KILOMETERS WEST of the Israeli Negev city of Beersheva lies the Chalcolithic site of Shiqmim. Excavated by Thomas E. Levy and the late David Alon from 1979 to 1993, the site provides a fantastic view of Chalcolithic (4500–3500 B.C.E.) life along the Wadi Beersheva. Underground tunnels, house foundations, human burials, copper artifacts, ivory ornaments, and a wealth of other items have been uncovered. Levy has argued persuasively for a model of chiefdom for this place and its time period.

One cannot visit Shiqmim easily. The site is in a restricted military zone and is far from any roads. However, the Israel Museum in Jerusalem displays some of its artifacts. Numerous publications discuss the site, excavations, and cultural history. A web page based at the Department of Anthropology of University of California, San Diego, is an accessible means of learning about and seeing the site. Shiqmim is an important archaeological site; the architecture and artifacts are engaging; the desert is simply beautiful.

We both excavated at Shiqmim. Coincidentally, so did three other contributors to this volume (Morag Kersel, Jonathan Golden, and Joel Bauman). We both use Shiqmim in our teaching. Shiqmim provides wonderful stories for teaching undergraduate anthropology—the dramatic landscape, the hardships of excavating far from electricity, water, and information outlets. And the rich array of material culture offers adventure, science, and a portal to the past. When either of us is asked about our most interesting excavations, as happens often to archaeologists, Shiqmim is usually the story told. Yet there is no marketing of Shiqmim for tourists by the state of Israel.

Based on our experiences at Shiqmim, and with a contrast to the nearby actively promoted sites like Masada and Petra in mind, we wrestled with how ancient periods and sites are selected and prioritized for promotion and consumption, by the state, by the academy, by individuals. Discussions with colleagues underscored a commonality across continents—that "the past" was becoming more than a concept useful for provoking political action and reaction, but a resource that could be utilized for widening the profit margin for various endeavors. These conversations concerning the growing phenomenon of marketing archaeological heritage continued through the last decade and eventually culminated in a session at the American Anthropology Association meetings in 2001, organized by Rowan and Jonathan Golden. All of the contributors to this volume noticed in one way or another the ways in which archaeology and heritage are becoming commodities in the marketplace. It's a global phenomenon and we tried to draw on examples from all areas of the world in order to examine this trend.

We thank all of the contributors for their work on the case studies and for helping integrate the concerns in a single volume. We would also like to acknowledge the efforts of David Ilan, Art Keene, Alfredo Minetti, and K. Anne Pyburn, who helped launch the project. Mitch Allen of AltaMira Press was supportive in our endeavor, providing enthusiasm and great suggestions.

Uzi Baram acknowledges New College for travel grants to the Middle East. He thanks the New College students who attended the session and returned to campus excited about the issues presented. Baram thanks Amy Reid, who was willing to visit archaeological sites in Israel during what we supposed to be a vacation, and listen to the concerns and analysis.

Yorke Rowan thanks Pennsylvania State University–Erie for funding to attend the American Anthropological Association meetings in Washington, D.C. He also thanks the Department of Anthropology at the National Museum of Natural History, Smithsonian Institution, where much of the research and work on this volume occurred.

INTRODUCTION   I

Archaeology after Nationalism: Globalization and the Consumption of the Past

I

UZI BARAM AND YORKE ROWAN

Archaeology in the Contemporary World

THE POLITICAL IMPLICATIONS OF interpreting and presenting the past continue to challenge archaeologists and complicate archaeology. Trigger's (1984) seminal work provided an initial consideration of the intersection of archaeology and politics, opening up terminology and case studies of archaeologies that support imperialism, colonialism, and nationalism. Silberman (1989, 1995), Arnold (1990), Gathercole and Lowenthal (1990), Kohl and Fawcett (1995), Trigger (1995), Patterson (1995), Díaz-Andreu and Champion (1996), and Meskell (1998), among others, expanded on the intersection of nationalism and contemporary archaeology.

These studies delineate how twentieth-century states employed archaeology for fostering national identity, in terms of presenting a positive portrayal of the nation and obscuring other histories that exist within the state boundaries (Trigger 1984). The point has been emphasized for the Middle East, where Trigger (1984) and Silberman (1989) have shown that archaeology is political and is employed to construct nationalist themes for the past. Archaeology, as the study of the past, is dominated by attempts by varied nations to "resurrect their greatness in the past" (Silberman 1989, 10). Trigger (1984, 358–60) defines nationalist archaeology as an approach championing "pride and morale of nations." But at the start of the twenty-first century, nationalism is not the only political force impinging on archaeology, and it may not be the most significant.

Just as the intersection of nationalism and archaeology becomes clarified, the bundle of processes involved in globalization is weakening the nation-state and subsuming nationalism. Although scholars have exposed the impact of nationalism on archaeology, a new task comes to the study of the past. Addressing the obstacles to good scholarship and possibilities for archaeology in the global age, several publications have examined the intersection of archaeology and education (Stone and Molyneaux 1994; Smardz and Smith 2000), public memory (Shackel 2000), the contemporary past (Buchli and Lucas 2001), the public benefits of archaeology (Little 2002), repatriation of cultural objects (Greenfield 1989), and the destruction of archaeological sites (Layton et al. 2001). All of these studies relate to the sociopolitics of archaeology, which Wobst (1995) explains as the acknowledgment that choices are made by the practitioners in what is focused on in the study of the past rather than being simply the product of the archaeological record. Here we consider archaeology's intersection with globalization.

This volume embraces a global perspective to consider a range of archaeological sites and objects, some well-known (e.g., the Parthenon Marbles, Stonehenge, Colonial Williamsburg) and others less examined. In providing a geographically expansive collective (from Cambodia to Jordan, Avebury to Orlando) and the variation in the types of representations and marketing of the past (from trinkets to theme parks), we hope to illuminate a set of issues and their implications for archaeology and globalization. The sociopolitics of the endeavor revolves around the concern for how archaeology, broadly defined to include historic preservationists, museum specialists, and tourism promoters, works with contemporary issues at archaeological sites and through artifacts. The objective is to open up a theoretical discussion on the intersection of material remains and access to the past in a global context. The underlying thread focuses on the contemporary consequences and long-term scholarly implications of globally generated and situated presentations of the past.

The consumption of the past includes people visiting and knowing places with historic content. Tourism is a massive and extensive global industry. The literature on tourism is becoming immense and archaeo-tourism is an important subset. But rather than investigate tourism, this volume follows the trajectory of scholarship that interrogates the intersection of archaeology and its contemporary context. Poria et al. (2001, 1047) note the common assumption that heritage tourism is a grouping within tourism based on the historic attributes of an attraction; they argue a more appropriate approach focuses on the "motivations and perceptions" of the tourists rather than on the place, the social aspect of the visit is the key to their definition. By separating the attributes of a place from the motivation to visit locales embodying heritage, Poria et al. (2001) open up the context of a heritage attraction, the politics of the presentation, and understanding of heritage, specifically in terms of archaeology.

After Nation

Archaeologists have been evaluating the question of ownership of the past (Skeates 2000) as manifest in international conventions, ownership versus management of sites and artifacts (Messenger 1999), the rights and interests of indigenous peoples, and the commodification of the past. Such research is frequently bound by nation-states and their practices. But as the nation-state loses supremacy to global forces and transnational corporations, similar forces are sweeping up archaeology in complicated, even contradictory ways.

The term "globalization" covers several layers of processes and interactions. Tsing discusses globalization as

> a set of projects that require us to imagine space and time in particular ways. These are curious, power projects. Anthropologists need not ignore them; we also need not renaturalize them by assuming that the term they offer us are true. . . . an analyst of globalism cannot merely toss it out as a vacant description. Instead, an ethnographic study of the global needs careful attention not only to global claims and their effects on social life but also to questions of interconnection, movement, and boundary crossing that globalist spokepeople have brought to the fore. To take globality as an object of study requires both distance and intimate engagement. (2002, 476)

Within obvious limitations of length, the contributors to this volume have tried to capture that dynamic. Studying local expressions of heritage, archaeology, and the consumption of the past, the contributors provide examples that illustrate the variation within the global arena. The imagining of space and time—the archaeological quest to reconstruct and represent the past of a place—requires anthropological details, the types found across the chapters in this volume.

Heritage as a Commodity

In employing the term "marketing," these investigations identify the active construction of the past toward specific purposes as their goal. But we do not stop with the production of a past in a particular location; studies can link the production (Bauman, this volume) with its distribution (Ardren, this volume) and consumption. Cheung (1999) argues that most tourism studies simplify the contest over heritage as foreign tourists versus local peoples. There is much greater complexity, as Stark and Griffin (this volume) show for Cambodia. Heritage is a complex notion, involving the past, contemporary social understandings of places, and the active construction of the past. Exploring heritage in their case studies, many contributors to this volume cite Lowenthal (1985, 1996), highlighting the fundamental role his ideas play in investigating and understanding the past in its contemporary context.

Lowenthal (1996) provides straightforward imagery for studying heritage. He (1996, 2–3) notes heritage's "potential for both good and evil is huge. On the one hand, it offers a rationale for self-respecting stewardship of all we hold dear; on the other, it signals an eclipse of reason and a regression to embattled tribalism." Heritage is a particular version of the past that belongs to a group. That fragmentation of the past by heritage leads to the assumption by various countries that

> their problems (are) unexampled elsewhere. In Australian eyes the attribution of heritage by populist mockery is a problem solely their own. Italians imagine that they alone have a heritage too burdensome to live with. Greeks feel uniquely bereaved by the classical legacy's global dispersal; none but Israelis suffer a suicidal Masada complex; Egyptians uniquely lack empathy with ancient roots. Only Americans parade their past with patriotic hype, debase it with Disney, and feel guilt on both counts. Or so they all think. But they are wrong; most of these heritage ailments are pandemic. (Lowenthal 1996, 249)

What is seen as unique can be placed in a global, comparative context. The wealthy can travel to heritage sites everywhere and anywhere in the world. The marketing of heritage takes the unique and universalizes it as a commodity.

Not only has heritage become a commodity, it is a wildly popular one around the planet. Wolf (1982, 310) defined commodities as "goods and services produced for a market . . . they can be compared and exchanged without reference to the social matrix in which they are produced." Wolf situated commodities in a historical anthropological perspective with the emergence of the modern world. Stone et al. (2000, 21) provide case studies of commodities in globalization, laying out a wide-ranging collection of goods in order to show the interconnections among consumers of the wealthy countries and the primary producers of poor nations within global networks. The power dynamics illuminated by Wolf (1982) and discussed by Stone et al. (2000) are important components to understand the implications of accelerating commodity production, distribution, and consumption in our increasingly interconnected world. During the modern period, a greater variety of goods and services have been made into commodities. Heritage sites are the product of archaeological excavations and historical investigations, and are now significant commodities in the global tourist market. The skill or labor required to extract an understanding of the past is less significant, it seems, than the postcards, refrigerator magnets, and entrance fees that can be charged for visiting a site. Heritage as commodity is not simply the place, its past, or its materiality. The complexity of what is made into a commodity can be illuminated, we believe, by global comparison to other commodifications.

The commodification of the past is part of a trajectory on which more and more aspects of social life and localized resources become objects for consumption. For instance, nature has become a good that can be evaluated via the market as well as visited or even bound into a theme park (Davis 1997). As nature becomes a subject of tourism, it is not surprising that the past, whether represented by artifacts in cabinets of curiosities, museums, or by the places excavated, is also made into a commodity for the world's largest industry—tourism. As a commodity, there are complex bargains for the stewards, managers, excavators, and interpreters of the places.

Davis (1997, 235) engaged in a long-term ethnographic study of a theme park based on nature. She discusses a shift in the theme park from an incoherence based on an underfunded collection of things that people liked versus the result after ample resources were poured into the complex. With coherence, with great care placed in the details, "the theme park has become more overbearingly persuasive, more beautiful and likeable. Its efforts to shape perceptions and feelings work, at least a lot of the time." Davis views this packaging of nature as the corporation winning. Archaeologists and historic preservationists can imagine, and probably are aware of, the tremendous number of sites and places uncared for, the excavation units overgrown with weeds or the old houses vandalized with graffiti. That incoherence is not positive yet the alternative, as discussed by Davis (1997), raises a concern that slick marketing of the past might remove authenticity. Success has its price (see Gable and Handler, this volume, for a more comprehensive consideration of similar issues).

Success can come from the marketing of heritage, from convincing people and institutions to fund the preservation of places. Preservation, according to Murtagh (1993, 19–22), is an umbrella term that includes preservation, restoration, reconstruction, and rehabilitation. There are several spectacular examples of successful preservation around the planet: Masada (Silberman 1989; Ben-Yehuda 1993) in Israel, Colonial Williamsburg (see Gable and Handler, this volume) in the United States, and the Jorvik Viking Center (Jones 1999) in Britain. The critiques of these famous sites raise unease on behalf of the less famous ones, the ones with less coherence due to lack of funding. This volume includes discussion of sites that are nonspectacular in terms of their marketing, and the range of examples illustrates the tensions involved in trying to save sites and make them accessible. In order to understand why the reification of the archaeological past as heritage and tourist site is a significant concern, one can turn to Eric Wolf (1982, 7), who explained his concern about reification in the teleological construction of human identities: "Names thus become things, and things marked with an X can become targets of war." Layton et al. (2001) and Golden (this volume) provide numerous examples of reification of heritage into monuments and sites that lead to destruction of those places and to violence against people. As Anderson (1991) showed in his study of nationalism, groups are willing to fight and die for their imagined communities; the same premise seems to hold for heritage sites, the imagined connection between present and past.

Global Presentations of the Past

Although there is much discussion of the new heritage boom, South (1997) points out that historical archaeologists in the United States have been engaged in the public presentation of the past for more than half a century. In critiquing calls for public engagement, South (1997, 55) recommends touring parks and historic sites to "see what has been going on outside." He argues that archaeologists have been engaged with the public, struggling with political decisions against the evidence from the archaeological record. Presentations of the past are similarly seen as a long-term issue for archaeology, with South (1997, 61–62) advocating generalized attempts to stimulate the imagination over focused attention on themes. South focuses on his experiences in the United States.

According to Tsing (2002), the power relations involved in globalization are seen as integral to the United States hegemony in world affairs and the impact of American tourists visiting sites in every corner of the planet. The inspiration for American and other Western tourists has implications in non-Western settings as well as within the United States. While South (1997) celebrates the presentations of the colonial past in the United States, Handsman (1978) raises concerns. Focusing on the tourist town of Colonial Litchfield, Connecticut, Handsman (1978, 65) argues for "analyzing Litchfield as a cultural production associated with the past . . . to interpret modern Litchfield as myth and symbol and past Litchfield as myth, history, and symbol." Handsman's goal is to theorize how history is reified. His concern is that the "dividing line between the genuine and the spurious is the realm of the social-commercial, where often what is spurious may become genuine and vice versa" (Handsman 1978, 65). The concern radiates from Colonial Litchfield's construction in the early twentieth century and now "a genuine touristic phenomenon, the sort of sight that, when combined with spurious elements such as guided house tours, local histories, postcards, and photographs, could easily establish itself as an alternative reality contributing to the alienation of individuals from their histories of everyday existence" (Handsman 1987, 69). Those concerns have been globalized.

Hoffman et al. (2002, 30) follow the National Trust for Historical Preservation's definition of heritage tourism as "travel to archaeological and historical sites, parks, museums, and places of traditional or ethnic significance. It also includes travel to foreign countries to experience different cultures and explore their prehistoric and historic roots." To encourage Americans and other Westerners to experience difference means making that difference accessible to them. Ebron (1999) explores the predicament of McDonald's restaurants sponsoring travel to Gambia and Senegal for African Americans to see their heritage. The company's "efforts capitalized on the possibility of selling identity and community along with company products" (Ebron 1999, 913). The notion of "McMemories"

(Ebron 1999, 912) should be added to the concerns of archaeologists working to present and represent the past.

Other aspects of corporate packaging can include popular novels about the past, television programs, and the mass manufacture of pseudo-artifacts as well as antiquities trading online. New technologies are creating an acceleration of concerns. Dealing in antiquities, which had been restricted to specific locations, is now open to anyone with Internet access. Online trading, such as eBay, facilitates the commodification of the past, encouraging more artifacts, particularly less expensive ones, to be bought and sold (Lidington 2002). Manipulation of the past is becoming easier; rather than nationalism, commercialization seems to be the next frontier of challenges for archaeologists and others concerned about accurate and meaningful presentations of the past. With the commodification of the past, scholars are raising concerns for authenticity in tourist displays (e.g., Bruner 2001; Little 2002). Tourists want an educational experience during visits to heritage sites, but that education is not simply a good; the intersection of travel and education has a long genealogy in the West, which helps illuminate the power dynamics involved.

Intersections of Travel and Education

The "grand tour" is a term used to describe the convention of Western European travel to the south and east as a foundation for elite education and social polish. European Christians have gone on pilgrimages to the Holy Land since St. Helena discovered the sites associated with Jesus; and pilgrimage to holy places is a pan-human phenomenon. But with the fifteenth century, a new motivation for Western European travel arose: education and experiences. The grand tour represents the intersection of travel and education. With its origins in the sixteenth century among the British elite, the grand tour became a fixture in seventeenth- and eighteenth-century English university education and a shared experience of aristocratic and landed men and many women throughout Western Europe. By the eighteenth century, the pattern of the grand tour was firmly in place, and specific sites of national and cultural importance were identified as required stops on the tour: Paris, Florence, Rome, Venice, Athens, Istanbul, and, if possible, the religious sites of the Holy Land. By the nineteenth century, the intersection of travel and education became fixed as part of Western leisure. Accounts of those travels, the records of experiences and observations, were popular. The number of publications related to travel to the Holy Land increased greatly over the nineteenth century as regular steamboat travel encouraged visits. Yehoshua Ben-Arieh (1989) notes that in 1800 there were nearly 1,600 books published on travel to Palestine; by 1877 there were more than 3,500.

In considering a genealogy for marketing heritage, we should note that Westerners once would travel to see the exotic, whether present or past, or they went to exhibits of alterity at home. Today tourists travel to see exhibits of the past. The genealogy of the grand tour is helpful for bringing out the multiple facets of the presentations of the past since there has been an acceleration of the processes over the last two centuries. Just as there were many types of travelers on the grand tour—merchants, explorers, and pilgrims—there are multiple types of tourists. Nevertheless there are commonalities in their motivations.

People going to distant places included pilgrims, merchants, explorers, and travelers. Leed (1995, 172) labels merchant travel as nonheroic, people seeking places for products and profit. The explorer seeks adventure, the unknown, the unmapped. Explorers discover and open pathways for others. Travelers go along routes created by the explorers. Tourism, a late-nineteenth-century invention, involves mass movement of people along avenues marketed by capitalist firms. Thomas Cook conceived of tours with the famous Cook's Tours of the East starting in 1869 (Shepherd 1987, 170–73). Cook's Tours stands as the prime example of early tourism, making travel accessible to the middle classes by standardizing the process. The *Quaker City* was the first steamship bringing North Americans on package tours of the eastern Mediterranean (Shepherd 1987, 173); Mark Twain ensured its fame. Although explorers, particularly to the Middle East, went in disguise, the tourists on the *Quaker City* "became instantly identifiable by their long overcoats (the English wore tweed), the veils which floated from beneath their sun helmets, their sunglasses, and their green lined umbrellas" (Shepherd 1987, 173). No longer did Westerners change to see the Middle East; they went as themselves, demanding security and ease of travel. As travel became even more accessible, the places visited were changed to meet Western interests. Silberman (1997) raises the specter for the next stage of archaeological sites, when they are transformed into theme parks for even greater ease of visitation.

The Israeli case is particularly instructive for exploring these issues (Trigger 1984; Silberman 1989; Trigger 1995; Silberman 1995; Abu el-Haj 2001, among many others), as it has been in the literature on the intersection of archaeology and nationalism. In this volume, there is one chapter based in Israel, another in its neighbor Jordan, and another that discusses representations of the Holy Land in Florida. Here, we use this exemplary case to illustrate the transition from nationalism to globalized heritage.

Although the site of Masada and the presentation of Jerusalem are the most famous case studies for exposing the construction of the past in Israel, those examples are oversimplified. The rationale for exploring the marketing of heritage is not that there is a new manipulation of the past in the contemporary world.

Rather, the point is that we can train our gaze toward new phenomena regarding the manipulation of the material record. The examples most often cited for Israel come from a particular context, one that is being erased by globalization. In the early twenty-first century, Israel is becoming deeply embedded in the global economy, with its computer industry, integration in global communication networks, and consumption of globalized goods. In the globalized economy, Israel continues to need tourists and the state actively recruits tourists with its archaeological history. The archaeological past, as seen in excavations, artifacts, and the cultural landscape, is a major draw for wealthy tourists. But the state and its institutions seem to be moving away from ideological support for the nationalist-based presentations of the archaeological past and toward a more consumerist approach, exemplified by the state authorizing the selling of antiquities. Tourists can visit the past and take a piece home with them.

To illustrate the dynamics of change, we will discuss three phases in Israeli archaeology and its presentation of the past. The first we label the Beit Alpha phase, the second, Masada, and the third, Beit She'an. The phases are based on sites that will be used to illuminate, briefly, the new configurations between archaeology and its context.

In 1928, a group of socialist Zionist workers at the Beit Alpha kibbutz near the Sea of Galilee were digging an irrigation ditch when they uncovered mosaics with Hebrew writing and Jewish symbols. During this time, the British, through their League of Nations mandate over Palestine, sought a balance between their own imperialist aims, the push for a Jewish national home in Palestine, and Arab Palestinian rights to self-determination. Tensions were high. With the enthusiasm of Eliezer Lipa Sukenik of Hebrew University, the mosaics were excavated and preserved. As Elon (1994, 14) explains, the discovery had a cathartic effect on the settlers. It was as if "they were recovering checked baggage from a storage room." This is archaeology for the sake of creating an identity, a distinctiveness based on a temporal depth in a place.

In the 1960s, under Sukenik's son, Yigael Yadin, the ancient fortress complex at Masada was excavated during a time when the state of Israel felt besieged. Masada was in a small corner near the Dead Sea, a region surrounded on three sides by the Hashemite Kingdom of Jordan. An impressive feat of coordination and discovery, the Roman period site of Masada became famous for the stories that Yadin told of recovering the history of the Jewish Revolt during the first century C.E. The excavations at Masada opened up new knowledge of the land, and archaeology became understood as a means to expand Israelis' experience with territory and history. The excavated story of Masada supported a notion of "them against us" and unified Israelis. Ben-Yehuda (1993) calls the visits to Masada a ritual, for Israelis and those who share the ideology of the state.

At the end of the twentieth century, the largest state-supported excavations were no longer focused on recovering Jewish symbols or reconstructing heroic tales of the past. At Beit She'an, not far from Beit Alpha, massive excavations exposed a Roman/Byzantine city with few evocative ties to nationalist history. Here archaeology provides employment for people in the modern town of Beit She'an, whose former mayor was a key member of several governments. By creating a tourist attraction, and hopefully providing future employment opportunities in a poor corner of Israel, this current phase of archaeology works within the realm of global tourism. Where ideology was once used to settle the land, drain the swamps, irrigate the deserts, and the communalism of the kibbutz and moshav were taken as national ideals, Israelis build malls that house stores like Toys R Us, they use cellular telephones, they watch CNN and FoxNews, and they eat at McDonald's, Domino's, and Subway. The role of the past, and the uncovering of the past, has changed as well.

Israel at the end of the twentieth century presented itself for Western consumption (according to some of its advertising) as a "country blessed with historical, archaeological, and religious treasures," containing many places and many landscapes. Different audiences are encouraged to see different components of the country. Recent advertising campaigns can be seen in this light. In magazines and newspapers (such as the general readership of the *New York Times* as well as the more specific audience of, for example, *Biblical Archaeology Review* and *Archaeology* magazines), Israel is presented with the line, "No one belongs here more than you." That slogan, found on GoIsrael (www.goisrael.com), promoted as "Israel's Official North American Tourism Web Site," is then split into three sections: Jewish interest, Catholic interest, and Protestant interest. The "Jewish interest" link leads to an image of a bar mitzvah at the Western Wall in the Old City of Jerusalem, with a menu of other choices specifically targeted to Jewish visitors (e.g., planning for a bar/bat mitzvah). The link to "Catholic interest" uses the image of the pope visiting the Western Wall, while the "Protestant interest" section uses the image of baptisms. "Muslim interest" is found only under the link labeled "photo gallery" and is not an option on the main web page.

These advertising campaigns reflect the routes offered to tourists in Israel. For Jewish tourists from the West, a tour guide can select case after case to provide concrete evidence—buildings, tombs, and artifacts—of people who were symbolically, if not genetically, ancestors. The totality of a tour of this Israel will attest to two unmistakable lines—an unbroken link between the Jewish past and the Jewish present in *Eretz Yisrael* (Hebrew for the Land of Israel) and another line linking all Jews in the Diaspora to the state of Israel. And the image serves to frame the historical questions that are asked by the tourists. The places and histories invoked create a discourse for the landscape as Jewish with the activities of Romans,

Crusaders, or Arabs at various points in the past injecting themselves into the dominant narrative rather than being part of it. A nationalist agenda is clear.

A Christian tour group will likely see a different Israel, a different landscape, and a different heritage in the land advertised as holy. The places of the New Testament follow the "footsteps of Jesus" through Nazareth, Jerusalem, and the Sea of Galilee. Because Bethlehem is now in the Palestinian National Authority, Israel has constructed a tourist Bethlehem on the outskirts of that city (and within the boundaries of the greater Jerusalem metropolitan area) for Christian visitors to see (and, more importantly, consume) that aspect of Jesus' life story. Rowan (this volume) shows the trajectory of presenting the past in a more and more accessible location, rather than a Holy Land experience in the Middle East, one can consume a similar experience in central Florida. This is not a twenty-first-century development. Rowan shows that its roots are in the nineteenth century; but the audience for the Holy Land Experience, and marketing, far surpasses that of its North American predecessors.

This is not to suggest these are the only venues for tourism found in the increasingly globalized Israel. There are vacationers from northern European countries visiting Eilat, the beach resort on the southern Red Sea coast, who have no interest in Jewish or Christian heritage narratives. There are "spa tourists" who are primarily interested in the restorative powers of the Dead Sea and the geologically associated mud and mineral baths. The potential for fragmentation seems endless. And the most striking part of these different tours is not their success in encouraging tourists to see very different heritages, to learn and experience different aspects of the past in the region; it is the ability to carve a small country into these separate landscapes. Two tour groups might return to the West with separate images of Israel. The collective goal for all the tourism, though, is the same: economic resources for the state. A simple equivalence of archaeology to nationalism in the state of Israel—the useful critiques of Israeli archaeology during the Beit Alpha and Masada phases—removes the complexity of the current phase of the marketing of the past in Israel and oversimplifies what is happening to the past in its territory. Israel provides an example of the processes; the case studies in this volume offer the opportunity to explore similar issues and concerns in depth.

Impact of Archaeology on the Local Level

The Israeli example provides the details to recognize the diversity of causes, results, and implications of marketing the past. The critiques of archaeology in Israel examine the issue of controlling time through space, supposedly to ensure social stability for the nationalist project by fixing spatial forms and thus borders for the state and temporal depth for its people. Does establishing archaeological sites as heritage sites work toward that end?

It is easy to cast archaeologists, historic preservationists, and other professionals as one-dimensional caricatures, particularly in opposition to indigenous or local peoples. They can be made into unwitting agents of the state or of transnational global processes. But people who become archaeologists are usually (hopefully) interested in the past beyond their professional responsibilities and obligations. Wobst (1995) asserts that in his experience, archaeologists have humanistic intentions regarding understanding the past. In that light, we should accept that archaeologists could be tourists, members of local communities, and concerned citizens. Their observations can be helpful in pulling together the strands of globalization on the marketing of heritage. Throughout the chapters, we see what the professional saw. Rather than telling archaeologists what they should do, the contributions illustrate the complex issues and concerns from a wide range of sites. In a sense this volume represents a multisite ethnography, following Marcus's (1995) challenge to follow the commodity, in this case heritage sites, organized for tourist consumption of the past. This collection employs archaeologists touring archaeological sites as part of their research as well as exploring the impact of globalization and tourism on their research interests. Not surprisingly, such research has a personal tone in describing visits to heritage sites as well as the researchers using themselves as examples of the phenomenon they are analyzing.

Consuming the Past at Sites

Across the case studies in this volume, one can find a common dynamic. Rather than presented for nationalist purposes, sites and historical places seem to be arranged, organized, and made accessible for tourists, whether local or foreign. The message is clearly that of heritage consumption rather than simply history presentation. The local specificity for each approach varies greatly. The significance of this dynamic for understanding the past is illustrated by Trouillot's (1995, 10–11) consideration of the Alamo. In raising a series of questions about the veracity of the stories of the 1836 siege, he covers the details of the battle, the reasons for the war, the courage of the defenders, and even whether Davy Crockett wore a coonskin cap when he died at the Alamo,

> That last question may sound the most trivial of a rather bizarre list; but it appears less trifling and not at all bizarre when we note that the Alamo shrine is Texas's main tourist attraction, drawing some three million visitors a year. Now that local voices have become loud enough to question the innocence of a little *gringo* wearing a Davy cap, mom and dad may think twice about buying one, and the custodians of history shiver, afraid that the past is catching up too fast with the present.

They are shivering, according to Trouillot (1995, xix) about these concerns, because at stake are "history and power." With globalization, the concerns are found everywhere. The uneven distribution of resources, the competition among groups and interests, and the forces ranging from performances at theme parks to violence are part of the contemporary concerns with heritage and the consumption of the past. The case studies offer the opportunity to delve into the concerns.

Organization of This Volume
Following the introduction, this book includes the following sections.

Part II: The Legal and Historical Context for Marketing Heritage
While there is a diversity of how peoples and nation-states organize and recognize their past, the international community, under the United Nations, has a specific set of rules and concerns. Bonnie Magness-Gardiner (chapter 2) provides a legal overview regarding heritage, specifically international conventions and protections implemented to protect cultural property. Her overview details the effects of the 1970 UNESCO Convention on the Means of Prohibiting and Preventing the Illicit Import, Export and Transfer of Ownership of Cultural Property, in particular, the 1983 Convention on Cultural Property Implementation Act that enables the U.S. government to implement that convention. The notion of cultural ownership has received much attention in the case of marbles from Athens. Examining the Elgin/Parthenon Marbles as a case study of issues surrounding the repatriation of cultural property, Morag Kersel (chapter 3) finds that this particularly contentious example demonstrates the overlapping interests of nationalism, economics, and politics behind calls for the return of material culture.

Reminding us that present debates are not unique to this historical moment, Steve Vinson (chapter 4) focuses an interpretation of contemporary concerns for a historical analysis of heritage. As a concept managed by national and political entities, long-standing attitudes toward how to manage heritage and its manifestations continue to be enforced or promulgated by these national and political bodies. Definition of that heritage, and how to manage it, continues to be defined by, or in opposition to, the same forces responsible for creating the dominant political paradigms.

Part III: The Past as Commodity
As Kelli Ann Costa (chapter 5) points out, while history ends, heritage continues. Costa discusses examples from Ireland, where the packaging of sites and landscapes taps into a sense of connection with the past by both creating the past as

exotic and unique, while at the same time, deflating time so that ancient themes and connections seem less remote to the modern visitor. This works particularly well with those of Irish descent who wish to visit ancestral lands. Costa's research also indicates that visitors' preferences for visits are affected as much by the visitors' centers and amenities as by the ancient sites themselves.

The growing power of tourism in many economies is leading to the rapid growth of the role of archaeological sites in commercializing the past and heritage. National tourism agencies use ancient sites and landscapes to create and promote tourism in a variety of ways. Archaeology may be used to market commodities unrelated to the past, but the concern in this part is the promotion and marketing of archaeology and the use of the ancient past to promote tourism and sell commodities as well as the intersection of promoting knowledge of the past with commerce. Archaeology may be employed as a tool for certain goals, such as local economic development projects, or to encourage the protection of ancient sites. Ancient sites and monuments are also the setting for modern material culture consumption, and thus they provide useful indicators of particular images actively promoted by archaeological site managers, as well as what material culture interests the visitors. Amy Gazin-Schwartz (chapter 6) uses these indicators to contrast two World Heritage sites in Great Britain, Avebury and Stonehenge. Gift shops attached to, or part of, archaeological sites market heritage via souvenirs, as a means of reaching or creating a sense of past. Tourists may experience an idea of the past via modern material culture, making the past seem more familiar and personal through the recognizable process of selecting items for purchase. In this way, Gazin-Schwartz suggests, the trinkets offered for sale may influence tourists' perceptions of the past.

Archaeology may serve only as a tourist curiosity, as the teaser, the backdrop, or another exoticized image to attract potential tourists. Traci Ardren (chapter 7) discusses the role of archaeological sites and symbols for advertising and promoting state run tourism in Mexico. Highlighting the exotic aspects of archaeology appropriates Maya symbols to create national symbols, while at the same the indigenous Maya are routinely excluded from the interpretation or benefits of the increased tourism. Despite the growing success of Mundo Maya—a multinational cooperative effort to foster tourism—and its manipulation of imagery drawn from the indigenous people, archaeological sites, and the natural environment, the revenue anticipated for the indigenous Maya, and local people, has largely remained unfulfilled.

Part IV: Archaeology in the Global Age

The relevance of heritage in the global age is increasingly evident. Awareness of the role of archaeology in the sociopolitical world is not new, but conflicting views of the past are intimately entwined with the formation of identities of all types, and the ways in which the past plays a legitimating role to group identity formation is only recently receiving serious attention. In this section, authors present different manifestations of struggles over the past and the impact of conflicts over the past.

Miriam Stark and P. Bion Griffin (chapter 8) examine the tensions between heritage and archaeological research, in particular the friction between the economics affecting those at the local level and the objectives of national programs for archaeological research and cultural heritage management in Cambodia. The rapacious demand for Khmer artifacts contributes to the continuous looting of Cambodia's archaeological heritage, yet the linkage between nationalism and heritage management deems the preservation of Cambodia's past essential not only for the potential of cultural tourism potential, but also for preservation of national heritage icons.

Jason James (chapter 9) examines the conflicts between West and East, modern and traditional, as seen through restoration efforts within the unified German state. Specifically focusing on cultural policies for the restoration of historical and architectural landmarks in East Germany, James notes that German leaders seek less provocative ways to concurrently claim ethno-cultural and civic definitions of national being, yet nevertheless promote West German hegemony. Although issues of preservation and reproduction of cultural property are not necessarily insidious, James highlights how in the German example cultural property may be used in creation of difference and identity, the notion that poverty is preservation, and the assertion or maintenance of boundaries between inclusion and exclusion.

Eric Gable and Richard Handler (chapter 10) discuss the construction of the past at Colonial Williamsburg. In order to counteract kitsch and inauthenticity, planners initiated attempts to reintroduce "dirt, ruin and decay" into restorations in the last decades of the twentieth century. This dirt, viewed as more realistic, albeit reintroduced as more representative of the people, is distinct from the cleanliness representing the upper classes. Performances intended to put life into the Williamsburg experience, however, reinforced the notion of the past as primitive—loud, unsanitary, and barbaric. The advent of social history at Colonial Williamsburg not only includes management's introduction of dirt and untidiness, but also the "deskilling" of craftspeople whose skills exceeded those for general consumption during the eighteenth century. General agreement that Colonial Williamsburg was too clean and tidy to be an accurate portrayal of the past nevertheless leads to the conclusion that if dirtied enough to be authentic, the public will not accept it.

Cultural property and symbolically infused monuments occasionally inspire more than subtle dissonance over cultural or identity politics. Drawing on the examples of the Ayodhya Mosque, Bamiyan Buddhas, and Jacob's Tomb, Jonathan Golden (chapter 11) examines attacks on symbolically charged buildings and monuments as reflections of ethnic, political, and religious conflicts over heritage claims. Although preservation of similar types of monuments at times fosters international consensus, we must guard against an assumption that marginalized groups will perceive the same buildings and monuments as important, or that the very idea of preservation carries with it the same emotive appeal. As Golden points out, claims to understanding the history of a building or monument often rely on archaeological data, or claims to data, and thus archaeologists have become increasingly aware that their interpretation of the past can have an effect on future events.

Part V: Representing the Past

In this section, three different case studies are bound by the commonality of places focused on the Holy Land as the object. Joel Bauman (chapter 12) investigates the ancient site of Sepphoris, a national park in Israel with importance to Judaism and Christianity, and prior to 1948, the site of a large Palestinian village, Saffouriye. Widely featured in popular and academic media, Sepphoris highlights evidence for cohabitation of the village by Jews, Romans/pagans, and early Christians, suggesting that the wealth of the city arose from such pluralistic traditions. Through extensive interviews and repeated site visits, Bauman's analysis illustrates the process of constructing an Israeli vision of place and heritage, and those professionals responsible for the design and manufacture of such landscapes and sites of collective memory.

Erin Addison (chapter 13) examines the choices of presentation of past material remains for the purposes of tourism in Jordan. Utilizing a novel approach, she finds that the emphasis on the Christian past, to the detriment of the Islamic remains, is reflected in the signs that direct visitors to ancient sites considered worthy of tourism by the Jordanian government. Moreover, Islamic heritage is deliberately obscured from Western visitors as well as those who would read Arabic language signs, and signs that would guide Islamic pilgrims are distributed or oriented away from first- and second-class roads.

The complexity of representing the past may be simplified if there is a perception of greater audience homogeneity. Whereas Bauman's analysis highlights the intricacies and multiple perspectives visible just below the surface of an ancient site's representation to the public, a modern theme park may appropriate specific aspects of the past to propagate a particular narrative of the past. Visiting the Holy Land Experience, a theme park in Orlando, Florida, Yorke Rowan (chapter 14) finds that images, replicas, and media are incorporated to provide an overt proselytizing message by commodifying the past for a particular audience.

Although geographically remote from the Holy Land, the creation of "constructed experience" is enhanced through use of authenticating elements such as ancient texts and agricultural implements, not dependent on them.

Part VI: Archaeologists and the Marketing of Heritage

Representing the past includes interpretation, and the intersection of the public and archaeology in the creation and promotion of the past is the focus of Barbara Little's discussion of interpretation as conducted in the National Park Service (chapter 15). Interpreters and archaeologists may find it difficult to communicate and agree on what the public "should" appreciate, and what that public is likely to retain. Little underscores the importance that the role of interpretation plays in how effectively messages are conveyed to the public, and this accentuates the importance of the responsibility that archaeologists have to become engaged not just with the stories of the past, but how those stories are narrated to the public.

Joan Gero (chapter 16) discusses the political context for the origins of the World Archaeological Congress in 1986, and the efforts to create a new, broader forum for the many voices of archaeologists from around the globe. In Gero's view, WAC represents not only a nonprofit organization for worldwide archaeology, but a reformulation toward "engaged archaeology," one that recognizes the historical and social role of archaeology and hence the necessity that archaeological work should be relevant to communities beyond the narrower confines of Western academia. WAC explicitly seeks to counter institutionalized views that could marginalize the cultural heritage of indigenous peoples, minorities, and the poor.

Philip Kohl, who played a key role in helping archaeologists recognize the intersection of archaeology and nationalism (Kohl and Fawcett 1995; Kohl 1998), provides the conclusions for this volume (chapter 17). His assessment underscores concerns voiced in these chapters about issues of authenticity of the past, the multivocality of representations, and the potential for the use and abuse of archaeology in globalization.

This volume is not meant to be all-inclusive. Aspects of the marketing of heritage not covered here include the replication of artifacts, the explosion of Internet antiquities trading, and marketing of Atlantis, El Dorado, and other pasts of the Western imagination. Our purpose is to raise questions; since archaeologists are witnessing the transformations in presentations of the past, it is hoped that this volume will encourage more explorations of the concerns and issues.

Conclusion

As scholars concerned about the preservation of the past, these studies raise questions regarding the relationship among multinational capital, local marketing schemes, local communities and descendant populations, and tourists. As Hoffman et al. (2002, 30) note,

> Archaeological parks—prehistoric or historic sites preserved and interpreted for the public—have always been obvious tourism magnets for the communities in which they are located, and in many cases this has been a driving concern for their preservation and development. As interest in heritage tourism grows, archaeological parks will attract greater attention, resulting in benefits to, as well as pressures on, the resource. Guidance from archaeologists can aid in the process.

Heritage marketing insists on, even requires, a focus on the unique. The tourist market uses the unique as a tool to encourage visits and consumption. Archaeological excavations can provide the material for such marketing. Yet, particularly in an archaeology grounded in anthropology, as is the case in the United States, there is the notion of a common human heritage for the archaeological record. The notion of a common human heritage can help challenge the racialist or primordialist ownership of sites, the type of exclusion used in the ethnic conflicts of the last decade.

The tension between the unique and the common that form the past raises an important challenge, is a site and its stories unique, open for use in the marketplace of global tourism or universal for all peoples? This question, we posit, should haunt archaeologists and others concerned about the presentation, preservation, and protection of the past. Globalized processes are experienced and mediated locally so the topic is explored via case studies. The diverse examples in this volume have common strands. That is not accidental or created: Whether in Cambodia, Jordan, Ireland, or Orlando, Florida, there are pressures being brought to bear on the presentation of the past. This volume offers the concerns, themes, and examples. The studies in it point out problems, pressures, and possibilities in the marketing of heritage around the world. We hope that the collection indicates some trends in the presentation of the past and opens up some concerns for archaeologists and others interested in preservation and presentation of the past.

References

Abu el-Haj, Nadia. 2001. *Facts on the Ground: Archaeological Practice and Territorial Self-Fashioning in Israeli Society.* Chicago: University of Chicago Press.

Anderson, Benedict. 1991. *Imagined Communities: Reflections on the Origin and Spread of Nationalism.* London: Verso.

Arnold, Bettina. 1990. "The Past as Propaganda: Totalitarian Archaeology in Nazi Germany." *Antiquity* 64(244): 464–78.

Ben-Arieh, Yehoshua. 1989. "Nineteenth-Century Historical Geographies of the Holy Land." *Journal of Historical Geography* 15(1): 69–79.

Ben-Yehuda, Nachman. 1993. *The Masada Myth: Collective Memory and Mythmaking in Israel.* Madison: University of Wisconsin Press.

Bruner, Edward W. 2001. "The Maasai and the Lion King: Authenticity, Nationalism, and Globalization in African Tourism." *American Ethnologist* 28(4): 881–908.

Buchli, Victor, and Gavin Lucas, eds. 2001. *Archaeologies of the Contemporary Past.* New York: Routledge.

Cheung, Sidney, C.H. 1999. "The Meanings of a Heritage Trail in Hong Kong." *Annals of Tourism Research* 26(3): 570–88.

Davis, Susan G. 1997. *Spectacular Nature: Corporate Culture and the Sea World Experience.* Berkeley: University of California Press.

Díaz-Andreu, Marguerita, and Timothy Champion, eds. 1996. *Nationalism and Archaeology in Europe.* Boulder: Westview.

Ebron, Paula. 1999. "Tourists as Pilgrims: Commercial Fashioning of Transatlantic Politics." *American Ethnologist* 26(4): 910–32.

Edensor, Tim. 1998. *Tourists at the Taj: Performance and Meaning at a Symbolic Site.* New York: Routledge.

Elon, Amos. 1994. "Politics and Archaeology." *New York Review of Books,* September 22, 14–18.

Gathercole, Peter, and David Lowenthal, eds. 1990. *The Politics of the Past.* London: Unwin Hyman.

Greenfield, Jeanette. 1989. *The Return of Cultural Treasures.* Cambridge: Cambridge University Press.

Handsman, Russell G. 1987. "Machines and Gardens: Structures in and Symbols of America's Past." In *Ethnography by Archaeologists,* edited by E. Tooker, 63–78. Washington, D.C.: American Ethnological Society.

Hoffman, Teresa L., Mary L. Kwas, and Helaine Silverman. 2002. "Heritage Tourism and Public Archaeology." *SAA Archaeological Record* 2(2): 30–32, 44.

Jones, Andrew. 1999. "Archaeological Reconstruction and Education at the Jorvik Viking Centre and Archaeological Resource Centre, York, UK." In *The Constructed Past: Experimental Archaeology, Education, and the Public,* edited by Peter G. Stone and Philippe G. Planel, 258–68. London: Routledge.

Kessing, Roger M. 1989. "Creating the Past: Custom and Identity in the Contemporary Pacific." *Contemporary Pacific* 1(1): 19–42.

Kohl, Philip L. 1998. "Nationalism and Archaeology: On the Constructions of Nations and the Reconstructions of the Remote Past." *Annual Review of Anthropology* 27: 223–46.

Kohl, Philip L., and Clare Fawcett, eds. 1995. *Nationalism, Politics, and the Practice of Archaeology.* Cambridge: Cambridge University Press.

Layton, Robert, Peter G. Stone, and Julian Thomas, eds. 2001. *Destruction and Conservation of Cultural Property.* London: Routledge.

Leed, Eric. 1995. *Shores of Discovery: How Expeditionaries Have Constructed the World.* New York: Basic.

Lidington, Helen. 2002. "The Role of the Internet in Removing the 'Shackles of the Salesroom': Anytime, Anyplace, Anything, Anywhere." *Public Archaeology* 2: 67–84.

Little, Barbara J., ed. 2002. *Public Benefits of Archaeology.* Gainesville: University Press of Florida.

Lowenthal, David. 1985. *The Past Is a Foreign Country.* Cambridge: Cambridge University Press.

———. 1996. *Possessed by the Past: The Heritage Crusade and the Spoils of History.* New York: Free Press.

Marcus, George. 1995. "Ethnography in the World System." *Annual Review of Anthropology* 14: 95–117.

Meskell, Lynn, ed. 1998. *Archaeology under Fire: Nationalism, Politics, and Heritage in the Eastern Mediterranean and Middle East.* New York: Routledge.

Messenger, Phyllis M., ed. 1999. *The Ethics of Collecting Cultural Property.* 2d ed. Albuquerque: University of New Mexico Press.

Murtagh, William J. 1993. *Keeping Time: The History and Theory of Preservation in America.* New York: Wiley.

Patterson, Thomas C. 1995. *Toward a Social History of Archaeology in the United States.* Fort Worth: Harcourt Brace.

Poria, Yaniv, Richard Butler, and David Airey. 2001. "Clarifying Heritage Tourism." *Annals of Tourism Research* 28(4): 1047–49.

Shackel, Paul A. 2000. *Archaeology and Created Memory: Public History in a National Park.* New York: Kluwer Academic/Plenum.

Shepherd, Naomi. 1987. *The Zealous Intruders: From Napoleon to the Dawn of Zionism—The Explorers, Archaeologists, Artists, Tourists, Pilgrims, and Visionaries Who Opened Palestine to the West.* New York: Harper & Row.

Silberman, Neil A. 1989. *Between Past and Present: Archaeology, Ideology, and Nationalism in the Modern Middle East.* New York: Henry Holt.

———. 1995. "Promised Lands and Chosen Peoples: The Politics and Poetics of Archaeological Narrative." In *Nationalism, Politics, and the Practice of Archaeology,* edited by Philip L. Kohl and Clare Fawcett, 249–62. Cambridge: Cambridge University Press.

———. 1997. "Structuring the Past: Israelis, Palestinians, and the Symbolic Authority of Archaeological Monuments." In *The Archaeology of Israel: Constructing the Past, Interpreting the Present,* edited by N. A. Silberman and D. Small, 62–81. Sheffield, U.K.: Sheffield University Press.

Skeates, Robin. 2000. *Debating the Archaeological Heritage.* London: Duckworth.

Smardz, Karolyn, and Shelley J. Smith, eds. 2000. *The Archaeology Education Handbook: Sharing the Past with Kids.* Walnut Creek, Calif.: AltaMira Press.

South, Stanley. 1997. "Generalized versus Literal Interpretation." In *Presenting Archaeology to the Public: Digging for Truths,* edited by J. H. Jameson, 54–62. Walnut Creek, Calif.: AltaMira Press.

Stone, M. Priscilla, Angelique Haugerd, and Peter D. Little. 2000. "Commodities and Globalization: Anthropological Perspectives." In *Commodities and Globalization: Anthropological Perspectives,* edited by A. Haugerd, M. P. Stone, and P. D. Little, 1–29. Lanham, Md.: Rowman & Littlefield.

Stone, Peter G., and Brian L. Molyneaux, eds. 1994. *The Presented Past: Heritage, Museums, and Education.* London: Routledge.

Trigger, Bruce G. 1984. "Alternative Archaeologies: Nationalist, Colonialist, Imperialist." *Man* 19(3): 355–70.

———. 1995. "Romanticism, Nationalism, and Archaeology." In *Nationalism, Politics, and the Practice of Archaeology*, edited by Philip L. Kohl and Clare Fawcett, 262–79. Cambridge: Cambridge University Press.

Trouillot, Michel-Rolph. 1995. *Silencing the Past: Power and the Production of History.* Boston: Beacon.

Tsing, Anna. 2002. "Conclusion: The Global Situation." In *The Global Situation*, edited by Jonathan X. India and Renato Rosaldo, 453–85. Malden, Mass.: Blackwell.

Wobst, H. Martin. 1995. "Commentary: A Socio-Politics of Socio-Politics in Archaeology." In *Critical Traditions in Contemporary Archaeology: Essays in the Philosophy, History, and Socio-Politics of Archaeology*, edited by V. Pinsky and A. Wylie, 136–40. Albuquerque: University of New Mexico Press.

Wolf, Eric R. 1982. *Europe and the People without History.* Berkeley: University of California Press.

THE LEGAL AND HISTORICAL CONTEXT FOR MARKETING HERITAGE

II

International Conventions and Cultural Heritage Protection

2

BONNIE MAGNESS-GARDINER

L
AWS AND REGULATIONS DESIGNED to protect artifacts, sites, monuments, and landscapes most often are the product of national legislation and are directed at internal management of state cultural resources. International regulation also plays a role in national resource management and protection. The global dimension of the issue is encompassed by the resources that often cross national boundaries, the symbolic and historical importance of individual sites, objects, or natural resources, and the transnational source of certain threats. The most notable of the transnational threats are war and First World market forces on Third World resources. After World War II, many states recognized the need for a global approach to the protection of cultural and natural heritage. The context of their concern was rapid postwar development that endangered the very resources that were proving valuable for economic expansion.

The 2001–2002 International Council on Monuments and Sites (ICOMOS) report on world heritage at risk illustrates the ways in which that concern is still valid. The report (Burke 2001) provides a laundry list of well-documented contemporary threats to sites and monuments, including "maintenance deficiency, lack of financial and human resources; economic and social changes, particularly changing State responsibilities and unsettled ownerships; insufficient conservation standards; tourism-related issues; the effects of globalization; military activity and political change; cultural displacement—forced migration; and lack, loss or inappropriate devolution of protective heritage legislation." Many of these threats cross international boundaries and international laws, and conventions are the only means of addressing them.

UNESCO (United Nations Educational, Scientific and Cultural Organization) developed and implemented most of the legal instruments that address problems of heritage protection and management. Membership in that body is not necessarily a criterion for participation in a specific convention. The following is a list of problems with a global dimension. Each is addressed by corresponding conventions. The complete text of these conventions and the most up-to-date list of ratifiers can be found on the UNESCO website, www .unesco.org/culture/legalprotection.

- Protection of sites/artifacts during warfare—Convention for the Protection of Cultural Property in the Event of Armed Conflict, known as The Hague Convention, 1954
- Prevention of illicit traffic in artifacts—Convention on the Means of Prohibiting and Preventing the Illicit Import, Export and Transfer of Ownership of Cultural Property, known as the 1970 UNESCO Convention
- Management of sites of global importance—Convention concerning the Protection of the World Cultural and Natural Heritage, known as the World Heritage Convention, 1972
- Protection of underwater archaeological sites—Convention on the Protection of the Underwater Cultural Heritage, known as the Underwater Cultural Heritage Convention, 2001

This chapter will focus on the two legal instruments to which the United States is a party: the World Heritage Convention and the 1970 UNESCO Convention.

World Heritage Convention (WHC)

The decision to build the Aswan High Dam precipitated the development of the WHC. It was clear from the outset that the dam would flood Abu Simbel, one of the treasures of Pharaonic Egypt. An appeal from the governments of Egypt and Sudan in 1959 led to a successful international campaign by UNESCO to save the monument (UNESCO 2001). At a cost of around $80 million, the Abu Simbel and Philae temples were dismantled, moved to dry ground, and reassembled. Over fifty countries donated half the funds to save the monuments, signifying international interest in heritage preservation and a willingness to offer concrete assistance. The success of the initial campaign led to other preservation campaigns: Venice in Italy, Mohenjodaro in Pakistan, and Borobodur in Indonesia, for example. The recent international outcry over the destruction of the Buddhas at Bamiyan, Afghanistan, illustrates the continuing worldwide concern for monuments that transcend local interest as well as the vulnerability of such monuments to political radicalism (Burke 2002) as well as to economic development.

In 1960 UNESCO initiated, with the help of ICOMOS, the preparation of a draft convention on the protection of cultural heritage from natural and man-made threats (UNESCO 2001). A few years later, after a White House conference designed to promote international cooperation to protect natural and scenic heritage, the International Union for Conservation of Nature developed similar proposals for its members. Proponents of the heritage convention combined the two texts (cultural heritage and natural heritage) for presentation to UNESCO. The General Conference of UNESCO adopted the Convention Concerning the Protection of World Cultural and Natural Heritage on November 16, 1972 (UNESCO 2000).

The WHC links the concept of nature conservation with site preservation. For the purposes of the convention, these are treated as complementary ideas relating cultural identity associated with sites to the natural environment in which they occur. The focus here will be on the cultural heritage component of the convention. The World Heritage list is the concrete result of the WHC. Inscription on the list qualifies the site for support through the World Heritage Fund. As noted by Schuster (2002, 2), the World Heritage list designation became an important symbol to be used by various interests in bringing political pressure on local and national institutions and many resources to bear on these internationally recognized sites.

The WHC defines the type of cultural sites that can be considered for inscription on the list as

> monuments: architectural works, works of monumental sculpture and painting, elements or structures of an archaeological nature, inscriptions, cave dwellings and combinations of features, which are of outstanding universal value from the point of view of history, art or science;

> groups of buildings: groups of separate or connected buildings which, because of their architecture, their homogeneity or their place in the landscape, are of outstanding universal value from the point of view of history, art or science;

> sites: works of man or the combined works of nature and of man, and areas including archaeological sites that are of outstanding universal value from the historical, aesthetic, ethnological or anthropological points of view. (WHC, art. 1)

The WHC also sets out the responsibilities of each member state for identifying potential sites and the role of that state in protecting and preserving them. Each state that is party to the convention pledges to conserve its own World Heritage sites and its national heritage. The World Heritage Committee administers the convention. Members are elected from the states that are party to the convention and serve set terms. The convention itself stipulates which professional advisory bodies will be used in evaluating the sites proposed for the list. According to article X of the WHC, each property nominated should:

1. Represent a masterpiece of human creative genius
2. Exhibit an important interchange of human values, over a span of time or within a cultural area of the world, on developments in architecture or technology, monumental arts, town planning, or landscape design
3. Bear a unique or at least exceptional testimony to a cultural tradition or a civilization that is living or has disappeared
4. Be an outstanding example of a type of building or architectural or technological ensemble or landscape that illustrates (a) significant stage(s) in human history
5. Be an outstanding example of a traditional human settlement or land use that is representative of a culture (or cultures), especially when it has become vulnerable under the impact of irreversible change
6. Be directly or tangibly associated with events or living traditions, with ideas, or with beliefs, with artistic and literary works of outstanding universal significance (the committee considers that this criterion should justify inclusion in the list only in exceptional circumstances and in conjunction with other criteria cultural or natural)

Any country may ratify the WHC; membership in UNESCO is not a requirement. The number of current states that are party to the convention is 172 (UNESCO 2002). Only states that are party to the WHC may nominate sites for the World Heritage list. The cost of membership is dues equal to 1 percent of UNESCO dues (for members of UNESCO) and voluntary contributions from all others. Benefits include

1. Financial assistance and expert advice from the World Heritage Committee as support for promotional activities for the preservation of its sites as well as for developing educational materials
2. Access to the World Heritage Fund, $3 million, for least developed countries and low-income countries, to finance technical assistance and training projects, and for states requesting help to prepare their nomination proposals or develop conservation projects
3. Emergency assistance for urgent action to repair damage caused by humanly made or natural disasters

In the United States, the Department of the Interior, National Park Service, and the United States Committee, International Council on Monuments and Sites

(US/ICOMOS) oversee World Heritage Convention activities. There are twenty-two World Heritage sites in the United States, including Mesa Verde National Park, Chaco Culture National Historical Park, the Statue of Liberty, and Monticello. The Department of the Interior, in cooperation with the Federal Interagency Panel for World Heritage, has identified many more sites (cultural and natural) as likely to meet the criteria for future nomination to the World Heritage list (Charlton 2001).

Although inscription on the World Heritage list brings international recognition, as well as potential for attracting funding and visitors (Schuster 2002; Wulp 2001), it is not without controversy. In the United States, there has been some concern about the protection of private and state property rights and the lack of congressional input in the selection process. In July 2000, the House passed the FY 2001 Foreign Operations bill that contained language prohibiting use of funds in the bill for the U.N. World Heritage Fund (McHugh 2000). In 2001, H.R. 883 was introduced in the House "to preserve the sovereignty of the United States over public lands and acquired lands owned by the United States." It specifically prohibits the secretary of the interior from nominating lands owned by the United States for inclusion on the World Heritage list unless certain restrictions are met concerning commercial development in surrounding areas. Although H.R. 883 has not passed into law, the concerns expressed in the bill are mirrored in community reaction to proposals for World Heritage status for sites in their region. For example, the proposal to create heritage sites in Tennessee met with accusations that the United Nations would control the property and that the region would suffer job loss due to restrictions on mining (Owens 1997).

Recent developments at Machu Picchu, a World Heritage site in Peru, illustrate how the World Heritage Convention brings together government, local agencies and interests, and international professional groups to strengthen the management and preservation of a cultural heritage site. In the mid-1990s, weaknesses in the management of the site, a government concession to build a cable car to increase accessibility, and plans for a large-scale hotel project led to concern for the long-term preservation of the site.

In 1997, the first World Heritage Committee task force assessed the site and asked Peru to formulate and institute a management plan. By 1999, a management plan was adopted and a management unit put into place. Plans for increased tourism were still an issue, and in 1999 the World Heritage Committee urged the Peruvian government to delay the planned cable car and hotel until another special task force assessed the situation. The task force issued a report in 2000, having already made preliminary observations and recommendations to the Peruvian government agencies responsible for Machu Picchu at the conclusion of the mission. The report includes very specific recommendations on the operation of the management plan, the lack of known carrying capacity, and the need to maintain its environmental integrity. Among other things, the report recommended a thorough study of carrying capacity before undertaking any new means of access to the site (UNESCO 2000a). In May 2001, the government of Peru suspended the cable car project indefinitely (UNESCO 2001a).

In countries where tourist dollars are a significant addition to the gross national product (GNP), the balance between development of spectacular sites and conservation of their infrastructure and ambiance will always be difficult. The World Heritage Convention, through the interest and recommendations of the committee and task force, provides world-class expertise to suggest the means of making choices regarding the development of Machu Picchu and other sites endangered by their own success in a sensitive way.

1970 UNESCO Convention

The UNESCO Convention on the Means of Prohibiting and Preventing the Illicit Import, Export, and Transfer of Ownership of Cultural Property (1970) seeks to protect cultural property against theft, illicit export, and wrongful alienation. States that are party to the convention are bound to return to other states cultural property stolen from a museum or similar institution and is inventoried, to take measures to control the acquisition of illicitly traded cultural objects by persons and institutions in their country, to cooperate with other states having severe problems of protection of their heritage by applying import controls based on the export controls of other states, and to take steps to educate the public.

UNESCO helps combat illicit traffic by drawing attention to International Criminal Police Organization (Interpol) notices of stolen cultural property and helping states draft legislation for the protection of movable objects. It also organizes regional training courses in cooperation with the International Council of Museums (ICOM) and Interpol. When appropriate, states involved in a cultural property dispute may request that the twenty-two-member state Intergovernmental Committee for Promoting the Return of Cultural Property to Its Countries of Origin or its Restitution in Case of Illicit Appropriation try to resolve the problem.

Unlike the WHC, with its active World Heritage Committee and funds for site conservation and management, the 1970 UNESCO Convention has no managing policy body, dues, or funds for programs beyond the training sessions conducted by UNESCO staff. Each state party implements the convention according to its own internal policies and legislation. Until 1997, very few market countries, notably the United States and Canada, had ratified the convention and thus its effectiveness was limited. The ratification by France in 1997, by Japan and the United Kingdom in 2002, and the planned accession of Switzerland in the near future enhance the potential of the convention as an active instrument to limit the traffic in illicitly excavated and exported antiquities.

U.S. Implementation of the 1970 UNESCO Convention: The Convention on Cultural Property Implementation Act

The 1983 Convention on Cultural Property Implementation Act (Public Law 97-446, 19 USC 2601 et seq., as amended, hereinafter CCPIA) enables the government of the United States to implement the 1970 UNESCO Convention on the Means of Prohibiting and Preventing the Illicit Import, Export, and Transfer of Ownership of Cultural Property. The United States, however, does not implement every article in the 1970 UNESCO Convention. Under the CCPIA, it implements articles 9 and 7(b). For article 9, the CCPIA authorizes the imposition of U.S. import restrictions on categories of cultural property originating in another country when the cultural patrimony of the country is in jeopardy from pillage. It must be noted that the import restrictions do not preclude all trade in antiquities from specific countries, but rather the import restrictions require documentation that the archaeological or ethnological article left the country of origin prior to the date that the import restrictions came into effect (Kouroupas 2000). Material already in circulation is allowed to continue to circulate without impediment. The imposition of import restrictions is intended to reduce the incentive for further pillage by discouraging trade in undocumented items. The intention is to keep archaeological sites and monuments intact and available for scientific excavation by making the objects in those sites less attractive in the international marketplace.

The search for those artifacts with a market value destroys many others artifacts as well as their context. For article 7(b), the CCPIA authorizes imposition of U.S. import restrictions on any cultural property stolen from an inventoried collection in a museum or other institution in a state that is party to the 1970 UNESCO Convention. The import restriction is from on the date the state became party to the convention.

The president of the United States carries out the numerous executive functions of sections 303 and 304 of the CCPIA (http://exchanges.state.gov/culprop/97-446.html). Most of these functions have been delegated to the secretary of state, who performs the principal executive functions under the CCPIA. The secretary of state, in turn, designates a member of his staff, usually in the Bureau of Educational and Cultural Affairs, to carry out these functions. The U.S. State Department has primary responsibility for support of the executive and advisory functions under the CCPIA. The Cultural Property Advisory Committee reviews foreign government requests for U.S. import restrictions on cultural property and submits its recommendations to the president's designee at the State Department. Appointed by the president, the committee is composed of eleven persons who are experts in archaeology or related fields, experts in the international sale of cultural property, and representatives of museums and the general public. The president's designee in the State Department considers the recommendation of the committee when it is received within the time constraints stipulated by the CCPIA, and he renders a decision in consultation with the Department of the Treasury.

U.S. Customs has the responsibility of enforcing import restrictions. When a decision to impose import restrictions is reached, U.S. Customs publishes a designated list of restricted objects in the *Federal Register*. In U.S. territories or areas outside the jurisdiction of the U.S. Customs Service, import restrictions under the CCPIA are enforced by the Department of the Interior.

The CCPIA draws a distinction between pillaged cultural property and stolen cultural property. Sections 303–307 of the CCPIA concern the problem of pillage and illicit export of uninventoried material. Pillaged material, in the context of the CCPIA, is archaeological or ethnological material that until the moment of its illicit extraction was in situ in an archaeological site or cultural context. Thus pillaged material is not inventoried, photographed, described, or otherwise known to the authorities with any specific, identifying details. Section 308 provides ongoing protection for material that is stolen after it has been documented or inventoried within a collection.

Protection from Pillage

Protection from pillage under the CCPIA is only applied on a country-by-country basis. Under article 9 of the 1970 UNESCO Convention and section 303 of the CCPIA, a state party to the 1970 Convention may ask the United States for help in a situation of pillage in their country by having the United States impose import restrictions on certain categories of archaeological or ethnological material. The Cultural Property Advisory Committee reviews the request and makes a recommendation to the president or his designee. When certain positive determinations have been made on the basis of criteria outlined in section 303, the president or his designee responds to the request from another state party by entering into an agreement to impose U.S. import restrictions on archaeological or ethnological material. Since the United States cannot enforce the export laws of another country, import restrictions create a mechanism for recovering the restricted material if it enters the United States without an export permit issued by the country of origin. An agreement under section 303 may be bilateral or multilateral. Import restrictions imposed within the context of an agreement have a five-year effective period and may be renewed in five-year increments if certain conditions apply. Import restrictions imposed under agreements and emergency actions are not retrospective. The United States currently has agreements with seven countries: Cyprus,

El Salvador, Guatemala, Italy, Mali, Nicaragua, and Peru. The full text of the agreements can be found on the International Cultural Property Protection website (http://exchanges.state.gov/culprop).

It has been noted that the provisions under the CCPIA have been implemented slowly since 1987 (Kaye 1998, 88). In that time, ten states have requested and received protection under the CCPIA, through either emergency action or bilateral agreement. A chart illustrating the chronological implementation of agreements and emergency actions under the CCPIA can be found at http://exchanges. state.gov/culprop/chartdate.html. The import restrictions imposed under the agreements and emergency actions have met with serious opposition by the art trade (Fitzpatrick 1998), including the support for a proposed amendment to weaken the legislation (Lufkin 2000). Yet, as Kaye (1998) points out, import restrictions and subsequent seizures and repatriation of unlawfully imported cultural property that are contemplated under the CCPIA allow underdeveloped and developed countries with a problem of pillage and looting to reclaim that heritage and protect the contextual integrity of their archaeological sites. Moreover, a recent poll conducted by Harris Interactive indicates strong popular support for this concept in the United States (Ramos and Duganne 2000, 27).

A recent case of illegal importation of pre-Columbian objects from El Salvador illustrates how an agreement works. The United States and El Salvador entered into an agreement on March 8, 1995, following an emergency action imposed on September 11, 1987. By the terms of the agreement, the United States imposed import restrictions on certain categories of pre-Columbian material from El Salvador described in a *Federal Register* notice on March 10, 1995, continuing protection for the list published on September 11, 1987, under unilateral emergency protection. The categories of restricted artifacts are also illustrated in an image database hosted by the State Department (http://exchanges.state .gov/culprop/esimage.html). As the agreements are not retroactive, all artifacts matching the categories in the *Federal Register* notices are required to have an export certificate from El Salvador or verifiable documentation that they left El Salvador prior to the imposition of import restrictions in September 1987.

In October 2000, a U.S. Customs inspector at San Francisco airport opened two crates shipped on board a direct flight from El Salvador containing approximately forty-five objects with a manifest marked "craft goods." The Customs officer was suspicious and detained the shipment for further investigation. Having seen similar objects on the State Department website, the officer asked a local archaeologist with expertise in this area to identify and authenticate the objects (Bruhns 2001). The archaeologist verified that most of the objects were authentic, dated to the pre-Columbian period, and Salvadoran in origin. She also produced a detailed inventory. Customs was then able to seize the objects as a violation of the Cultural Property Implementation Act, since the importer did not have the appropriate export certificates from El Salvador as the country of origin. All interested parties were notified of the seizure and forfeiture proceedings began. The original importer did not contest the seizure, the artifacts were then forfeited to the U.S. government and returned to El Salvador in a ceremony at the Organization of American States building in Washington, D.C.

However, the deterrent to pillage offered by seizure and return of looted objects crossing U.S. borders is not the only, or even the most important, feature of the agreements. The agreements also contain provisions that ask the United States and the partner country to work together to improve the security of sites and museums, institute public education programs, carry out site and museum inventories, and institute exchanges of personnel and objects, among other things. These provisions are intended to strengthen everyone's appreciation of cultural heritage and to provide measures to keep sites and monuments intact for future research and the appreciation of future generations. In El Salvador, both countries agreed that El Salvador should use its best efforts to reestablish the national museum, destroyed by an earthquake some years earlier (Krecke 2000). With this expression of U.S. interest and support, the Salvadorans asked their national legislature to fund a new museum. The funding was forthcoming and the museum officially opened in 2000. In addition, the U.S.-El Salvadoran agreement provided opportunities for professional exchanges in support of museum development. The exchanges were facilitated by the State Department Bureau of Educational and Cultural Affairs programs for international exchange. The exchange of professionals is an important part of every cultural property agreement.

Section 304 enables the president or his designee to take unilateral emergency action by imposing import restrictions for a limited period of time, not to exceed eight years. This provisional action may be taken in response to an article 9 request by a state in accordance with section 303 of the CCPIA. Provisional emergency protection may be in effect until the terms of an agreement are negotiated. In order for emergency protection to be authorized by the president, the requesting state must submit, in addition to information relevant to criteria in section 303 authorizing an agreement, information that supports a finding of an emergency as described in section 304.

Emergencies are just that: cases of extreme need that demand immediate action. The United States currently has two emergency actions in force: one for Khmer stone sculpture from Cambodia and one for Byzantine archaeological material from Cyprus. The same implementation provisions apply: material designated under the emergency action cannot enter the United States without a valid export certificate from the country of origin or verifiable documentation that it left the country of origin prior to the imposition of the emergency action.

Stolen Cultural Property

Section 308 provides a blanket import restriction on articles of stolen cultural property. It is an ongoing action and does not require that a state party make a request. It implements article 7(b)(i) of the 1970 UNESCO Convention. Article 7(b)(i) prohibits the importation of articles of cultural property (broadly defined to include painting, sculpture, manuscripts, the decorative arts, etc., and not limited to archaeological or ethnological material) documented within an inventory of a museum or religious or secular public monument or similar institution in any state party and that are stolen from such institutions.

Under section 308, no article of stolen cultural property originating in a state party to the 1970 UNESCO Convention may be imported into the United States after the date the convention entered into force with respect to the state party or the effective date of the CCPIA (April 12, 1983), whichever date is later. The enforcement of sections 303, 304, and 308 of the CCPIA rests with the U.S. Customs Service.

A recent case in New York illustrates how section 308 operates (Levine 2002). An intricately carved tenth-century relief of a warrior guarded the tomb of Wang Chuzhi for over a thousand years until spring 1994, when thieves used dynamite to blast their way into the burial site in mountainous Quyang County of Hebei Province in northern China. The looters removed approximately ten reliefs from the rich tomb, damaging many of the surrounding art works. Six years later, in March 2000, Christie's in New York advertised the relief for sale at auction on consignment from a gallery in Hong Kong. Valued at between $400,000 and $500,000, the relief was seized by U.S. Customs agents before it went on the auction block. Christie's cooperated fully with the investigation. The fact that this was stolen was brought to the attention of Customs by a scholar who recognized the style and subject matter of the piece as belonging to this specific archaeological site. When the Chinese authorities measured the gap in the tomb wall where the relief had been removed, it was found to be the exact dimension of the warrior relief in New York. As the tomb was a registered monument, part of the inventory of national patrimony in China, relief could be claimed under section 308 of the CCPIA. The dealer voluntarily offered the piece back to China. When it was returned, China said the panel would become part of its National Museum's permanent collection.

Conclusion

Globalization brings with it benefits and costs to world archaeological heritage. Wealth, leisure, and the ability to travel to once remote archaeological sites allow more people to appreciate this heritage. But the presence of more people may jeopardize the integrity of the sites. Local and international appreciation of archaeological heritage leads to support of research projects, preservation efforts, and museum exhibits, but may also lead to acquisition of objects illegally excavated or exported. Both the World Heritage Convention and the 1970 UNESCO Convention offer protection for countries with important archaeological sites and monuments from the jeopardy in which they are placed by their own popularity, as well as by development, looting, and lack of management and planning. Both conventions need to be more widely known and utilized in the appropriate circumstances.

Note

Bonnie Magness-Gardiner is a senior cultural property analyst at the State Department. The views in this article are her own and do not necessarily reflect those of her employer.

References

Bruhns, Karen Olsen. 2001. "An Hour in the Life: Archaeologists at Work." http://archaeology.about.com/library/hour/blbruhns.htm. Accessed September 3, 2002.

Burke, John. 2002. "The Path to Destruction." *Guardian*, May 5, 2002. www.observer.co.uk/afghanistan/story/0,1501,710471,00.html. Accessed August 23, 2002.

Burke, Sheridan. 2001. *Trends, Threats, and Risks: ICOMOS World Report 2001–2002 on Monuments and Sites in Danger.* www.international.icomos.org/risk/2001/synthesis.htm. Accessed August 23, 2002.

Charlton, Jim. 2001. "World Heritage Sites in the United States." National Park Service. www.cr.nps.gov/worldheritage. Accessed September 6, 2002.

Fitzpatrick, James. 1998. "Stealth UNIDROIT: Is USIA the Villain?" *New York University Journal of International Law* 31: 47–77.

ICOMOS (International Council on Monuments and Sites). 2000. *Trends, Threats and Risks: ICOMOS World Report 2000 on Monuments and Sites in Danger.* www.international.icomos.org/risk/trends_eng.htm. Accessed August 30, 2002.

Kaye, Lawrence M. 1998. "Art Wars: The Repatriation Battle." *New York University Journal of International Law* 31: 79–94.

Kouroupas, Maria Papageorge. 2000. "The International Pillage of Cultural Property." *Cultural Resource Management* 23: 69–71.

Krecke, Dave. 2000. "Cultural Property Protecting the World's Heritage." *State Magazine*, May. www.state.gov/www/publications/statemag/statemag_may2000/bom.html. Accessed September 3, 2002.

Levine, Jane. 2002. "Returning Stolen Cultural Property: Tomb of Wang Chuzi Marble Wall Relief." *Cultural Resources Management* 27: 17–18.

Lufkin, Martha. 2000. "New Law Would Weaken US Ability to Keep Out Loot." *Art Newspaper.* www.allemandi.com/TAN/news/article.asp?idart=2350. Accessed September 6, 2002.

McHugh, Lois. 2000. *World Heritage Convention and U.S. National Parks.* CRS Report for Congress 96-395. http://cnie.org/NLE/CRSreports/international/inter-1.cfm. Accessed August 19, 2002.

Owens, Pat. 1997. *Clinton Expands Sovereign Land Theft, National State Sovereignty Coalition.* Document 126, 2/14/97. Wisconsin State Sovereignty Coalition. www.cascadian.com/NANS/News/LandTheft.html. Accessed August 19, 2002.

Ramos, Maria, and David Duganne. 2000. "Exploring Public Perceptions and Attitudes about Archaeology." Harris Interactive.

Schuster, J. Mark. 2002. "Making a List and Checking It Twice: The List as a Tool of Historic Preservation." The Cultural Policy Center. http://culturalpolicy.uchicago.edu/workingpapers/Schuster14.pdf. Accessed September 6, 2002.

UNESCO. 2002. "World Heritage Committee Gives New Impetus to Protection of Endangered Sites." Press release no. 2002-42. www.unesco.org/bpi/eng/unescopress/2002/02-46e.shtml. Accessed August 15, 2002.

———. 2001. "The International Safeguarding Campaign of the Monuments of Nubia —Egypt." www.unesco.org/culture/heritage/tangible/egypt/html_eng/index_en.shtml. Accessed August 16, 2002.

———. 2001a. "Cable Car Project for Machu Picchu Suspended." WHNEWS 29.04 (May 25, 2001). http://whc.unesco.org/news/2904.htm. Accessed August 29, 2002.

———. 2000. "World Heritage Information Kit." http://whc.unesco.org/infokit.htm. Accessed August 16, 2002.

———. 2000a. "Special Mission Report." www.mpicchu.org/unesco_mission.html#reducehotel. Accessed August 29, 2002.

Wulp, Patricia. 2001. "World Heritage Designation Poses No Threats to U.S. Parks, UN Association-USA." www.unamich.org/Main/Advocacy/Articles/worldheritage.htm. Accessed August 19, 2002.

The Politics of Playing Fair, or, Who's Losing Their Marbles?

3

MORAG KERSEL

HERE IS FIERCE ANTAGONISM BETWEEN those who possess cultural property and those who seek its return. Competing claims for cultural artifacts
such as Greece's Parthenon Marbles engender some of the most intractable and contentious debates in the realm of international cultural heritage.
A large number of cultural artifacts in Western museums, stately mansions, or hidden away in the private collections of businessmen have had a politically contentious history. Much of this cultural property has come under scrutiny by a
burgeoning postcolonial consciousness, highlighting the inherently problematic
nature of their current venues. Concurrently, the claims of ownership by indigenous communities are equivocal as issues of the "right" of ownership, the identity of the owner, the disposition of cultural artifacts as symbolic capital
(Bourdieu 1990) in the global economy, and modern property law persistently in-
fringe on these repatriation claims. Unrepatriated cultural property is caught in a
type of limbo—never entirely connected to the countries where it is situated or to
the places from where it originates. The questions of who owns the past and where
cultural property belongs consistently arise.

The answer to the question of who owns the past is, with increasing frequency,
the artifact's country of origin. A significant number of these objects have already
been returned in response to popular demand, international initiatives, and legal
pressure. Notable examples include the Director of the Supreme Council of Egyptian Antiquities Zahi Hawass's campaign to have many Egyptian antiquities returned to Egypt (Lufkin 2002); the repatriation of the artifacts from the Sinai by
Israel to Egypt in accordance with the 1979 peace treaty (Einhorn 1996; Hassan-
Gordon 2000); the Metropolitan Museum in New York's return of the Lydian
Hoard to Turkey (Kaye and Main 1995); and recent announcement of the intention of Italy, after years of international pressure, to return the Axum Obelisk to

Ethiopia (Williams 2002). The marble sculptures taken from the Parthenon in the first years of the nineteenth century are the best-known claim for the repatriation of cultural property, and the request for repatriation remains unfulfilled. As with other political and highly emotional controversies, there seems to be no middle or common ground in the dispute over where the Marbles should reside.

Superficially, this case appears to be little more than one nationalistic argument pitted against another. Even the name calls into question allegiances—the common term "Elgin Marbles" implicitly denoting British ownership. On closer inspection, the dispute is more complicated. The motives for requesting the repatriation of the Marbles may not be as multifarious as some voices in the debate would suggest but boil down to the economic benefit of owning the Marbles. Heritage tourism is a growth industry and in 2004 with additional visitors for the Olympic Games, Greece could see an unprecedented year of economic gain. The Marbles as an important tourist attraction in Britain continue to draw large crowds to the British Museum. This chapter illustrates the deployment of the Marbles in the global economy of cultural commodities, and the ambiguities and ironies surrounding these transactions. The central issue of this chapter is not the repatriation of the Marbles (although the issue is discussed to some extent), but the motives of each country to "own" the Marbles.

Historical Background

An acropolis, literally "high city," was a central feature of most ancient Greek city-states. "No other acropolis was as successful as the Athenian: a massive urban focus that was always within view and that at various times throughout uninterrupted 6,000-year-long cultural history served as a dwelling place, fortress, sanctuary and symbol—often all at the same time" (Hurwit 1999, 4). With high sheer rock walls on all sides it was an easily defendable location. By the end of the sixth century B.C., the Acropolis was no longer a protected residential area. Relatively more peaceful times, and resulting expansion of the city, meant that Athens was no longer limited to this citadel and now stretched around its lower flanks. By this time, the Acropolis had become the site of the city's most important religious cults and, most importantly, the center of the city's titular deity, Athena. Herodotus records that in 480 B.C., at the time of the second Persian invasion, the entire Acropolis was plundered and then burned by the invaders. Among the buildings lost were the temple to Athena Polias and the temple to Athena Parthenos, the latter still under construction at the time of the attack.

After their victory against the Persians at Plataea in 479 B.C., Athenians returned to their abandoned city and found all the buildings on the Acropolis had been laid to waste. Pericles wanted to rebuild the city and make it an artistic, cultural, and political center. The Parthenon and the temple of the Maiden (Athene Parthenos), from which the Marbles came, were erected between 447 and 438 B.C. We know the architects, we know where the marble was quarried (Matthews et al. 1992; Korres 1995; Pike 2002), we know that the votive statue of Athene was by Phidias and that he supervised the carving of the Marbles (St. Clair 1998, 46), and we also know in some detail what payments were made in the drachmas of antiquity (St. Clair 1998, 48). The construction of the Parthenon and the Acropolis involved a large workforce, many resources, and a vast amount of gold. The project was an exercise in conspicuous consumption, with clear political symbolism communicating the Athenian military victory over the Persians (Hamilakis 1999, 305) and sending a clear message to those city-states and warring nations contemplating a challenge to Athenian political dominance.

In the *History of the Peloponnesian Wars*, Thucydides writes that "if only the temples and the foundations remained . . . one would conjecture that [Athens] had been twice as powerful as in fact it is." Plutarch in his *Pericles* emphasizes that the reconstruction (at public expense) was a testament to the city's wealth and power. Both Plutarch and Thucydides believe that architecture conveys both the power and the glory of its makers. In the past, as today, the question of whether the Parthenon serves as an outstanding and enduring achievement as suggested by Plutarch or only as propaganda, as Thucydides seems to suggest, is still relevant. Over the centuries changes in the symbolic meaning of the Parthenon illustrate a transformation in how the space and material culture was co-opted for different audiences. Emptied of its deities and treasures, the Temple withstood its conversion into a church, a mosque, and, finally, an arsenal.

In 1686 an alliance of European powers led by Venice and financed by the pope renewed their long-standing war on the Ottoman Empire. In 1687 Italian general Francesco Morosini led an army to free Greece from the Turks. During the siege the Ottoman military used the Acropolis as a vantage point and turned the Parthenon into a storage facility for ammunition. The fortifications were no match for modern warfare; the strategic significance of the Acropolis was negligible (Hurwit 1999, 291). Still the symbolic importance of the site was evident and Morosini reluctantly ordered his troops to surround the area. "Though it was now a mosque, the Parthenon had once been the cathedral of Athens and the Turks, overestimating European reverence for holy buildings and the Classical past, thought that Morosini's men would not attack" (Hurwit 1999, 192). During the siege by the Venetians, a single shell pierced the roof of the Parthenon, directly hitting the gunpowder, igniting a colossal explosion that blew away the roof, two-thirds of the old cella walls, and brought down a series of colonnades that supported the metopes and frieze slabs (Hurwit 1999, 292).

Not only did Morosini and his men attack but they also took home some spoils of victory:

> When the garrison surrendered and Morosini took possession of the Acropolis he decided to take home to Venice a trophy of his conquest the large group of sculptures from the west pediment which had survived the explosion. But when his engineers were lowering the massive statues their cables broke and the whole group was shattered. A head from one of the pedimental figures, now in Paris, was taken back to Venice by Morosini's secretary. Two heads from a metope, now in Copenhagen, were taken by another officer in his army. The following year Morosini was compelled to withdraw from Athens leaving the Acropolis a heap of marble rubble. More damage was done to the Parthenon in half a year that in all its previous history. (St. Clair 1998, 57)

For the next century or so the rubble from the Parthenon provided hearthstones and doorsteps for Athenian peasants and mortar for the building trade, while Ottoman soldiers used the carved figures for target practice. With every earthquake tremor more of both the building and the sculptures fell.

From the seventeenth century, with the onset of Classicism as one of the main ideological forces in the West, the classical monuments of Greece and Rome again became the center of European attention. Western Europeans traveled to Greece for inspiration and to experience the Classical ideal. This led to a corpus of travel writings and memoirs, as well as the "collecting" of many pieces of antiquity (Hamilakis 1999, 306). British readers became familiar with the features and sculptures of the Parthenon from the descriptions and illustrations in *The Antiquities of Athens* (1762) by James Stuart and Nicholas Revett. The designs in their book became the templates and models for many British stately homes and public buildings.

In 1795, Thomas Bruce, the seventh earl of Elgin (known as Lord Elgin), a career diplomat posted to Constantinople in the Ottoman Empire, went in search of classical inspiration. Elgin had been occupied for some years building a grand country house in Scotland, Broomhall. He engaged a rising young architect, Thomas Harrison, an excellent designer in the Greek style and passionate admirer of Greek classical architecture. Harrison strongly encouraged Elgin to arrange for drawings to be made of the Greek antiquities in Athens and especially "to bring back plaster casts in the round of the actual surviving objects. There was no suggestion at that time that the original remains themselves should be removed" (St. Clair 1998, 34).

Lord Elgin approached Sultan Selim III in November 1799 for permission to sketch and to make casts of the statuary and architectural elements of the Acropolis. Here the tale grows murky. Did he bribe the Ottomans, the ruling power? Did he exceed the authority given him by the permit? Did he remove sculptures that were safe and secure in their high original positions? Did his appetite for rescue develop into greed, unscrupulous, corrupt, and unethical?

The original Turkish firman (an official letter from the Ottoman government conferring favors) has long since been lost and the remaining copy is in Italian, subject to varied interpretations. The initial legal controversy of the Marbles turns on the seventeenth-century meaning of the Italian word *qualche*. Usually translated as "some," it should read "some pieces of stone with inscriptions and figures." But it can also be translated as "any." Whether or not the original firman gave Lord Elgin this sweeping permission, Elgin's men, led by the Italian landscape painter Giovanni Battista Lusieri and the less scrupulous Reverend Phillip Hunt, liberally interpreted the vague document. With Elgin's enthusiastic if long-distance support (Elgin visited Athens only twice, and very briefly), they immediately began dismantling the Parthenon frieze (Hurwit 1999, 296).

Under the law of the time the acts of the Ottoman officials with respect to persons and property under their authority were presumably valid (Merryman 1985, 1897). Some scholars believe that the Ottomans had a solid claim to legal authority over the Parthenon because it was public property, which the respective successor nation acquires on a change of sovereignty (O'Connell 1956, 226–27). In a series of articles based on extensive research into the question of the Turkish firman, legal scholar David Rudenstine has come to the conclusion that Elgin did not request or receive permission to remove the Marbles (Rudenstine 2000, 2001a, 2001b, 2002). Other experts have also questioned the Ottoman claim to legal authority over the Athenian Acropolis (Eagan 2001; Reppas 1999). In absentia, Elgin was convinced by Lusieri and Hunt that the sculptures were in grave danger from Turkish neglect. By the end of the expedition Elgin had accumulated much of the best of what the Acropolis had to offer. Elgin thought he was rescuing and preserving sublime examples of a culture that was the heritage of the West rather than specifically that of an Athenian culture. As Vinson (this volume) notes, "The British Empire wished to identify with the prestige of the Greek culture. This was not out of racial identification with the ancient Greeks. Rather, there was a sense that the British, as the greatest, freest, people on Earth, were the most natural possessors of the objects."

Elgin left Constantinople in January 1803. The sculptures ended up in London's custom house in 1804, after a long and adventurous journey involving the sinking of the ship *Mentor*, which carried one shipment of sculptures, subsequently recovered by Greek fishermen (Hamilakis 1999; Hitchens 1997). The remaining shipments of the Parthenon frieze remained in the custom's house for two years during Lord Elgin's French imprisonment. Napoleon's forces seized Elgin on his way back to Britain and held him hostage using the Marbles as their ransom demand. Elgin refused to give up his beloved Marbles; he even lost his nose to a disfiguring disease. On returning to England, Elgin found himself destitute and with no means or motive for returning to Broomhall, and his only option was to sell the Marbles. He placed the Marbles in the dirty, damp shed and grounds of his Park Lane house, where they remained for years, decaying in London's damp climate, while he tried to find a buyer. As the Marbles languished in Elgin's musty storerooms, they became the stuff of legend in London, inspiring artists, poets, authors, architects, and the general populace.

The classical style of architecture swiftly adopted by the nation and the mystique of the Marbles added to this craze. Some twelve years later, in 1816, the Marbles were bought by the British government through an act of Parliament. When Elgin offered the Marbles for sale, there was much public debate on the issue, specifically centered on whether Elgin illegally exported the Marbles, whether he abused his position as ambassador to obtain the Marbles, and whether he was trying to get rich by selling the collection (St. Clair 1998, 274). Both the government and the public opposed the purchase. In the end the Parliament purchased the entire collection for far less than the original asking price, by a vote of 82–30 (Trade Environmental Database 2002). Intriguing, the thirty members voting against felt Elgin improperly took the Marbles from Athens (Greenfield 1996, 59–63). Once purchased, the Marbles were subsequently transferred to the British Museum, where a special gallery was built and where they reside today.

According to Richard Prentice (2001, 8), museums are today immersed in a wider commodification of culture: the extensive proffering of artifacts as a means of attaining the real. The majority of the Parthenon sculptures now reside at the British Museum (Hitchens 2001, 84), where the visitor can experience the "real" Parthenon by viewing the sculptures on display in the Duveen Gallery. In the earlier part of this century Lord Duveen had the Marbles scrubbed with wire brushes to make them look more attractive. The British Museum buried the report of this treatment and kept the sculptures out of view for ten years, hoping that the damage wouldn't be noticed (St. Clair 1999). Arguments have been made that removing the sculptures from the Parthenon saved them from the pollution and earthquakes that plague Athens (Daley 2001, 88). But is this really for the best? Is the museum providing the best educational experience for the viewers by exhibiting the Marbles out of their original context? And is the audience having the "real" experience that the sculptor Phidias intended by considering the Marbles at eye level against the backdrop of a stone wall instead of hundreds of feet in the air against the brilliant blue of the Athenian sky?

In the very first years of the nineteenth century it must have seemed inconceivable to Elgin that the Greeks would in 1821 begin to wrest their independence from the Ottoman Empire and be a Christian kingdom by 1829 that took up the heritage of the ancient Greeks as its patrimony; he could only see his precious Marbles in terms of more hearth stones, more marble dust for mortar, more fingers, toes, and noses knocked off by potshot musketry. Had Attica remained under Ottoman rule—as did Epirus, Macedonia, and Roumelia throughout the nineteenth century—even the Greeks might be grateful for his preservation of the Marbles, rather than vilifying Elgin's rescue operation. Elgin "saved" the Marbles, but should Britain now possess them?

To whom should the Marbles belong? According to Christopher Hitchens (2001, 88), the eminent political writer, the Marbles belong to the collective:

> Not to us, not to Greece, not to London, not to Lord Duveen nor to the Elgin family heirs. They belong to Phidias and Pericles. To whom does the whole belong? The whole belongs to us, because it is the nearest definition of the global continuity and artistic patrimony.

Professor J. H. Merryman (1985, 1916), a noted legal expert on cultural repatriation, argues that "everyone has an interest in the preservation and disposition of the Elgin Marbles; the matter does not touch only on Greek and English interests. The Marbles are the cultural heritage of all mankind." The idea that the Marbles represent the heritage of all people is based on the preamble of the 1954 Hague Convention for the Protection of Cultural Property in the Event of Armed Conflict, which states that "cultural property belonging to any people whatsoever is the cultural heritage of mankind." It is this sense of collective ownership that forms the basis for the concept of cultural internationalism (Merryman 1984) and begs the question of where and how cultural artifacts should be stored, displayed, and interpreted.

The Greek government has officially requested the return of the Marbles on a number of occasions. The first request was submitted to the British government on October 1983 through diplomatic channels. "The Greek Minister of Culture, Mrs. Mercouri played into the hands of the museum authorities by asking the British 'to make a sentimental and political gesture' by returning the Parthenon frieze to Athens" (Wilson 1985, 99). The appeal was made so that the Marbles might be reunited in one collection, in a museum to be built at the foot of the Acropolis Hill where the remains of the Parthenon temple stand.

An interesting topic that is often debated when the issue of the Marbles arises is that of laches, the legal doctrine whereby those who take too long to assert a legal claim lose their entitlement to compensation. According to Merryman (1985), Greece may no longer be able to claim ownership due to the extensive passage of time, regardless of whether or not the acquisition was legal. Greek independence from the Ottomans dates to 1828, and thus the Greeks had over 150 years to pursue their legal remedies before they finally demanded the return of the Marbles in 1983 (Merryman 1985, 1900). It appears that Greece may have lost any right of action they might have had for the recovery of the Marbles before an English court, where the application statute of limitations is six years (United Kingdom

Statute 1980). Thus far Greek governments have avoided making a narrow legal claim, wishing to avoid a judgment asserting that they have no legal standing in this case (Allan 2000).

The British have done everything in their power to keep the Marbles in England. They have refused official requests by the Greek government, refused international arbitration, and as of this writing, have steadfastly clung to the conviction that the Marbles belong in Britain (Greenfield 1996, 107).

A Question of Restitution

Why should the Elgin Marbles be returned to Greece? From the Greek perspective, there are four points supporting their claims. First, the monument to which the sculptures belong is in Athens (Hellenic Ministry of Culture 2002). Second, in Athens the Marbles will be exhibited within sight of the Parthenon, and the visitor can form a complete image of the temple in its entirety (Prunty 1984, 1178). Third, the cultural and historical significance of the sculptures as well as their aesthetic importance to Greece act as symbols of national heritage—the symbol of Greek Classical civilization at its apogee. And fourth, "the Marbles were removed during a period of foreign occupation when the Greek people had no say in the matter" (Greenfield 1996, 83). Following this argument, the Marbles were wrongly taken by Lord Elgin and have never legally or morally belonged to him or Britain (Merryman 1985, 1897).

The British have consistently provided four arguments justifying their retention of the Marbles. First, the Marbles were removed legitimately on the basis of a legal document—the Sultan's firman. Second, returning the Marbles to Greece would constitute a precedent for the universal removal of major acquisitions of the world's museums, thus limiting the role of the museum in the education of the populace (Trade Environmental Database 2002). Third, the removals were necessary on conservation grounds, and they have proved highly beneficial in preserving the sculptures from 150 years of high levels of pollution in Athens. Fourth, the Marbles have become an integral part of the British cultural heritage (Reppas 1999, 917).

In theory, repatriation should be easy. Cultural property is, for most legal purposes, like other property; the owner can recover it, subject to the possible rights of good faith purchasers (Merryman 1985, 1889). In many analyses of this case the legal issues come down to two positions; first, the Marbles were wrongfully taken by Lord Elgin and have never legally or morally belonged to Britain and, second, even if they are British property, ethically they should be returned to Greece. The issue of repatriation, however, is not the only question. Why do the countries involved really want the Marbles and are their motives as selfless as they may appear at first glance?

Why Do Britain and Greece Really Want the Marbles?

Greece

In a 1999 article on the Marbles, Yannis Hamilakis, a Greek archaeologist living in Britain, states, "throughout history the Parthenon Marbles have at the same time been singularized and commoditized" (Hamilakis 1999, 313). They have been referred to as symbolic capital (Hamilakis 1999; Hamilakis and Yalouri 1996), as something that can be exchanged for economic capital or national profit. Placing the Marbles in Bourdieu's definition of symbolic capital, the Marbles are traded for symbolic capital (Greek pride and nationalism) that is then converted back into economic capital in the future museum. The Marbles as symbolic capital are therefore a resource whose value derives from the ability to access and mobilize the symbols and symbolic resources of a culture (Bourdieu 1990, 118). Is Greece requesting the Marbles under the guise of nationalism, when perhaps their immediate motives are of an economic nature? In its request for the Marbles in time for the 2004 Olympics, is Greece exchanging its symbolic capital—the remains of the past—for potential national profit?

During their original conception and creation the Marbles functioned in the conspicuous consumption that accompanied the competition and power dynamics between Athens, other classical Greek city-states, and the Persians (Hamilakis 1999, 313). The Parthenon was about politics and commemoration of a glorified past. We witness their transition from a political instrument to commodity through a series of exchanges. In the eighteenth and nineteenth centuries, they were given away as part of broader political transactions between the Ottoman Empire and other global powers, including Britain and France. Napoleon's attempt to ransom the Marbles for the safe return of Elgin, and then Elgin's subsequent sale of them to the British public by way of an act of Parliament, further illustrates the utility for political purposes of the Marbles over time, although at this point they have made the evolution to commodity, which can be bought and sold. Today the Marbles represent symbols of the glories of the Classical era, the seed of Western democracy; but they have become commodities to be consumed by a global audience.

Their value is not only as a Greek icon but also as a contested commodity in the sphere of nationalistic movements. Nations all over the globe, as well as the collective European Community, have weighed in on this repatriation issue. In the United States, the 107th Congress introduced a concurrent resolution, "Expressing the Sense that the Parthenon Marbles Should be Returned to Greece" (H. Con. Res. 436). The resolution states "whereas the Parthenon is a universal symbol of culture, democracy, and freedom, making the Parthenon Marbles of concern not only to Greece but to all the world" (H. Con. Res. 436). This resolution has been referred to the House Committee on International Relations where it will undoubtedly languish for an unspecified period of time.

Do the Marbles just stand for democracy and the Classical ideal or do they represent something further? Hamilakis suggests that "this issue stands for the broader negotiations of the Hellenic Nation in the present-day world arena, it operates as a metaphor for its attempt to escape marginalization, to remind the West of its 'debt' to Hellenic heritage" (Hamilakis 1999, 313). To be seen as a key symbolic monument, the Parthenon must be viewed in its entirety, a sentiment echoed in a concurrent resolution of the 107th Congress: "Whereas the United Kingdom should return the Parthenon Marbles in recognition that the Parthenon is part of the cultural heritage of the entire world and, as such, should be made whole" (H. Con. Res. 436). In a June 2000 address to the British Parliament, the Greek minister of foreign affairs, George Papandreou, reminded the Members of Parliament (MPs) that he did not want to "rake over" the events of two hundred years ago when Britain was an empire and Greece a "subject" nation, but he went on to suggest that Britain took advantage of its global powers in the acquisition of the Marbles (Westminster 2000).

In an interesting turn of events Papandreou then introduced a more conciliatory overture by suggesting joint ownership, the Marbles back in Athens and the British Museum the beneficiary of rotating loan exhibitions of other antiquities. "We are talking about the Parthenon," he said to MPs, "we are talking about the greatest national symbol of Greece. What we are saying is that this masterpiece must be reunified and its integrity restored" (Westminster 2000).

Unwittingly, Papandreou uses the Marbles as symbolic capital in the global marketplace as he barters with Britain for the return of Greek cultural property. By suggesting joint ownership the Marbles are firmly established as a commodity, which can be possessed by two different parties, or exchanged for other Greek items. It is not the antiquities as physical objects, which will be jointly owned, but their value and symbolic meaning, which will be exchanged.

The reunification of the Marbles is somewhat of a falsehood. The facts are these: there are no plans to restore the Marbles to the Parthenon, the Acropolis is not to be significantly renewed, and nothing on the site will ever again be as it was in the days of Pericles. If the Marbles were returned to Athens they would not glitter in the hot sun against the bright blue of an Athenian sky, but would merely exchange one museum for another—an essential precaution, against the polluted Athenian air—and what is the point of that? "The Greeks just want an additional tourist attraction," says Michael Daley (2002), director of ArtWatch, a U.K. group that monitors the effects of restoration on works of art in museums. The bottom line is that the Greeks want to have those sculptures in a museum in Athens that would charge fees to the public and would be part of its tourist industry. Daley sees no point in taking the Marbles out of a museum with free public access and placing them in what he predicts will be an Athenian theme park.

In perhaps a counterconciliatory gesture in August 2001, the *Guardian* reported that the British Museum "was conducting talks with the Greek authorities about a temporary loan for the period of the Olympic Games" (Ezard 2001). The focal point of the debate has shifted from one of ownership to one of location, thus reinforcing the idea that the core issue may be more about the economics of the Marbles than the nationalistic pride engendered by the sculptures. Essentially the Marbles, like almost all of the antiquities of Greece, are seen as commodities that have material value and viable economic potential.

In anticipation of the extra tourism generated by the Olympic Games, Greece has stepped up the pressure on the repatriation of the Marbles. Over a million people a year pay to visit the Acropolis. During the Olympics, tourism estimates are at 3 million. In the final statement of the 107th Congress concurrent resolution, it was "Resolved by the House (the Senate concurring), that Government of the United Kingdom should enter into negotiations with the Government of Greece as soon as possible to facilitate the return of the Parthenon Marbles to Greece before the Olympics in 2004" (H. Con. Res. 436), stressing the importance of returning the Marbles before the 2004 Olympics. The timeliness of the restitution is predicated on the underlying assumption that there will be an economic windfall accompanying the repatriation of the Marbles to Athens. Reinforcing the notion of the Marbles as symbolic capital, the Marbles are indirectly exchanged for economic capital. Olympic visitors will pay to see the Marbles, the symbol of Greek greatness.

In October 2001, the board of the new Acropolis Museum in Athens announced that Swiss American architect Bernard Tschumi had won the design competition for the museum. The groundbreaking ceremony took place in early June 2002; the museum is scheduled for completion in time for the 2004 Olympics. The Acropolis Museum will remain an empty testament to the colonial attitudes of the West if the Marbles do not appear in time for the games (Alberge 2001).

Britain

Over 6 million (4.5 million of them foreign) people visit the British Museum for free (Trade Environmental Database 2002). At the British Museum, the magnificently displayed Marbles are seen in the context of wider Greco-Roman antiquity vis-à-vis the treasures of other civilizations (Daley 2001, 85). At no cost, visitors can experience the splendors of Egypt, Greece, Rome, Africa, and the Far East in an afternoon visit to the British Museum galleries. Through private parties such as champagne receptions, the British Museum reaps monetary benefits from the Marbles. The Marbles have become prized settings for corporate parties, perhaps precisely because of their dual symbolism: Western democracy and British Empire at its height of global power.

The Marbles have been in England for more than 180 years and have become part of the British cultural heritage and the British Museum experience. The Marbles and other works in the British Museum have inspired British arts and architecture. In the view of the British government it would not be in the public's best interest to remove the sculptures from one of the world's richest museums where they form an integral part of the museum's collection and where they are available for study by scholars in the context of the collection as a whole. Even if it were accepted that the removal of the sculptures from the museum could be justified in the public interest, the necessary repatriation could only take place if compensation was paid to the museum. The jurisprudence of the European Court of Human Rights suggests that such compensation must bear some relation to the market value of the possessions. Although in one sense the sculptures are priceless, it is clear that their market value is many millions of pounds.

As quoted in an article in the *Economist* (2000) British Museum spokesman Andrew Hamilton says "the Museum is forbidden by law to dispose of any objects from the collection, even if we were so minded. And the trustees are adamant that any piecemeal dismemberment would be a betrayal of their role as trustees, and spoil one of the finest museums in the world in comparative culture." In April 2001, British Prime Minister Tony Blair announced—in Athens, of all places—that he has no intention of returning the Marbles to Greece. His reason? They are being well looked after where they are. Besides, more people can see them in London. This stance fairly drips with imperial condescension, implying that the Greeks cannot take care of their own national treasures (*North Jersey Record* 2001).

In a recent panel discussion on ownership and protection of cultural property, James Cuno, former director of the Harvard University Art Museums, stated that one of the only reasons that there might be for Britain to return the Marbles would be that of political expediency. "Repatriation is based, not out of favor, but out of interest. For example, if Greece allows for British air bases so the British would have easy access to the Middle East, then Britain may repatriate the Marbles as a return gesture" (Cuno 2001, 314). Once again the Marbles are conveyed as symbolic capital, exchanging the Marbles for military favors. Conventional wisdom is that Britain will never return the Marbles, but in the prevailing world sentiment toward repatriation and the political pragmatism of the move, Britain may see that the economics of returning the Marbles may be in the best interests of global goodwill.

In its latest move, the British Museum is considering a radical plan to return the Marbles in exchange for a series of rotating exhibitions of Greek artifacts in order to reduce their £6 million debt. Even though the museum has never charged for entry, in a swap they would be able to charge for admission, a lucrative new source of income (Morrison 2002). The symbolic capital that represents the height of British Classicism is exchanged for economic capital.

The Resolution?

Merryman (1983, 759) states, "if the matter were to be decided on the basis of direct emotional appeal, the Marbles would go back to Greece tomorrow." They originated in Greece and they should be returned to Greece as the primary symbol of Greek nationalism. "Their value stems not only from their origin and association with the Parthenon with its enormous symbolic value, but also from their additional value as a disputed commodity, involving one of the political and economic superpowers" (Hamilakis 1999, 313). Elgin's removal of the Marbles may have deprived Greece of part of its national heritage, but at the same time it has contributed to the increase in their value as an international cultural commodity. Their placement in the British Museum contributed to the worldwide recognition of the greatness of Greece in the age before globalization. Hamilakis (1999) suggests that their return to Greece may in fact diminish part of their value. The Marbles will be removed from the international market of cultural economy, losing their ability to stand as symbols of the heated debate over cultural patrimony, the entire body of unrepatriated cultural property in the world's museums and private collections and continued postcolonial dominance.

If Britain surrenders to Greek nationalistic pleading and returns Elgin's trophies to the land of Pericles, are they establishing a precedent that will inevitably be exploited without scruple and result in the impoverishment, even the dismantling, not only of the British Museum, but of all the major Western museums? If the Greeks back down from this debate and settle for a "loan" of their cultural patrimony, are they not acquiescing to thousands of years of colonial domination and setting the stage for continued abuses of cultural property by occupying nations? There is no easy answer to the debate surrounding the "ownership" of the Marbles but the exercise of thinking critically about the motives for claims of possession suggests a broader inquiry into who should lose "their" Marbles.

Acknowledgments

I would like to thank Yorke Rowan and Jonathan Golden for inviting me to participate in the AAA session out of which this chapter was generated. The topic was a case study in my master's thesis and I would be remiss not to thank James Reap and Mel Hill for providing supervision and direction. John Carman, Uzi Baram, and Yorke Rowan provided helpful comments and editorial advice on earlier drafts of this chapter. All errors and omissions are solely my own.

References

United Kingdom Statute 1980, Limitation Act, chapter 58, section 2.

Alberge, Dayla. 2001. "Greece to Build £29m Home for Elgin Marbles." www.thetimes .co.uk/article/0,3-2001,372400,00.html. Accessed October 26, 2001.

Allan, Elkan. 2000. "Will Britain Lose Its Marbles?" www.salon.com/travel/ feature/2000/02/05/marbles/index.html. Accessed October 26, 2001.

Beard, Mary. 2002. *The Parthenon.* London: Profile.

Bourdieu, Pierre. 1990. *The Logic of Practice.* Cambridge: Polity.

Cuno, James. 2001. "Ownership and Protection of Heritage: Cultural Property Rights for the Twenty-first Century: Panel Discussion." *Connecticut Journal of International Law,* Spring 2001, 313–24.

Daley, Michael. 2001. "Antiquities: International Cultural Property?" In *Who Owns Culture? Cultural Property and Patrimony Disputes in an Age without Borders,* edited by Michael Janeway and András Szántó, 72–90. New York: National Arts Journalism Program.

———. 2002. Interview by David D'Arcy. NPR *Morning Edition.* July 25.

Dryden, John, trans. 1984. *Plutarch: Life of Pericles.* New York: Warner/Penguin.

Eagen, S. 2001. "Comment: Preserving Cultural Property: Our Public Duty: A Look at How and Why We Must Create International Laws That Support International Action." *Pace International Law Review,* Fall 2001, 407–46.

Economist (2000). "Not Carved in Stone." March 18, 98.

Einhorn, Talia. 1996. "Restitution of Archaeological Artifacts." *International Journal of Cultural Property* 5(1): 133–53.

Ezard, John. 2001. "Greece Presses for Loan Deal on Marbles." www.guardian.co.uk/ elgin/article/0,2763,539547,00.html. Accessed November 3, 2001.

Gazi, A. 1990. "Museums and National Cultural Property II. The Parthenon Marbles." *Museum Management and Curatorship* 9: 241–57.

Greenfield, Janette. 1996. *The Return of Cultural Treasurers.* 2d ed. Cambridge: Cambridge University Press.

Hamilakis, Yannis. 1999. Stories from Exile: Fragments from the Cultural Biography of the Parthenon (or "Elgin") Marbles. *World Archaeology* 31(2): 303–20.

Hamilakis, Yannis, and Eleana Yalouri. 1996. "Antiquities as Symbolic Capital in Modern Greek Society." *Antiquity* 70: 117–29.

Hassan-Gordon, Tariq. 2000. "Egypt to Set Up a Museum for Artifacts Returned by Israel." www.metimes.com/2K/issue2000-48/eg/egypt_to_set.htm. Accessed September 20, 2002.

H. Con. Res. 436. *Concurrent Resolution Expressing the Sense of the Congress That the Parthenon Marbles Should Be Returned to Greece.* July 2002.

Hellenic Ministry of Culture. 2002. "The Restitution of the Parthenon Marbles, Why Athens and Not London?" http://apollo.culture.gr/6/68/682/e68201.html. Accessed June 14, 2002.

Hitchens, Christopher. 1997. *The Elgin Marbles: Should They Be Returned to Greece?* London: Verso.

————. 2001. "Antiquities: International Cultural Property?" In *Who Owns Culture? Cultural Property and Patrimony Disputes in an Age without Borders,* edited by Michael Janeway and András Szántó, 72–90. New York: National Arts Journalism Program.

Hurwit, Jeffrey M. 1999. *The Athenian Acropolis: History, Mythology, and Archaeology from the Neolithic Era to the Present.* Cambridge: Cambridge University Press.

Jones, Jonathan. 2000. "Tainted Love." www.guardian.co.uk/elgin/article/0,2763, 349870,00.html. Accessed October 25, 2001.

Kaye, Lawrence, and Carla Main. 1995. "The Saga of the Lydian Hoard Antiquities: From Usak to New York and Back and Some Related Observations on the Law of Cultural Repatriation." In *Antiquities Trade or Betrayed, Legal Ethical and Conservation Issues,* edited by Kathryn Walker Tubb, 150–162. London: Archetype.

Korres, Manolis. 1995. *From Pentelicon to the Parthenon.* Athens: Publishing House "Melissa."

Lufkin, Martha. 2002. "Egypt Demands Return of Antiquity at Virginia Museum, Threatening Lawsuit: Object Had Been in Collection since 1963." *Art Newspaper,* August 4, 2002.

Matthews, K. J., Luc Moens, S. Walker, Marc Waelkens, and Paul de Paepe. 1992. "The Reevaluation of Stable Isotope Data for Pentelic Marble." In *Ancient Stones: Quarry, Trade, and Provenance,* edited by Marc Waelkens, Norman Herz, and Luc Moens, 203–12. Leuven: Leuven University Press.

Merryman, John H. 1983. "International Art law: From Cultural Nationalism to a Common Cultural Heritage." *Journal of International Law and Politics* 15: 757–93.

————. 1984. "Trading in Art: Cultural Nationalism vs. Internationalism." *Stanford Lawyer* 18: 24.

————. 1985. "Thinking about the Elgin Marbles." *Michigan Law Review* 83: 1880–1923.

Morrison, James. 2002. "British Museum Considers Elgin Marbles 'Swap' to Reduce £6m Debt." www.independent.co.uk/story.jsp?story=350574. Accessed November 11, 2002.

North Jersey Record. Editorial. 2001 April 3, A12.

O'Connell, Daniel P. 1956. *The Law of State Succession.* Cambridge: Cambridge University Press.

Pike, Scott. 2002 "Intra-Quarry Sourcing of the Parthenon Marbles: Applications of the Pentelic Marble Stable Isotope Database." Paper presented at the Parthenon and Its Sculptures in the Twenty-first Century: The Current State and Future Directions of Research Conference, University of Missouri–St. Louis, St. Louis, April 27.

Prentice, Richard. 2001. "Experiential Cultural Tourism: Museums and the Marketing of the New Romanticism of Evoked Authenticity." *Museum Management and Curatorship* 19(1): 5–26.

Prunty, Anne. 1984. "Toward Establishing an International Tribunal for the Settlement of Cultural Property Disputes: How to Keep Greece from Losing Its Marbles." *Georgetown Law Review* 72: 1155–75.

Reppas, Michael J. 1999. "The Deflowering of the Parthenon: A Legal and Moral Analysis on Why the 'Elgin Marbles' Must Be Returned to Greece. Fordham Intellectual Property." *Media and Entertainment Law Journal* 9: 911–84.

Rudenstine, David. 2000. "Did Elgin Cheat at Marbles?" *Nation,* May 29, 43–51.

————. 2001a. "Symposium: IV. Cultural Property: The Hard Question of Repatriation, the Rightness and Utility of Voluntary Repatriation." *Cardozo Law Review* 19: 69–82.

————. 2001b. "A Tale of Three Documents: Lord Elgin and the Missing, Historic 1801 Ottoman Document." *Cardozo Law Review* 22: 1853–83.

————. 2002. "Lord Elgin and the Ottomans: The Question of Permission." *Cardozo Law Review* 23: 449–71.

St. Clair, William. 1998. *Lord Elgin and the Marbles.* 3d rev. ed. London: Oxford University Press.

————. 1999. "The Elgin Marbles: Questions of Stewardship and Accountability." *International Journal of Cultural Property* 8(2): 391–521.

Stuart, James, and Nicholas Revett. 1762. *The Antiquities of Athens.* London: John Haberkorn.

Thorpe, Vanessa, and Helena Smith. 1999. "Return Elgin Marbles, Says Clinton." www.guardian.co.uk/elgin/article/0,2763,195556,00.html. Accessed October 29, 2001.

Trade Environmental Database. 2002. "The Elgin Marbles." http://gurukul.ucc.american.edu/Ted/monument.htm. Accessed June 14, 2002.

Warner, Rex, trans. 1972. *Thucydides: History of the Peloponnesian War.* Rev. edition. London: Penguin.

Westminster, David. 2000. "PM Rejects Greek Push for Marbles." www.guardian.co.uk/elgin/article/0,2763,328604,00.html. Accessed November 3, 2001.

Williams, Daniel. 2002. "Italy Vows to Return Ethiopia's Obelisk: Homecoming of Relic Taken by Mussolini's Forces Would End Long Dispute." *Washington Post,* July 20, A15.

Wilson, D. 1985. "Return and Restitution: A Museum Perspective." In *Who Owns the Past?* edited by I. McBryde, 99–106. New York: Oxford University Press.

Yalouri, Eleana. 2001. *The Acropolis: Global Fame, Local Claim.* New York: Berg.

From Lord Elgin to James Henry Breasted: The Politics of the Past in the First Era of Globalization

4

STEVE VINSON

WHAT DO WE MEAN BY GLOBALIZATION? Is it a set of wholly new economic relationships between those with capital and those who work, between an older world in which traditions and human relationships were paramount and a new world in which unrestrained free trade has reduced everything to its cash value? Is it a world in which a few industrialized nations have managed to dominate the many less-developed countries of the world, and a world in which a handful of wealthy men with no particular loyalties to anything have hijacked those nations to further their own agendas? Is it a world in which the need for creating ever new markets for ever new products forces global business enterprises into every corner of the world, remaking societies at will in order to expand business opportunities? Is it a world of dazzling new technologies, barely dreamed of by our parents and inconceivable to our grandparents, that have facilitated all of these changes?

If so, then globalization is nothing new because this is a reasonably close paraphrase of Karl Marx's description of the world as it existed for him in 1848, when he and Friedrich Engels published the *Communist Manifesto*. Yet there is little in Marx's analysis of the causes and consequences of capitalism that would be unfamiliar or uncongenial to modern antiglobalization protestors.

In fact, globalization really began two centuries ago with the extension of Western economic and political power mediated by advanced industrial technology and the ideologies of free trade and imperialism. More importantly, the first period of globalization had some profound effects on how the global past came to be viewed. In the eighteenth and early nineteenth centuries, interest in the ancient past was as spiritual as it was strictly historic. But as the nineteenth century progressed and passed over into the twentieth, the past no less than the present became increasingly nationalized and racialized, to the point that James Henry

Breasted, the founder of American Egyptology, could claim racial kinship with the ancient Greeks and Egyptians and thereby a share in their history.

Let us consider briefly how the world changed from 1789 to the early 1920s. Forces were unleashed that might be described as centripetal and centrifugal. The centripetal forces—those that tended toward unity—included the development of industrial capitalism and the perfection of mechanized transportation and electronic communications. Until 1800 or so, Europe had existed in a rough economic and political equilibrium with the rest of the world. Europe had long experienced a net drain of precious metals to Asia, sustainable only because the inflow of free precious metals obtainable from the New World considerably exceeded the outflow (Morineau 1999, 124ff.). Europeans may have chafed at restrictions on trade but lacked the means to dominate Asia or Africa. With steam-powered vehicles, with industrial, mass-produced weapons, and with instantaneous electronic communication, all of that changed. Midcentury saw the Opium War of 1839–1842, the consolidation of British rule in India, and the opening of Tokugawa Japan by Admiral Perry. By the 1890s, Africa was mostly colonized and the American West was fully conquered. After the turn of the century, Latin America was the backyard of the United States, which, in possession of Hawaii and the Philippines, was on the way to becoming a global power.

The Third World had been created, and for reasons that are all too familiar today. As non-European states modernized, most had to borrow capital from the West. As modernization projects faltered, reforms were demanded to protect Western creditors. In extreme cases, as with the Ottoman Empire, state finances might be taken over by Western experts, much as modern Third World states find themselves shackled with demands from the International Monetary Fund (IMF). And cultural imperialism had appeared. In the age of high imperialism, new waves of missionaries set forth to win souls for Christ. The rhetorical justification for imperialism and globalization depended greatly on the self-evident superiority and universal validity of Christianity (e.g., Lugard 1893, 1:69ff.) in ways that prefigured today's insistence on the noncontingency of Western concepts of human and political rights.

The centrifugal forces were the forces of liberalism and nationalism, which began a two-pronged attack on the remaining absolute monarchies and polyglot empires of Europe and the Middle East. In Europe, this began with the French Revolution, but the American Revolution was probably the first step in this direction, as Benedict Anderson (1991, 47ff.) has emphasized. If eighteenth-century revolutions were inspired by Enlightenment ideals of a transcendent political equality of all men, the roots of nineteenth-century revolutions—in Europe and the Americas—lay elsewhere: in the principle of nationalism, of self-determination in a largely ethnic sense.

In nineteenth-century Europe, nationality was closely related to language and came to be closely tied to the idea of race. On one hand, nationalism and racism were inherently particularizing forces. On the other hand, nationalism made its contribution to this first era of globalization, and remains crucial today, since it provided a unifying paradigm for thinking about the world as a whole and a structure for the dominant international order. In any case, as one surveys the changes that swept the world after 1800, one need not be a revolutionary socialist to agree with Marx: everything was new. And perhaps paradoxically, one result of this newness was an obsession with the past. Archaeology, philology, anthropology, folklore, and history all owe their beginnings as modern academic disciplines to this first period of globalization. This had to do with the ease of access to the Africa and the Middle East after 1800; it had to do with an upsurge in Western religiosity, which provided a research agenda for Western archaeologists and philologists working in the Holy Land; it had to do with the paradigm of evolution, which offered a research agenda to anthropologists working among tribal peoples; it had to do with the Romantic movement, which sought the essentially human in the wildness of antiquity; and it had to do with nationalism, which drew its strength from a posited primordial existence of nations. The Romantic conception of both nationalism and race structured the world into a neat pattern of mutually exclusive but interlocking racial and national spaces, each with its own history and destiny.

The creation of new states legitimated by this Romantic belief in the primacy of the nation created what Benedict Anderson has characterized as one of the central paradoxes of nationalism: objective modernity versus subjective antiquity (Anderson 1991, 5). These brand-new states labored, as they still labor, to discover suitable national histories and historical symbols, even if such symbols fit current reality only approximately, or even contradicted it. One example: Greece today sees the Parthenon Marbles as a *national* symbol, despite their origin as a statement of a specifically Athenian patriotism that defined itself as much or more in opposition to rival Greek *poleis* as in opposition to the Persian barbarians. As Rhodes (1995, 41) has pointed out:

> The Parthenon was the first building constructed on the Acropolis following Athenian release from the Persian threat, the first building constructed out of the rubble left untouched for all those years as a reminder of that threat. As such, it must certainly be associated with the intention to present Athens as the final victor over the Persians, as the new leader of Greece, the mistress of an empire formed to defend Greece against barbarian destruction.

Fifth-century B.C.E. Greeks knew this only too well; one imagines that Archidamus II, the Spartan king who led the first phase of the Peloponnesian War precisely to defend the Greeks from the ambitions of Athens, would have been none to happy with a modern Greek patriotism which elevated the Athenian to the paradigmatically Greek. Thucydides (2.11) has Archidamus say, as he prepares the Peloponnesians for war, "the whole of Hellas is eagerly watching this action of ours, and, because of the general hatred of Athens, wishing us success in our undertakings" (Warner 1972, 130).

Yet the fractious warring classical Greek city states became, in the nineteenth century, the nation of Greece; and so nationalism and ancient history were joined, as it were, at birth. A specifically racialized ancient history, however, was relatively slow to appear, at least in the Anglophone world. The Romantic Hellenism that developed in the eighteenth century was above all an aesthetic movement. That is not to say that interest in things Greek was apolitical. A good early example is John Gillies's dedication of his 1786 history of Greece to George III. In this dedication, Gillies describes Greek history as an indictment of "the incurable evils inherent in every form of Republican policy" (Webb 1982, 179–80). But what is evident even here is a view of history much like that of the ancients themselves: as a series of moral lessons that were valuable precisely because they were universal, not because they legitimated specific political claims in the present.

It is against this background that the appropriation of the Parthenon Marbles should be seen. The British Empire wished to identify with the prestige of Greek culture. This was not out of racial identification with the ancient Greeks. The Aryan theory, which might have bolstered such an argument, had only recently been made possible by the philological research of William Jones, and would receive its most explicit formulation by Gobineau (1884) only in midcentury. Rather, there was a sense that the British, as the greatest, freest, people on Earth, were the most natural possessors of the objects.

This is the gist of the argument that Elgin himself put forward to persuade the British Parliament to buy the Marbles, which they did in 1816. In the pro-Elgin pamphlet *Memorandum on the Subject of the Earl of Elgin's Pursuits in Greece*, by William Richard Hamilton (1815), a letter from an anonymous "friend of Lord Elgin" was included as appendix E, which laid out Elgin's position. Possession of the marbles would enable England's artists to perfect their craft through imitation of the greatest models known from the history of art. Moreover, no other nation's artistic community could take the fullest advantage of this opportunity. As the "friend" wrote:

> For the creation of a school, she possesses advantages, which have never been enjoyed in the same degree: she is wealthy, and she is free. Whatever encouragements are offered to improvement by those rewards which it is the power of wealth to bestow, are afforded here. But as the Patron of the Arts, her proudest distinction is her free government, which gives to the human faculties their fullest energies;

and secures to every individual the most entire enjoyment of those advantages, which the exertion of his faculties can command.

But there was a practical side to England's claim as well:

The advancement of the Fine Arts, and the facility of studying specimens of acknowledged merit, has a peculiar claim to favour in a manufacturing and commercial country. . . . In fact, there is no manufacture, whether of utility or decoration, that would not derive great benefit, were the means of . . . adopting the purest forms and designs, at all times accessible to the manufacturer and the purchaser.

And beyond all this, there was a desire to bolster England's political greatness. As one member of Parliament expressed it: "The possession of these precious remains of ancient genius and taste would conduce not only to the perfection of the arts, but to the elevation of our national character, to our opulence, to our substantial greatness" (Hitchens 1987, 134).

And so, through the appropriation of the marbles, Britain sought to link itself to Greece not racially or even historically but spiritually. But by the end of the century, the past was being thought of in other ways. The case of Sir William Matthew Flinders Petrie, the great originator of scientific archaeology in Egypt, is an interesting one. Petrie was born in 1853 and first went to Egypt with the intention of studying its pyramids in 1881, just three years before the Berlin Conference of 1884, which laid the groundwork for European colonial domination of Africa (cf. Hochschild 1998, 84–87). One of Petrie's greatest achievements was the definite identification of Egypt's predynastic culture—the late prehistoric culture (conventional dates c. 5000–3050 B.C.E.; cf. Hoffmann 1979) that immediately preceded Egypt's pharaonic civilization. Petrie's basic results remain fundamental for all work on this period. But considering the period in which he was working, it is no surprise that Petrie interpreted the transition from predynastic to dynastic Egypt in terms of invasion and conquest by a superior race, to which he referred as the "Dynastic Race."

Petrie argued in his 1917 *A History of Egypt* (1991, 2–3) that, at the end of the predynastic period, a dynastic race had entered Egypt—probably from the Red Sea—and had inaugurated pharaonic civilization by conquering "a decadent civilization of the prehistoric age," whose "highest development . . . had taken place perhaps a thousand years before." This dynastic race was the sixth of a series of distinct races that had inhabited late prehistoric Egypt, which Petrie identified through analysis of the nasal physiognomy of human figures in predynastic Egyptian art: (1) "The old aquiline race of the Libyo-Amorite type, to which belongs the bulk of the prehistoric remains"; (2) "a people with curly hair and plaited beards, most like a type found later in the Hittite region"; (3) "a people with pointed nose and long pigtail of hair, who probably lived in the mountains by the Red Sea"; (4) "a people with short and tilted nose, who seem to have occupied Middle Egypt"; (5) "a somewhat similar people, with rather longer nose, and a projecting beard, who may belong to the Delta"; (6) the dynastic race: "An entirely different race, having a straight bridge to the nose, and a very vigorous and capable type of face."

In his *History*, Petrie withheld judgment on the origin of these straight-nosed invaders, although in his later synthesis *Prehistoric Egypt* (1920, 49), he expressed the view that they came from Elam—a region in contemporary southwestern Iran. But Petrie always thought of them as a superior race from outside of Africa, bringing civilization to the natives.

It would be interesting to know whether and to what extent Petrie consciously drew parallels between his view of Egypt's terminal prehistory and the present that he himself was living out. Petrie was interested in racial theory and especially in theories of history that identified race as a central force in human events (Silberman 1999). His immediate forebears and his contemporaries attempted to define parallels between British and/or French imperial history and the history of Rome (Hingley 2000; Reid 2002, 140ff.). It is fair to say that Petrie's historical hermeneutic resembles more than a little the contemporary self-assessment of British imperialism in Africa, as we see in an 1893 apologia from Frederick Lugard, a British diplomat who served in many imperial posts in Africa and Asia. For Lugard, the British were in Africa as apostles of civilization: "The African holds the position of a late-born child in the family of nations, and must as yet be schooled in the discipline of the nursery" (Lugard 1893, 74).

Lugard's combination of progressivism and racism was packaged more crudely by U.S. Senator Albert Beveridge in a notorious 1900 defense of America's conquest of the Philippines:

> God has not been preparing the English-speaking and Teutonic peoples for a thousand years for nothing but vain and idle self-contemplation. . . . No! He has made us the master organizers of the world to establish system where chaos reigns. He has given us the spirit of progress to overwhelm the forces of reaction throughout the earth. (Garraty and Divine 1968, 2ff.)

Americans too saw world history in racial terms, and a more explicitly political racial discourse on ancient Egypt soon surfaced in the work of American Egyptologist James Henry Breasted. In his 1926 synthesis of the history of the ancient world, *The Conquest of Civilization*, Breasted placed the ancient Egyptians in the "Great White Race"—notwithstanding their "tanned skins." This great white race included the Egyptians, all Europeans, and the Semites of the ancient Near

East. These peoples were responsible, collectively, for the creation of civilization (J. Breasted 1926, 112).

What is striking about Breasted's racism is his evident desire to dehistoricize civilization. Breasted did not imagine that the civilizations of the ancient Near East and the modern West were linked solely by a chain of contingent events. The real linkage was racial: "The evolution of civilization," he wrote, "has been the achievement of the Great White Race." That is: one civilization, one achievement, one race. This kind of inclusive racism was at odds with much contemporary European thinking on race—contrast Petrie's fragmented racial typology for predynastic Egypt, or the Aryan theory and its spin-offs that conflated race, nationality, and language—and perhaps reflected Breasted's American roots. It is noteworthy that even today, the U.S. government—though dropping Breasted's "great" from its name for the white race—regards whiteness in much the same way Breasted did: as a class comprising "people having origins in any of the original peoples of Europe, the Middle East, or North Africa" (Grieco and Cassidy 2001). Though examples of the race/nation equation are found in American contexts (e.g., Beveridge; cf. Garraty and Divine 1968, 2ff.), it seems that the melting pot character of the United States, in both its self-image and its lived reality, has often worked to favor a broad, prenational conception of race more along the lines of Blumenbach than Gobineau.

In any case, Breasted clearly had abundant reasons—emotional and professional—to defend the racial honor of the ancient Egyptians and Hebrews. Breasted's son and biographer, Charles Breasted, reports that as a student in Berlin in 1891, Breasted was disturbed at the extreme German nationalism he encountered (C. Breasted 1943, 37ff.). As an Egyptologist, Breasted naturally had a stake in the historic centrality of Egyptian culture. And Breasted's original vocation for the ministry (C. Breasted 1943, 16ff.) suggests a feeling of spiritual connectedness to the Near East. Underneath it all, however, was an implicit claim to an actual share in the history of the ancient Near East. As an American, Breasted's heritage may have stretched back only to the seventeenth century. With his mixed Dutch and Anglo-Saxon heritage (C. Breasted 1943, 5), Breasted could trace his history back no further than Caesar's western campaigns. But as a charter member of the great white race, Breasted could claim a very impressive heritage indeed. This suggests a conception of heritage that is somewhat at a variance with the notion proposed by, say, Edward Said, who considered that Orientalist scholarship of the era of high colonialism was oriented toward control of the other (Said 1978), or of Anderson (1991, 178ff.), who thought of the colonial museum as a sort of advertisement intended to convince the natives of the superiority of the colonial regime. For Breasted, at least, the Orientalist project was at least as much leading the "great white race" to the truth of its own past—about reclaiming what was, in fact, rightfully its own—as it was about political or economic domination of inferiors and aliens.

We now face forces much like those of that first globalizing era—a homogenizing world capitalism that opposes itself to particularist claims, all of them invoking history as a source of legitimation. And no less than did our nineteenth- and early-twentieth-century forebears, we too fight out our historical battles on racial and national terrain, whether we consider the Parthenon Marbles, Afrocentrism, or the repatriation of cultural and human remains to indigenous peoples. It would be hard to locate terms more question begging than these last two: Afrocentrism as a discourse could not, of course, exist without explicit acceptance of the relevant European racial and geographic categories, which obviously have a history of their own, one that has little to do with Africa. And repatriation as a political issue could not, of course, exist in the absence of a nearly total subsumption of indigenous forms of social organization under the concept of a patria, a defined geographic space possessed by a specific group of people with diachronic cultural coherence, who operate through a formal governmental and bureaucratic structure. As real as such structures may now appear to be, they were products of a particular historical moment, and one in which bureaucrats rather than indigenes held the upper hand.

Yet the dominant forms of political organization, created in the first era of globalization, continue to make national political bodies and their cultural wings inevitable—from a local tribal council or county historical association up to the level of a major national museum or a multinational organization like UNESCO. And these organizations enforce particular types of attitudes toward the past and its material remains. They create the concept of heritage as a kind of property that has to be managed and used for the benefit of its putative owners, and as a tool to this end they create culture-historical maps that are supposed to be congruent with some version of the modern political map, as it is or as it should be. Even those who desire to escape the dominant political paradigm—say, indigenous peoples who inhabit territories north of the United States, and who desire to be known by the term "First Nation" (rather than "Canadian Indian")—find themselves invoking, willy-nilly, the rhetoric of history ("First") and of nationalism. Historicizing the concepts of race and nation—and the concept of history itself—can help us remember how contingent heritage actually is, and it may encourage us not to claim too much scholarly authority for the positions we take in what are, ultimately, political and legal, rather than historical or anthropological, questions.

References

Anderson, B. 1991. *Imagined Communities: Reflections on the Origin and Spread of Nationalism.* 2d ed. London: Oxford University Press.

Breasted, C. 1943. *Pioneer to the Past: The Story of James Henry Breasted, Archaeologist.* New York: Scribner's.

Breasted, J. H. 1926. *The Conquest of Civilization.* New York and London: Harper & Bros.

Emery, W. 1961. *Archaic Egypt.* Middlesex, U.K.: Penguin.

Garraty, J., and R. Divine, eds. 1968. *Twentieth-Century America: Contemporary Documents and Opinions.* Boston: Little, Brown.

Gobineau, J. A. 1884. *Essai sur l'inégalité des races humaines.* 2d ed. Paris: Firmin-Didot.

Grieco, E. M., and R. C. Cassidy. 2001. "Overview of Race and Hispanic Origin." Census 2000 Brief (March).

Hamilton, W. R. 1815. *Memorandum on the Subject of the Earl of Elgin's Pursuits in Greece.* 2d ed. London: John Murray.

Hingley, R. 2000. *Roman Officers and English Gentlemen: The Imperial Origins of Roman Archaeology.* London: Routledge.

Hitchens, C. 1987. *The Elgin Marbles: Should They Be Returned to Greece?* London: Chatto & Windus.

Hochschild, A. 1998. *King Leopold's Ghost.* Boston: Houghton-Mifflin.

Hoffmann, M. 1979. *Egypt before the Pharaohs.* New York: Knopf.

Lugard, F. D. 1893. *The Rise of Our East African Empire.* London: Blackwood.

Mark, S. 1997. *From Egypt to Mesopotamia: A Study of Predynastic Trade Routes.* College Station: Texas A&M University Press.

Morineau, M. 1999. "The Indian Challenge." In *Merchants, Companies, and Trade: Europe and Asia in the Early Modern Era,* edited by S. Chaudhury and M. Morineau, 116–44. Cambridge: Cambridge University Press.

Petrie, W. M. F. 1920. *Prehistoric Egypt.* London: British School of Archaeology in Egypt.

———. 1991. *A History of Egypt—Part One.* Rev. 10th ed. London: Reprinted Histories and Mysteries of Man.

Reid, M. 2002. *Whose Pharaohs? Archaeology, Museums, and Egyptian National Identity from Napoleon to World War I.* Berkeley: University of California Press.

Rhodes, R. 1995. *Architecture and Meaning on the Athenian Acropolis.* Cambridge: Cambridge University Press.

Said, E. 1978. *Orientalism.* New York: Pantheon.

Silberman, A. 1999. "Petrie's Head: Eugenics and Near Eastern Archaeology." In *Assembling the Past: Studies in the Professionalization of Archaeology,* edited by A. Kehoe and M. Emmerichs, 69–79. Albuquerque: University of New Mexico Press.

Warner, R., trans. 1972. *Thucydides: History of the Peloponnesian War.* Rev. ed. London: Penguin.

Webb, T., ed. 1982. *English Romantic Hellenism, 1700–1824.* Manchester: Manchester University Press.

THE PAST AS COMMODITY   III

Conflating Past and Present: Marketing Archaeological Heritage Sites in Ireland

5

KELLI ANN COSTA

> *Cultural landscapes—cultivated terraces on lofty mountains, gardens, sacred places . . . testify to the creative genius, social development and the imaginative and spiritual vitality of humanity. They are part of our collective identity.*

(UNESCO 1993)

THE IDEA OF "HERITAGE"—that inherited past which ranges from language, names, property, habits, and customs to waterways, landscapes, cultures, and objects—is often so broadly defined as to defy any real agreement or understanding. Heritage has become a commodity; something that can be marketed and managed and presented as evidence of longevity, brilliance, perseverance, and power. That archaeological sites and the practice of archaeology itself have become part of the "process" of heritage making is linked to the idea that heritage needs stewardship and preservation. Heritage carries with it a sacred cast. Unlike history—which is over and done with—heritage continues despite its often perceived connection with a historical past. The marketing of "heritage" and the management of heritage sites is a global movement. Much the way Newport, Rhode Island, reinvented its colonial and merchant past to attract twentieth-century commerce in the form of tourism, countless other areas of the world have re-created pasts with mass appeal. Many other places have simply been created: the Disney phenomenon and other massive theme parks have, in a very short time, become "traditional" vacation spots for the touring public. In Ireland the archaeological landscape has been reintroduced to the visitor and local alike both to exoticize Ireland's past as unique and superior and to conflate the past with the present by establishing connections and familiar themes with it (Cooney 1996).

Visitors to the sites may know nothing about them, but they are sure they have some deep connection to them—especially if they are of Irish descent. They inherit the cultural landscape through some ethereal and tenuous (nonetheless "blood") tie from an ancestor (usually male and usually noble—or at least terribly brave) who strolled across this very landscape. "Ignorance, like distance, protects heritage from harsh scrutiny" (Lowenthal 1998, 135).

Recently I was able to go along on an organized bus tour of Ireland with twenty-five Americans ranging in age from thirty-five to sixty-five. The tour organizer's goal was to introduce the mostly first-time travelers to some of Ireland's unique cultural heritage. Discussion at the airport prior to departure seemed to center on the recent violence in Belfast and Omagh, the possibility of being robbed, and the amount of Guinness that would be consumed (and the "fact" that it would be warm beer). There was little interest or discussion regarding the culture and history of Ireland beyond what could be offered to them as durable goods. They seemed to have a notion of homeland, but Ireland was supposed to be entirely idyllic and backward. "Dublin," as one tour mate told me, "isn't really Irish at all." Urban areas were the "fault" of the English and should be expunged from the Irish countryside. My fellow tour takers all possessed that misty eastward gaze toward the green of a homeland generations removed, but most, if not all, were reluctant to meet their potential brothers and sisters of Eire face-to-face.

As a group they held fast to a fictionalized, reified memory of Ireland, a collective "brokered image" (Costa 2001) that has been gleaned from popularized versions of a mythologized (but fairly recent) past. To visit an Ireland *not* precisely reminiscent of the image is disappointing at the very least. The "new Ireland" (that of Celtic Tigers, computers, and million-dollar flats) is a fabrication born of and through the poisonous influence of the United States and Europe. Many of the tourists were high school teachers who were incredibly unprepared for the minor culture shock of the comfortable and controlled tour. On a loop through Limerick the driver showed everyone the street made famous in Frank McCourt's book *Angela's Ashes* where he collected coal as a boy. Though interested in the driver's comments, one teacher turned to me and said, "Everyone knows that (meaning abject poverty) never happened in Ireland—it's always been heaven on earth here. McCourt only wrote that nonsense for pity money." Clearly she had never heard of famine, war, or colonialism.

When a modern organized tour goes to Ireland, even the Irish of today are caricatured to represent a timelessness embodied in the landscape. One doesn't go to see the Irish as much as one goes to see Ireland; which may or may not include the "Irish" in a tourist sense. Likewise when people come to New Hampshire where I live, they don't come to see me—or any other New Hampshirite for that matter. They come by the busloads to see a representation of my state's unique cultural heritage that includes its seasonal landscapes. The appropriation of "a culture" of Ireland for consumption by the tourist industry and their patrons has been instrumental in the formation of borders and frontiers that few outside the "indigenous" culture will cross. "Knowing the Irish" means having been to Ireland, spoken to a few "authentic" Irish in a pub in Dublin, Killarney, or Galway, and quite possibly having found that small out of the way village where no one has ever been (except of course the 3,000 other people who just left). And it means seeing the sites, especially the ones with visitor centers, whether one has any knowledge of the site's history or not. What matters is their presence on the heritage landscape: must-see venues of pristine unaffected glory.

The heritage landscape in Ireland is there for consumption. As it belongs to the nation of Ireland so it belongs to the world; it draws the world to it and they keep coming to be mesmerized and mystified by a past beyond their imaginations. Archaeology is a process by which treasures are brought to the surface for public display. It hovers on the same plane as the mytho-historical past of Ireland itself. But, like the heroes Cú Chulainn, Cormac, Diarmaid, Grainne, and Fergus, archaeology's part in creating heritage is soon enveloped in an insular mist of perplexity and legend; it is meant to be seen, not heard.

Navan Fort

Since 1997 I have been researching heritage sites and their marketing and management in both Ireland and Scotland. Since 2000 I have concentrated on three well-known archaeological sites in Ireland: Tara, Navan Fort, and Newgrange. Navan Fort—*Emain Macha*—is located near Armagh City in Northern Ireland. Prior to resuming work in 2001, I had been in contact with the Navan Center, a large education and visitor center adjoining the fort. I was very interested in how the center was interpreting and presenting the fort and several other sites of the Navan complex to school groups and other visitors. Dudley Waterman's excavations undertaken from 1961 to 1971 have been the most extensive thus far completed at the site, and his original work has been a driving force behind the popularization of the site and its presentation to the public. After his untimely death in 1979 efforts to preserve the site were stepped up in response to a proposal to expand a nearby quarry. This proposed extension would have put the entire site in danger of destruction and was met with a strong outcry from the entire archaeological community of Ireland. Barry Raftery (1985) and many others were compelled to testify against this proposed action in order to preserve the site. In 1986 the Navan Research Group was established to continue research at the complex and has regularly published the journal *Emania* since. Further, the Navan at Armagh charitable trust opened the Navan Center in 1993 to serve as an educational center dedicated to the history, archaeology, and literary traditions of the area (Hamlin 1997). In this section I examine the archaeological history of Navan Fort, its cultural attributes, its connections to Irish epic literature, and finally, the Navan Center.

Navan Fort/Emain Macha: History and Archaeology

The Navan complex is a group of sites that includes Navan Fort, Loughnashade, the King's Stables, Haughey's Fort, and some smaller Neolithic through Iron Age sites (Warner 1994).

Navan Fort is considered one of the four major royal sites in Ireland that include the Hill of Tara, Co. Meath, Knockaulin/Dún Ailinne, Co. Kildare, and Cruachan/Rathcroghan, Co. Roscommon. Navan Fort is located on a natural drumlin somewhat south and west of the city of Armagh. This large glacial hill is one of many in the surrounding landscape of greater Armagh. There is evidence of occupation from the Neolithic in levels beneath the constructed mound (Simpson 1989; Mallory and McNeill 1995; Waterman 1997; Lynn 1997a; Waddell 2000). The Neolithic is generally referred to as Phase I following the excavations done by Dudley Waterman from 1961 through 1971. The phases are described using his designations. Recently revised phases (see table 5.1) are based on recalibrated C14 dates. Phase II is a transitional phase marking a horizon between the Neolithic and Bronze Age indicated by plow marks across much of the interior and surrounding areas of the extant ditch and bank (Raftery 1994; Waterman 1997; Waddell 2000). The evidence suggests little activity at the site for several centuries following this. There then appears to have been increased interest in Haughey's Fort and the King's Stables during the Middle Bronze Age, after which Navan returns to prominence.

Phase III, a long period of intense activity at the site, shows evidence of human occupation and alteration from the ninth century B.C. through the first cen-

Table 5.1.   Original Phases at Navan Fort as Described by Waterman, with Revised Phases That Correspond with Radiocarbon Dates in Right Column

Phase I	Neolithic	c. 4000 B.C.	Lithics, pottery	Phase 1
Phase II	Neo/Early Bronze Age	c. 3500–2800 B.C.	Plow marks	Phase 2
Phase IIIi	Late Bronze Age	c. 900–450 B.C.	Ditch and bank	Phase 3
Phase IIIii	Early Iron Age	c. 450–250 B.C.	Circular enclosures	Phase 4a
Phase IIIiii	Iron Age	c. 250–100 B.C.	Middle enclosures	Phase 4b
Phase IV	Iron Age	c. 95 B.C.	Timber "temple"	Phase 5a
Phase V	Iron Age	c. 95 B.C.	Cairn	Phase 5b
Phase V	Iron Age	c. 95 B.C.	Destruction	Phase 5c
Phase V	Iron Age	c. 95 B.C.	Mound	Phase 5d

Source: Lynn 1997b.

tury B.C. (Herity and Eogan 1996; Lynn et al. 1997; Waddell 2000). The earliest phase (IIIi) defines the construction of the unusual ditch and bank structure where the ditch occurs inside of the bank (Herity and Eogan 1996). Univallate (single line of defense) forts (there are four known in Ireland) are mainly found in landscapes of low hills and broad plains (Herity and Eogan 1996, 228). Phase III falls into Ireland's Late Bronze Age and Early Iron Age, 1200–300 B.C., a time of visible social stratification and increased obsession with warfare and defensive structures (Mallory and McNeill 1995).

Phase IIIii took place during the later fourth to second centuries B.C., placing it in the Early Iron Age. At this time a series of circular structures were constructed (Waterman 1997; Waddell 2000). A number of nearby sites that may have been forms of defensive earthworks are thought to have been constructed at this time, including the Black Pig's Dyke and the Dorsey, which have provided a variety of radiocarbon dates corresponding to Phase III and Phase IV occupation at Navan Fort (Lynn 1989, 1991). The famous Barbary ape skull and mandible (now in the British Museum) correlates with the IIIii phase. This unusual and unique skull testifies to the growing importance and power of the occupants at Navan Fort and may indicate contact or trade with groups in North Africa or other areas of the Mediterranean. The ape has engendered much speculation as to its actual reasons for being at Navan. It may have been a gift to the local king; Barbary apes were often kept as pets in the Mediterranean region (Pilcher et al. 1997) long before the medieval period. They even bear mention in the occasional classical text, and remains have been found at later sites in Ireland such as at Carrickfergus, Co. Antrim from the fourteenth or fifteenth centuries (Pilcher et al. 1997). Phase IIIiii is indicated by the middle enclosures shown through a series of concentric rings on the drumlin's apex.

While the concentric rings of phase IIIiii indicate a shift in the use of the site, the exceptional structural changes that took place over the fourth and final fifth phase of Navan Fort's development would seem to support widespread cultural changes in the Ulster area (Lynn 1991). The construction of a massive wooden structure around 95 B.C. at Navan Fort, as well as an explosion of further defensive structures at the Dorsey and others, suggests a drastic transformation of Irish culture during the time of Phase IV (Raftery 1994). The structure, thought to be a massive conically roofed building, would likely not have served as a house due to its size (literally 40 meters in diameter), but may have been used for ritual, tribal, or ceremonial purposes by the *Ulaid*—the people who gave Ulster its name. This time period in Ireland was a time of general unrest as new peoples challenged established groups for power throughout the island. The Celts may have arrived at Navan and begun to enculturate a people not especially interested in joining them. The construction of the Forty Meter Structure may have been a response to this pressure and a physical display of the existing people's power or the new power of the incoming group. We know from the archaeological record that the effort may have been made in futility.

Shortly after its creation the structure was purposefully filled with limestone boulders and then apparently burnt to the ground in Phase V. It is generally felt this final act of destruction was deliberate; that the burning may have been seen as an act of cremation. Navan Fort was then covered with turf and abandoned. The Waterman excavations found little evidence of activity at the site once the mound (which is prominent in the countryside today) was constructed (Aitchison 1994), although it remained symbolically powerful for several centuries.

Navan Fort and Emain Macha: Cultural and Historical Considerations

Beginning in the Late Bronze Age, Ireland's cultural landscape experienced profound changes. Archaeological evidence throughout the island indicates increased construction of defensive earthworks that may have marked tribal territories (Champion 1988; Brindley 1994). The "royal centers" to which Navan Fort belonged were often associated with defensive earthworks. Speculation about the purpose of surrounding local bank and ditch structures, such as the Black Pig's Dyke, the Dorsey, and the Dane's Cast, has led to suggestions that these massive linear structures may have served as "frontier defenses of ancient Celtic kingdoms" (Raftery 1994, 86; Mallory and McNeill 1995). Other suggestions such as their use as cattle enclosures, ritual avenues, or race courses have found little evidential support, and their actual purpose remains a mystery.

Chris Lynn's excavations in the late 1970s at the Dorsey produced evidence of a possible palisaded structure (Aitchison 1993) and the Black Pig's Dyke shows evidence of a timber palisade (Walsh 1987; Raftery 1994). Their geographic situation and relationship to the entire Navan complex seem to support the notion of defensive earthworks set up to protect the area of Navan Fort.

By the Bronze Age, Irish agriculture was flourishing and with it the establishment of strong kin-based chiefdoms. Pollen analysis from the area of Navan Fort indicates large-scale deforestation and an increase in grass (*Gramineae*), weeds such as buttercups (*Ranunculus acris*-type), and nettles (*Urtica*), as well as cereal pollen that likely indicate farming (Pilcher et al. 1997). Cereal pollens continue to increase throughout the Bronze Age.

At Navan Fort itself pollen analysis seems to indicate a fairly continuous pastoral use (Pilcher et al. 1997). This is further supported by the number of pig bones found at the site. Unlike grazing cattle (which pigs outnumber), pigs are dependent on oak mast (Pilcher et al. 1997). The amount of pig remains also may indicate the status of the inhabitants at Navan Fort. Pork is considered a "royal feast" and is reported as such in both classical literature and the Irish epics such as the *Táin Bó Cuailnge* (The Cattle Raid of Cooley). The values obtained for oak "suggest that some oak forest existed in the vicinity" (Pilcher et al. 1997, 116). As might be expected around 100 B.C.—the time of the ritual destruction of the fort—a marked increase in forest regeneration supports the notion that most cultural activity ended at the site at that time.

The Fort in Epic Tradition

Who were the people of Navan Fort? The archaeological evidence indicates they were people of considerable status. Another indication of their status comes from the stories of oral tradition written down by Christian monks in Ireland and elsewhere from the eighth through the fifteenth centuries A.D. The *Táin Bó Cuailnge* is the most famous of these and is part of the Ulster Cycle. The *Táin* is the "oldest vernacular epic in Western literature" according to its most widely read translator Thomas Kinsella (1969). The *Táin* recounts the lives and exploits of King Conchobar MacNessa and the Red Branch Knights, and the hero Cú Chulainn. The stories center on the "royal enclosures" of Tara, Cruachan, and especially Emain Macha. Though no exact location is given in the sagas, equating the *Táin's* Emain Macha with Navan Fort is generally accepted (Mallory 1985). Descriptions of the general area and the fort itself indicate that it was a ringed fort ("The women settled on the ramparts of Emain" [Kinsella 1969, 15]) surrounded by a "green" located near the market town of Macha. Ard Macha is the Irish name for the city of Armagh. There is also mention in the Kinsella translation of the fort being burned: "Before the morning Dubthach had massacred the girls of Ulster and Fergus had burned Emain" (Kinsella 1969, 15).

The kings of Ulster had residence at Emain Macha where there was a great enclosure used as a gathering place for the Knights of the Red Branch. Passages such as "Conchobar and the nobles of Ulster were at Emain" (21) and "the men of Ulster were assembled in Emain Macha" (23) and references to the Knights and boy troops meeting and training there strongly support the interpretation of the extensive site of Navan Fort as the saga's Emain Macha. Flanagan traced the anglicization of the Irish "Emain" (variously *Eamhain* or *An Eamhain*) to Navan beginning in the seventeenth century. Emain is pronounced "Evin" (or "owen") and Flanagan suggests the typical Irish *An Eamhain* became, over the course of a century or so, the form known today as Navan by the eighteenth century (Lynn et al. 1997, 8).

Emain Macha is mentioned in many other tales as well, including *The Courtship of Etaine*. Its prominence in the literature suggests the site and its occupants were held in high regard. Linguistic and archaeological evidence supports the idea of Navan Fort and Emain Macha being one and the same (Lynn 1994). Even in the later historic period "kings" of Ireland would pay homage to the greatness of Emain Macha. It is known that Brian Boru camped at the site in the eleventh century. During the time these epics were being penned, Ireland itself was under a high degree of duress from Viking invasion and the influence of both the English and the Scots. The air of desperate acts is palpable in the annals. The preservation and presentation of sites such as Emain Macha help remind the Irish of their turbulent and glorious past, and give visitors a tangible point of reference to the tales they may only be vaguely familiar with.

The Navan Center Dilemma

The Navan Center was closed abruptly in the summer of 2001. Rumors were swirling among the people of Armagh who suggested anything from management embezzling money to unwanted influence from the European Union. The Navan Center was located in a specially designed building with "dynamic audio-visual techniques, narration, (and) interactive devices . . . to bring the area's archaeology and mystery to life" (Navan at Armagh brochure). Several colleagues at the county museum (and past employees of the center) explained that the center had closed due to some long-term financial difficulties related to gross overestimations of earnings and a large fire that destroyed some of the audiovisual equipment causing thousands of pounds worth of damage. There have been several lawsuits filed by former employees regarding the closure.

Without the center, entry to Navan Fort is free, unguided, and unsupervised. Over the course of several days few visitors entered the site. Had a visitor stopped by the site who was not familiar with anything beyond the historical/mythical past of cattle raids, heroes, and royalty, their archaeological education would have been brief and in English only. The trip around the site is aided by a series of plaques that describe the archaeology, history, and literary sources related to the fort. Several of these have been damaged and are now missing, their metal stands covered with an assortment of graffiti. Absent the educational and organizational services the Navan Center provided, Navan Fort and the rest of the complex are static, arbitrary mounds of earth. In 2001 Navan Fort's presence at tourist shops and visitor centers (such as St. Patrick's Trian) and its prominence in shop windows and bookstores in and around Armagh City were obvious. By the summer of 2002 reference to the fort was difficult to find even at St. Patrick's Trian.

The Hill of Tara

The Hill of Tara is a related site located in County Meath south of Armagh. It is known as the seat of the ancient kings of Ireland and home to one of St. Patrick's earliest Christian triumphs over the pagan Irish. Like Navan Fort, Tara's historical reputation was something I assumed would help attract visitors to the site. As part of the Boyne Valley monument system, the site is part of the prehistoric drive through County Meath beginning with Knowth, Dowth, and Newgrange in the east and ending at Maeve's Fort just beyond Tara at the southwestern end of the drive.

This large, complex site contains many elements ranging from the Neolithic "Mound of Hostages" to several ditch and bank structures to the large ring fort at the center with the legendary crowning stone to the "banqueting hall." Tara's mythological history is steeped in the mystery and magic of Ireland's best story-tellers and includes tales of the Nemedians, the Fir Bolg, the Tuatha De Danann, the Milesians, and the "Great Kings of Ireland." The invasion legends that surround Tara secure Ireland's bold, magical, and heroic past in the memories of both visitors and the Irish alike. Tara represents the Irish diaspora in reverse—only the greatest of men and women would survive through these tumultuous changes, therefore only the greatest of their descendants inhabit Ireland today.

Tara: History and Archaeology

Like Navan Fort, Tara developed in stages over several thousand years. While only about 150 meters above sea level, the Tara ridge offers a commanding view of the surrounding plains (Fenwick 1996). Radiocarbon dating from several areas of the Hill indicate activity at the site ranged from before 3000 B.C. to 400 A.D. or later. The Mound of Hostages (Dumha na nGiall) is thought to be the most ancient of the more than thirty monuments at the site. Radiocarbon dates ranging from 3355–2465 B.C. to 2875–1945 B.C. suggest its construction around 3000 B.C. (Waddell 2000). The Mound of Hostages is a small passage tomb that contained at least two hundred burials, most of which were cremations. Many of the cremation burials in the mound were associated with urns and food vessels. Other grave goods including a stone battle ax, bronze daggers, and knives, and, with one flexed male burial a jet, bronze, and amber necklace suggest the mound was used by both Beaker and Urnfield cultures and possibly by an earlier "Bowl Food Vessel" people (Raftery 1994; Herity and Eogan 1996; Waddell 2000).

A central focus of the site is the Ráth na Ríogh (Fort of the Kings). This huge bank and ditch structure (similar to the internal ditch at Navan Fort) encloses 70,000 square meters and five or more additional monuments, including the Mound of Hostages described above (Raftery 1994; Herity and Eogan 1996; Roche 1999; Waddell 2000). The Teach Cormac and An Forradh are also located within the ditch and bank. Teach Cormac, or Cormac's House (named for the Irish King Cormac mac Airt), is a double-ringed or bivallate fort that is joined to the Forradh, or Royal Seat, another larger bivallate mound where the Lia Fáil, or Crowning Stone, is now located.

South of the Ráth na Ríogh is Ráth Laoghaire (Leary's Fort), which has been partially destroyed by agricultural activity. This massive ditch and bank fort is named for King Leary, who was challenged to accept Christianity by St. Patrick in the fifth century. The condition of the area makes it difficult to discern the overall structure, but it once had a high rampart encircled with a ditch that enclosed an area of about 130 meters in diameter; clearly this was an imposing structure at one time. Its southern location to the Ráth na Ríogh may have been principally defensive, unlike the suggested ceremonial or ritual function of the King's Fort itself.

North of the Mound of Hostages and just outside the Ráth na Ríogh is the Ráth of the Synods, another ditch and bank structure enclosing a flat-topped mound. Named for a series of ecclesiastical meetings supposedly held in the eighth century (Herity and Eogan 1996; Waddell 2000), the Ráth of the Synods has undergone several series of changes since its initial construction. Originally a funerary structure, it then shows evidence of a defensive palisade, followed again after a period of disuse by burial activity, and finally in the early centuries A.D., its use as a multivallate ring fort becomes clear (Raftery 1994; Waddell 2000). Ring forts were not only large structures built to protect many people, but were usually smaller protected homesteads for a farm family and a few domesticated animals (Herity and Eogan 1996). These homestead forts average 25 meters in diameter; the Ráth of the Synods, which measures about 27.5 meters diameter, can be interpreted as a protected homestead. This is supported as well by its multivallate structure.

Other structures include the Banqueting Hall, or Teach Miodhchuarta, which consists of two parallel earthen banks that extend over 200 meters in length. Located north of the Ráth of the Synods, this structure has often been interpreted as a place where the royal families, their champions, and honored guests would feast. Archaeological evidence does not support this medieval fancy. More likely this served as a kind of ceremonial avenue or some other processional or ritual area related to Tara's activity. The Sloping Trenches (Claonfhearta) ring barrows and Ráth Grainne are located north and west of the primary enclosure and also consist of ditch, bank, and central raised platforms. Ráth Grainne incorporated a number of barrow sites into its construction. Finally, several sacred wells are located within or near the Ráth na Ríogh, one particularly associated with St. Patrick, whose statue is also erected in the site.

Recent excavations at Tara undertaken by the Discovery Program reopened an area of the ditch and bank of the Ráth na Ríogh previously excavated by Sean P. Ó'Ríordáin and Ruaidhrí de Valera in the late 1950s. These new excavations provided an opportunity to more accurately date the construction of the ditch and bank of the Ráth na Ríogh to the "first century BC, which is broadly contemporary with the date postulated for the figure of eight features found . . . (at) the

Ráth of the Synods . . . and the central timber from the large circular structures at Emain Macha (Baillie 1988, 39)" (Roche 1999, 29). As it grew in importance to the Iron Age cultures surrounding it, Tara became a recognized area of ritual and ceremony. This is supported by the abundance of horse and dog bones (both "valuable" symbols of status) that appear within the bank and ditch above the furnace "floor" found during the Discovery Program excavations. Previous status objects found at Tara include twisted gold torcs that date to the Late Bronze Age (Raftery 1994, 69). The site's antiquity is obvious from the Neolithic presence at the Mound of Hostages and its continuous use through the early Middle Ages as the crowning place of the high kings of Ireland. Later conflicts between Brian Boru and Malachy II in the eleventh century as well as more contemporary gatherings such as the Battle of Tara in 1798, Daniel O'Connor's Monster Meeting in 1843, and the Irish Volunteers gathering there during the Easter Rising in 1916 have kept the Hill of Tara alive in the collective consciousness of the Irish today (Slavin 1996).

Tara: Culture Change

While parallels can be drawn between Navan Fort and Tara regarding their long histories, Tara seems to have figured more prominently as the symbolic "center of Ireland." Tara's importance as an area of burial activity, bronze and iron production, and defense are also clearly defined in the archaeological record. This history of cultural evolution is briefly outlined below and is followed by a discussion of Tara's importance as a royal center and finally with the coming of St. Patrick and its subsequent waning importance in the eighth century A.D.

The Neolithic in Ireland is marked by an increase in agricultural activity and settlements. This typical pattern in Europe is accompanied by widespread deforestation as seen in the palynological evidence indicative of a coeval increase in weeds, herbs, and grass (O'Kelly 1990; Pilcher et al. 1997). The appearance of polished stone implements and various ceramics including Beaker pottery in the Late Neolithic and evidence of both round and rectangular houses—often in small village clusters—support the idea that Ireland had become a land of territories. This time period also marks the use of megalithic monuments including burial chambers like the Mound of Hostages and Newgrange, and standing stones such as those found throughout Ireland.

The establishment of tribal territories and the defense of them, the influx of outsiders ("invaders"), increases in population, and the development of metal working mark the cultural horizon between the Neolithic and Bronze Age in Ireland. As stated above in the discussion of Navan Fort, the Late Bronze Age is the time when hill forts and other territorial landmarks came into use. Many of these landmarks take the form of tumuli of various sizes, most of which are believed to be burial chambers. As at Navan Fort, Tara's natural raised geographic position may have helped establish its early prominence as an important and highly visual site. The ridge not only provides a wide and unobstructed view of the surrounding areas, but can also be seen from some distance. Tara seems to have been a territorial marker that increased in importance as the cultures of Ireland moved from tribal organizations to chiefdoms and succumbed to the influence of increasing contact with the continent and Britain.

Paralleling the cultural developments at Navan Fort, the Bronze Age at Tara is indicated by an increase in defensive structures, weaponry, and symbols of status such as gold and bronze torcs and lunulae. It is clear that a social hierarchy had developed throughout Ireland at this time although these types of high status objects represent only a very small number of inhabitants. Most Irish in the Bronze Age would have been of a peasant class—a relatively invisible class in the archaeological record. By the end of the Bronze Age new economic and technological patterns were emerging through increased trade abroad. Cattle were becoming important, horses may have been used for both transportation and farm work, grain was grown, and lakeside settlements were increasing. Pins, dress fasteners, spindle whorls, and an assortment of fibulae indicate that the production of woven fabrics became increasingly important during the Bronze Age. Irish goods began to appear in Britain and many other areas of Europe, a new material—iron—found its way into the Irish tool kit, and a new people known as the Celts landed on Ireland's shores.

As the Bronze Age gave way to the Iron Age between 600 and 400 B.C., palisaded structures and defensive earthworks increased. The Celts—a people who first appear in Central Europe during the Hallstatt period about 800–750 B.C.— brought new artistic, political, and linguistic customs to Ireland. As was common in Europe the Celts absorbed the local peoples and formed loose confederacies centered on charismatic leaders and local kings. It was during the Iron Age that royal centers became the focal points of warring factions. Tara's presence as a ceremonial site and the place of the Lia Fáil (Crowning Stone) made it an even more important—and often contested—area than the other royal sites.

The Iron Age was a time of clear social hierarchies. Associated grave goods found with inhumations in and around royal sites are rich and often reflect the warlike nature of the times. Cyclical festivals held at Imbolc, Lughnasa, Beltane, and Samhain were often presided over by druids and kings. Óenachs, or assemblies, were commonly held in Ireland and, according to Raftery, "a law tract of the eighth century (A.D.) stipulates that it was the duty of every king to convene an óenach at regular intervals" (1994, 81). While óenachs apparently were not held at Tara, the king at Tara presided over ones held at Tailtiu (modern Teltown) a short distance from the royal site at Lughnasa in late summer (Raftery 1994).

With the Iron Age and the succeeding Christian era, evidence of habitation at Tara, such as may have been at the Ráth of the Synods earlier, disappears. The Ráth na Ríogh is built during the Iron Age, enclosing the Mound of Hostages; the Teach Cormac and An Forradh are built as conjoining monuments. According to Herity (1993) these conjoined embanked mounds are found only at royal sites. The Iron Age and the Celts also brought the tradition of storytelling and oral histories, passed on and later written down by literate monks in the Middle Ages and the early Christian era.

St. Patrick's statue at Tara reminds visitors that change in Ireland came quickly between 400 and 600 A.D. Patrick was particularly convincing in bringing Christianity to pagan Ireland by going to challenge King Leary at Tara (Ross 1995). Patrick apparently moved between several areas of Ireland according to the *Memoir of Tírecháin*, written in the seventh century (Chadwick 1970; Dillon and Chadwick 1967). Armagh is considered the ecclesiastical center of Ireland, and Patrick's choice of Armagh may have been tied to the importance of Navan Fort and the powerful influence of the area over the surrounding territories. Nonetheless, with the coming of Patrick and many other Christian monks and missionaries, archaeological evidence supports a rapid waning of activity at Tara and its final abandonment as the seat of the high kings of Ireland sometime in the middle of the eighth century A.D.

Tara: Literary Evidence

Like Navan Fort/Emain Macha, Tara also figures prominently in many of the Irish epics of the eighth to fifteenth centuries. These epic tales helped establish Tara as the center of ancient Irish culture in the consciousness of Ireland's people. Unlike Emain Macha there is no question that the Tara of legend (*Témair* in Irish) is the Tara known today. The Lia Fáil is referred to numerous times in many of the tales of both the Finn Cycle and the Cycle of Kings. Also clearly described are Ráth Grainne, the Sloping Trenches, and Teach Cormac. Teach Cormac is the "power center" of Cormac mac Airt and his ancestors and descendents.

Of particular interest to Tara are the tales of Diarmaid and Grainne, Etaine, and the stories of Conn of the Hundred Battles. In one tale of Art, Son of Conn, Tara is called "the noble conspicuous dwelling of Ireland." Tailtiu is referred to as one of the main burial places in Ireland with Brug (Newgrange, Knowth, and Dowth on the Boyne River) and Cruachan. Tara itself was the gathering place for men to wait in assembly for the king. It was a place of magic known to gods like Lugh and Mananan mac Lir; a place where a king's family could be gambled away for the promise of honor and greatness. It was a place of truth, knowledge, and purity. A place inhabited by gifted youth, noble warriors, great (though fallible) kings, and druids. Its power was undeniable and legendary—even in the eighth century when it had fallen into disuse.

A Walk across Tara

Despite its famous past Tara often languishes for want of visitors. Over the course of my visits in 2001, which took place over several days and at various times, the largest number of visitors to the site was seven at one time. This may in part be due to the foot and mouth scare that gripped Europe at the time. On two of the occasions I was there, the small visitor center was "closed for lunch" (once at 10:30 A.M. and once at 2:30 P.M.). Visitors who chose to bypass the center when it was open were free to wander across the landscape, read the small guideposts (above eye level and difficult to read), and climb up the mounds, rings and into the ditches. I observed people happily snapping pictures and chatting quietly with one another at each signpost. When asked if they knew about the site and its place in Irish history or folklore, their responses inevitably were amalgamations of Druidic sacrifices (the Stonehenge response), Christian salvation (the St. Patrick response), and fairy mounds (the Leprechaun response). While native Irish visitors were familiar with Tara's history, nonnative visitors were without a frame of reference beyond fairy tales, public television, or popularized histories of Ireland in general. Tara was no different than any other hill fort or tumulus on the Irish (or English) landscape. Its uniqueness resided in the fact that the visitor had been there, had the photographs, postcards, and fridge magnets to prove it, and that they would remember it in a context probably quite unlike its actual history.

The visitor center, located in the refurbished St. Patrick's church, carried the usual guide books, maps, introductory film, and offered short guided tours for a small fee (1.90E). It also had a few souvenirs and information on the rest of the Boyne Valley. Outside the site there is a used book shop owned by a local author and a small café/gift shop where visitors have access to the Tara China pattern and more souvenirs. Upon my return in the summer of 2002 business had picked up appreciably. Even during the worst weather (the summer had been the worst anyone could remember) there was a steady stream of tour buses, rental cars, and other visitors. The Lia Faíl still attracted the bulk of the crowds with most visitors going directly toward it for photographs and a chance to see if their proximity would cause the stone to scream their royal kingship. Few visitors during my four days of observations ventured out to Leary's Fort, the Sloping Trenches, or Ráth Grainne.

Newgrange and the Brú na Bóinne

In 2001 I decided to get the "tourist experience" to Newgrange. I hiked to the tourist center off Grafton Street, reserved my coach and tour pass, and waited in a crowded, noisy, cavernous converted church for my bus. I was excited about seeing Newgrange—a site that had intrigued me since childhood with its enigmatic

mound and gleaming facade. I was beginning to feel unsure of the way I was going to see it as more and more people gathered in the "meeting spot" with their
fanny packs, windbreakers, baseball caps, and umbrellas. Nonetheless, when our
guide arrived I climbed on board and settled in for the hour-long ride to the Brú
na Bóinne visitor center and Newgrange beyond. The guide pointed out landmarks along the way, commented on housing expenses, and was generally ignored
by the fifty or more mostly Americans on the bus. On my return in 2002 I rented
a car and avoided the frantic nature of the Dublin tourist centers. I was surprised
that I was able to get right on scheduled tours of both Newgrange and Knowth
due to the reputation of the crowds and long waits, but according to several of the
employees at the Brú na Bóinne Center, it is rare that people have to wait more
than one hour to have a tour of the tombs' interiors.

Once at the visitor center, visitors are herded along the passageway to the building entrance, given ID stickers to gain entry to Newgrange, Knowth, or the center
only and instructed to either view the seven-minute film that recounts the entire
5,000-year history of the site or to go to the "library" one level down. The library
is actually a gift shop with an assortment of books, posters, and other souvenirs.
There is also an extensive and very informative exhibition area that seems to very un-
derutilized by visitors. With few exceptions they quickly pass through the area on
their way to the film; those who take their time are often there to revisit the exhibition after a rushed tour on a previous visit.

Within a short time of arriving at the center visitors are herded onto buses
and driven to Newgrange, gleaming in the distance in the Irish summer sun. Unlike Navan Fort and Tara, entry into Newgrange is highly controlled by a number
of gates, fences, passes, and guards. Upon arriving, visitors are placed in a locked
"holding corral" to wait for their guide while a turnstyle type of tour through the
magnificently rebuilt vision of Michael O'Kelly proceeds ahead of them. And it is
magnificent.

O'Kelly excavated at Newgrange from 1962 through 1975 through the encouragement of the Irish Tourist Board (Bord Fáilte) (O'Kelly 1982). A truly international undertaking (teams from the United States, Great Britain, and other
European countries worked there), the massive passage tomb was reconstructed
with painstaking care. O'Kelly was unable to restore certain areas as he had "envisioned" them, including the entrance, which would not have accommodated the
number of tourists expected postexcavation. The mound itself was shored up with
a concrete cap now covered by the turf itself and not visible from the outside (it
is not mentioned by the guides). The exterior revetment wall sparkles in the sun-
shine with its carefully placed quartz and granite "pebbles"; the wall had collapsed
soon after its construction. O'Kelly conducted several slip studies to ensure an accurate rebuilding of the wall. He accomplished this by building and collapsing

sections of the wall several times in order to discern the fall patterns of the quartz and granite pebbles. The result is the spectacular outer revetment wall of the cairn with its encircling standing stones and decorated curbs. In response to detractors to his re-creation, O'Kelly stated that they "can see for themselves *how much more impressive* it now is than if it had been restored to a bogus hemispherical shape in accordance with the misconceptions of earlier days" (1982, 73, italics mine).

The archaeological significance of Newgrange and the Brú na Bóinne is emphasized by the tour guides. However, the re-creation of the site's exterior and the attractive facade and landscaping are presented as authentic and pristine. Visitors are also titillated by the story of Newgrange and the winter solstice whose light illuminates the passageway each year. To see the splendor of this event involves a ten-year waiting list and a lottery system, but all visitors get to see the re-created show—done with spotlights and electric switches dozens of times a day. After a brief visit to the awe-inspiring interior (where visitors are crammed shoulder to shoulder into the central chamber), visitors are asked to exit the tomb and are allowed to wander around outside examining decorated curb stones and the few remaining standing stones. Then they are called back to the buses and rushed back to the center. Tours are then immediately whisked back to Dublin—all in the space of a few hours.

Newgrange: Archaeology and History

Because I have described many of the cultural attributes of the Neolithic in discussing Navan Fort and Tara, I will only briefly touch on the Neolithic as it pertains to Newgrange, the Boyne Valley, and chambered tombs in Ireland. Of particular interest is the archaeology completed by O'Kelly in the 1970s at Newgrange and his reconstruction of the monument's facade mentioned above. An important aspect of the Neolithic generally is the florescence of megalith building in the form of burial chambers, stelae, stone circles, and monuments.

Newgrange is a massive passage tomb of about eighty-five meters in diameter that is part of the Boyne Valley Cemetery in County Meath. The cemetery complex includes Newgrange and its associated sites, Dowth and Knowth, all located along the River Boyne. Like Tara and Navan Fort, Newgrange was constructed on a ridge that allows a wide view of the surrounding landscape and the river. It is a striking presence in the Boyne Valley landscape. It has twelve extant standing stones associated with it and has ninety-seven curb stones surrounding it, many of which are decorated with incised, stone-pecked cup and ring, chevron, and spiral designs. There has been endless speculation regarding the meanings of these designs; they are very common throughout Europe and occur in a number of megalithic situations including burial chambers, standing stones, alignments, stone circles, and monuments (Green 1989).

At Newgrange evidence of Neolithic habitation is found prior to the construction of the mound and sometime after the collapse of the mound (C. O'Kelly 1982; M. Kelly 1990; O'Kelly, Cleary, and Lehane 1983; Sweetman 1985, 1987). Within the mound itself are three "cells" and a large chamber with a high, corbelled stone roof. The passage itself is about twenty meters in length and is in a west-northwest orientation. This orientation allowed the winter solstice sunrise to shine through an opening called the "roof box" and illuminate the interior passage, at one time shining on an intricately carved triple spiral on one of the rear orthostats (Waddell 2000).

When the agricultural communities in the Boyne Valley were compelled to construct Newgrange they began to strip away the surrounding landscape. The great mound itself is constructed of layers of turf as well as massive stone slabs and quartz pebbles. Pollen analysis from the turfs supports the notion that the communities disturbed their own cereal grains and pasture fields in order to construct this part of the mound (Waddell 2000; M. O'Kelly 1982).

O'Kelly excavated at Newgrange in the 1960s and 1970s. Few portable artifacts were found within the chamber itself because the site had been left open to free public access since the 1700s. Cremation remains were found and some "typically Neolithic" artifacts such as beads, polished stone celts, and possible bone pins were found in association with the cremated bone. Excavation of the turf mound itself revealed some Roman period coins and glass that may have been inadvertent or may suggest the site's timeless attraction to a visiting public (Eogan 1991).

Newgrange: The Landscape of Imagination

While Tara and Navan Fort clearly have their place in the epic literature, Newgrange may or may not. Claire O'Kelly (1982) suggests Newgrange appears in the early chronicles and dindshenchas (place lore) several times. In particular she mentions The Pursuit of Diarmaid and Grainne, where Oengus of the Brú brings Diarmaid's body after his death. "Brú" means "abode, hall, mansion, or castle" (O'Kelly 1982, 43) and, in the case of Newgrange, is most often understood as the mansion of the Dagda, god of the Tuatha de Danann, the mythological inhabitants of old Ireland who retreated to the underworld (fairy mounds or sidhe) with the Celtic invasions and his son Angus or Oengus Mac Oc.

In Cross and Slover's 1936 edited version of The Pursuit of Diarmuid and Grainne, Angus mourns wildly at the death of Diarmuid by the great boar on Ben Gulban. At one point Angus sings:

> Raise ye fairy shouts without gainsaying,
> Let Diarmuid of the bright weapons be lifted by you;

> To the smooth Brug of the everlasting rocks—
> Surely it is we that feel great pity.

Although Grainne requests Diarmuid's body be brought to her at Ráth Grainne at Tara, Angus refuses. He carries the body on "a gilded bier, with his (Diarmuid's) javelins over him pointed upwards, and he went to the Brug of the Boyne" (Cross and Slover 1936, 417).

Another recurring character is that of "Boann"—literally the Boyne—as a woman messenger, mother goddess. Boann, or Eithne-Boann, is the daughter of the Dagda as well as the sister-mother of Oengus. In *The Dream of Oengus* Boann is sent to search Ireland for a girl Oengus has seen only in his dreams. This symbolizes the river as far-reaching and powerful, perhaps all-seeing. Even though Boann fails (the girl is not to be found on the Boyne), she is called into service again by her nephew Fraech to provide him with clothes and gifts from the fairy mounds in Fraech and Finnabair. The River Boyne passes by many of the sites said to be inhabited by the Tuatha de Danann—the mounds of Newgrange, Knowth, and Dowth included. Boann eventually drowns herself in the River Boyne and is ever after associated with it.

Michael O'Kelly's excavations and his stunning reconstruction of the monument have helped establish the site as one of the premier stops on a trip through Ireland. Its importance to Irish prehistory is uncontested; its continued importance to modern Ireland is obvious through the funding made available to preserve and conserve the site, the construction of the state-of-the-art Brú na Bóinne visitor center, and its designation (with Knowth and Dowth) as a U.N. World Heritage site in 1993.

Situating Identities: Marketing Heritage

The idealized Ireland is essentially premodern, damp, green, and tweed. This model may include a landscape of ancient sites, but the sites are magical, eerie, and to be avoided—the ancient landscape is as separate from an imagined Ireland as the city with its cars and noise and haute cuisine. It is beyond reality: opposite of Baudrillard's (1988) hyperreality (a created truth or history), the ancient landscape exists outside the limited vision of Ireland that most visitors have. A visit to the sites inspires awe; the depth of their history and the context of their positions as essential to Ireland and Irish identity do not inspire a need to know more. They are too ancient. They are too pagan. They are too wild. They are too uninhabited.

The temporal space between the ancient sites and the visitor is further emphasized by the visitor centers associated with the sites themselves. Whether absent, discreet, or highly visible, without some prior knowledge of site context, visitors leave awestruck but no more informed than before they arrived at the site.

Often the information is rapid-fire; it is also glossy and high-tech. Knowing full well that low-tech approaches are unappealing to short attention span visitors on a rushed, abbreviated tour, the presentations are reduced to Cliffs Notes that benefit no one but the centers themselves. When a center is absent (or closed as at Navan Fort), visitors are often in a position of learning on their own or experiencing the landscape with no understanding or contextual barometer to lean on. The meanings of the sites, even the temporal positions of the sites, are beyond their realm of experience. A discreet visitor center such as the one at Tara may offer the visitor the most intimate experience with its small tours, opportunity to ask questions, and detailed, though vernacular, information. The discreet center is becoming a rare occurrence on the Irish landscape. In most cases, the authentic experience of the ancient cultural landscape is empty or over controlled. Much the way a visitor to an unfamiliar culture may be temporarily (or permanently) put off due to language barriers or cultural differences they are unprepared to accept, visitors to ancient sites are often confused by the amount and degree of information; overwhelmed, the standard reaction seems to be to shut down, ignore sign posts or guides, and retain only the most titillating memories. An example would be a number of the American tourists visiting Newgrange who were amazed by the Neolithic use of concrete in erecting standing stones. Despite the tour guide's quite clear explanation of the use of concrete in the outer ring, the group had clearly reached the point where the information was background noise.

Left on their own, visitors often flock to the ancient sites with the most widely advertised visitor's center such as at Brú na Bóinne. This may have much to do with restricted access, and may also be due to transportation: the larger the visitor's center, the more tourists that can be transported there, and the more revenue that can be generated in a single visit. The bells and whistles of the center are folded into the "positive experience" of the visit: is it comfortable? Attractive? Airconditioned? Clean? Appropriately flashy? Does it have bathrooms? Parking? A restaurant? Do the personnel understand their audience? Is it in English (Japanese, German, Italian)? Can we get back before dinner to the comfort of our hotel, bed and breakfast, guest house? Will we be entertained? Unlike "the sharing of mythic space" (Kelly 1996, 45), which occurs at historically familiar venues, often the visitor to the ancient sites of Ireland is simply overwhelmed. The more theme-parked the visitor center, the more memorable the visit. The idea is to have been there, not necessarily to have been enlightened.

Conclusion

What accounts for the differences in organization, presentation, and access to these ancient sites? It may be due in part to the EC regional development policy begun in the 1980s, in which "unprecedented levels of capital funding

[were] directed toward the provision of visitor facilities at heritage sites in Ireland" (Cooke 2000, 375). Clearly the Brú na Bóinne visitor center and the Boyne Valley experience have been heavily promoted as one of the premiere heritage site activities in Europe—and indeed it is. The architecture of the building is bold and aesthetically exciting, and it reflects the symbolism of Newgrange in complex and interesting ways. Sites located some distance from the focal point of Newgrange receive "less press"—mention of Tara or the elegant Maeve's Fort is practically nonexistent at the center. Tourist offices in Dublin and Meath do a brisk business selling access to Newgrange, whereas entry to Tara is free when the tour is self-guided. An organized tour to Tara from Dublin (or elsewhere) can only be had as part of a larger tour—it cannot stand alone as an attraction.

The walls surrounding Newgrange tantalize the visitor by prolonging the mystery—the information is highly controlled, access is timed, interior photography forbidden. At Tara the visitor need only follow the signs along the highway to the narrow lane where the site rests. Access is unfettered and without frills. Information is available through either signposts or maps and short histories—a guided tour can be organized in minutes. Tara is peaceful, belying its extraordinary past of battles, coronations, and brilliance. Newgrange is frantic, making it difficult to grasp its past as a somber ritual mound of high symbolism and death.

Navan Fort rises silently in the Armagh countryside, a mute representative of a glorious and horrifying history. Equally silent are the darkened rooms of the Navan Center, which only a short time ago bustled with activity. Of the three sites Navan Fort held its mysteries closest. One of the most important sites in Europe, located in one of Ireland's most historically important cities, the fort has survived when its champions—both ancient and modern—have not. Is the Navan Center necessary? The fort and the remaining sites of the complex existed for millennia without it. Does the organization and information given out at "visitor facilities" help visitors relate to and understand Ireland's remarkable past? Curators and managers would like us to think so. Perhaps more important or insidious is that the centers become the attraction and the sites become a repetitious theme of "seen one hole in the ground, seen them all." Access to sites such as Newgrange has become tied to the tourist centers like those in Dublin, which may or may not offer transportation to Tara as well (three out of four "day tripping" schemes do not). Visitors to Ireland who may be reluctant to drive "on the wrong side of the road" are restricted to travel on the available tours. The absence of a modern visitor center at Tara may also lend to its apparent lack of popularity (which admittedly had increased after the foot and mouth scare had passed). The once active center at Navan Fort reflects the emptiness of the site, while the bustling and frantic center at Newgrange demonstrates a well-orchestrated, highly organized effort to present a controlled and attractive (and revenue generating) experience for the visitor.

Acknowledgments

I would like to extend my thanks to Uzi Baram and Yorke Rowan for organizing such an interesting session at the 2001 American Anthropological Association meetings in Washington, D.C., and for inviting me to be a part of it. I would also like to thank Greer Ramsey of the Armagh County Museum and Michael Slavin of Tara for their assistance. Mention needs to be made of the gracious help and advice given by the Ulster Archaeological Society, the Environment and Heritage Service (NI), Christopher Lynn, and the team excavating Navan Fort in 2002. Kate Sweetman offered friendship and insight and breakfasts. Clare Tuffy of Dúchas shared invaluable information as did the management of the Cruachain Ai center in Tulsk, Co. Roscommon. This research was made possible through a Franklin Pierce College Faculty Research Fellowship (2001) and a Marion and Jasper Whiting Foundation Fellowship (2002). As always, my husband, Bill, is owed the greatest debt for his enduring support and encouragement. This is for Michael Slavin himself.

References

Aitchison, Nicholas B. 1993. "The Dorsey: A Reinterpretation of an Iron Age Enclosure in South Armagh." *Proceedings of the Prehistoric Society* 59: 285–301.

———. 1994. *Armagh and the Royal Centres in Early Medieval Ireland.* Woodbridge: Boydell & Brewer.

Baillie, Michael G.L. 1988. "Dating of the Timbers from Navan Fort and the Dorsey, Co. Armagh." *Emania* 4: 37–40.

Baudrillard, Jean. 1988. *America.* Translated by Chris Turner. London: Verso.

Brindley, Anna L. 1994. *Irish Prehistory: An Introduction.* Dublin: Rinehart.

Chadwick, Nora. 1970. *The Celts.* East Rutherford, N.J.: Pelican.

Champion, James M. 1988. "From Bronze Age to Iron Age in Ireland." In *The Bronze Age-Iron Age Transition in Europe,* edited by M. L. Stig Sorensen and R. Thomas, 287–303. Oxford: British Archaeological Reports International.

Coles, John M. 1967. "Some Irish Horns of the Late Bronze Age." *Journal of the Royal Society of Antiquaries of Ireland* 97: 113–17.

Collins, A. E. P., Sheridan, A., McCorry, M., and Lynn, C. J. 1997. "Objects of Flint, Polished Stone, and Pottery from Site B." In *Excavations at Navan Fort 1961–1971,* edited by Dudley Waterman, 61–82. Belfast: Stationery Office.

Cooke, Pat. 2000. "Principles of Interpretation." In *The Heritage of Ireland,* edited by Neil Buttimer, Colin Rynne, and Helen Guerin, 375–84. Wilton, Co. Cork: Collins.

Cooney, Gabriel. 1996. "Building the Future on the Past: Archaeology and the Construction of National Identity in Ireland." In *Nationalism and Archaeology in Europe,* edited by M. Díaz-Andreu and T. Champion, 146–63. London: Westview.

Costa, Kelli Ann. 2001. *Brokered Image: Material Culture and Identity in the Stubaital.* Lanham, Md.: University Press of America.

Cross, Tom Peete and Slover, Clark Harris, eds. 1936. *Ancient Irish Tales.* New York: Henry Holt.

Dillon, Myles, and Chadwick, Nora. 1967. *Celtic Realms: The History and Culture of the Celtic Peoples from Pre-History to the Norman Invasion.* London: Phoenix.

Eogan, George. 1991. "Prehistoric and Early Cultural Change at Brugh na Bóinne." *Proceedings of the Royal Irish Academy* 91C: 105–32.

Fenwick, James. 1996. "A Panoramic View from the Hill of Tara, County Meath." *Ríocht na Midhe* 9: 1–11.

Green, Miranda. 1989. *Symbol and Image in Celtic Religious Art.* London: Routledge.

Green, Miranda., ed. 1995. *The Celtic World.* London: Routledge.

Hamlin, Anne. 1997. Foreword to *Excavations at Navan Fort 1961–71,* edited by D. M. Waterman, iii. Belfast: Stationery Office.

Herity, Michael. 1982. "Irish Decorated Neolithic Pottery." *Proceedings of the Royal Irish Academy* 82C: 247–404.

———. 1993. "Motes and Mounds at Royal Sites in Ireland." *Journal of the Royal Society of Antiquaries of Ireland* 123: 127–51.

Herity, Michael, and Eogan, George. 1996. *Ireland in Prehistory.* London: Routledge.

Kelly, Marjorie. 1996. "Enshrining History: The Visitor Experience at Pearl Harbor's USS Arizona Memorial." *Museum Anthropology* 20: 45–57.

Kinsella, Thomas, trans. 1969. *The Táin: From the Irish Epic Táin Bó Cuailnge.* Oxford: Oxford University Press.

Lowenthal, David. 1998. *The Heritage Crusade and the Spoils of History.* Cambridge: Cambridge University Press.

Lynn, Christopher J. 1989. "An Interpretation of 'The Dorsey.'" *Emania* 6: 5–14.

———. 1991. "The Iron Age Mound in Navan Fort: A Physical Realization of Celtic Religious Beliefs?" *Emania* 10: 33–57.

———. 1994. "Hostels, Heroes, and Tales: Further Thoughts on the Navan Mound." *Emania* 12: 5–20.

———. 1997a. "Site B Excavation: Phase 4, Multi-Ring Structure." In *Excavations at Navan Fort 1961–1971,* edited by Dudley M. Waterman, 35–48. Belfast: Stationery Office.

———. 1997b. "Site B Excavation: Phase 5, the Composite Mound." In *Excavations at Navan Fort 1961–1971,* edited by Dudley M. Waterman, 49–60. Belfast: Stationery Office.

———. 1997c. "Interpretation of Structural Evidence." In *Excavations at Navan Fort 1961–1971,* edited by Dudley M. Waterman, 147–72. Belfast: Stationery Office.

———. 1997d." Comparisons and Interpretations." In *Excavations at Navan Fort 1961–1971,* edited by Dudley M. Waterman, 209–30. Belfast: Stationery Office.

Lynn, Christopher J., Flanagan, D., Waterman, Dudley M. 1997. "Introduction to the Excavations at Navan Fort." In *Excavations at Navan Fort 1961–1971,* edited by Dudley M. Waterman, 1–12. Belfast: Stationery Office.

Mallory, J. P. 1985. *Navan Fort: The Ancient Capital of Ulster.* Belfast: Institute of Irish Studies.
———. 1997. "*Emain Macha* and Navan Fort." In *Excavations at Navan Fort 1961–1971,* edited by Dudley M. Waterman, 197–208. Belfast: Stationery Office.
Mallory, J. P., and Brown, D. M. 1999. "Dating Navan Fort." *Antiquity* 73: 280, 427–32.
Mallory, J. P., and McNeill, Timothy E. 1995. *The Archaeology of Ulster: From Colonization to Plantation.* Belfast: Institute of Irish Studies.
Mitchell, Franklin. 1976. *The Irish Landscape.* London: Collins.
O'Kelly, Claire. 1982. "Newgrange in Early Irish Literature." In *Newgrange: Archaeology, Art, and Legend.* Edited by Michael J. O'Kelly, 43–64. London: Thames & Hudson.
O'Kelly, Michael J. 1982. *Newgrange: Archaeology, Art, and Legend.* London: Thames & Hudson.
———. 1990. *Early Ireland: An Introduction to Irish Prehistory.* Cambridge: Cambridge University Press.
O'Kelly, Michael J., Cleary, R. M., and Lehane, D. 1983. "Newgrange, Co. Meath, Ireland." In *The Late Neolithic/Beaker Period Settlement.* British Archaeological Reports International Series, 190. Oxford.
Pilcher, J. R., Larmour, R. A., Weir, David A., McCormick, Finbar, Hodgson, G. W. I., Jones, A., Jenkins, P., Napier, P., and Raftery, Barry. 1997. "Environmental and Faunal Studies." In *Excavations at Navan Fort 1961–1971,* edited by Dudley M. Waterman, 107–26. Belfast: Stationery Office.
Raftery, Barry. 1985. "Navan Fort Enquiry." *Journal of the Royal Society of Antiquaries of Ireland* 115: 152–55.
———. 1987. "The Loughnashade Horns." *Emania* 2: 21–24.
———. 1994. *Pagan Celtic Ireland: The Enigma of the Irish Iron Age.* London: Thames & Hudson.
Roche, Helen. 1999. "Late Iron Age Activity at Tara, Co. Meath." *Ríocht na Midhe* 10: 18–30.
Ross, Anne. 1995. "Ritual and the Druids." In *The Celtic World,* edited by Miranda Green, 423–44. London: Routledge.
Slavin, Michael. 1996. *The Book of Tara.* Dublin: Wolfhound.
Simpson, D. D. A. 1989. "Neolithic Navan?" *Emania* 6: 31–33.
Sweetman, P. David. 1985. "A Late Neolithic/Early Bronze Age Pit Circle at Newgrange, Co. Meath." *Proceedings of the Royal Irish Academy* 85C: 195–221.
———. 1987. "Excavation of a Late Neolithic/Early Bronze Age Site at Newgrange, Co. Meath." *Proceedings of the Royal Irish Academy* 87C: 283–98.
UNESCO. 1993. *Cultural Landscapes.* www.unesco.org/whc/exhibits.
Waddell, John. 2000. *Prehistoric Archaeology of Ireland.* Bray, Co. Wicklow: Wordwell.
Walsh, Aidan. 1987. "Excavating the Black Pig's Dyke." *Emania* 3: 5–11.
Warner, Richard B. 1994. "The Navan Complex: A New Schedule of Sites and Finds." *Emania* 12: 39–44.
Waterman, Dudley M., ed. 1997. *The Excavations at Navan Fort 1961–1971.* Belfast: Stationery Office.

Mementos of the Past: Material Culture of Tourism at Stonehenge and Avebury

6

AMY GAZIN-SCHWARTZ

The secretary-general of the Society of Antiquaries provided me with a particularly fine example of an English Heritage souvenir. It is a snow globe, and if one shakes it, it produces a snowstorm over Stonehenge. It is very fine, especially because it has the word "Stonehenge" emblazoned on the front in Greek letters. English Heritage obviously knows something about the construction of Stonehenge that we do not.

(LORD REDESDALE, HOUSE OF LORDS, OCTOBER 31, 2001)

O N OCTOBER 31, 2001, the House of Lords in London debated a National Heritage bill that included provisions governing the trading functions of English Heritage, as well as underwater archaeology and the sharing of authority among heritage agencies. English Heritage is a quasi-governmental organization created in 1983 to oversee protection and management of historic buildings and archaeological sites in England. The problem of providing funds to preserve, conserve, and interpret heritage sites, and to manage them as tourist attractions, is a major focus of discussion not only in governmental arenas but among archaeologists and others with professional or personal interest in the sites (Chippindale 1989; Lowenthal and Binney 1981; Seaton and Bennett 1996; Williams 1998). Many sites supplement other sources of revenue by providing gift shops where visitors can purchase souvenirs or mementos of their travels, and tourists have come to expect such amenities. In a study of what people want from visits to historic sites, nearly one-third of the responses to the question "What makes a visit to a historical site particularly enjoyable to you?" involved physical amenities such as shops, restaurants, bathrooms, and cleanliness (Cameron and Gatewood 1998, 4).

In this chapter I want to examine these shops as archaeological sites themselves. The shops are, after all, places where a concentration of material culture can provide evidence about the meanings of the sites to the people who use them. Do the gift shops help to promote understanding of the sites to which they are attached? What kinds of pasts are represented in the items for sale at the shops? How does the act of purchasing souvenirs engage people with history? How do gift shops connect these consumers of archaeology, the "ordinary" tourists, with the sites they are visiting?

My interest in these questions has its origins in a 1994 trip to Stonehenge and Avebury, two World Heritage sites located within twenty miles of each other in Wiltshire in southwestern Britain. Both sites contain Neolithic and Bronze Age stone circles surrounded by intensively utilized landscapes that include stone avenues, numerous burial mounds, enclosures, medieval and modern villages. Both sites have been intensively and extensively studied as archaeological sites. Both sites are also part of the modern world, major tourist attractions, and the sites of contested interpretations, uses, and meanings (Bender 1998; Chippindale 1989, 1994).

Stonehenge

In the summer of 1994, I was among the thousands of tourists who visited Stonehenge. Visitors drove up (or were driven by bus) to a parking lot; to get to the stone circle you had to pay an entry fee (currently £4.40 for adults and £2.20 for children), pass the gift shop, and walk under the road through a concrete tunnel containing a mural time line leading you back from the present, through the Middle Ages, to the Iron Age and Bronze Age, until you emerged onto the World Heritage site itself. Some tourists just wandered around by themselves; others took advantage of various guided tours, with either a taped tour and headphones or human guides. I overheard one of the guides explain that no one knew for sure what the purpose of the stones was: "Whatever your ideas are, you may well be right." Many visitors expressed amazement at the circle; they were stunned that "primitive people" could have made it "without modern technology."

On the way out, the path once again guided tourists past the gift shop; like many other people, we went inside hoping to get a souvenir that would suitably remind us of our visit. According to Bender (1998, 125) most tourists at Stonehenge spend more than half their visit buying souvenirs and food, and using the toilets. Certainly the gift shop is a treasure trove for souvenir hunters!

The English Heritage gift shop at Stonehenge was all Stonehenge all the time. There was something here for everyone: pens, buttons, pins, fridge magnets, and many different T-shirts, all with pictures of Stonehenge on them; books, posters;

erasers, pencils, diaries, mugs, shot glasses. It seemed that anything you could imagine putting an image of the henge on, this gift shop had. There were also model Stonehenges: trilithon models, make-your-own-cardboard-Stonehenge-cutout models, and already made models in many sizes, from tiny to several feet in diameter (£15.95 for the smaller model). It was even possible to get bits of bluestone or sarsen stone like the rocks that are used in Stonehenge, glued to pieces of cardboard—these stones were a bargain at £3.95. (In Victorian times, people could rent hammers in the nearby town and chip bits off Stonehenge itself [Chippindale 1994]; for perhaps obvious preservation reasons, tourists are no longer allowed to wander among the stones.) Books in the shop ranged from children's picture books with stories about ancient folk to professional archaeological studies.

The shop at Stonehenge admits that the site exists in the present—although the Druids claim the henge as a sacred site, it is managed today as a tourist site. It exists as the focus of millions of short visits—day trips from London, one stop on a packaged tour, a few hours, a couple of souvenir pencils or chips of stone, and the tourists are on their way. For those interested in the site as a historic site, there are indeed informational brochures and books; for those who view it as just one more old thing in England, there are shot glasses. English Heritage is actually quite welcoming to everyone at what they describe as "Europe's most famous prehistoric monument."

The tourist gift shop, in my experience, complicates Bender's argument that the version of history presented at English Heritage sites is conservative, "a top-down past that ends when the last stone was put in place . . . a bulwark against the forces of modernity" (Bender 1998, 118–19). Bender argues that the official presentation of Stonehenge has denied complexities inherent to the site: complexities of class, gender, and history. Rather than recognizing that Stonehenge has now, and probably always had, multiple meanings, the official presentations promote one perspective—that the monument was created in the deep past, by "our" ancestors, for ritual purposes probably having to do with the changes of seasons and perceived motions of sun and moon.

While official guide books and signs surely do present Stonehenge as belonging to the "deep rooted past" (Bender 1998, 125), in the tourist shop all interests are catered to. Tourists can take away whatever bit of the monument seems to them a worthwhile souvenir. There are multiple levels of taste, authority, and interpretation.

This inclusive tone and open, welcoming stance fits surprisingly well with the monument. Stonehenge is visible on the horizon from many directions from miles away; coming along the road one spots it many minutes before arriving. It invites people at a distance to visit and explore its mystery.

For specialist tourists, like archaeologists, the shop and other amenities at Stonehenge detract from the site. Druids, pagans, and others who view Stonehenge as a sacred site may recognize the importance of having a shop to support the preservation of the monument, but also decry the commercialization of a holy place. Archaeologists may feel that the presence of these modern facilities detracts from the special feeling of the site. In a "dialogue" in Bender's 1998 book, archaeologist Christopher Tilley explains why he doesn't much like Stonehenge:

> One of the reasons is because Stonehenge has lost its aura of the past, it's much more a contemporary monument. That's because of the car-park, the thousands of people there, all the information signs, and the guards and the fencing. . . . It's always much larger in the imagination that it is on the ground. I'm always a bit disappointed. (Christopher Tilley, in Bender 1998, 79–80)

Avebury

Avebury is both a working rural village and the center of a World Heritage site. It is possible to stay in a bed and breakfast just outside the mile-long bank and ditch surrounding the complex of stone circles. Two roads run through the bank and ditch, and a pub sits at their intersection. Sheep graze among the stones, and there is also a Medieval church in the village. The monuments at Avebury are managed by the National Trust, a private heritage organization founded in 1895 "to act as a guardian for the nation in the acquisition and protection of threatened coastline, countryside and buildings" (National Trust 2002).

One woman who runs a B&B talked about the differences between Stonehenge and Avebury, and about the controversy in the village over plans to build a new parking lot just outside the circle. It was clear that Avebury residents were quite concerned about the "Stonehengification" of Avebury. They were content with their tens of thousands of visitors a year, and had no wish to get all the coach tours that visit Stonehenge, where more than half a million people visit each year (Golding 1989).

The gift shop at Avebury is run by the National Trust. It is located in a sturdy, rural-style wooden building just next to a large, thatched, seventeenth-century barn, now used for exhibits. Inside the shop were books on Avebury; tasteful linen tea towels with wildflowers and calendars printed on them, or perhaps with the words Avebury and a picture of a stone. You could buy pencils, postcards, calendars; you could also buy lovely handwoven woolen shawls (similar to the shawls available at National Trust shops all over Britain), craft items including ceramic tea sets (with wildflower decorations but not Avebury stones), hand-turned wooden bowls, and watercolor paintings.

At the Avebury shop, the massive stone circle just outside (the twenty-foot-high bank and ditch are feet away from the entrance) was almost an afterthought—there were Avebury postcards there rather than Roman Bath ones, but otherwise, you could be in any shop in any part of the country. The Avebury shop seemed to strive to present souvenirs that would re-create an idealized image of rural, upper-class Britain; the prehistoric circle only fits into this vision as a feature of the managed and idealized landscape—a folly, if you will. Indeed, National Trust policy is to provide a particular type of souvenir in its gift shops: "The National Trust's overwhelming style of representation continues to be that of the country landowner, as its main subject of concern is still represented by itself as the country heritage and estate" (Boniface 1996, 113).

Avebury, as the B&B lady implied, is not as welcoming as Stonehenge, and neither is the site. The circle is actually invisible from the approach roads until you are inside it; the bank and ditch hide its view, and the road bends in such a way that coming to the village in a bus you all of a sudden find you are inside a prehistoric monument. You have to know it is there to find it. Unlike Stonehenge, there is also a village right in the middle of the circle. So Avebury, more than Stonehenge, actually exists in the present as a part of everyday life. It may not be used for its original intention, but those stones make great scratching posts for the sheep grazing around them. Avebury seems to be the home of prosperous farmers, English villagers who would be familiar to Miss Marple. It is tidy and well managed. The post office notice board contains notices of local political meetings and social gatherings. The gift shop also reflects this aspect of the site. Avebury is not just about tourists; it is also not just about the ancient site. It is more than anything about an image of Britain that has photogenic sheep grazing on bright green fields under blue, cloud-dotted skies; a lovely stone church and a village with a pub lined along one street, honey-colored stone houses with well-tended gardens. The souvenirs available to those discriminating tourists who get there reflect this ideal of a long, continuous history of pastoral life, complete with beautifully hand-crafted, useful objects and romantic images.

Comparing Tourist Shops and Ancient Monuments

The Stonehenge and Avebury gift shops represent two variations on the theme of tourist shops in Britain. Stonehenge creates a past that is clearly in the past, no longer important in the world except as an old thing; it belongs to everyone and has something for everyone. It is all about how people got those stones there, what they did to them in the past. It is not so comfortable with how people use it in the present. Since 1978, for example, tourists are no longer able to wander freely among the stones, in a measure to protect the stones from damage. The English Heritage Stonehenge brochure states: "The view from the path will, however, allow you to see and photograph the monument in a more natural setting"—I assume that means, without all those people inside it! There is little on sale that deals with the use of the site in contemporary culture, as the focus for example of summer solstice Druid ceremonies, and even more controversially of a summer solstice rock music festival. The image in the photograph, and the interpretation each tourist makes for herself about the significance of the monument in the past, is the focus of both the gift shop and the presentation of the site. "You are as likely to be right about what happened there as anyone!"

Avebury's shop, like the monument, is more exclusive. It also deals with the past, and with an image of the past, but this is no longer just any past. It is a particular pastoral past that has its roots in particular class-based ideas about rural life, history, and landscape. It is a quite conservative image that situates the present-day gift shop and the stone circle together within a well-crafted and well-regulated historical continuum.

Tourists buying "tat" at Stonehenge may feel they have gained a piece of an ancient, but no longer living, mystery. Tourists at Avebury may instead feel that they have connected with the deeply continuous history of Britain. Both images are contemporary constructions and are incomplete representations of the actual histories of the two places. Like Avebury, Stonehenge has existed through all the times since it was first built. Though the purpose for which it was built did not, perhaps, persist, excavations and documents reveal that the monument was the focus of attention in the Roman period, in medieval times, in early modern times, and especially in Victorian times. The contemporary interpretation of its prehistoric astronomical significance is only the most recent attribution of meaning to the site (Chippindale 1994). In like manner, Avebury is not just a very pleasant rural English village, but it existed for thousands of years before the "invention" of this rural ideal. People conducted ceremonies there; were buried nearby; there was even possibly a battle between Anglo-Saxons and Vikings nearby (Burl 1979, 34). Since the 1980s, when limits were placed on festivals at Stonehenge, Avebury has increasingly become the site of pagan ceremonies including weddings and solstice rituals (Pitts 1996, 125). In fact, according to Pitts, the shop now includes "magical New Age paraphernalia" as well as magazines like *The Ley Hunter* and *Pagan Dawn* (Pitts 1996, 124). So, the meanings expressed by the material culture of the shops at these two heritage sites are incomplete. In this, of course, they are no different from archaeological interpretations of the monuments.

Shopping for Meaning

For many tourists, the connections with the past are created not only, and perhaps not even primarily, through their experiences of visiting these ancient sites. For many tourists, these connections are formulated through the act of shopping in the gift shops. According to Baker's 1988 study, the shop at the York Viking exhibit in the 1980s took in more money per square foot than every Marks and Spencers in England except the Oxford Street [London] branch (Bender 1998, 117 n. 14).

Shopping, as Miller has shown (2001), is one context for discourses about social relationships at many scales. People create understandings about the meaning of kinship, gender, and class in the context of purchasing items they deem appropriate for different purposes. He says norms about these social situations are not just adopted from the dominant culture, but are played with and negotiated in the act of shopping. Similar discourses are active in the process of shopping for appropriate souvenirs. Archaeologists select those items that affirm their identities as professionals, as keepers of knowledge about the sites. In a BRITARCH listserv discussion about the kinds of things that are appropriate or inappropriate for souvenir shops at archaeological monuments, lists of "acceptable" items included postcards, slides, local books and archaeology journals, relevant books and guides. Generic materials, things not directly related to the site, and popular images that "pretty up" the site were rejected as meaningless garbage. The act of shopping for people with an academic or other interest in the sites supports their professional identities, and positions them in contrast to the general tourist population that does not distinguish so readily between accurate and alternative images. "A colour-in-line drawing of a perfectly symmetrical, squared edges, stone multi-circle that bares [sic] passing historical resemblance to Stonehenge when it was built. But to many tourists who buy these souvenirs with this drawing on them, it is 'prettier' than the real thing" (Connely 2001).

Similarly, children are reportedly attracted to brightly colored plastic insects, erasers with images on them, and expensive chocolates. Archaeologists, historians, and to some extent pagans seek information, education, and confirmation of their beliefs about the sites in the items they purchase. Clearly, many other tourists have other goals for their shopping.

Those who manage these shops—the institutions responsible for the management of the archaeological or historical sites—argue that the shops serve more than one purpose: they are there to provide financial support to the upkeep of the monument; to offer educational materials to the visitors; to make the tourist experience more satisfying. Items for sale are chosen based on these goals. In speaking of the National Trust shops, one archaeologist wrote:

> There is a danger of too much cosy chintz and tweedom, and an excess of Peter Rabbit (however much Beatrix Potter is a Trust saint). It matters because it may damage the visitor's experience. The shop is usually at the end of the tour and becomes the visitor's last—and lasting—impression. That may distort the pleasure and learning of the visit. The ideal is to have a variety of well-designed goods that

present the best of modern British craftsmanship and live up to the excellence expected of the Trust. (Cadogan 1995, 126)

From the perspective of the shop owners, learning and pleasure are the goals of shopping; from the perspective of the archaeologist, it should be also learning and some pleasure; what of the tourist perspective? Archaeologists who visit these shops are often appalled by the cheap commercialism of the objects available for display, and by the superficial nature of the educational materials. What we fail to understand is that for tourists, the shop provides not education but an experience that links sightseeing, and also the ancient sites being seen, to their own world, a world that is in many ways constructed by commerce and consumerism. This is perhaps a blow to archaeologists who want the experience of visiting ancient sites to somehow change people's perceptions of the world. We want this experience to make people more aware of their own histories; to come to value protection of archaeological resources; to question or at least ponder important ideas about society, change, modernity, primitiveness, or hegemony (Bender 1998). Tourists may want anything from a pleasant day out, to an educational holiday, to an experience that engages them in a sense of unbroken, long-term nationalism.

These varied experiences and perceptions are rooted in contemporary culture. It should not be surprising that visitors to Stonehenge and Avebury have differing experiences and differing goals. Bender has argued (1998) the same was true when they were the loci of important prehistoric activities, and when people visited or interacted with them in every time period since their construction. Though archaeologists recognize that interpretations of the histories of the sites may be more or less well supported by the material evidence, we must also recognize that there is no single correct interpretation of such sites, and there never was.

Archaeologists experience the past through direct engagement with *its* material culture. In the gift shop, tourists experience a consumer idea of the past through its transformation into mass-produced (or even handmade) objects of modern material culture (fluorescent orange pencils with the word Stonehenge imprinted on them, or handmade pottery). In this way, the site may not be internalized as a locus of the past and history, but as a stylistically and geographically differentiated locus of modern consumer experience. In the gift shop, an unfamiliar and distant idea of the past is mediated and made familiar through the ubiquitous and immediately gratifying process of selecting objects for purchase.

It may well be, however, that shopping in the gift shops does not, in the minds of tourists, form connections to any past, but rather places the historic site in a contemporary context. The particular historical context of their purchases does not seem as meaningful as the cultural and personal experiences of shopping. *Shopping* is the point of buying souvenirs, not remembering or constructing an idea of history.

If half their time is spent snacking and buying tourist trinkets, and if those trinkets are purchased not for their historical significance but because they are suitable commodities to commemorate a trip, it is difficult to see how archaeologists' goals of engaging people with history may be accomplished.

Yet I would argue that, based on the contrasts between the Avebury and Stonehenge shops, tourists' perceptions of history are shaped differently by the different types of trinkets offered for purchase. In both cases, history has become a commodity. Versions of the historical past are linked to the present through shopping, and mementoes purchased represent what the tourist/shopper takes away from her experience of the site. Historical accuracy is not the primary item for sale in either shop. Rather, it is an idea of history, presented in multiple media. The tourist will chose the media that he or she can afford, and the image that is most meaningful or representative of his or her own experience. Shopping, rather than creating a "top-down" idea of the past, allows visitors to craft their own images. However, the different shops offer different ranges of possible images or ideas of the past, so that the particular tourist experience is crafted within these limits. I think it would be difficult to come away from Avebury with a perception other than of the continuity of a particular kind of idealized rural lifestyle, one that we can participate in by buying some of these objects. It would similarly be difficult to leave Stonehenge without thinking that the past was a very different, if welcoming, country.

Acknowledgments

I want to thank Uzi Baram and Yorke Rowan for inviting me to contribute to this volume. Their patience and attention to detail have been invaluable. Ave and Elizabeth both accompanied me to Stonehenge and Avebury, and tolerate my obsession with tourist traps. Without their support, writing would be impossible.

References

Baker, F. 1988. "Archaeology and the Heritage Industry." *Archaeological Review from Cambridge* 7(2): 141–44.

Boniface, Priscilla. 1996. "The Tourist as a Figure in the National Trust Landscape." In *"The Remains of Distant Times": Archaeology and the National Trust*, edited by David Morgan Evans, Peter Salway, and David Thackray, 108–15. London: Boydell Press for the Society of Antiquaries of London and the National Trust.

Bender, Barbara. 1998. *Stonehenge: Making Space*. Oxford: Berg.

Burl, Aubrey. 1979. *Prehistoric Avebury*. New Haven: Yale University Press.

Cadogan, Gerald. 1995. "Buildings." In *The National Trust: The Next Hundred Years*, edited by Howard Newby, 117–34. London: The National Trust.

Cameron, Catherine M., and John B. Gatewood. 1998. "Excursions into the Un-Remembered Past: What People Want from Visits to Historical Sites." www.lehigh.edu/~jbg1/numen .htm. Accessed October 10, 2001.

Chippindale, Christopher. 1989. "The Heritage Industry." *Archaeology* 42: 61–63.

———. 1994. *Stonehenge Complete*. Rev. ed. New York: Thames & Hudson.

Connely, Cerridwen. 2001. "Re: acceptable souvenirs." Message to BRITARCH discussion list, http://jcismail.ac.uk/lists/britarch. html (accessed November 6, 2001).

Evans, David Morgan, Peter Salway, and David Thackray, eds. 1996. *"The Remains of Distant Times": Archaeology and the National Trust*. London: Boydell Press for the Society of Antiquaries of London and the National Trust.

Fedden, Robin. 1974. *The National Trust Past and Present*. Rev. ed. London: Jonathan Cape.

Golding, F. 1989. "Stonehenge: Past and Future." In *Archaeological Heritage Management in the Modern World*. Edited by H. Cleere. London: Unwin Hyman.

Littrell, Mary Ann, Luella F. Anderson, and Pamela J. Brown. 1993. "What Makes a Craft Souvenir Authentic?" *Annals of Tourism Research* 20: 197–215.

Lowenthal, David. 1996. *Possessed by the Past: The Heritage Crusade and the Spoils of History*. New York: Free Press.

Lowenthal, David, and Marcus Binney, eds. 1981. *Our Past before Us: Why Do We Save It?* London: Temple Smith.

Miller, Daniel. 2001. *The Dialectics of Shopping*. Ithaca: Cornell University Press.

National Trust. 2002. www.nationaltrust.org.uk/main/nationaltrust. Accessed September 14, 2002.

Newby, Howard, ed. 1995. *The National Trust: The Next Hundred Years*. London: The National Trust.

Pitts, Michael. 1996. "The Vicar's Dewpond, the National Trust Shop, and the Rise of Paganism." In *"The Remains of Distant Times": Archaeology and the National Trust*, edited by David Morgan Evans, Peter Salway, and David Thackray, 116–31. London: Boydell Press/Society of Antiquaries of London and the National Trust.

Lord Redesdale. 2001. House of Lords, October 31, 2001. www.parliament .the-stationery-office.co.uk/cgi-bin/htm. Accessed November 12, 2001.

Seaton, A. V., and M. M. Bennett. 1996. *Marketing Tourism Products: Concepts, Issues, Cases*. London: International Thomson Business Press.

Williams, Stephen. 1998. *Tourism Geography*. London: Routledge.

Where Are the Maya in Ancient Maya Archaeological Tourism? Advertising and the Appropriation of Culture

7

TRACI ARDREN

O NE OF THE STRONGEST FACTORS in the commercialization of the archaeological record is the growing role of tourism in world economies. Archaeological sites and symbols are often used by national tourism agencies to promote their countries. These advertisements accentuate the exotic aspects of archaeological tourism while simultaneously appropriating and integrating prehistoric heritage into symbols of national identity. The use of archaeological knowledge in the promotion of state-run tourism in Mexico is particularly distinctive because indigenous Maya, who have the closest cultural ties to many archaeological sites, are largely excluded from the interpretation, management, and economic benefits of tourism. This chapter examines the role of advertisements in the commercialization of archaeological sites and the exclusion of indigenous views of the past.

Many studies have documented the important role of tourism in the modern Mexican economy; it is currently the third largest national industry, a primary focus of foreign investment, and the second largest employer after agriculture (Austin 1994; Clancy 1999). One of the two primary centers of archaeo-tourism is the southeastern state of Yucatán. Because Mexico has implemented a top-down approach to its tourism economy, giving the federal government a direct hand in planning, funding, and promoting tourism as a means to fund regional development, remarkable changes have occurred in the Maya area of Yucatán as a result of the increase in tourism since FONATUR (Fondo Nacional de Fomento al Turismo, or National Tourism Board) was created in the 1960s (Van Den Berghe 1995; Clancy 1999). The Mexican government depends so heavily on foreign tourism that it is willing to pursue tourism plans despite opposition from local groups, or at the very least with minimal local involvement (Long 1991).

103

Despite certain improvements in infrastructure, the economic benefits of this $6.4 billion dollar per year industry are small for local Maya communities. Hotel industry ownership and control is confined to large-scale Mexican chains and foreign investors while new electrical and telecommunications improvements are consistently targeted to places where large numbers of tourists are expected, like the Mayan Riviera or Cancún-Tulum corridor (Brown 1999; Clancy 1999). Objective evaluation of the tourism industry in Mexico leaves no doubt that the benefits for local communities are few, and multinational corporations or federal agencies control most touristic revenue (Clancy 1999; Pi-Sunyer et al. 1999).

Perhaps the most dramatic example of this policy of national development through tourism is the resort area of Cancún, where over 2 million people visit each year. Created by computer modeling in the 1970s as a new tourist destination, the population of Cancún has soared from 27,000 in 1950 to over 500,000 today (Pi-Sunyer et al. 1999, 5). Wage laborers have migrated to Cancún from throughout the rest of the Yucatán peninsula and elsewhere in Mexico looking for temporary or permanent work. Some live in company towns built by development corporations to house workers away from the gaze of tourists, others live well inland in squatter-style villages where it is illegal for them to hold title to land (Pi-Sunyer 1999, 29).

Throughout the Yucatán peninsula, Maya service industry workers are not satisfied with the wages and conditions of work that have resulted from the tourism boom, but are reluctant to dismantle the system that provides one of the very few options for earning cash in the present economy. As resorts and ecotourism preserves eat up the available land resources that have historically defined Maya cultural practices linked to communal corn agriculture, individuals work the system to minimize disadvantage to themselves (Norris et al. 1998).

While Cancún is primarily a destination known for its beaches, archaeological tourism plays a significant and growing role in the overall package of the Mayan Riviera, and an especially important role in the marketing of this area. Because Cancún was built in an area with minimal colonial or historic period occupation, developers were given free reign to create their own designs for resorts. Many resorts draw on the ancient past as creative inspiration and use pseudo-Maya temples and motifs as decorative themes. This appropriation of cultural imagery is very selective however, because none of the modern resorts draw on the recent local cultural heritage of fisher folk, but instead focus only on the exotic aspects of ancient ruins or the tropical locale. Ironically, actual postclassic temples that formerly dotted the coastline along the Maya Riviera have been only sporadically preserved, and are often engulfed by hotel resorts. These small structures often lack signage or guards and are rarely identified as actual ruins, leaving the visitor with the impression that they are a recent form of landscaping decoration. The result of this commercially driven improvisation on a Maya theme is the perpetuation of an inaccurate understanding of Maya culture as something extinct. In other words the total lack of authenticity in the depiction of Maya culture in the hotel zone only confirms the visitors' stereotype that the Maya have disappeared, leaving only relics and ornamentation behind.

Site visits are fundamentally involved in the commercial success of this region. Tourists from the beach resorts are bused to nearby sites such as Tulum, Chichén Itzá, and Coba; the archaeological zones of the states of Quintana Roo and Yucatán receive almost 3 million visitors a year (Vega 2002, 64). Most of these visitors will have no interaction with archaeologists, and their only access to archaeological information (besides reconstructed architecture) is through text panels at select locations on the sites. These same visitors will have extensive access to tour guides provided by the hotels and resorts, many nonlocal to Yucatán and without formal training in archaeology. A significant proportion of these visitors will also carry a popular book or magazine with which to navigate the largely uninterpreted or misinterpreted ruins, and the information in these popular sources takes on all the more significance when tourists realize the archaeological zone is largely lacking interpretive information and their guides are undereducated.

The Mexican government tightly controls archaeological site management; of the 31,887 sites in the country, only 173 are open to the public (Vega 2002, 62). This is explained as largely due to a lack of adequate funding for site excavation and conservation, although the massive tourism industry generates enormous gate receipts—it currently costs about US$10 to enter the most popular sites like Chichén Itzá and Teotihuacán. These gate receipts are funneled into state or national coffers presumably for site maintenance, although the federal institute of archaeology and history is also supported by these funds. Very few archaeological sites are owned by private trusts or corporations.

Further revenue is generated by concessions granted to shop tenders while local artisans are often prohibited from selling on site. Members of the town of Piste near Chichén Itzá are engaged in an ongoing struggle to participate in the economic activities that occur on the archaeological site and associated visitors center (Castañeda and Himpele 1997). Local woodcarvers and T-shirt venders were removed from the site when the new tourist complex was built in the early 1990s. Rents are too high for local independent vendors in the official visitors center, so they continue to enter the site and sell their wares, only to be removed by security staff. This process has continued uninterrupted for more than ten years and is not unique.

Few native communities in Mexico benefit economically from this massive ancient heritage industry (Ardren 2002). While local villages in Yucatán are often aware of the potential for archaeology to generate touristic revenue, and are receptive to excavations and consolidation in order to attract tourists, there are few examples of local or community-initiated control of archaeological tourism. Thus the archaeological past, represented both in reconstructed sites open to the public and as a design motif for modern vacation environments, is fundamentally implicated in the tourism industry and its inequities.

Whether conscious participants or not, archaeologists share some responsibility for the growth and influence of this industry, and should engage more actively in debate about how archaeological knowledge is used, manipulated, and commodified. Discussions within the discipline have focused on how archaeological interpretation can be appropriated by nationalistic or political agendas but relatively little attention has been paid to the commercialization of archeological inquiry (Gero and Root 1990; Dietler 1994; Kohl 1998; Pyburn 1998).

As part of an effort to more critically engage in the commercial uses to which archaeological data are put, I conducted a survey of three popular archaeology magazines in order to examine how archaeology is being used to promote a touristic agenda in the Maya area. In particular I wanted to see how archaeological images were used in relation to indigenous peoples, and whether any patterns of exclusion or appropriation were apparent.

The study of archaeological representation addresses the ways in which knowledge about the past is constructed through different modes of presenting our disciplinary findings. A recent contribution to this literature asserts that both academic and nonacademic modes of representation should be viewed as important avenues for the construction of theories of the past because archaeologists—those who privilege themselves with the ability to generate knowledge about the past—are just as influenced by popular culture as nonarchaeologists (Moser 2001). Often we distance ourselves from images of the ancient past that appear in popular media because we assume a false dichotomy between science and culture (Moser 2001, 263). Other studies have documented how popular archaeological literature uses the discipline of archaeology in the formation and maintenance of dominant Western cultural ideals such as the inherent good of Western technology, or the universal value of family relationships (Gero and Root 1990; Lutz and Collins 1993; Hervik 1999). It is clear that archaeological knowledge can be manipulated easily for many reasons, and the advertising industry, with its aim of income generation rather than accurate representation, seems to be an arena in which archaeological knowledge is particularly vulnerable.

I chose to examine three mainstream magazines widely available to the public reader. *Arqueología Mexicana* is published by the National Institute of Anthropology and History in Mexico, and is sold on newsstands. It has a high academic content, few advertisements, and articles in Spanish that focus primarily on the high civilizations of ancient Mexico such as the Aztec and Maya past. *Mundo Maya* is published by the marketing arm of the Mundo Maya, a confederation of five countries from the Maya area that seeks to promote and encourage intercountry travel; this magazine is often given away free to hotel guests or sold on newsstands. *Mundo Maya* has articles in Spanish and English at a very introductory level, a high percentage of advertisements, and a significant number of articles that concern traditional Maya cultural practices described in essentializing language. *Archaeology* magazine is published in English by the Archaeological Institute of America and is widely available in North America on newsstands. Articles are written for both scholarly and public enjoyment, and the percentage of advertisements is very high, especially for tour agencies and collectibles.

In a mostly complete survey of the 2000–2001 issues of these magazines, almost thirty advertisements were found that use archeological sites or images, excluding small ads for private companies. Two themes deserve comment, among the many that emerge in an analysis of the commercial purposes to which archaeological images can be put.

The first theme concerns what is really being sold. Most advertisements deliberately blurred the boundary between the commodity and the vender, featuring the archaeological site prominently with a national tourism agency tag discretely tucked in a corner. Almost all of the advertisements have a nationalistic aspect, which is not surprising given that all the countries of the Maya area maintain national control of archaeological properties, and these advertisements were created and paid for by the institutional organizations that manage these properties. The selective use of the same sites over and over again, especially those with large pyramids and other monumental architecture, creates an image of powerful nations able to control vast resources. To this end, only elite culture is portrayed as interesting or important; house mounds, ceramic sherds, and the minutia of daily life nowhere appear in the commercial portrayal of the ancient history of the Maya area. Instead, the history of Honduras or Belize is told by the most rare and unique artifacts, such as jade mosaic masks and two-meter-high carved stelae. Mexico in particular has redefined itself as a nation of Mexicans, rather than diverse indigenous peoples, and has done so by appropriating the cultural symbols of indigenous groups that have often had contentious or conflictive relationships with the state. It is extremely ironic that the archaeological monuments of Quintana Roo have become widespread symbols of Mexican identity because this state has a long history of peripheral relations with the nation of Mexico. Granted statehood in the 1970s, Quintana Roo was the refuge of Maya independence movements during the nineteenth-century caste wars (Reed 1964). The view held by powerful Mexicans of Quintana Roo as an uncivilized frontier has certainly played a role in the vigorous use of tourism as a civilizing force.

Yet even more disturbing than the nationalistic uses of Maya cultural heritage for the purposes of the Mexican state is the supranational organization of the Mundo Maya. Many magazine advertisements have been sponsored and created by the Mundo Maya, which remains a vaguely defined organization known primarily through advertising campaigns. The concept of the Mundo Maya debuted in the pages of *National Geographic* magazine, and was heralded as a multinational cooperative effort to facilitate tourism across the region and ultimately spread wealth throughout the Maya area (Garrett 1989, 424). Beyond extensive advertising campaigns, and a ubiquitous Mundo Maya symbol that appears on the doors of hotels and restaurants affiliated with the program, very little of the original mandate has been realized. Certainly local Maya groups have been left out of Mundo Maya development programs, and the organization often seems little more than another advertising strategy (Norris et al. 1998; Alexander 1999). Most disturbing is the multinational corporation framework utilized by Mundo Maya, which manipulates images of local people, archaeological sites, and natural wildlife to fulfill a program not tied to even a national agenda, but an international or multinational one. The designation of key sites within the Mundo Maya as UNESCO World Heritage centers has generated more advertising capital than actual managerial support and contributes to the sense that Mundo Maya is geared to an international commercial agenda rather than local or regional concerns.

A second theme concerns how people are used in these advertisements. Rarely was a foreign tourist depicted, but it was quite common to have indigenous people included in an advertisement for an archaeological park or holiday vacation in the Maya area. Alongside indigenous people, animals and other elements of the local environment were often balanced so that the impression given is one where nature, archaeology, and people are equally interesting and equally important to the tourist. The tradition of conflating people with aspects of natural history has been extensively commented on by indigenous scholars as well as postprocessual analyses of museum exhibits and other arenas of anthropological discourse (McGuire 1992; Deloria 1995; Hervik 1999). Clearly the advertising world does not see this association as problematic, and continues to communicate to the public an essential equation between the exoticism of the jaguar, the pyramid, and the native dancer.

Of the advertisements that portray an indigenous person in association with archaeological ruins, only one depicts an indigenous man, all the others use native women in a potent double whammy of exoticism. This combination of exotic women and exotic ruins plays on a long history of the portrayal of non-Western women in the pages of *National Geographic* and other Western travel magazines (Lutz and Collins 1993). Female images are abundant in all types of advertising, but the role of non-Western women in popular media has been particularly important in the development of an eroticized stereotype best exemplified by the frequent use of photos showing nearly naked women in the pages of *National Geographic* (Lutz and Collins 1993). The association of indigenous women with archaeological sites, while perpetuating the view of native people as unchanging or timeless as mentioned above, also allows advertisers to play with issues of desirability and escapism. The theme of longing versus fear is the perfect metaphor for exotic women and foreign travel.

The deliberate use of this powerful stereotype is made all the more clear by the clothing worn by women in these advertisements (see figures 7.1 and 7.2 at the end of this chapter). Nowhere does a native woman in business dress appear; instead women are either clothed in traditional/exotic dress that highlights their cultural affiliation and distance from the observer, or they are barely clothed at all, which highlights their desirability and the equation between desire and tourism. Presented as an ethnographic fact, it is clear that just as archaeological images are selectively chosen for commercial and nationalistic purposes, the inclusion of native people in these advertisements is a deliberate act of cultural appropriation to benefit corporate interests.

In these popular magazines, archaeological sites and their descendant communities have become commodities used to sell vacations, escapism, trinkets, and the magazines themselves. Clearly these media are not a forum for the free exchange of ideas, or pure entertainment, or the education of the public as they claim, but a stylized representation of select themes with specifically economic goals. The more often images of the archaeological past are commodified in advertisements, the more acculturated both archaeologists and the public become to the idea that prehistory is something to consume. This belief is consistent with a colonial past and a multinational or globalized future. As academics, archaeologists are trained to use words precisely, but they are less familiar with visual language and how symbols or illustrations often create a visual ideal that persists (Moser 2001, 268). Studies of representations show that these powerful visual forms of archaeological knowledge do not just replicate academic ideas about the prehistoric record, but often actively construct their own meanings or take on a life of their own (Hervik 1999). I advocate anthropological archaeologists become more involved in the ways in which archaeological images are utilized by the popular media to perpetuate cultural stereotypes and inequalities of power (Kohl 1998). Archaeologists have abdicated this responsibility by distancing themselves from popular culture, but as custodians of prehistory they must do more than that.

What avenues do archaeologists have for redressing the abuses of archaeological data by the advertising industry? Professional organizations such as the Society for American Archaeology, the American Anthropological Association, and the World Archaeological Congress can support justice in advertising with educational material and strongly worded position papers that discourage the use of indigenous people in tourism advertisements unless and until documentation can be provided that demonstrates local people benefit from this tourism. More effort should be directed toward entering into dialogue with local, state, and national tourism agencies about locally appropriate advertising strategies. A billboard displaying blond tourists drinking beer on a postclassic Maya temple alienates indigenous Maya children from their heritage and reinforces the impression that the ruins are entertain-

Figure 7.1.   Guatemalan cultural tourism advertisement from *Archaeology,* March 2001–December 2001. Used with permission.

Figure 7.2. Mexican cultural tourism advertisement from *Archaeology*, November 2000–December 2001. Used with permission.

ment for wealthy foreigners, not places of cultural meaning and history. Archaeologists working in the Maya area could increase the amount of information they channel to local school systems, encouraging young people to understand and appreciate archaeology on its own terms, rather than just a tool of state run tourism. Further support of indigenous students of archaeology holds some promise for a more diverse and local set of archaeological interpretations. When local communities experience a reorganization or restriction of access to archaeological sites, archaeologists must speak against this discrimination.

Ultimately academic archaeologists must acknowledge their own role in the production of archaeological knowledge that often excludes indigenous people and benefits the state (Kohl 1998, 225). By understanding the manipulation of academic investigation by powerful economic and political interests, archaeologists can proactively adjust research strategies to create new models for local control of tourism and thus local economic return. By acknowledging the power of commercial images to create a visual ideal, archaeologists can decide to engage in the creation of more accurate and hopefully less deliberately exploitative images of the ancient cultures investigated. By working in partnership with local indigenous peoples whenever possible, we circumvent the multinational forces which threaten to control archaeological knowledge and return to the anthropological mandate to dignify the human experience.

Acknowledgments

I would like to thank Uzi Baram and Yorke Rowan for the invitation to participate in the 2001 session, Marketing Heritage: Global Goods and the Endangered Past, and for their constructive comments and patience. I also thank Michael Dietler for my introduction to the vulnerability of archaeological interpretation, Joan Gero for her encouragement of an engaged perspective, and Lisa Breglia for her suggestion to examine marginalization in *Arqueología Mexicana*. The people of Yaxuna, Chunchucmil, and Kochol are to be thanked for their resilient tolerance of our conversations about tourism.

References

Alexander, Sara E. 1999. "The Role of Belize Residents in the Struggle to Define Ecotourism Opportunities in Monkey Sanctuaries." *Cultural Survival Quarterly* 23(2): 21–23.

Ardren, Traci. 2002. "Conversations about the Production of Archaeological Knowledge and Community Museums at Chunchucmil and Kochol, Yucatan, Mexico." *World Archeology* 34(2): 379–400.

Austin, Amanda A. 1994. "Fonatur Leads Efforts to Mold Mexico's Resorts." *Hotel and Motel Management* 209(9): 4–6.

Brown, Denise Fay. 1999. "Mayas and Tourists in the Maya World." *Human Organization* 58(3): 295–304.

Castañeda, Quetzil, and Jeff Himpele. 1997. *Incidents of Travel in Chichen Itza.* Watertown, Mass.: Documentary Educational Resources.

Clancy, Michael. 1999. "Tourism and Development: Evidence from Mexico." *Annals of Tourism Research* 26(1): 1–20.

Deloria, Vine. 1995. *Red Earth, White Lies: Native Americans and the Myth of Scientific Fact.* New York: Scribners.

Dietler, Michael. 1994. "Our Ancestors the Gauls: Archaeology, Ethnic Nationalism, and the Manipulation of Celtic Identity in Modern Europe." *American Anthropologist* 96(3): 584–605.

Garrett, Wilbur E. 1989. "La Ruta Maya." *National Geographic* 176(4): 424–79.

Gero, Joan, and Dolores Root. 1990. "Public Presentations and Private Concerns: Archaeology in the Pages of National Geographic." In *The Politics of the Past,* edited by P. Gathercole and D. Lowenthal, 19–37. London: Unwin Hyman.

Hervik, Peter. 1999. "The Mysterious Maya of National Geographic." *Journal of Latin American Anthropology* 4(1): 166–97.

Kohl, Philip L. 1998. "Nationalism and Archeology: On the Constructions of Nations and the Reconstructions of the Remote Past." *Annual Review of Anthropology* 27: 223–46.

Long, Veronica. 1991. "Government-Industry-Community Interaction in Tourism Development in Mexico." In *The Tourism Industry: An International Analysis,* edited by M. Thea Sinclair and M. J. Stabler, 205–22. Oxford: CAB International.

Lutz, Catherine A., and Jane L. Collins. 1993. *Reading National Geographic.* Chicago: University of Chicago Press.

McGuire, Randall H. 1992. "Archaeology and the First Americans." *American Anthropologist* 94: 816–36.

Moser, Stephanie. 2001. "Archaeological Representation: The Visual Conventions for Constructing Knowledge about the Past." In *Archaeological Theory Today,* edited by I. Hodder, 262–83. Cambridge: Polity.

Norris, Ruth, J. Scott Wilber, and Luís Oswaldo Morales Marín. 1998. "Community Based Eco-Tourism in the Maya Forest: Problems and Potentials." In *Timber, Tourists, and Temples: Conservation and Development in the Maya Forest,* edited by R. Primack et al., 327–42. Washington, D.C.: Island.

Pi-Sunyer, Oriel, R. Brooke Thomas, and Magalí Daltabuit. 1999. *Tourism and Maya Society in Quintana Roo, Mexico.* Latin American Studies Consortium of New England Occasional Paper no. 17. Storrs: Center for Latin American and Caribbean Studies, University of Connecticut.

Pyburn, K. Anne. 1998. "Consuming the Maya." *Dialectical Anthropology* 23: 111–29.

Reed, Nelson. 1964. *The Caste War of Yucatan.* Stanford: Stanford University Press.

Van den Berghe, Pierre. 1995. "Marketing Mayas: Ethnic Tourism Promotion in Mexico." *Annals of Tourism Research* 22(3): 568–88.

Vega, Verónica. 2002. "Deterioradas mas de 31 mil zonas arqueológicas." *Vertigo* 2(67): 62–64.

ARCHAEOLOGY IN THE GLOBAL AGE IV

Archaeological Research and Cultural Heritage Management in Cambodia's Mekong Delta: The Search for the "Cradle of Khmer Civilization"   8

MIRIAM T. STARK AND P. BION GRIFFIN

MORE THAN A CENTURY AFTER ITS BIRTH as a professional discipline, archaeology has grown beyond its conventional boundaries. One direction of this growth involves the development of international cultural heritage management, and another lies in the growing recognition that political and social factors constrain archaeological practice (see Kohl 1998 for review). Nationalism and heritage management have shaped the nature of much archaeological research in Southeast Asia (e.g., Bray and Glover 1987; Glover 1986, 1993, 1999; Peterson 1982–1983). Nowhere is this linkage between nationalism and heritage management more evident than in Cambodia, a country wracked by political instability for nearly five decades. Angkor Wat, and its many associated temples, has provided a powerful icon for Cambodia's colonial administrators, for its royal leaders, for its communist cadres, and for the current government under Hun Sen. To the Khmers, Cambodia is Angkor, and their Angkorian heritage is their future.

Of growing importance to Khmers today is the Mekong delta of southern Cambodia, where some of the earliest Khmer archaeological sites have been found. Since 1996, the Lower Mekong Archaeological Project (hereafter LOMAP) has worked at the site of Angkor Borei. This site has produced the earliest dated Khmer inscription and a distinctive art style that scholars associate with pre-Angkorian Khmer. To many Cambodians, Angkor Borei represents the cradle of Khmer civilization. But it is also a living community, and looting its archaeological resources has provided many residents with supplemental income.

This chapter examines tensions inherent in archaeological research and cultural heritage management in Cambodia at both the national and local levels. We begin by discussing the importance of archaeology in heritage management in Southeast Asia, and its connection with cultural tourism. We will then focus on Cambodia and its history of archaeological research. Archaeological research is intimately tied to marketing heritage in Cambodia, and today involves two components: (1) the development of historical (archaeological) sites as destinations for cultural tourism and (2) the illicit trafficking in antiquities. The archaeological site of Angkor Borei, where the Lower Mekong Archaeological Project has worked since 1996, provides a case study for discussing some of these issues.

Heritage Management and Archaeology in Southeast Asia

Southeast Asia is one of the world's more culturally diverse geographic regions, with hundreds of languages and all of the world's major religions. The region's archaeological heritage is equally diverse, with roots in the Paleolithic and involvement in world trade systems as early as the Roman era, and expressions of most social and political formations (kingdoms, states, and empires) for centuries before European contact (for reviews, see Bellwood 1997; Hall 1985; Higham 1989).

Most archaeological work undertaken today across Southeast Asia involves the identification, investigation, conservation, restoration, and management of archaeological sites. Each country now has a centralized governmental agency that administrates heritage management, although countries vary in the size and effectiveness of their heritage management agencies. Four countries have outstanding examples of heritage management organizations, with well-trained archaeologists and (at least until recently) adequate funding: Thailand, Vietnam, Malaysia, and Indonesia.

One regional organization, SPAFA (SEAMEO [Southeast Asian Ministers of Education Organization] Program in Archaeology and the Fine Arts), is responsible for integrating human and material resources for heritage management across the ten countries of Southeast Asia. SEAMEO reestablished the Applied Research Centre for Archaeology and Fine Arts (ARCAFA) in 1978 as the SEAMEO Project in Archaeology and Fine Arts SEAMEO SPAFA), essentially maintaining the goals of ARCAFA as guidelines for action. Since then, the government of Thailand has hosted SPAFA, and this organization runs regional training workshops in aspects of heritage management. Other international organizations, such as UNESCO, International Centre for the Study of the Preservation and Restoration of Cultural Property (ICCROM), and World Monuments Fund also contribute funding and expertise to managing the region's cultural resources.

The bulk of heritage management attention is devoted to religious monuments of the second millennium A.D., when classical states arose throughout the mainland and in some areas of island Southeast Asia. Disarticulating nationalist interests from tourism concerns in Southeast Asian heritage management is thus difficult, since national and international visitors routinely include visits to historic monuments as part of their tourist itineraries to these Southeast Asian countries. Cambodia epitomizes this situation, since tourism revenue comprises at least 30 percent of its national economy. The magnet for most international tourism to Cambodia lies in the country's northwest, where Angkor Wat and more than 250 other temples that date from the Angkorian era (A.D. 802–1432) are found (map 8.1). The following section provides a historical framework for understanding the development of a linkage between archaeology and marketing heritage in Cambodia.

History of Heritage Management in Cambodia

The French Colonial Period, 1861–1953

To say that Cambodian archaeology equals Angkorian archaeology is no exaggeration. At the beginning of the French period in Indochina, nineteenth-century colonial administrators considered most things Cambodian to be culturally depauperate and economically uninteresting in contrast with neighboring Vietnam in all ways but one: the extraordinary archaeological ruins that represented Cambodia's magnificent past (see also Stark 2001). The wealth of archaeological ruins inspired the French to develop a research institute for the Far East, or L'École Française d'Extrême Orient (or EFEO), in 1898. This institute focused on conserving and restoring ruined Khmer (Cambodia, Laos) and Cham (Vietnam) monuments of Indochina (for reviews of the French colonial period, see Bezacier 1959; Coedès 1951; Grousset 1951; Malleret 1969).

In Cambodia, the roots of heritage management (and its marketing) took hold during the early twentieth century. In 1907, France signed a treaty with Siam that assured the return of three western provinces of Cambodia containing Angkor and its associated monuments. In 1908, EFEO launched its systematic program of conservation and restoration of Khmer monuments. EFEO founding directors Louis Finot and Alfred Foucher also established the Service Archéologique as one arm of the institution. The French also began restoration and conservation activities at the temples of Angkor. The primary goal of work at Angkor lay in conservation of the monuments: the Conservation d'Angkor was created in 1908 after Siam returned Cambodia's three western provinces, and the Archaeological Park of Angkor was established in 1926.

Developing museums and exhibiting artifacts is one effective tool for marketing heritage. French colonials were also busy collecting Cambodia's archaeological heritage, with a particular interest in the pre-Angkorian and Angkorian period statuary that they found curated at Buddhist temples across southern Indochina. In 1879, French industrialist Emile Guimet established a museum in Lyon to

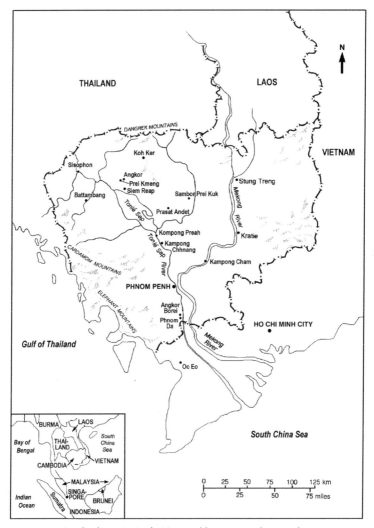

Map 8.1.   Cambodia, principal cities, and key pre-Angkorian Khmer sites.

house his extensive Asian collections. When he subsequently established a museum in Paris in 1899, it was named the Musée National des Arts Asiatiques-Guimet (hereafter Musée Guimet). French explorer Louis Delaporte's journeys in Siam and Cambodia had already provided a valuable collection of Khmer art that formed the nucleus of collections in the Paris Musée Indochinois at the Trocadéro, founded in 1882. In Cambodia, Georges Groslier founded the first museum of Khmer art in 1920 in Phnom Penh and named it the Musée Albert Sarraut. Renamed the National Museum of Cambodia, the museum serves as the repository for Khmer sculptures, inscriptions, and other Cambodian antiquities. By the time that France granted judicial powers and technical responsibilities to countries in its former colony in 1951, EFEO had identified 1,256 monuments: 780 in Cambodia, 401 in Vietnam, and 75 in Laos.

From Independence to War, 1953–1975

Cambodia's independence from France brought with it attendant problems of administering its cultural heritage. Although Cambodians assumed responsibility for running their country, French colonial institutions continued heritage management work in the country. Bernard-Philippe Groslier became the conservator at Angkor by 1956, and this era witnessed an acceleration of conservation and research on the country's heritage (Stark 2001). Although few Cambodians pursued academic training in archaeology, Angkor Park had a large contingent of trained Cambodian professionals on staff. In fact, the origins of Southeast Asia's regional organization, SPAFA, can be traced back to 1971, when the Khmer Republic of Cambodia initiated ARCAFA. Based in Phnom Penh, the urgent priority of AR-CAFA was to discover and preserve the cultural heritage of Southeast Asia. The operation of a two-year interim phase (1975–1977) was planned, but political instability in Indochina prevented implementation of this plan. With the rise to power of the Khmer Rouge in April 1975, Cambodia's archaeological heritage fell into disarray.

The Khmer Rouge Period, 1975–1979

Although the Khmer Rouge took control of Phnom Penh in April 1975, their ideology and practice began to damage Cambodia's heritage management by 1970. With the onset of widespread civil war, all archaeological research activities ceased. Political instability during the next five years ultimately forced the closure of Conservation d'Angkor in 1972, the end of its preservation work in 1973, and the departure of its staff. The Khmer Rouge used Angkor to commemorate a former glory, and spared the ruins from destruction that they wrought on Buddhist temples throughout the country. Angkor was completely abandoned until the end of the Pol Pot regime in 1978, and forces of nature undid much of the clearing work EFEO undertook to protect the monuments from destruction.

Like their predecessors, the Khmer Rouge used Cambodia's cultural heritage to support their vision of the perfect society (also see Chandler 1993). As Lindsay French (1999, 179) notes, the Angkor temples were seen as examples of a golden age of Khmer political and cultural supremacy, and were put forward as symbols of highest Cambodian achievement. Massive irrigation projects by the Khmer Rouge were fueled, in part, by an effort to restore the hydraulic society that they believed characterized Angkor (following work by Groslier). The Angkorian temples were among the few religious monuments left standing in the country; Khmer Rouge officials destroyed Buddhist temples and statues in their quest to eradicate religion from the countryside. Most of Cambodia's trained archaeologists and technical experts also perished between 1975 and 1978 as part of the Khmer Rouge plan to eliminate educated elements of the society.

So perhaps it is no surprise that the entry of Vietnamese soldiers in 1979, as part of Vietnam's occupation of Cambodia, involved the destruction of Angkor's antiquities (McDonald 1999). Subsequently, a variety of Angkorian artifacts (sculpture, architectural elements, artifacts) flooded the international antiquities market. Cambodian archaeology continued to suffer through the 1980s, as the country struggled to recover from the Khmer Rouge era and to cope with the Vietnamese occupation. Civil war continued in the northern and western portions of the country, in areas with high densities of Angkorian era monuments. Only one international conservation team, from India, dared return to Angkor Wat soon after 1979, when fighting continued in the region between the Vietnamese and the Khmer Rouge.

Following the Vietnamese withdrawal in 1989, Cambodian archaeology witnessed a gradual resurgence that began with conservation activities in the Angkor region. Such work has been difficult because fighting between government troops and the Khmer Rouge continued in parts of northern Cambodia for nearly a decade after the Vietnamese left. In 1989, after a hurricane ripped through the Angkor region, the Cambodian government appealed to international agencies to help with restoration efforts. And so work resumed in the Siem Reap area, after a hiatus of more than fifteen years. In 1992, Angkor Wat was added to the World Heritage list. Since that time, some international organizations like UNESCO have launched projects in the region, and the influx of major development support by the UNESCO Japanese Trust Fund (Japanese Government Team for Safeguarding Angkor, or JSA) at Angkor Wat and Angkor Thom has revitalized the region. So, too, has Sophia University's ongoing work at Banteay Kdei. In all, more than thirty countries are now engaged in conservation efforts in the area; these include France (EFEO), Hungary, the United Kingdom, Italy, Indonesia, China, and the United States (World Monuments Fund and the Center for Khmer Studies). A useful review of recent activities is found in Bhandari (1995, 105–44).

Legacy of Angkor Today

After the U.N.-sponsored elections in 1993, the royal government resumed power in a coalition government (see also French 1999). Prince Norodom Ranariddh, who was elected prime minister during those elections, noted that "unity is the only way to the survival of our nation. There is no other symbol for that unity except Angkor Wat temple" (Fairclough 1995, 38). This national pride in Cambodia's cultural heritage is a major catalyst behind efforts to resume archaeological work throughout the country and also to showcase its heritage on the international scene. During this time, the Cambodian government helped mount two international art exhibitions of Khmer art: one in Canberra, Australia (1992) and a grand exhibition that toured the United States, France, and Japan in 1997 entitled "Millennium of Glory: Sculpture of Angkor and Ancient Cambodia" (Jessup and Zephir 1997).

The Cambodian governmental has also taken political steps to preserve its country's national heritage since 1993. A governmental organization, with the acronym APSARA (Autorité pour la Protection du Site et l'Aménagement de la Région d'Angkor), was created in 1995 to assume responsibility for managing the Angkor area. Sites located in the remainder of the country are administered by the Ministry of Culture and Fine Arts in Phnom Penh. On January 25, 1996, the Cambodian National Assembly passed the Law on the Protection of Cultural Heritage (Sok 1998). APSARA and UNESCO worked jointly with UNDP (United Nations Development Program) and SIDA (Swedish International Development Agency) to produce a zoning and management plan for the Angkor region (APSARA 1996). Since 1999, a force of nearly three hundred French-trained "heritage police" has patrolled the Angkor Archaeological Park (Gittings 2001).

Today archaeology provides one of the greatest sources of tourism revenues in Cambodia, and the politics of heritage management are highly complex: the volume of visitation to the Angkor Archaeological Park has quadrupled since 1998, with 171,000 foreign visitors in 2000 (Gittings 2001). The first half of 2002 saw an even more marked increase, one of about 75 percent. Foreign tourists numbered some 212,690. Japanese are reported to be the most numerous, followed by Americans (Puy 2002). Cambodia's archaeological heritage today is thus important on two fronts: as a symbol of national pride and unity and as a source of economic revenue. Each year, the Archaeology Faculty of the Royal University of Fine Arts accepts approximately thirty students into its five-year program to pursue degrees in archaeology.

Beginning in late 1999, local tourism began to increase. By 2001 the Angkor Archaeological Park was, during national holidays, deluged by Khmer tourists from all but the poorest walks of life. People arrive by airplanes, speedboats, private cars, and even by trucks, coming from Phnom Penh, Battambang, and towns throughout the country. The growing middle class is especially in evidence (photo 8.2). Unlike most foreigners, Khmer visitors are coming with a great sense of heritage and identity, but few have a sense of care of the monuments and the cultural landscape.

Photo 8.1.   Crowds at the interior entrance of Angkor Wat. Photo by P. Bion Griffin.

Photo 8.2.   Affluent Khmer tourist at Angkor Wat, posing on a photographer's pony. The water tank is the location of the village scene in the film *Lara Croft: Tomb Raider*. Photo by P. Bion Griffin.

Photo 8.3.   Khmer tourists unloading at Banteay
Srei, Angkor. Photo by P. Bion Griffin.

Given the lack of sanitation facilities, the trashing of the sites is increasing. Institutional interest in development of facilities remains oriented toward the paying foreigners.

In Cambodia, heritage management is big politics and big business. The administration of the Angkor Archaeological Park exemplifies this linkage: in 1999, the Sokha Hotel company (a unit of the politically well-connected Sokimex oil and gas firm) cut a deal with Prime Minister Hun Sen to handle gate receipts from the park. Under this arrangement, Sokimex gives US$1 million each year of ticket revenues to APSARA. In its first year of operation (1999–2000), Sokimex collected almost $3.9 million from ticket sales; more than half that amount was clear profit for the company. Recent and growing criticism with this arrangement may require a renegotiation of the contract, so that more ticket revenues go into the heritage management organizations that preserve and protect Cambodia's archaeological past (Turnbull 2000).

Marketing Heritage: Looting and Archaeology at Cambodia's New Millennium

When Cambodia opened Angkor Wat for tourism, antiquities became one of the country's greatest attractions (Shoocondej 1999, 38). Antiquities looting has a long tradition in Cambodia, and the first large-scale looting was done by French author André Malraux, who removed nearly a ton of stones from Angkor Wat in 1924 (Dagens 1995, 105–6). Struggles between the Khmer Rouge and the central Cambodian government from 1979 to 1997 involved people, land, and wealth; the Khmer Rouge moved precious gems and antiquities across the Thai border to finance their war efforts (e.g., Wilkinson 1999). The shift in governmental control in 1997 (during which Hun Sen assumed control of the country) led to the demobilization of the Khmer Rouge. The collapse of the Khmer Rouge has led to a surge of unbridled looting in the country's remote provinces (e.g., Mydans 1999). Since 1990, once sacred Khmer temples and sculptures have been transformed into commodities in the international (and illicit) antiquities market. Virtually no Khmer temple is left unscathed (French 1999, 171).

In the past decade, interest in Asian antiquities has grown substantially in the West (Vincent 1996). For example, Asian sales for Sotheby's worldwide reached $112.6 million in 1997—nearly double the sales only two years previously (McCord 1999, 34). Cambodia's ancient sculptures and ceramics are considered among Southeast Asia's finest, and can be compared to the value of Egyptian or Roman or Chinese antiquities on today's art market (Shoocondej 1999, 37). This demand for antiquities is widespread, and illicit Khmer art has been found in the collections of major museums, like the Metropolitan Museum of Art (ICOM 1997, 11) and the Honolulu Academy of Art (see below).

Great profit comes from marketing Cambodia's heritage, and looters are willing to take great risks. In 1993, perhaps as many as three hundred well-armed bandits used rockets to blast their way into the Angkor Conservancy; they took eleven statues worth up to US$1 million on the international art market. As early as 1996, a single Khmer sculpture could net $100,000 on the international art market, and even ancient Buddhist and Hindu amulets go for $20,000 to $30,000 (Vincent 1996, 138–39). By 1997, international presses carried stories of the seizure of vast shipments of Khmer antiquities from ancient temples beyond the reach of the international police—from sites in northern Cambodia, in northeastern Thailand, in Laos, and even in Vietnam.

The scale of this looting ranges from the mundane to the truly breathtaking. One recent report (McCarthy 2002) describes villagers near Siem Reap who excavate and sell Khmer glazed ceramics (likely dating from the ninth to twelfth centuries) along the road to Phnom Kulen, a newly de-mined tourist destination for Khmers and foreigners alike.

Take, for example, the seventh-century Bodhisattva statue from Vietnam that the Musée Guimet acquired in 1990 through a Paris dealer: the price was the equivalent of US$1 million. Or consider the hoard of sixty-one Khmer sandstone sculptures and friezes that the Cambodian military confiscated in 1997. These sculptures come from the twelfth-century mountaintop temple of Preah Vihear, near the Thai border (Doole 1999; Ker 1997), and were part of the private collection of a top Khmer Rouge leader named Ta Mok.

One of the most remarkable cases of looting was discovered in 1999 and implicates both the Cambodian and Thai military. In January, Thai police seized a tractor trailer full of 117 stone carvings in Prachinburi province near the Cambodian border. The director of heritage protection at the Ministry of Culture,

Uong Von, noted that pneumatic drills had been used to dismantle tons of stone bas-relief at the temple (Mydans 1999). Sources said that allegedly six hundred Cambodian soldiers spent a month loading the wall segments onto trucks for cross-border transport (McPhillips 2001). One of the leading scholars in Khmer history, Claude Jacques, believes that the seizure recovered perhaps half of the missing material from this Angkorian site (ABC interview, January 27, 1999). These carvings, when reassembled, constitute an eleven-meter-long breach in the wall around the twelfth-century temple of Banteay Chhmar, which is valued at more than US$1 million on the international art market (McCarthy 2002).

Cambodia's cultural heritage is leaving the country through all its borders, but much of the antiquities traffic moves from Cambodia to Thailand with the assistance of the Thai and Cambodian military (Wilkinson 1999). Today one of the biggest markets for Khmer antiquities is Bangkok (Thailand), where art stores carry not only Khmer antiquities, but also catalogs of intact architectural elements at Khmer temples that can be removed (i.e., looted) to order. Compounding the problem is the fact that antiquities trafficking is not illegal in Singapore, Hong Kong, or Taiwan. Khmer antiquities freely flow through these cities, which are free ports with minimal regulations on exports (Polk 2001). Since the Thai government has not yet signed the 1970 UNESCO Convention against trafficking in antiquities (Thosarat 2001), Thailand is one of the leading transit points for trafficking in Cambodian antiquities. Only recently has UNESCO developed a website that inventories Khmer artifacts, detailing their nature, in order that illicit

Photo 8.4.   Aspara beheaded by looters, Angkor Wat. Photo by P. Bion Griffin.

Photo 8.5.   Aspara damaged by time, not vandals, Ta Nei, Angkor.
Photo by P. Bion Griffin.

commerce may be hindered (Shoocongdej 1999). Looted antiquities "rediscovered" in western locations, especially museums, are slowly beginning to be repa-
triated. The Honolulu Academy of Art, for example, in May 2002 returned two
pieces of statuary to the National Museum in Phnom Penh. Previously donated
to the museum, their recognition led to de-accessioning, and with great fanfare, a
ceremonial journey home.

Vast numbers of people are involved in the illicit and highly lucrative antiquities trade. Thieves handle the objects, and secure Cambodian police or military
protection to guard the transport of stolen goods through military-controlled territory. Thieves smuggle these goods out of Cambodia, to Singapore, Thailand, or
Hong Kong, overland or by sea. Some sell the goods immediately, while others
store them in unlikely places; in July 1999, officials dredged the ponds of Thailand's ancient capital of Ayutthaya and recovered forty tons of stone carvings
thought to have been smuggled from Cambodia. Others ship sculptures out of
southern Cambodia to Singapore, and then to Bangkok to sell to dealers whose
shops are found in fashionable shopping malls in Bangkok like River City. Thai
authorities periodically undertake—and publicize—crackdowns on these shops,
but the scale and tempo of trafficking in Khmer antiquities continues unabated.

The Cambodian and international public generally associates archaeology
with Angkor, because of its splendid monuments and because the Angkor region
has experienced the greatest investment of energy and funding for restoration and
preservation in the country. Yet the Angkor area—which consists of a rather

Photo 8.6.   Aspara damaged by oil from people's hands, Angkor Wat. Photo by P. Bion Griffin.

bounded area around the northern end of the Tonle Sap Lake—represents a small
section of the country's archaeological resources. The Khmer empire's historic
monuments stretch south to the Vietnamese border in Takeo province (Phnom
Bayang), east to at least central Cambodia, north into Laos (Wat Phu), and west
into central Thailand (Lopburi).

Equally impressive are the many archaeological sites that predate the eighth
century A.D., and that are scattered around Cambodia along its major rivers and
its secondary tributaries. Civil war and its lingering effects (particularly land
mines) have limited archaeological survey in many of these areas, so we still have
little idea of the distribution of sites for different time periods. As new sites are
found during development projects or by archaeologists, the logistics of heritage
management become equally harrowing to those associated with the Angkorian
monuments. One recent example, from the northern Cambodian province of Banteay Meanchey, involves the Iron Age site of Phum Snay (Pottier 2000). Exposed

Photo 8.7.   Reconstructed aspara at Ta Prohm, Angkor. Photo by P. Bion Griffin.

through road construction activities in 2000, this Iron Age site once contained a huge cemetery and represents the only documented site of its time period in the country. Despite numerous visits to the site by representatives of Cambodia's heritage management agencies and the installation of military police at the site, looting continues at such a vast scale that the site resembles a lunar landscape (also see

Thosarat 2001). Salvage excavations in 2000 and 2001 recovered a range of important archaeological material, but it is not clear whether research at the site will be possible in the future because of the wholesale looting by local villagers, for sale to foreign collectors in the United States, Europe, Singapore, and Japan.

One important region that the French described during the heyday of the colonial era is now undergoing archaeological investigation and political negotiation: Cambodia's Mekong delta. The next section of this chapter briefly introduces the region and uses the archaeological site of Angkor Borei (Takeo province) as a case study for exploring global goods and Cambodia's endangered past.

Archaeological Work at Angkor Borei

Heritage management and archaeological research are intimately linked on the Lower Mekong Archaeological Project, which was a direct outgrowth of the University of Hawaii/East-West Center/Royal University of Fine Arts Cambodia Project. That broader project was begun in 1994 by the East-West Center (Honolulu, Hawaii) as a form of capacity building for Cambodia's heritage community (for review of project, see Griffin et al. 1999). This broader Cambodia project was instigated to provide training to graduates of the Royal University of Fine Arts (Phnom Penh) in archaeology, art history, and historic preservation in a research context (Griffin et al. 1996; Griffin et al. 1999). The Lower Mekong Archaeological Project was established to study the early historic period of southern Cambodia, from 500 B.C. to A.D. 500 (Stark et al. 1999).

At the invitation of Cambodia's Ministry of Culture and Fine Arts, LOMAP has concentrated most of its archaeological research on the archaeological site of Angkor Borei. Our fieldwork combines archaeological research and training and uses a variety of field techniques, from excavation and survey to geoarchaeological prospecting and coring. Several American students from the University of Hawaii, and more than twenty graduates from the Archaeology Faculty of the Royal University of Fine Arts have participated in LOMAP fieldwork since 1996.

Southern Cambodia contains a rich yet poorly understood record of early historic period occupation, from approximately 500 B.C. to approximately A.D. 500. Archaeological research in the last two decades suggests that the Mekong delta experienced extensive settlement and human land use that predated the Angkorian period, or before about A.D. 802. Historians and art historians have identified the endpoint of the early historic period about A.D. 500, when we see the emergence of statuary, writing, and a more complex political organization that may have been integrated through religious ideology (Coedès 1968; Vickery 1998).

The archaeological importance of Angkor Borei lies in its historical role as an inland center of Cambodia's earliest state, which Chinese emissaries called "Funan" (see reviews in Hall 1985; Stark 1998; Stark and Bong 2001). Founded in the late centuries B.C., the settlement grew into a major population center by the early first millennium A.D. and housed sizable populations. Perhaps as early as A.D. 100, people began to dig a series of canals that radiated southward from the settlement and ultimately connected most major first millennium settlements in the delta. At some point later in the sequence, the people of Angkor Borei erected a massive earthen and brick masonry wall around its borders; we see the construction of brick monuments and stone statuary in the later first millennium A.D., and the earliest dated Khmer inscription (Stark et al. 1999).

Archaeological, bioarchaeological, and geoarchaeological research continues at and around the site of Angkor Borei to trace its occupational history and relative importance through time (Stark and Bong 2001). At its apex during the first millennium A.D., Angkor Borei was at least three hundred hectares in area, housed more than a dozen brick structures that served either as Indic shrines housing stone sculptures, or as mortuary monuments that contained cremation ashes and associated grave goods. At its peak, the settlement could have housed several thousand inhabitants (as it does today) and helped integrate the northern delta both politically and economically (Stark 1998). Cambodians view Angkor Borei as the cradle of their civilization, and researchers are still in the process of defining the site's historical role in the development of complex society in the Mekong delta.

Angkor Borei as a Contemporary Community and a Heritage Site

Unlike the abandoned tells of the Near East, the archaeological site of Angkor Borei is located beneath an eponymous district. At the western edge of the Mekong delta, Angkor Borei today has approximately 6,000 inhabitants who live within its walled boundaries; about 22,000 others live within the general area. Cambodian political boundaries operate at several levels: the village (the *phum*), the subdistrict *(khum)*, and district *(srok)*, and the province *(khet)*. Angkor Borei's population is a mixture of Khmers and Vietnamese. The southeasternmost subdistrict of the Angkor Borei district is called Khok Thlok, and its southern boundary abuts the Vietnamese border.

Khmers associate Khok Thlok district in particular, and this area in general, with the origin story of Preah Thaong or Nagi Soma (Gaudes 1993; Ledgerwood 1996). In the origin story that Funan residents recounted to visiting Chinese emissaries in the third through sixth centuries A.D., an Indian Brahmin priest named Preah Thaong (or Kaundinya) left India for Southeast Asia and arrived at the shores of the Mekong delta. There he saw a beautiful local princess, named Soma, on the shore. She was the daughter of the king of the *nagas*, serpents that lived beneath the ocean. Preah Thaong and Nagi Soma battled each other for control of the region; he defeated her, they fell in love, and married. It is said that

King Preah Thaong introduced Hindu customs, legal traditions, and the Sanskrit language to the population. Nagi Soma's father "drank the waters" that covered the land (this might have involved draining parts of the delta for farming) and gave the people a kingdom that he called Kambuja (also see Gaudes 1993).

Southern Cambodia, including Takeo province, was largely under the control of the Khmer Rouge between 1970 and 1974 (Quinn 1976, 4). Takeo province was known as Area 13 to the Khmer Rouge (Quinn 1976, 19). Vietnamese residents occupied the area associated with the archaeological site of Angkor Borei until 1970 (Boua and Kiernan 1989, 3). Some of the population abandoned this area during the early 1970s because of American bombing and Khmer Rouge–imposed restrictions on clothing and on activities such as cross-border movement (Quinn 1976, 15). The Cambodian government organized a variety of development projects in this region after the collapse of the Khmer Rouge in 1979. Land reclamation schemes developed by the provincial administrators established Angkor Borei as a district in 1982, and settlers from across the province have moved into the region in the past twenty years (Boua and Kiernan 1989).

Looting at Angkor Borei

Cambodia's heritage officials selected Angkor Borei for LOMAP because of its historical importance, political stability, and accessibility from Phnom Penh. Work at this site, however, underscores the intimate relationship between heritage management and preservation, on the one hand, and heritage destruction (looting) and cultural tourism on the other. The site of Angkor Borei is located a few kilometers from Cambodia's border with Vietnam. Riverine traffic between Vietnam and Cambodia is continuous: people, their animals, and their goods move into and out of this Angkor Borei en route to (or arriving from) Vietnam. The community's key location and large size makes it ideal for trafficking goods, both legal and contraband. According to interviews with local villagers and with officials, the looting of the settlement's archaeological past extends back at least a decade.

Before 1970, antiquities were revered in Cambodia: Indic statues and artifacts were stored and venerated in Buddhist temples across the country. French collectors visited these temples in the 1930s and took most seventh- and eighth-century (pre-Angkorian) Indic statues from Cambodian communities for curation in the National Museum (Phnom Penh) and in France. With the conclusion of the U.N.-sponsored elections in 1993 and the resumption of relative stability in the country, more statuary moved onto the international art market. After the 1993 elections, local people report that outsiders began to visit Angkor Borei in search of antiquities. The rising demand for antiquities was irresistible to the military troops stationed in the region, and villagers report that they were given screens to use in their excavations of areas that might yield gold. In interviews with LOMAP members in 1999, the head monk of the Buddhist temple at Phnom Da (the hill with temples south of Angkor Borei) reported that he was approached by armed villagers and ordered to relinquish antiquities that were stored at his temple. Today, Angkor Borei/Phnom Da–style sculptures are now available for purchase on the web through vendors in Asia and Europe.

The fact that Angkor Borei is a regular destination for field trips from the Royal University of Fine Arts may aggravate the local looting situation. For a few days each February and March, busloads of college students descend on the district office at Angkor Borei to camp out, visit the ruins with their teachers, and learn about Cambodia's pre-Angkorian past. Faculty members from the Royal University are also members of the Ministry of Culture and Fine Arts, and various faculty members involved with these trips have regular contact with the district (local) officials. Periodically, Royal University faculty members talk with local officials about site preservation concerns. While this contact minimizes visible looting activities at all levels of local government, our interviews with villagers suggest that the level of looting activity may have actually escalated between 1993 and 1999: the very period during which field trips had taken place.

In 1999 and 2000, LOMAP was privileged to excavate the first documented pre-Angkorian cemetery in the country. This cemetery was exposed through illicit excavations south of the Buddhist temple called Wat Komnou, and the landowners responsible for those excavations reported finding and selling numerous artifacts (particularly whole earthenware vessels and beads). Through the two-year period that fieldwork involved, villagers approached us repeatedly in efforts to sell their artifacts to us. By the end of the 1999 field season, we learned enough about the local antiquities trade to ascertain that many district officials were involved; the district governor, for example, was busy making his own collections of local antiquities during the 1999–2000 period. It was also said that the provincial governor had a substantial collection of pre-Angkorian statuary in the province's capital. With political reorganization in 2000, many of these officials have been given new assignments elsewhere.

LOMAP efforts to halt trafficking in antiquities were admirable but limited. We were only able to persuade the landowners to stop looting the excavation area through monthly compensation for "guarding" the area. The month that our funding stopped in January 2001, landowners resumed their digging. Moreover, 2001 reports from the markets in Phnom Penh, and from web searches that turn up pre-Angkorian statuary from southern Cambodia, suggest that looting of Angkor Borei continues.

Threats to the archaeological resources in the region stem as much from economic development activities that cause unintentional damage as from active efforts by local residents to mine the site for antiquities for sale. With settlement and land reclamation in the region has come landscape modification, which includes opening new fields for cultivation and animal husbandry. Efforts since 1998 by the European Union's development program, called PRASAC (Le Programme de Réhabilitation et de l'Appui au Secteur Agricole du Cambodge), involve canalization projects in the area. These new canals irrigate new fields and facilitate transportation but occasionally cut through archaeological sites. The region floods annually, and these floods destroy local unpaved roads. Repairing local roads requires road fill, and in 1996 the Angkor Borei district governor authorized local villagers to dismantle one of the largest standing brick monuments on the site to grind its bricks into road fill. Angkor Borei is thus under imminent threat of destruction from all angles, from villagers digging their gardens to massive construction activities that eradicate ancient brick monuments.

LOMAP members have participated in three activities that may help to stem the problem: regular meetings with members of Cambodia's heritage ministry, public outreach, and the development of a local museum. Meetings throughout the 1999 and 2000 field seasons brought the highest ministry members to Angkor Borei, where they talked with district officials. We also met with the deputy provincial governor at the end of 1999 to discuss methods for both protecting the site and encouraging tourist visitation. Work continues to find funding to develop a zoning and management plan that might afford Angkor Borei (and its environs) some protection against a range of factors that threaten the integrity of its archaeological resources. A second, and perhaps equally effective, strategy involved public outreach.

Public Outreach

LOMAP field investigations from 1996 to the present have attracted great attention to the area by its local inhabitants, and the proximity of our excavation unit to one of the community's two Buddhist temples meant that many of the area's residents took an intense interest in our work. So, too, did villagers living near the area, schoolteachers, and leaders of the temple community, who often stopped by several times a week to observe our progress. This work offered public education for community members, as well as for a number of Khmer and foreign visitors to the ongoing excavations. Dr. Miriam Stark and Mr. Bong Sovath visited the Angkor Borei high school to make a presentation on our research and to answer questions, and we explained our work to various village leaders at Wat Komnou throughout the archaeological field season.

In 1999, the Ministry of Culture also sent down a delegation in the second week of March to sanctify the site. This event drew many residents from Angkor Borei. In 1999 and 2000, LOMAP members also conducted tours to cohorts of archaeology and architecture students from the Royal University of Fine Arts (Phnom Penh) throughout the field season. The tours provided a culture historical background to the site and then concentrated on findings from the cemetery. Audience members were encouraged to ask questions, and visitors (regardless of background) asked the same set of questions regarding the age of the deposits, the nature of the findings, and the relationship between the site of Angkor Borei and Cambodian oral traditions regarding Khmer origins.

Angkor Borei as Tourist Destination?

To the Cambodian government, the cultural resources of Angkor Borei may represent a potential source of economic revenue. Angkor Borei's proximity to Phnom Penh (if the roads are repaired) and its cultural significance to the Khmers make Angkor Borei an excellent candidate for protection and tourism development. The Department of Tourism has already begun to highlight Angkor Borei and Phnom Da as a tourist destination. The European Union's agricultural development program, PRASAC (*Programme de Réhabilitation et d'Appui au Secteur Agricole du Cambodge*), began an effort toward tourism development in 1997 by constructing an on-site museum at Angkor Borei. LOMAP members have assisted the European Union since 1997 in developing the on-site museum at Angkor Borei through photography, consultation on exhibits, and displays.

The Angkor Borei museum celebrated its official opening on May 5, 1999. Representatives of the Ministry of Culture and Fine Arts, the Ministry of Tourism, PRASAC, the European Union, and the University of Hawaii attended the opening. For the first time, the museum was also opened to residents of Angkor Borei and several hundred people came to see the museum. Hundreds of visitors (foreign and Khmer) came to the Angkor Borei museum in 1999 and in 2000, based on the museum's visitor book. The Ministry of Culture and Fine Arts continues to struggle with the Ministry of Tourism over control of the museum, and particularly over control of entrance fees. Local officials insist on running the museum, while provincial authorities express frustration over their lack of participation in the maintenance of the museum. Efforts to enhance the area's attractiveness to tourism continue as LOMAP works collaboratively with the European Union and with Cambodia's Ministry of Tourism and Fine Arts. Yet the looting continues at Angkor Borei.

Discussion and Conclusion

Heritage management, nationalism, and archaeological research are inextricably linked to marketing heritage in Cambodia, in a complex web of relationships that implicate people and organizations from the bottom up. Angkor Borei is one of the largest, and certainly one of the oldest, early historic period sites in the Mekong delta on either side of the border. The fact that Cambodians today live in Vietnam's Mekong delta today (the Khmer Krom) adds fuel to the claim that the Mekong delta was Khmer for centuries or millennia before the Vietnamese took it from Cambodia in the seventeenth century. So, too, do chronometric dates produced through work by the Lower Mekong Archaeological Project (Stark et al. 1999; Stark and Bong 2001). The foregoing examples have illustrated how Cambodian archaeology, regardless of location or time period, has become a political arena. In the case of Angkor Borei, studying the origins of Angkor places research in a delicate position between identity politics and good scholarship.

We hope that the Angkor Borei example illustrates how economic development is associated with looting. At the local level, archaeological work and the establishment of a local museum pits community concerns against provincial interests in a struggle over private land ownership and tourism potential. At the national level, an ongoing dialogue involves both bureaucrats and scholars who disagree about the ownership, management, and meaning of this important archaeological site.

Archaeological resources in and around Angkor Borei comprise an important part of Cambodia's cultural heritage. Through our outreach efforts, LOMAP members and our colleagues in the Ministry of Culture and Fine Arts seek to encourage a sense of stewardship among Angkor Borei residents that might transcend their preoccupation with Angkor Borei as a resource to be mined for its marketable heritage. Such community education efforts are best done regularly, and by an onsite staff. Cambodia is one of the world's poorest countries, and heritage management outside of Angkor is a luxury. No resources are thus available for such work at Angkor Borei, and the future of that archaeological site is in great jeopardy.

Grinding poverty, corrupt governmental officials, a poorly compensated military, and—most of all—a voracious international demand for Khmer antiquities all contribute to the continued looting of Cambodia's archaeological heritage. This taste for antiquities has been most publicized for Cambodia's Angkorian past because of the vast scale of destruction in recent years. Yet poor Cambodians, with few economic alternatives and powerful economic incentives, also view pre-Angkorian sites as potential gold mines both literally and figuratively. On March 6–9, 2001, Cambodia hosted the eleventh session of UNESCO'S Intergovernmental Committee for Promoting the Return of Cultural Property to its Countries of Origins. Perhaps such widespread international efforts can help Cambodians stem the flow of their past beyond the boundaries of their country.

Cambodia's archaeological heritage is vital to its people, and the archaeological heritage of Angkor Borei is valuable to many different constituencies. To archaeologists, its resources hold a story that describes the origins of the earliest civilizations in the Mekong delta. To schoolteachers and educators, Angkor Borei represents the cradle of Khmer civilization and the Khok Thlok of oral traditions. To Cambodian and foreign tourists, Angkor Borei and Phnom Da represent an intriguing destination to learn about Cambodia's ancient past. The challenge now is to preserve it—and the artifacts from this site that appear on the global market—for Cambodia's future generations.

Acknowledgments

Our thanks go first to Yorke Rowan, who invited Miriam Stark to participate in this symposium. We would also like to acknowledge Bonnie Magness-Gardiner for supplying us with articles and encouraging us to participate in this symposium. Miriam Stark is also grateful to many Cambodian colleagues who assisted her in the Lower Mekong Archaeological Project in so many ways. Special thanks go to the Ministry of Culture and Fine Arts and to Her Royal Highness Princess Norodom Bopha Devi (Minister). We also thank His Excellency Chuch Phoeurn, His Excellency Tuy Koeun, His Royal Highness Prince Sisowath Pannara, and His Excellency Pen Yet for their ongoing support of the project. Thanks also to Jim Bayman for comments on an earlier draft of this chapter. Bion Griffin thanks the many Khmer students at the Royal University of Fine Arts for years of insightful commentary, and to Judy Ledgerwood, Kim Sedara, and Bong Sovath for ongoing advice. We are also grateful to the residents of Angkor Borei, and particularly to the community of Vat Komnou, for their encouragement and support during our field research. Responsibility for the final form of the chapter rests with its authors.

References

ABC News. 1999. "Industrial-Scale Temple Looting in Cambodia." Interview with Claude Jacques, January 27, 1999. www.abc.net.au/ra/asiapac/archive/1999/jan/raap-27jan1999-2htm. Accessed June 17, 2003.

APSARA [Autorité pour la Protection du Site et l'Aménagement de la Région d'Angkor]. 1996. Angkor: A Manual for the Past, Present, and Future. Phnom Penh: Royal Government of Cambodia.

Bellwood, Peter. 1997. Prehistory of the Indo-Malaysian Archipelago. Rev. ed. Honolulu: University of Hawaii Press.

Bezacier, Louis. 1959. L'archéologie au Viêt-nam d'après les travaux de L'École Française d'Extrême Orient. Saigon: France-Asie.

Bhandari, C. M. 1995. Saving Angkor. Bangkok: White Orchid.

Boua, Chanthou, and Benedict Kiernan. 1989. "Oxfam in Takeo." Manuscript in the possession of the author.

Bray, Warwick, and Ian Glover. 1987. "Scientific Investigation or Cultural Imperialism: British Archaeology in the Third World." Institute of Archaeology Bulletin 24: 109–16.

Chandler, David. 1993. A History of Cambodia. 2d ed. Bangkok: Silkworm.

Coedès, Georges. 1951. "Études indochinoises." *Bulletin de la Société des Études Indochinoises* n.s. 26(4): 437–62.

———. 1968. *The Indianized States of Southeast Asia.* Edited by Walter F. Vella. Translated by Sue B. Cowing. Honolulu: University of Hawaii Press.

Dagens, Bruno. 1995. *Angkor: Heart of an Asian Empire.* Translated by Ruth Sharman. New York: Abrams.

Doole, Jenny. 1999. "Post-War Cambodia." *Culture without Context: The Newsletter of the Illicit Antiquities Research Centre* 4: 2–3.

Fairclough, Gordon. 1995. "Potent Symbol." *Far Eastern Economic Review,* January 19, 1995, 38.

French, L. 1999. "Hierarchies of Value at Angkor Wat." *Ethnos* 64(2): 170–91.

Gaudes, Rudiger. 1993. "Kaundinya, Preah Thaong, and the 'Nagi Soma': Some Aspects of a Cambodian Legend." *Asian Folklore Studies* 52: 333–58.

Gittings, John. 2001. "Buddhas of Angkor under Threat from Looting." *Guardian Unlimited,* August 28, 2001.

Glover, Ian. 1986. "Some European Contributions to the Prehistory of Indonesia: A Personal View." *Indonesia Circle* 40: 5–16.

———. 1993. "Other People's Pasts: Western Archaeologists and Thai Prehistory." *Journal of the Siam Society* 81: 45–52.

———. 1999. "Letting the Past Serve the Present: Some Contemporary Uses of Archaeology in Viet Nam." *Antiquity* 73: 594–602.

Griffin, P. Bion, Judy Ledgerwood, and Chuch Phoeurn. 1999. "The Royal University of Fine Arts, East-West Center, and University of Hawaii Program in the Archaeology and Anthropology of the Kingdom of Cambodia, 1994–1998." *Asian Perspectives* 38(1): 1–6.

Griffin, P. Bion, Ledgerwood, Judy, and Stark, Miriam T. 1996. "Education and Cultural Resource Management at Angkor Borei, Cambodia." *CRM: Cultural Resources Management* 19(3): 37–41.

Grousset, René. 1951. "Figures d'orientalistes." *Bulletin de la Société des Études Indochinoises* n.s. 26(4): 413–26.

Hall, Kenneth R. 1985. *Maritime Trade and State Development in Early Southeast Asia.* Honolulu: University of Hawaii Press.

Higham, Charles F.W. 1989. *The Archaeology of Mainland Southeast Asia.* Cambridge: Cambridge University Press.

ICOM [International Council of Museums]. 1997. *One Hundred Missing Objects: Looting in Angkor.* Paris: ICOM-EFEO.

Jessup, Helen I., and Thierry Zephir, eds. 1997. *Sculpture of Angkor and Ancient Cambodia: Millennium of Glory.* Washington, D.C.: National Gallery of Art.

Ker, Munthit. 1997. "Stolen Cambodia Artifacts Recovered." Associated Press.

Kohl, Philip L. 1998. "Nationalism and Archaeology: On the Construction of Nations and the Reconstructions of the Remote Past." *Annual Review of Anthropology* 27: 223–46.

Ledgerwood, Judy. 1996. "Myth/history and the Study of Angkor Borei." Paper delivered at the Khmer Studies Conference, Monash University, Australia. Manuscript in the possession of the author.

Malleret, Louis. 1969. "Histoire abrégée de l'archéologie Indochinoise jusqu'à 1950." *Asian Perspectives* 12: 43–68.

McCarthy, Terry. 2002. "Reclaiming History: After Decades of Official Neglect and Rampant Theft, Cambodia Is Finally Recovering its Artistic Heritage." *Time.* www.time.com/time/asia/features/ontheroad/cambodia.relics.html. Accessed June 17, 2003.

McCord, A. 1999. "Sotheby's Rochell: Riding a Rising Market." *Art & Auction,* March 15, 1999, 34.

McDonald, Mark. 1999. "World Teams Work to Restore Ancient Site in Cambodia." *San Jose Mercury News,* March 1, 1999.

McPhillips, Jody. 2001. "Lost and Found: Ordinary People Return Extraordinary Artifacts." *Cambodia Daily,* March 31, 2001.

Mydans, Seth. 1999. "Raiders of Lost Art Loot Temples in Cambodia." *New York Times,* April 1, 1999.

Peterson, Warren. 1982–1983. "Colonialism, Culture History, and Southeast Asian Prehistory." *Asian Perspectives* 25(1): 123–32.

Polk, Kenneth. 2001. "The Antiquities Trade Viewed as a Criminal Market." *Hong Kong Lawyer,* October 2001.

Pottier, Christophe. 2000. *Rapport sur la visite d'une nécropolie de l'âge du fer.* Report submitted to the Ministry of Culture and Fine Arts, Kingdom of Cambodia. École Française d'Extrême Orient, Centre de Siemreap-Angkor, Cambodia.

Puy, Kea. 2002. "Tourists to Angkor Wat increases 75.3% in 1st Half of 2002." *Cambodia Today,* July 11, 2002. http://go.to/CambodiaToday. Accessed July 2002.

Quinn, Kenneth. M. 1976. "Political Change in Wartime: The Khmer Krahom Revolution in Southern Cambodia, 1970–1974." *Naval War College Review,* Spring, 3–31.

Shoocondej, Rasmi. 1999. "Destruction of Southeast Asia's Past through Looting." *World Archaeological Bulletin* 9: 37–40.

Sok, Siphana. 1998. *Laws of Cambodia.* Vol. 2. Phnom Penh: Cambodian Legal Resources Development Center.

Stark, Miriam T. 1998. "The Transition to History in the Mekong Delta: A View from Cambodia." *International Journal of Historic Archaeology* 2(3): 175–204.

———. 2001. "Archaeology in Cambodia." In *Encyclopedia of Archaeology: History and Discoveries,* edited by Tim Murray, 239–48. Santa Barbara, Calif.: ABC-Clio.

Stark, Miriam T., and Bong Sovath. 2001. "Recent Research on the Emergence of Early Historic States in Cambodia's Lower Mekong." *Bulletin of the Indo-Pacific Prehistory Association* 21(5): 85–98.

Stark, Miriam T., P. Bion Griffin, Chuch Phoeurn, Judy Ledgerwood, Michael Dega, Carol Mortland, Nancy Dowling, James M. Bayman, Bong Sovath, Tea Van, Chhan Chamroeun, and David Kyle Latinis. 1999. "Results of the 1995–1996 Field Investigations at Angkor Borei, Cambodia." *Asian Perspectives* 38(1): 7–36.

Thosarat, Rachanie. 2001. "Report from Southeast Asia." *Culture without Context: The Newsletter of the Illicit Antiquities Research Centre* [Cambridge], no. 8.

Turnbull, Robert. 2000. "Temples of Gloom." *Far Eastern Economic Review*, August 31, 2000.

Vickery, Michael. 1998. *Society, Economics, and Politics in Pre-Angkor Cambodia: The 7th-8th Centuries.* Tokyo: The Centre for East Asian Cultural Studies for UNESCO, the Toyo Bunko.

Vincent, Steven. 1996. "The Allure of Southeast Asia." *Art & Auction*, October 1996, 138–41.

Wilkinson, Gina. 1999. "Protectors Pillage Cambodian Artifacts." *Asia Times Online*, June 24, 1999.

Recovering the German Nation: Heritage Restoration and the Search for Unity

9

JASON JAMES

ERMANY HAS NOW BEEN FORMALLY unified as a nation-state for over a decade, yet the sense of national unity leaders invoked to justify unification remains painfully elusive. Although the unification of the western Federal Republic of Germany (FRG) with the eastern German Democratic Republic (GDR) in 1990 was presented as a return to normalcy after a forty-year interruption, the reality proved much more complex. A wall in the mind has long outlived the old physical barrier between the two populations. While many West Germans resent the cost of revitalizing the Eastern economy, many East Germans complain that unification proceeded rather like colonization and that they remain second-class citizens. There is some truth behind the Easterners' claim: rather than a joining of two equals, unification amounted in legal and practical terms to an absorption of the GDR into the existing FRG. And despite West German Chancellor Helmut Kohl's 1990 promise of "blooming landscapes" of prosperity in the Eastern states, they still lag behind the West in earnings and economic growth while unemployment remains significantly higher (Endres 2000; Heuser 2002).

Since 1990, a host of policies, programs, and pronouncements have been implemented to mitigate the economic inequalities between East and West Germans as well as overcome the prejudices and resentments they often harbor toward each other. In comparison to economic measures, however, policy and rhetoric focused on national culture have received little attention in commentaries on the East–West divide. One area of cultural policy, the restoration of architectural landmarks in East Germany, calls for closer examination.

Restored heritage sites in the East are regarded as vital to the region's prosperity, specifically as a magnet to draw new residents, investors, and, most importantly, tourists. Historic landmarks have been presented as one of East Germany's few positive contributions to the unified nation. Yet West Germans' approach to

heritage in the East has worked to reinforce a sense of inequality. More specifically, I suggest that West Germans' initial discovery of what they described as untouched heritage in the East, along with their subsequent efforts to rescue it, are
implicated in what John Borneman (1998, 112) has referred to as the orientalization of East Germany. The "backward" East figures here as a place less altered
by history than the West, which appears as more modern and thereby further removed from the older, antimodern traditions blamed for the rise of fascism. If the
East is more "German" in this negative sense, it also represents a locus of cultural
authenticity in much the same way that rural peasant communities functioned for
nineteenth-century Romantics. The people and historic places in East Germany
represent an earlier Germanness the West once rejected but now wishes to recover.

Heritage restoration as such is a realm of potent symbolism, not only in the
material symbols it produces but also in the practices of (re)producing them as
cultural property. Recovered historic landmarks in East Germany offer ideal symbols of national totality because they seem to capture Germanness in a tangible,
discrete form. They appear both unequivocal and, because of their age, uncontro-
versial. More precisely, they embody the German *Kulturnation* (cultural nation),
which figures here as both a locus of continuity and a victim of recent history. It
remains conceptually and morally separate from the tainted aspects of German
history and identity.

The project of restoring these landmarks therefore represents, I suggest, a kind
of redemptive labor. That is, it serves as a means of compensating for and undoing the damage inflicted on national culture over a sixty-year period marked by
fascism, war, national division, and state socialism. In this way, landmark restoration casts German nationhood in a decidedly traditional (ethno-cultural, commu-
nitarian, primordial) form. This representation of nationhood finds some
legitimacy in international discourses of cultural property, but it sits uneasily with
claims to the effect that Germanness has become a civic identity—a matter of up-
holding democratic values rather than laying claim to a biological and cultural inheritance.

Before examining these issues in more detail, it is important to set the theoretical stage by examining the symbolism of buildings and historic landmarks as
well as the relationship between the concept of cultural property and the nation.
I then establish the historical context of current restoration efforts by taking a
closer look at the role of heritage in visions of national unity prior to 1989 and
West Germans' (re)discovery of cultural landmarks in the GDR. My argument in
these initial sections draws on published texts as well as observations made during
two years of field research in East Germany between 1996 and 1998. I then present the case of the Frauenkirche (Church of Our Lady) in Dresden to illustrate
the symbolism of national restoration attached to such projects. The analysis then

turns to a second case, a federal program called Cultural Lighthouses, which is-sued a catalogue of national landmarks in East Germany. This project reflects both the production of national patrimony as a means of recuperation, and the orientalization of East Germany in the context of heritage restoration.

Architectural Symbolism and Cultural Property

Built structures generally carry multiple layers of significance. Architecture also frequently serves as a rich source of metaphors for collective life. It can give ma-terial form to the economic and social power of its creators, to utopian visions of the future and nostalgic fantasies of the past, and to notions of cultural achieve-ment. Architecture provides a powerful medium for representing, shaping, and at-tacking identities. Structures can stand as both icons and sacred objects whose tangibility and durability offer ideal symbolic form for collective claims to unity and continuity. Historic buildings in particular often come to embody an objec-tive, unmovable link between the present and the past that confirms the continu-ity of national being (see Barthel 1995). In this and many other cases, individual structures and sometimes entire cities stand in a metonymic relationship to a given group: they are discrete objects that capture something much larger, parts that stand for the whole. Sacred sites and monumental structures in particular are of-ten cast metaphorically as the physical body of the group that claims them, and their loss, injury, survival, or reconstruction registers the group's suffering or re-covery.

The logic underlying such architectural and iconoclastic symbolism becomes clearer when we understand the role of architectural landmarks as a consummate form of cultural property. In his study of Québécois nationalism, Richard Han-dler (1988, 6–14) argues that the idea of cultural property combines a fetishism of material culture with a model of the nation as collective individual. (The cen-tral aspects of Handler's argument could also apply to other groups that make claims to cultural property, although those organized as nation-states do so with greater legitimacy and force.) Together they form what Handler calls the nation-alist model of "possessive individualism," in which culture appears as the exclusive possession of a distinct group. That is, like the human individual, the unique qual-ities claimed by the nation are thought to find expression in its material posses-sions, its cultural icons. Cultural property represents, in other words, a permutation of what Slavoj Zizek (1990) calls "the Nation-Thing"—that which national subjects claim as their exclusive inheritance and entitlement, that which others wish to damage or take away (see also Clifford 1985).

The value attributed to cultural artifacts, Handler (1988, 14) maintains, fol-lows from a misrecognition similar to the mystification by which commodities be-come objects of fetishism under capitalism. According to Marx (1977, 435ff.), commodity fetishism involves perceiving the world in terms of relations between things rather than the social relations behind those things. Gottfried Korff (1994) makes a parallel argument regarding the authenticity of historic landmarks. The sacred qualities attached to landmarks do not reside in the material structures themselves, but derive instead from the society that treats them as authentic relics. In other words, although stone and wood usually remain the center of attention in historic preservation, it is actually the symbolic practices surrounding them that make them heritage in the first place. From this perspective, national cultural property is not simply out there to be discovered, but is instead produced and reproduced.

The production of these symbols involves a selection and framing of cultural objects, eras, and themes as illustrious while submerging events and traditions that do not fit that vision of heritage. Historic landmarks are produced by being placed under legal protection, being catalogued in lists of heritage sites, and undergoing restoration or reconstruction. Their appearances on tourist itineraries and postcards, in glossy pictorial volumes, and in television portraits participate in their production and reproduction. Public figures also frequently use them as sites for important speeches and meetings, while tourists visit them as sites of pilgrimage and citizens contribute funds to their refurbishment. In other words, these myriad practices not only serve as a performance of devotion to the collective that landmarks represent, but also reproduce their sacred value as heritage.

Handler concludes that the model of possessive individualism goes hand in hand with an essentialist vision of national totality. The metaphor of the collective individual and the treatment of culture as a singular thing each work to vest the nation with qualities of boundedness, continuity, and homogeneity. Yet the nationalist desire for totality can never be fulfilled, Handler argues, and for that very reason it drives an endless process of objectifying an "authentic national culture" through selecting, sanctifying, and paying homage to cultural artifacts. Through these practices, "the national totality will know its own essence, will control the definition of its own being. It will acknowledge the existence of other national entities, . . . but its identity will not depend on interrelationships and exchanges. 'Our true being' can only be an inner quality, a natural essence" (Handler 1988, 194). Although the nation's collection of cultural property can therefore never be truly complete, I would add, imagining the possibility of its completion goes hand in hand with the fantasy of totality. The status of the collection as a whole can hold as much importance as the individual artifacts it contains.

Cultural Heritage and the German Nation

As a vision of totality, the concept of the German *Kulturnation* (cultural nation) has long been, in one form or another, extremely powerful precisely to the degree that German nationhood has remained problematic. The vision of a single German cultural landscape was central to nationalist aspirations in the nineteenth century, when the area referred to as Germany consisted of numerous feudal territories. The term "cultural nation," first coined by the German historian Friedrich Meinecke (1919) in contradistinction to the French *Staatsnation* (state nation), fell out of use after World War II because of its association with German exceptionalism. Yet the idea of German culture still proved central in efforts to sustain an image of a unified nation in the decades after 1949, when East and West Germany officially became two separate states and the legacy of National Socialism rendered other expressions of national belonging suspect. Most recently, in 1990 the cultural nation returned implicitly in the rhetoric of national continuity used by leaders to portray unification as natural and necessary. And in the years since unification it has proven as important as ever due to persisting East–West tensions, a continuing (albeit mitigated) uneasiness surrounding the concept of the German nation, and the increasing integration of the European Union. Although the idea of German national heritage itself arguably carries a problematic historical charge, it has proved an especially useful concept because it can be rendered as separate from and untouched by Germany's tainted pasts. While many historic landmarks and sites recall these burdened pasts (the excavated Gestapo headquarters in Berlin is a good example), *Kulturerbe* (cultural heritage) refers by and large to positive emblems of cultural continuity and identity.

In order to fully appreciate the role of historic landmarks and their restoration in the context of unification it is necessary to examine briefly the ways East and West German leaders sought to resurrect the idea of the nation. Although the East and West German states each represented themselves as the other's negative mirror image (Borneman 1992), they did so in part by virtue of what they held in common, namely the desire to create a sense of legitimate nationhood. In the 1970s and 1980s, both governments began to refurbish the concepts of German national history and heritage (von Bredow 1983) while trying to skirt the tainted historical connotations of those terms, usually by attributing them to the Germans on the other side of the Iron Curtain.

The FRG claimed to be the sole legitimate German state. Its constitution legally applied to the entire German people, which meant that East Germans were technically citizens of the FRG; they merely had to cross the border to enjoy this status, which of course became an extremely difficult and dangerous venture after the Berlin Wall was erected in 1961. The *Ostpolitik* or "Eastern policy" later adopted by West German leaders signaled a de facto acceptance of division, yet the FRG never officially abandoned the goal of unification.

In contrast to the FRG, the GDR never officially claimed to represent all Germans and effectively abandoned the goal of reunification. The regime led by Erich Honecker from 1971 to 1989 did, however, revive the idea of national culture in the 1970s with the aim of shoring up its flagging domestic and international legitimacy. This included returning a statue of Frederick the Great to its place in East Berlin as well as increasing funding for the restoration of landmarks associated with traditions and figures once disparaged as bourgeois or imperialist (Sheehan 1992, 166). Martin Luther, for example, once again became an accepted object of veneration.

In 1986, West German Chancellor Helmut Kohl (1986, 289) praised the East German regime's expanded efforts in the realm of historic preservation as a sign of renewed historical consciousness in the East that would, he hoped, deepen their sense of commonality with their fellow Germans in the West. This was hardly what the socialist leadership had intended. Yet Kohl's remarks did resonate among those in the West who felt that it was time for West Germany to become a normal nation, which included removing taboos on concepts like German culture and fatherland. Indeed, Kohl's talk of historical consciousness reflected a concerted effort to create a healthier sense of national identity among West Germans, whose sense of pride remained limited, some argued, to "D-Mark nationalism."

The most protracted domestic confrontation over issues of normalization and relativization, however, was the 1986 Historians' Debate, in which Jürgen Habermas (1989a,b) attacked "revisionist tendencies" emerging in German historiography and political rhetoric (see Evans 1989; Maier 1988). More specifically, he argued that some historians and conservative politicians were promoting a dangerous relativization of the Nazi period. Jeffrey Olick (1998, 553) sums up the message of relativization thus: "The German past had its horrors, but so did the pasts of other countries. The twelve short years of Nazi rule do not exhaust the extent of the German past, which must be 'accepted with all its highs and lows.'" Although Kohl's efforts in this regard were not unprecedented, Olick continues, "his style . . . was more aggressive, embodied in an ideological program for cultural change."

In Habermas's view, this ideological program aimed at resurrecting a traditional sense of national belonging founded on primordial qualities of shared culture and history. Although he did not use the term "essentialism," Habermas can be read as attacking the essentialist core of this project and the search for continuity that accompanied it. In light of modern German history, Habermas insisted, the FRG was obliged to adopt a "postconventional" identity based on *Verfassungspatriotismus* (constitutional patriotism), a civic identity founded on commitment to reason and democratic values rather innate qualities or organic traditions. Germanness should reside in political practice rather than an ethnic fact. This does not exclude historical consciousness, Habermas explains, but it does insist on a critical awareness of the past.

Unification and the Discovery of the Past in East Germany

The events of 1989–1990 seemed to vindicate Kohl and render his ideological program unnecessary. East Germans' quick abandonment of calls for reformed socialism in favor of the slogans "Germany, one fatherland!" and "We are one people!" was interpreted by Kohl and many others as clear evidence that the bedrock of national commonality remained intact. (Skeptics responded that East Germans' enthusiasm for unification actually reflected less lofty sentiments, namely the desire to share in West German prosperity.) Along with East Germans' calls for national unification, the fact that the international community ultimately sanctioned the move suggested that terms like nation and fatherland might at last be free of their former taboos. The desire to be a normal nation like others finally seemed capable of fulfillment.

Kohl and his supporters presented unification as a restoration of normalcy, but it was also crucial to cast it as a new beginning in order to calm worries about a Fourth Reich. Unification, they asserted, would once again give political form to the nation that had existed before division and had survived it, yet this enduring national community bore no resemblance to the *Volksgemeinschaft* of the Nazis. The Federal Republic (which would now incorporate the "new states" of the former GDR) stood for freedom and democracy within a framework of both national and European unity (Kohl 1990). Despite such assurances, however, the argument for unification ultimately proceeded from the kind of primordialist claim that Habermas had attacked in 1986: Germans belong together in one state because they constitute a single historical people with a common heritage. As we shall see, this desire to have it both ways—to present German nationhood as based on natural, prepolitical commonalities but also founded on democratic principles—has persisted beyond Kohl's tenure as chancellor. (Kohl's Christian Democrats were defeated by a coalition of Social Democrats and Greens in 1998.)

Given the tension between the historical stigmas that plague Germanness and the claim that unification represented a return to normalcy, it is not surprising that historic landmarks figured prominently in attempts to cast national unity as a natural fact. In his address to the first session of the unified German parliament on October 4, 1990, Chancellor Kohl singled out prominent architectural monuments in the East as icons of shared Germanness:

> Among the contributions of the [new eastern] states [to the unified nation] . . . we should not overlook an invaluable cultural heritage. They include old landscapes rich with tradition that hold unique documents of our history. The palaces in Schwerin and Potsdam, the marvelous form of the Naumburg Cathedral, the

Semper Opera in Dresden—they all stand for a single Germany. At the Wartburg [Castle] Luther translated the Bible for all Germans, and Weimar has become a worldwide symbol of German classicism. We are pleased that these monuments to our common history and culture are now accessible to all. [1990, 554, my translation]

Kohl's tour of national treasures in the East reflects the possessive, objectifying logic described above. His statement can also be read as a symbolic retrieval of these buildings into the common national collection. That is, he converts or reproduces them as national heritage to be claimed by all Germans. Not only are they now accessible to West German pilgrims, they have also returned to the unified nation's possession after having been held hostage in the GDR for forty years.

Although Kohl may not have consciously intended this, his attention to historic landmarks resonated with the perception shared by many East Germans that the terrible condition of historic buildings and old town centers reflected the GDR regime's own advanced stage of deterioration. Indeed, along with the sense of imprisonment symbolized by the Berlin Wall, the exclusive and repressive power of the party, and the scarcity of goods ranging from cars to bananas, East Germany's crumbling inner cities and demolished historic buildings contributed significantly to the simmering disenchantment that culminated in the protests of 1989. Among the groups that came to be known collectively as the *Bürgerbewegungen* (citizens movements), several had formed in the 1980s in response to state plans to demolish historic buildings and neighborhoods. Several hundred residents of Erfurt, for example, formed a human chain around the old city core to protest plans to demolish the historic Andreas Quarter. When representatives of these citizens' groups later sat down with socialist officials to work out the terms of reform, they immediately demanded the suspension of all construction and demolition projects and the dismissal of incumbent city planning officers.

East German preservation activists soon found support among West German experts and enthusiasts. On their first visits to the GDR after the border opened, these Westerners discovered a past they felt the FRG had lost. Having formerly imagined socialist cities as dominated by the gray concrete of Stalinist architecture, they were positively astounded by what they saw. In addition to the well-known landmarks highlighted by Kohl, these explorers found scores of villages, towns, and old city centers that in their eyes looked as though nothing had changed since the 1930s. "Where in the [old] Federal Republic," asked West German journalist Sebastian Preuss, "can one find so many buildings still preserved in their prewar state down to the last detail?" (1990, my translation). As architecture critic Günter Kowa recalls, "This wealth of architectural heritage, admittedly decaying but not yet falsified by . . . prosperity and still preserved in every detail, was for the one [Western] side part discovery and part revelation, and for the other [Eastern side] a fund of cultural property they had once given up for lost but that now demanded immediate rescue" (1996, my translation).

Although in most respects East Germans were expected to recapitulate the recovery West Germany had experienced in the 1950s and 1960s, when it came to heritage they were exhorted to avoid repeating its mistakes. Most postwar urban reconstruction in the West abandoned notions of heritage and tradition due to their association with fascism, favoring instead a modernist approach to architecture and planning that would signal a radical break with the past. By the late 1960s, however, some West Germans began to regret this sweeping rejection of history. The earlier desire to remake West German cities in a modern, democratic cast, some contended, had actually made them uniform and dysfunctional, lacking in character, memory, and community ties (Mitscherlich 1965, Soane 1994). Unlike most cities and towns in the East, one Bavarian preservationist claimed, modernized West German cities had mutated into "schematized Legolands" (Hampel-Zöllner 1990). Meanwhile, well-preserved historic towns in the West had lost so much of their original substance, some complained, that they offered something closer to the artifice of an amusement park than authentic heritage. Andreas Glaeser (2001, 187) suggests that West German architects and planners of the generation responsible for these developments saw in the East a chance to redeem themselves for the sins of their youth.

The unexpected chance to recover authentic German heritage represented in this view one of the few fortunate effects of socialism. "Poverty is the best preservation," German preservationists frequently muse, and the historic substance it had left standing in the GDR inspired a wave of nostalgia. "In the Eastern states, we rediscover our past," proclaimed Preuss (1990; see also Wagner 1996, 95ff.). The few West Germans who not only visited but eventually chose to settle in the East after 1989 often expressed similar sentiments. "When I walk along the cobblestone streets late at night," one young professional explained to me, "I have the feeling that a horse and carriage could turn the corner at any moment." The Eastern town where he settled exuded a flair that his own hometown in the West had lost long ago, he claimed.

Many Westerners initially seemed much more enchanted with East Germany's historic cities than with the people who lived in them, although they often expressed (and sometimes still do, I have observed) a patronizing admiration for Easterners' "natural," "uncomplicated" ways. This was not a new perception, but the direct contact possible after the fall of the Wall seemed to reinforce it. For many West Germans, Easterners offer a purer historical version of themselves in much the same way that "primitive" peoples and the "backward" rural peasantry provided early ethnologists' and folklorists with "noble savages" and images of unchanged tradition. West German praise for the seemingly unchanged cities and villages of the East rendered them as artifacts reflecting and confirming the authentic Germanness of their inhabitants. Both appear as from a different time, as having stood still for fifty years or more.

The preunification version of this perspective appears most clearly in the writings of Günter Gaus, who served as the West German envoy to the GDR from 1973 to 1981. Gaus's 1983 book *Wo Deutschland Liegt* (Where Germany Lies) insists that "the Germans . . . over there [in the GDR] have more roots in German history than we do here—history less in the sense of its external facts, but rather as a source of social conduct that reaches all the way into intimate, private habits, with many inherited virtues as well as flaws (*Unwerten*)" (1983, 26, my translation). East Germans live at a slower pace, he says, and the countryside remains devoid of neon signs and supermarkets. In a word, they have remained more German, which for Gaus means they have retained a stronger will to cling to old, familiar things—the things that the West Germans have given up (1983, 172–73). Gaus insists that one should not on this basis approach the GDR as an open-air museum of the German past, but his nostalgia remains evident. Stephan Wolle argues that Gaus saw the East Germans as "the 'noble savages' of the consumer age" (1998, 82, my translation). Recent texts echo Gaus's perspective. An article by Martin and Sylvia Greiffenhagen highlights the "flaws" of Germanness in the East (1994, 9). After seeming to distance themselves from the view of Easterners as more German, they proceed to cite sociological surveys as evidence for the persistence of old German (especially Prussian) ways, including tendencies toward naive hatred and cynical conformity (1994, 20).

Glaeser refers to this tendency to see East Germany as stuck in an earlier time as "distemporalization" (2001, 180). Johannes Fabian's (1983) term "allochronization," although originally developed in his critique of anthropological practice, seems adaptable to this context as well. Whatever the term, this perception includes a romantic component that renders East Germany as the locus of national authenticity while also asserting its backwardness. This ambivalent perception can also be seen in relation to what John Borneman (1998, 109) describes as a "double fiction" West Germans maintained about East Germany. On the one hand, the GDR figured as the external and antithetical other to the FRG. It was the negative mirror image that reinforced the West's self-image as democratic, anticommunist, and as having broken with the Nazi past more decisively than its "totalitarian" counterpart. On the other hand, the GDR was treated as internal to the West, as a lost part of the German nation whose retrieval would complete it.

Put differently, the preserved Germanness Westerners find in the East reflects the fundamental ambivalence of German nationhood. It contains qualities and ideas associated with fascism, but it also represents cultural roots. To deny continuity with burdened legacies while affirming it with cultural heritage requires treating the two as completely separate. To locate an essential Germanness in the East thus proves quite advantageous for the West insofar as the positive heritage found there can be incorporated as a national legacy, while the tainted aspects of Germanness remain at a safe distance from the West, lodged in the Eastern other. Cultural heritage, particularly in the form of architectural landmarks, offers what appears as an untainted and therefore easily assimilable aspect of this positive legacy. Not only does it usually predate both fascism and socialism, but it also suffered damage under both. It appears separate from these regimes to the degree that it appears as victim rather than perpetrator in the disasters of modern German history. Moreover, as suggested above, the restoration allows (Western-dominated) unified Germany to perform a kind of redemption by counteracting the failings of the GDR and compensating for Western sins against heritage at the same time.

Images of Unity, Continuity, and Recuperation

Since as early as 1989, federal, state, and local governments as well as national and local organizations have devoted enormous amounts of money and energy toward rescuing landmarks in East Germany. Public campaigns have called on Easterners and Westerners alike to assist in the effort and admire the results. In 1991 the federal budget included a total of 620 million marks (roughly $370 million) for the restoration of historic cityscapes in the East (Stade 1994). (This alone marks the project as exceptional since cultural affairs, including historic preservation, fall under the jurisdiction of regional state governments in the German federalist system.) Municipal and state contributions raised the total investment to approximately $900 million for that year alone, and the federal government later extended its subsidies to individual landmarks (Bickelhaupt 1994). In the first years after unification, seasoned preservation and planning officials from Western cities also volunteered to help East German officials struggling with a new body of law as well as unfamiliar political practices and economic principles. Ironically, protecting heritage frequently meant going to battle with the investors and developers who were to serve as the primary motors of urban redevelopment and economic growth for Eastern cities.

In the first decade following unification, historic architecture became a major attraction for West German tourists visiting the East, and for those unwilling or unable to explore in person, reports in various media offered the next best thing. The drama of preservation in the Eastern states enjoyed wide publicity, and in many cases the aim of symbolizing national unity was quite explicit. The people behind these initiatives were in most cases West German.

In a particularly ambitious example, the (originally West German) national public television network ZDF joined with the German Foundation for Monument Protection (Deutsche Stiftung Denkmalschutz, a nongovernmental organization founded in 1985 in West Germany) to produce a series of programs beginning in 1992. The series title Citizens, Save Your Cities! reiterates the exhortation that East Germans avoid the mistakes of the West. The program's stated aim was to portray the "cultural riches" contained in the "crumbling landscape" of the Eastern states (Zweites Deutsches Fernsehen 1997). Each of the series' fifty-nine editions profiled one or more "endangered" monuments and called on citizens to contribute funds and exert political pressure to help ensure their survival.

Reflecting on the series after its conclusion in 1997, moderator Werner von Bergen (1997, 6) writes in a decidedly Romantic vein that images of "grandiose ruins" in Eastern cities "deeply moved" the show's producers as well as its audience. Judging from the title of von Bergen's contribution to a retrospective booklet on the series, he also perceived the show and the project of restoration itself as having inspired feelings of national unity. The title, "Zusammen bauen was zusammen gehört" [Building together what belongs together], is an adaptation of a now legendary statement made by former West German Chancellor Willy Brandt at a 1990 unification rally: "Jetzt wächst zusammen was zusammen gehört" [Now what belongs together is growing together]. In von Bergen's title, the projects of historic preservation and national unification appear to reflect and confirm one another. Just as Germans belong together, so do the objects of their cultural patrimony.

The image evoked here of East and West Germans joining together to rescue their endangered cultural heritage is rich with overlapping connotations: cooperation in the national project of caring for endangered collective property; incorporating the East in the nation by restoring its decrepit landmarks; and recovering the nation by rebuilding its heritage. The essentialism discussed by Handler underlies all of these connotations. This is most apparent in the ambiguous implications of the term gehört (belong). Not only does the supposed cooperation between East and West Germans in this effort confirm that they belong together, but the cultural property they rescue together also already signifies their commonality because the property belongs to them in common.

The local structures restored under the auspices of programs like Citizens, Save Your Cities! all participate in the symbolism of recovered nationhood, but current projects to reconstruct prominent landmarks offer particularly vivid examples of the ways historic buildings have become poignant symbols of recuperation. The recent decision to reconstruct the facade of the Prussian royal palace in Berlin, for example, manifests a desire to reverse time and undo historical loss.

The reconstructed facade will replace the GDR's Palace of the Republic, which replaced the original royal palace after it sustained serious bomb damage and was eventually demolished. Many East Germans have contended that the plan reflects West Germans' desire to eradicate every vestige of the GDR from the cityscape (see Burkhardt 1996; Glaeser 2001).

The reconstruction of the Frauenkirche in Dresden incorporates a similar condemnation of the GDR while offering an especially poignant sign of restored continuity: its absence during forty years of socialism becomes an anomaly in the stream of national history, just as the GDR itself has come to represent a transient episode. Before its demise in the Allied firebombing of February 1945, the Frauenkirche formed the most prominent feature of Dresden's skyline for two hundred years. Once known as the Florence on the Elbe because of its magnificent baroque architecture, the city held no direct military importance but was considered one of Germany's most beautiful. The firebombing was thus essentially an act of psychological warfare intended to speed German capitulation.

The ruin of the Frauenkirche—two wall fragments and a massive pile of charred stones—remained essentially untouched through the years of socialist rule. While some saw the ruin as an admonishment against war, for others it represented the barbarity of bombing a city solely because of its cultural significance. By virtue of its location in Dresden and its status as a sacral structure, the lost church serves as an ideal touchstone for claims that Germany too—or at least some of its people and traditions—can be counted among the innocent victims of World War II. The 1990 "Call from Dresden" that marked the beginning of the reconstruction campaign begins with the statement, "On February 13, 1945, only a few weeks before the end of a war whose outcome was already clear, air raids left the Frauenkirche in ruins" (Bürgerinitiative 1990, my translation). One pamphlet soliciting donations for the project underscores the tragedy of the church's destruction and its victimhood by emphasizing its earlier endurance and portraying its demise in anthropomorphic language: "She [sic] withstood the canon balls of Friedrich II's army and even braved the devastating air raids of February 13, 1945, but on February 15, 1945, the *biggest sacred baroque building in Germany* collapsed with a sigh" (Telemundi 1994, emphasis in original).

The ruin was explicitly marked as a national symbol when Chancellor Kohl chose it as the backdrop for his first public speech in East Germany in December 1989, when he declared that West Germany would remain true to the goal of reunification. More recently, in concert with images of resurrection the former ruin seems to signify not only national loss in World War II, but also the failings of the GDR. According to one pamphlet, "Its rebuilding, planned since the end of the war, was prevented by the economic and political conditions which existed under communist rule" (Paul 1993). Another text casts the ruin as a sign of negligence:

"In the decades following [its destruction], only a sad pile of rubble was left to recall one of the most significant European cultural monuments" (Stiftung Frauenkirche n.d.; my translation). Socialism, it seems, lacked both the practical means and the national will that unified Germany has demonstrated.

The cost of the Frauenkirche reconstruction has been estimated at $156 million, with some funds coming from federal and state sources but more than half financed through donations. Begun in 1994 and still underway a decade later, the exact replication of the destroyed structure was made possible by the extensive documentation produced during a previous restoration from 1938 to 1943 (Paul 1993). Only by virtue of the careful attention to national heritage under National Socialism, it turns out, is the project possible at all.

It may be partly for this reason that the project's promotional literature speaks of local and European identity, seldom if at all mentioning Germany. Some texts cast the reconstruction as a gesture of peace and national reconciliation, while others take pains to portray it as recovering a piece of world culture. Echoing the rhetoric used by Helmut Kohl to calm anxieties about German unification, one pamphlet claims that "The reconstruction will symbolize to all the *unification* of Germany and Europe in *peace* and *freedom*" (Telemundi 1994; emphasis in original). References to national heritage are conspicuous in their absence, especially in light of the fact that even the European Union and the United Nations still treat nationhood as the primary category of cultural identity. Given the complications surrounding Germanness, however, the absence of overt reference to national heritage is not surprising.

The fact that the Frauenkirche reconstruction has been cast as an achievement made possible by national unification and as an undoing of socialist neglect suggests, however, that the church's resurrection parallels that of the nation. Indeed, images of healing and resurrection—equally applicable to Dresden, Germany, and Europe—appear frequently. The primary emblem of the reconstruction effort portrays a fully reconstructed church rising up behind the silhouette of the diminutive and overgrown ruin it has replaced. The accompanying text enjoins its readers to "Help us heal one of the most painful wounds in the heart of Europe" (Telemundi 1994). While the text offers yet another anthropomorphic image, the illustration calls to mind the proverbial phoenix rising from the ashes. The promotional literature employs this metaphor frequently.

The return of such a prominent architectural victim thus expresses a kind of closure, a final clearing of the rubble left by a catastrophic century. Yet opponents of the project have contended that the reconstruction amounts to a monumental sign of wishing to turn back the clock. It suggests that wounds can be healed, that one can retrieve what has been lost. Dieter Bartetzko, architectural critic for the national newspaper *Frankfurter Allgemeine Zeitung*, expresses this view with particular eloquence:

A window to yesterday has opened, a window that also opens to the future. A glimpse of something that was believed lost forever has been granted, the promise of return now takes tangible form. The myth of Orpheus and Eurydice comes spontaneously to mind, a story that insists on the irreversibility of time, life, and death. . . . Dangerous and obliging illusions are at work here: brand new, as though untouched by time and war, the three-dimensional likeness of this Baroque architectural wonder presents itself as immortal. [2002, my translation]

Plans for the reconstruction of the entire Neumarkt quarter surrounding the church—which will involve reproducing the baroque facades of sixty destroyed houses—offers further evidence, according to Bartetzko, that the project aims to conquer ephemerality (see also Simon 2002). He goes on to remark on the argument made by reconstruction proponents that the mixture of old and new building stones in the reconstructed church will prevent amnesia about its "death and return." "We shall wait and see," he concludes skeptically, apparently unconvinced by the implied claim that the "new-old Frauenkirche," even if it bears marks of its former absence, can signify loss more powerfully than the ruin it replaces. It seems more likely that its primary message will be, as Bartetzko suggests, an assertion of the possibility of resurrection, of recovering the past.

The Continued Search for the Cultural Nation

Although the architectural symbols and rhetoric of the cultural nation fit especially well with Helmut Kohl's conservative project of reawakening national consciousness, his party has by no means monopolized them. In his address to the World Tourism Conference in Hannover, Germany, the current chancellor, Gerhard Schröder (2000), highlighted architectural icons in a manner that closely echoed Kohl's 1990 speech. After beginning his address with a verbal tour of historical and cultural highlights in West Germany, he quickly added, "But that alone is not Germany." The approaching tenth anniversary of unification gave cause, he continued, to celebrate the East German "peaceful revolution" of 1989 as well as the fact that all Germans can now travel throughout the country without harassment. An important benefit of unification, it seems, lies in West Germans' freedom to visit historic landmarks in the East. Schröder explained that he himself had spent his last vacation touring East Germany, seeming to offer himself as an example of a devoted cultural pilgrim. But as much as East German recovery impressed him, he confessed that "I was ashamed at how little we all know of the great cultural treasures that suffered such neglect under the totalitarian regime of the communist party." Once again, the socialist regime's cultural delinquency counts among the many wrongs that the current state must undo, while East Germany appears as uncharted territory awaiting exploration. Moreover, the icons of a national heritage that endured so much damage and neglect seem to capture the suffering and recuperation of the nation itself. Chancellor Schröder has made significant commitments of personnel and funds to further the goals implicit in such statements. In his first year in office he appointed a special federal minister for cultural and media affairs. And according to official figures, his administration doubled federal spending for cultural institutions, which in addition to memorials and landmarks covers museums, theaters, and libraries. Along with these regular expenditures, the office has created a number of special subsidy programs devoted to heritage, including approximately $7 million for landmarks of local and regional significance and $19 million for Cultural Lighthouses in the East. This new category refers to cultural monuments that "manifest the . . . achievements of the German state (*Gesamtstaat*)" or "are vital to the identity of German cultural landscapes" (Naumann 2000). Federal funding for the restoration of historic landmarks stood at $87 million for 1999 alone, 88 percent of which went to projects in the Eastern states.

Michael Naumann, the first minister for cultural and media affairs, specifically promoted cultural heritage as a vehicle for achieving national unity. The task of recovering rare cultural artifacts in the East remains at the center of this effort. In response to a journalist's question about the role of culture in bringing East and West Germany together, Naumann emphasized the "old traditions" in the East that initially struck Westerners as a "previously undiscovered treasure" (Das Parlament 1999). Naumann also invoked the nation more explicitly than the promoters of the Frauenkirche reconstruction, but in doing so couched the idea of German cultural identity in a vision of the European Union as composed of distinct historical peoples. "Particularly now, as Europe continues to grow together," he explained in a 1999 interview, "it is necessary to place special emphasis on individual cultures and to strengthen the cultural dimension of the unification process. Europe consists of regions and states, each with their own cultural identity" (Das Parlament 1999). Naumann's successor Julian Nida-Rümelin (2002) has gone still further in normalizing the idea of the cultural nation by insisting, "To our shared political constitution that is binding for all Germans corresponds a deep-rooted (*gewachsene*), shared cultural disposition (*Verfasstheit*)." From this perspective, Germany's political being simply reflects its cultural being. It remains unclear where immigrants fit into this picture.

Naumann was more explicit than his successor, however, about the importance of cultural nation in the face of Germany's troubled legacies: "West and East Germans will become aware of what it means to be German in Europe first and foremost through culture and history. We need this sort of 'unifying tie' even more than others in the wake of the disastrous past" (Das Parlament 1999). Note that "culture and history" remain conceptually distinct from "the disastrous past." The need for unifying bonds and the splitting off of burdened German pasts that this entails point to what Glaeser (2001, 186) refers to as "longing for an admirable tradition" among contemporary Germans. I would call it a desire for redemption through the cultural nation. Historic buildings serve as ideal symbols for this ostensibly untroubled legacy.

Seeking Cultural Lighthouses in the East

The recent Cultural Lighthouses program offers a striking example of state efforts to include East German landmarks in the pantheon of the cultural nation. West German scholar Paul Raabe was contracted to conduct research on cultural landmarks and institutions in the East and produce a Blue Book describing their significance and condition. The first publicized draft of the book includes twenty historic monuments, museums, and archives as Cultural Lighthouses.

The Blue Book gives form to an otherwise elusive set of criteria that transform a building or institution into a historic artifact and ultimately endow it with national significance. In his foreword to the draft presented in December 2001, Minister Nida-Rümelin suggests that books of this sort can define a canon and thereby find use as a guidebook for cultural tourists. In other words, the book will serve as both a guide for and a means of consuming cultural artifacts. Books featuring historic landmarks, with their idyllic photographs and celebratory texts, can be seen as one mode of creating and appropriating these relics. If the government decides to publish the Blue Book for a popular audience, it will no doubt become a vehicle for acts of consumption and gift exchange that affirm landmarks' value as heritage—their ability to represent the collective. Like the pilgrimages of politicians and tourists, the consumption of these images can be read, in other words, as reproducing their symbolic value.

In addition to presenting a canon of national heritage in the East, the Blue Book contains passages that participate in the orientalization of East Germany. After noting the "difficult situation" faced by landmarks in the East and the need to "make them clearly visible, both nationally and internationally" (2001, 7), Raabe explains that his assignment required him to undertake a total of twelve trips to Eastern states. Driving his own car and accompanied by his wife, Raabe explored the Eastern cultural landscapes on behalf of the German state. Taken together, his West German background and his story of exploration indirectly reiterate the inequality of East and West. In addition to offering validation for East German complaints about the overwhelming predominance of West Germans in key political and bureaucratic positions, we find the image of an adventurous Westerner embarking for the East in order to discover its treasures, select the most worthy examples, and represent them to the rest of the populace, on behalf of the locals.

Raabe's explanation for the choice of the term "lighthouses" reinforces this impression. Like the monuments and institutions he describes, lighthouses are imposing, highly visible structures, and their light offers orientation in the dark (Raabe 2001, 24). The metaphor of light also carries the connotation of enlightenment, he explains. One wonders, however, about the relative need of enlightenment he finds in East and West: before unification, he explains, the East Germans seemed "stuck in the pre-modern era" and appeared to have forgotten all history prior to the Russian Revolution after years of indoctrination (Raabe 2001, 10–13). The East is apparently still emerging from socialist-imposed ignorance. This lack of historical awareness apparently explains the degree to which cultural treasures in the East remain "behind" those located in the West, as Raabe asserts, in both their physical condition and the attention they command (2001, 26). The unfortunate residents and landmarks of East Germany, it seems, have a long way to go to catch up to their Western counterparts.

Now that these landmarks are no longer subject to the neglect and political exploitation they suffered in the GDR, Raabe asserts hopefully, they can be properly maintained and promoted as a means for East and West Germans to once again internalize the shared sense of history that was "torn apart" by division (2001, 9–12). This goal, he points out, finds explicit support in the Unification Treaty of 1990. In addition to positing an enduring sense of cultural unity, article 35 emphasizes that German identity cannot focus on economic might alone, but must also emerge from its status as a *Kulturstaat* (cultural state). This formulation is echoed in the statement cited above in which Cultural Lighthouses are defined as reflecting the achievements of the *Gesamtstaat* (entire German state). Yet again we find a concerted effort to avoid reference to the nation. Raabe departs from the norm by explicitly noting his avoidance of the term *Kulturnation*, but fails to offer a reason. The problem lies, I contend, in its association with a prepolitical notion of belonging—Habermas's "traditional" form of national identity.

Although an understandable choice from this perspective, employing the terms *Gesamtstaat* and *Kulturstaat* appears as a rather strained and ultimately transparent effort to retain the sense of *Kulturnation* without using the word. The term *Gesamtstaat* suggests unity and totality. Yet the entity divided from 1949 to 1990 was not the German state, but the nation. *Kulturstaat* seems even less appropriate because the cultural property invoked here bears no inherent relationship to the state as a political entity, although it does fall under its legal protection and enjoys its financial support. Moreover, the current German state has, strictly speaking, existed for only fourteen years (or fifty-five years if one wishes to regard the FRG as having merely expanded in 1990).

The term *Kulturstaat* makes sense only as an implicit attempt to draw political legitimacy from cultural identity. It seeks to combine the ethno-cultural and political visions of nationhood that sit rather awkwardly side by side in contemporary Germany. The idea of national culture remains fixed at the center of discourse surrounding unity and identity, yet many Germans—leaders most especially—wish to assure themselves and the rest of the world that today's Germany is really about democracy, rights, and liberties.

Conclusion

Unification permitted the recovery of precious artifacts formerly missing from the national pantheon of German cultural heritage. Recovering cultural icons in East Germany works to recover a brand of Germanness that appears normal. As Kohl and other officials have described them, these monumental symbols populate a common national landscape where Germans can recognize themselves, just as other collectives find themselves in their monuments and landscapes. Superficially, at least, this seems entirely consonant with the widely accepted discourse of rights to cultural identity and programs to protect endangered heritage. Indeed, the project of rescuing landmarks in East Germany resonates particularly well with international heritage discourse (and appears especially compelling) insofar as these landmarks appear as unfortunate victims of willful destruction and neglect. Like other threatened cultural and natural treasures that stand on the verge of disappearing forever, these national icons seem fragile, vulnerable, and innocent. Protecting German national culture becomes thereby a moral imperative on par with ensuring the survival of marginalized languages, cultural traditions, and natural environments.

In the case of contemporary Germany, however, the image of suffering, endangered landmarks reinforces a useful but questionable distinction between national heritage on the one hand and the regimes implicated in its injury. My point is not that Germany's tainted pasts and cultural heritage form a single, onerous tradition, but rather that drawing a hard boundary between them is untenable. It makes the cultural nation available as a seemingly innocent foundation for national belonging without confronting the visions of essence and totality it reflects. It validates a conception of German culture as the inalienable possession of Germans traditionally defined. The Germany projected onto and read from historic landmarks possesses a discrete cultural and linguistic body—an image of the nation as a totality founded on cultural inheritance rather than civic practice.

My central concern is therefore the ways in which the current project of restoration indulges in fantasies of recovered authenticity and national recuperation at a time when more energy and resources could be devoted to actively engaging contemporary Germany's political and cultural complexities. The problem lies in the longings that restoration fails to question or expresses as natural—longings to undo the losses of this century by resurrecting its cultural victims, to identify the nation with those victims in such a way that their suffering appears as inflicted by outside forces, and the longing to retrieve icons of cultural and historical continuity that appear entirely unconnected to the burdensome "pasts" of this century. In the nation's "monumental time" (Herzfeld 1991) embodied by historic landmarks, the tragedies of national division and fascism fade into the background as temporary interludes in a larger story of continuity. Like the nation, they were in place before the GDR, before World War II and Hitler. Some have survived these catastrophes intact but stand in need of extra care; others once appeared lost forever but have returned through miracles of resurrection.

The attempt to simultaneously claim ethno-cultural and civic definitions of national being is hardly peculiar to Germany, but concerns surrounding essentialist nationalism and xenophobia make the contemporary German version of this alchemy particularly worthy of attention. The problems of national identity raised in West Germany in the 1980s did not, in fact, disappear with unification, but leaders have found less provocative ways of promoting redemptive national culture and history. The construction of a memorial to the murdered Jews of Europe in the center of Berlin seems to signal an unequivocal commitment to remembering the Nazi genocide, and new immigration policy combined with changes in German citizenship law suggest a new political tone regarding ethnic diversity. Yet the return to the cultural nation seems less than fully compatible with these messages, particularly to the degree that it directly or indirectly furthers the "cultural fundamentalism" (Stolcke 1995, 4) that often goes hand in hand with anti-immigrant sentiments in Europe.

Not only does the idea of German national heritage set aside the recent past in favor of sweeping cultural continuity, it also conveniently allows the West to incorporate the East as a cultural landscape into the Federal Republic while still treating the GDR as fundamentally other. It offers a way, in other words, of splitting off the national history and culture found in East Germany from tainted pasts. Since these pasts also include the GDR, the embrace of Eastern heritage ironically erases its four decades of existence except insofar as it appears as a negligent custodian of national treasures. It appears primarily in terms of what must be undone or corrected. There are certainly no designated Cultural Lighthouses from the socialist era. Focusing on heritage in the East allows the West to remain immune, as it were, from the ambivalent aspects of this primordial Germanness by keeping its most authentic exemplars at a distance. Making East Germany the locus of authentic, unaltered Germanness means that its artifacts and people represent an object of desire as specimens of heritage, but they also appear less modern, stuck in the past, and closer to the fascist legacy. This further naturalizes West German hegemony by both reinforcing its preeminence and implying that the task of *Vergangenheitsbewältigung* (mastering the past) is primarily an East German affair.

All of this does not mean that restoring landmarks and celebrating heritage are necessarily pernicious activities. Yet the reproduction of cultural property deserves close scrutiny, I contend, because it is implicated in the production of difference and identity, in the assertion of boundaries marking exclusion and inclusion, and in the maintenance of unequal power relations through boundaries of inclusion and exclusion.

References

Bartetzko, Dieter. 2002. "Der erste Blick: Dresdens Frauenkirche lueftet den Schleier." *Frankfurter Allgemeine Zeitung,* May 16, 43.

Barthel, Diane. 1995. *Historic Preservation: Collective Memory and Historical Identity.* New Brunswick, N.J.: Rutgers University Press.

Bergen, Werner von. 1997. "Zusammen bauen was zusammengehört." In *Bürger rettet Eure Städte: 5 Jahre Hilfe für den Denkmalschutz,* 6–7. Mainz: Zweites Deutsches Fernsehen.

Bickelhaupt, Thomas. 1994. "Das Ende der DDR war der Neuanfang für die Denkmalpflege." *Neue Zeit,* May 17.

Borneman, John. 1992. *Belonging in the Two Berlins: Kin, State, Nation.* Cambridge: Cambridge University Press.

———. 1998. *Subversions of International Order: Studies in the Political Anthropology of Culture.* Albany: State University of New York Press.

Bredow, Wilfried von. 1983. "Geschichte als Element der deutschen Identität?" In *Die Identität der Deutschen,* edited by Werner Weidenfeld, 102–18. Munich: Carl Hanser Verlag.

Bundesregierung der Bundesrepublik Deutschland. 2001. "Pflege des kulturellen Erbes." Press release, March 5. www. bundesregierung.de/frameset/index.jsp. Accessed May 22, 2002.

Bürgerinitiative für den Aufbau der Frauenkirche. 1990. "Ruf aus Dresden." www.frauenkirche-dresden.org/my_html/ histor1.htm. Accessed June 6, 2002.

Burkhardt, Armin. 1996. "Palast versus Schloß oder: Wem gehören die Symbole?" In *Von "Buschzulage" und "Ossinachweis" Ost-West-Deutsch in der Diskussion,* edited by Ruth Reiher and Rüdiger Läzer, 137–68. Berlin: Aufbau Taschenbuch Verlag.

Clifford, James. 1985. On Objects and Selves: An Afterword. In *Objects and Others: Essays on Museums and Material Culture.* Vol. 3, History of Anthropology, edited by George W. Stocking Jr., 236–46. Madison: University of Wisconsin Press.

Das Parlament. 1999. Interview with Dr. Michael Naumann. *Das Parlament,* March 4. www.bundesregierung.de/frameset/index.jsp. Accessed May 22, 2002.

Endres, Alexandra. 2000. "Zehn Jahre deutsche Einheit: Wo der Aufschwung Ost ausblieb." *Süddeutsche Zeitung,* September 27, 27.

Evans, Richard J. 1989. *In Hitler's Shadow: West German Historians and the Attempt to Escape from the Nazi Past.* New York: Pantheon.

Fabian, Johannes. 1983. *Time and the Other: How Anthropology Makes Its Object.* New York: Columbia University Press.

Gaus, Günter. 1983. *Wo Deutschland Liegt: Eine Ortsbestimmung.* Hamburg: Hoffmann & Campe.

Glaeser, Andreas. 2001. "Conclusion: Why German Remains Divided." In *A New Germany in a New Europe,* edited by Todd Herzog and Sander L. Gilman, 173–97. New York: Routledge.

Greiffenhagen, Martin, and Sylvia Greiffenhagen. 1994. "Die ehemalige DDR als das 'deutschere' Deutschland?" In *Die neue Bundesländer,* edited by Martin Greiffenhagen, Heinrich Tiemann, and Hans-Georg Wehling, 9–22. Stuttgart: Verlag W. Kohlhammer.

Habermas, Jürgen. 1989a. "Apologetic Tendencies." In *The New Conservatism: Cultural Criticism and the Historians' Debate,* edited and translated by Shierry Weber Nicholsen, 212–28. Cambridge: MIT Press.

———. 1989b. "On the Public Use of History." In *The New Conservatism: Cultural Criticism and the Historians' Debate,* edited and translated by Shierry Weber Nicholsen, 229–40. Cambridge: MIT Press.

Hampel-Zöllner, Manfred. 1990. "Laßt Euch nicht kaputt-sanieren!" *Thüringische Landeszeitung,* October 26.

Handler, Richard. 1988. *Nationalism and the Politics of Culture in Quebec.* Madison: University of Wisconsin Press.

Herzfeld, Michael. 1991. *A Place in History: Social and Monumental Time in a Cretan Town.* Princeton: Princeton University Press.

Heuser, Uwe-Jean. 2002. "Einig Katerland: Der Osten ist schon Chefsache, jetzt kommt der Westen dran." *Die Zeit* 41. www.zeit.de/2002/41/Politik/200241_einig_katerland.html. Accessed October 11, 2002.

Kohl, Helmut. 1986. "Regierungserklärung von Bundeskanzler Kohl vor dem Deutschen Bundestag am 14. März 1986 zur Lage der Nation im geteilten Deutschland (Auszug zu kulturellen Fragen)." *Europa-Archiv* 41(10): D289–92.

———. 1990. "Regierungserklärung des Bundeskanzlers der Bundesrepublik Deutschland, Helmut Kohl, über die Grundsätze der Politik der ersten gesamtdeutschen Bundesregierung, abgegeben vor dem Deutschen Bundestag am 4. Oktober 1990 in Berlin." *Europa-Archiv* (Dokumente) 45(21): D552–64.

Korff, Gottfried. 1994. "Von der Leidenschaft des Bewahrens." *Die Denkmalpflege* 52(1): 32–40.

Kowa, Günter. 1996. "Das taktische Spiel der Denkmalpfleger. Durchbrochene Stadtmauern, verkitschte Fassaden: In Ostdeutschland machen sich architektonische Mißgeburten breit." *Frankfurter Allgemeine Zeitung,* May 8.

Maier, Charles. 1988. *The Unmasterable Past: History, Holocaust, and German National Identity.* Cambridge: Harvard University Press.

Marx, Karl. 1977. *Selected Writings.* Edited by David McLellan. Oxford: Oxford University Press.

Meinecke, Friedrich. 1919. *Weltbürgertum und Nationalstaat.* 5th ed. Munich: Oldenburg.

Mitscherlich, Alexander. 1965. *Die Unwirtlichkeit unserer Städte: Anstiftung zum Unfrieden.* Frankfurt am Main: Suhrkamp Verlag.

Naumann, Michael. 2000. "Die Halbzeitbilanz von Staatsminister Naumann im Originaltext." October 27. www.bundesregierung.de/frameset/index.jsp. Accessed May 22, 2002.

Nida-Rümelin, Julian. 2001. Geleitwort to "Blaubuch: Kulturelle Leuchttürme in Brandenburg, Mecklenburg Vorpommern, Sachsen, Sachsen-Anhalt und Thüringen," 5–6. Draft copy. www. bundesregierung.de/frameset/index.jsp. Accessed May 29, 2002.

———. 2002. "Die kulturelle Dimension des Nationalstaates." March 8. www .bundesregierung.de/frameset/index.jsp. Accessed May 22, 2002.

Olick, Jeffrey K. 1998. "What Does It Mean to Normalize the Past? Official Memory in German Politics since 1989." *Social Science History* 22(4): 547–74.

Paul, Jürgen. 1993. *Dresden ruft/Dresden Calls.* Translated by Valérie Louverjat. Dresden: Gesellschaft zur Förderung des Wiederaufbaus der Frauenkirche Dresden e.V. Pamphlet in German and English.

Preuss, Sebastian. 1990. "Die Rettung Thüringens: Denkmalpfleger aus Ost und West diskutierten in Fulda." *Frankfurter Allgemeine Zeitung,* June 26.

Raabe, Paul. 2001. "Blaubuch: Kulturelle Leuchttürme in Brandenburg, Mecklenburg Vorpommern, Sachsen, Sachsen-Anhalt und Thüringen." Draft copy. www .bundesregierung.de/frameset/index.jsp. Accessed May 29, 2002.

Schröder, Gerhard. 2000. "Rede des Bundeskanzler Gerhard Schröder anlässlich des Welttourismusgipfels, 27.9 in Hannover." www.bundesregierung.de/frameset/index.jsp. Accessed June 6, 2002.

Sheehan, James. 1992. "National History and National Identity in the New Germany." *German Studies Review,* Winter, 163–74. German identity theme issue.

Simon, Axel. 2002. "Architektonische Maskerade in Dresden." *Der Tages-Anzeiger,* April 10, 63.

Soane, J. 1994. "The Renaissance of Cultural Vernacularism in Germany." In *Building a New Heritage: Tourism, Culture and Identity in the New Europe,* edited by G. J. Ashworth and P. J. Larkham, 159–77. London: Routledge.

Stade, Heinz. 1994. "Damit den Bewohnern ihre Stadt nicht abhanden kommt." *Thüringer Allgemeine Zeitung,* May 19.

Stolcke, Verena. 1995. "Talking Culture: New Boundaries, New Rhetorics of Exclusion in Europe." *Current Anthropology* 36(1): 1–24.

Stiftung Frauenkirche. n.d. *Ihr Engagement kann vielleicht keine Berge versetzen, aber Steine.* Dresden: Stiftung Frauenkirche. Pamphlet.

Telemundi. 1994. *Helfen Sie mit, eine der schmerzhaftesten Wunden im Herzen Europas zu schließen/Help us to Heal one of the Most Painful Wounds in the Heart of Europe.* Dresden: Telemundi. Pamphlet in German and English.

Veen, Hans-Joachim. 2000. "Vereint, aber noch nicht wirklich eins? Ein Plädoyer wider den völkischen Rückfall." *Deutschland Archiv* 33(2): 269–75.

Wagner, Wolf. 1996. *Kulturschock Deutschland.* Hamburg: Rotbuch Verlag.

Wolle, Stephan. 1998. *Die heile Welt der Diktatur: Alltag und Herrschaft in der DDR 1971–1989.* Berlin: Christoph Links Verlag.

Zizek, Slavoj. 1990. "Eastern Europe's Republic's of Gilead." *New Left Review* 183: 50–62.

Zweites Deutsches Fernsehen. 1997. *Bürger rettet Eure Städte: 5 Jahre Hilfe für den Denkmalschutz.* Mainz: Zweites Deutsches Fernsehen.

Deep Dirt: Messing Up the Past at Colonial Williamsburg

10

ERIC GABLE AND RICHARD HANDLER

*Kitsch is the absolute denial of shit, in both the literal and the figurative
senses of the word; kitsch excludes everything from its purview which is
essentially unacceptable in human existence.*

MILAN KUNDERA (1984, 248)

OLONIAL WILLIAMSBURG IS NOT A RUIN.[1] It is the reconstructed capital of
Virginia at the dawn of the American Revolution, and it has been a popular attraction for over half a century. A million paying customers come
each year to watch the fife and drum corps and militia parade down the Duke of
Gloucester Street or to observe the many craftspeople—blacksmiths, gunsmiths,
silversmiths, weavers, coopers, and cooks—hard at work. These visitors wait pa-
tiently in line to enter the well-appointed homes of the colonial burghers, where
they will admire the "furnishings" of a satisfying domesticity—the wallpaper, the
draperies, the furniture, the prints, the dried flowers, the china on which are set
simulacra of meats, pastries, and fruits. These visitors come also, so nearly every
one of them will tell you, to learn about "the past," "their past"—the collective
truth about the way life "really was" back at the Founding.

To most of Colonial Williamsburg's million visitors a year, a stroll down its
boulevards is at once pleasant and edifying. Indeed, it is so pleasant that some can
imagine themselves living there year-round, in a community that is charming and uncomplicated. And it is doubly edifying, for it is both inspirational and educational.
To visit Colonial Williamsburg is to get in touch with a patriotic past—hence the
museum's inspirational punch. Because that past has been reconstructed to be as "authentic" as possible, a visit to the museum is thought to be educational as well. And
even though visitors are more sophisticated about historical interpretation than

highbrow critics presume them to be, they nonetheless tend to accept the museum's claims to mimetic accuracy. For both staff and visitors, to tour Colonial Williamsburg is to experience "the real thing."

Yet, for other people, Colonial Williamsburg is the last place they'd choose to visit, let alone live. "The place leaves nothing to the imagination," a colleague of ours who prefers ruins keeps pointing out. In this critical perspective, a ruin invites visitors to populate and rebuild the past in their own minds, whereas a restoration like Colonial Williamsburg renders them passive spectators with no role other than the consumption of kitsch. For other critics, Colonial Williamsburg is simply "too clean" to be a faithful re-creation of the past. Cleanliness, here, has its literal meaning: Colonial Williamsburg's grounds and buildings are too well kept to be accurate to the eighteenth century. But critics also complain that Colonial Williamsburg is too clean in another sense: it presents a bowdlerized past, long on inspiration and high on the social ladder. Historical "dirt"—the chaotic and dismal facts about poverty, squalor, and class oppression—has been swept out of sight, to the detriment of realism and hence of the museum's educational mission.

Colonial Williamsburg's planners are sensitive to the too-clean critique. In poking fun at themselves, they sometimes call Colonial Williamsburg a "Republican Disneyland." Disneyland serves as a powerful symbol at this museum (and at many others), for it is a major competitor that is, in many ways, on the cutting edge of the "attraction industry." Disneyland both fascinates and repels Colonial Williamsburg staffers, who envy Disney's people-handling prowess, as well as its "Imagineering" acumen, but fear that their museum might easily become vulgar and ovecommercialized in the Disney manner. Indeed, as a symbol, Disneyland represents both kitsch and inauthenticity—the very qualities which Colonial Williamsburg, as a serious educational institution, wishes to avoid.

To avoid kitsch and inauthenticity, Colonial Williamsburg planners have for the past two decades sought to introduce dirt, ruin, and decay into the restoration. The incorporation of entropic natural processes, as well as greater historical attention to social conflicts, have come to be seen by administrators in many history museums as the logical next step to be taken in their quest for ever greater degrees of authenticity (e.g., Schlereth 1978, 1984). In other words, including processes of ruination as part of a historic "restoration" bolsters rather than detracts from the mimetic ideal of reproducing the past as it really was. However, Williamsburg's production of dirt and ruination in the pursuit of truth creates a series of tensions and paradoxes, and it is these that we explore in this chapter.

Putting the Pieces Together: The Mimetic Ideal

The notion that doing history is like piecing together a jigsaw puzzle is commonly articulated at Colonial Williamsburg. For instance, a permanent archaeological exhibit, with glass cases of fragmented artifacts juxtaposed to a reconstructed tableau, bears the following explanatory label:

> The purpose of archaeology in Williamsburg is to assist in reconstructing the environment in which both the great and small events of Virginia history took place. Excavated artifacts are pieces in the jigsaw puzzle of the past. Here eighty-eight objects removed from the earth of Williamsburg provide precedents for virtually everything seen in this recreated colonial bedroom.

The jigsaw puzzle image implies that the past is either a two-dimensional picture which has been shredded or a three-dimensional object which has been shattered. A primary goal of historians and archaeologists—and of Colonial Williamsburg itself—is to put back together the pieces in order to achieve a mimetically complete version of the past. The completed puzzle may be either a restored "original" or a newly fabricated "reconstruction," but in either case, the goal is to achieve "the real thing," a completely "accurate" or "authentic" facsimile of "the past."[2]

The first twenty years of restoration work at Colonial Williamsburg (until about 1950) were devoted to reconstructing the physical setting. This process was overseen by architectural historians whose main concern was "visual authenticity," as one commentator puts it (Brinkley 1990, 9). At a time when most historians had no interest in so-called material culture, these architects were documenting buildings and treating buildings as documents. They traveled throughout the Virginia Tidewater region to locate surviving period buildings and compose sketchbooks of architectural and decorative details (Kopper 1986, 176–77). Using such visual documentation, the restorers set about re-creating a city that would *appear* as it had in the eighteenth century. As the 1951 version of the Colonial Williamsburg guidebook put it, "during restoration work, modern conveniences and services were hidden rather than discarded." However, the visual authenticity of the project was guaranteed, according to the same text, by the fact that "architects have been guided by archaeological remnants, maps, drawings, and daguerreotypes; data from insurance records, diaries, and wills; and any other sources of evidence which research workers could discover" (CW 1951, 18–19).

Once the first major phase of reconstruction was accomplished and "visual authenticity" established, museum officials turned their attention to bringing their newly restored city to life. Such a project was meant to engage senses other than the visual: in particular, to re-create the sounds and smells of the eighteenth century. And beyond this authenticity of the senses, the museum became increasingly concerned to re-create an experience of the past, thereby allowing visitors to "feel" what life "was like" in the colonial capital of Virginia. This enlarged project began to take shape in the face of a new mass tourism that developed after World War II: as more and more visitors flocked to Colonial Williamsburg, the museum became increasingly concerned with "interpreting" their city to the public. "The real thing" that Colonial Williamsburg was to present to the public came more and more to be seen as the total life of the past.

An additional influence prompting museum officials to strive for more "life-like" presentations has been the persistently voiced criticism that Colonial Williamsburg is an idealized version of the past, too clean to be true. As noted at the outset, the too-clean critique has two dimensions. Literally, the restored city is said to afford a "prettified and over-sanitary view of eighteenth century Williamsburg" (Cotter 1970, 427). The real eighteenth century, Hogarthian in sensibility and appearance, means "death and poor health, rotten teeth, blindness and depravity . . . broken crockery, chicken bones, oyster shells . . . trash" (Olmert 1985, 30, 33); it means "smells, flies, pigs, dirt and slave quarters" (Whitehill 1966, 43; cf. Wallace 1986, 154; Huxtable 1992). Moreover, for many critics, the lack of literal dirt has come to stand for an antiseptic approach to the past. For them, the museum's whitewashed exterior is a symbol of a troubling absence in the story Colonial Williamsburg tells: the erasure of any but the "silk pants patriots" (to use an insider's term); that is, the almost exclusive focus on white Founding Fathers (Van West and Hoffschwelle 1984; Wallace 1986, 157). As the museum's head research historian put it, discussing his expectations for a more representative history, "I want [the public] to go away disturbed. I see this museum as a device to make Americans look at aspects of both the past and the present that they may not want to see" (quoted in Bordewich 1988, 31).

To bring Colonial Williamsburg alive, to make full use of the sumptuous setting that Rockefeller money created, and to respond to its critics, the museum's top management has modified its aesthetic and historical sensibilities. The turn to social history, that is, the inclusion of slaves, women, children, and everyday realities, began in the mid-1970s. But long before that, museum officials had experimented with ways to incorporate lifelike processes and touches into their presentation. In the 1960s, people spoke of introducing more "life-on-the-scene" into the museum: sheep, oxcarts, scarecrows, bee hives, and crafts demonstrations were all intended to make the Historic Area "come alive." As a typical newspaper item of the time explained, "Additional woodpiles . . . are appearing in the Historical Area as spring approaches. It's not [that] colder weather is anticipated. . . . [It's] just another attempt to give the area a more 'lived-in' appearance."[3]

Attention to such details comes from visitors as well as staff members. For example, a 1981 letter to the president of Colonial Williamsburg from a Florida man advised the museum to "create olifactory [sic] detail. In the palace, for instance, sprinkle liquid smoke . . . in the smoke house so that when people lean in to see the hams, etc., they can actually smell them. The same could be done in the cellar. Empty beer on the floor of the beer cask room and wine into the packing of the wine storage room. (The stables smell is taking care of things naturally!)"

To which a museum vice president responded understandingly, "We have recently introduced actual wood smoking in the smokehouses with the hope that the smell would linger, and we have had some improvement in that presentation. We achieve an aroma in the wine cellar by placing a few apples in a concealed bucket. They add a fermented cider smell that has been quite effective."[4]

Such lifelike "touches" as those mentioned here are myriad, and new details are always forthcoming. In general, to bring their city to life, Colonial Williamsburg planners have relied on animals and a growing force of costumed employees who engage, to varying degrees, in eighteenth-century activities. And with particular reference to dirt and disorder, the burden of the ongoing attempt to make the Historical Area more realistic has been carried by three vehicles: unmown grass, peeling paint, and animal shit.[5] In our fieldwork, we heard references to all three frequently, and all were, in a manner of speaking, featured when Colonial Williamsburg was featured on NBC television's *Good Morning America* on December 11, 1991. Interviewing the foundation's president, Charles Longsworth, Charlie Gibson commented on the changes he noticed:

CG: I visited here many many times, but years ago. And I know it's an ever-changing place. I gather you are beginning to show it, not as the idealized colonial town that some people may remember if they visited here long ago, but showing it a little bit warts and all.

CL: Well, we used to look like what many American small towns try to imitate, the idealized colonial city. Now we try to look more authentic. We let the paint go, we let the grass grow. But more importantly, we're interpreting the lives of all the people who were here. . . .

Later Gibson introduced another segment of the program with the following euphemistic reference to shit:

CG: Good morning everybody, I'm Charles Gibson . . . we are this morning on the Duke of Gloucester Street that comes up the middle of Colonial Williamsburg. They say it's a mile long, a hundred feet wide, and two feet deep in the rainy season back in colonial times—there was that much mud.[6]

Deep Dirt: The Ruin in the Restoration

The notion that the gritty processes of real life, that dirt and ruination, must be added to an overly idealized vision of the world replicates, in a sense, the rise of the ruin as a category in the Western sensibility. The eighteenth-century passion for ruins can be seen as a moment in the history of both romanticism and realism. In the eighteenth century, the ruin—and, more generally, the picturesque—became a valid aesthetic category alongside the beautiful and the sublime. People interested in ruins sought that category alongside the beautiful and the sublime. People interested in ruins sought reality as it was rather than idealized visions of what reality might be. Yet the picturesque could become a fantasy in its own right, when the quaint, the exotic, the irregular were aestheticized for their own sake, thereby leading away from, rather than to, what might be seen as a renewed connection with "real life." Indeed, the aestheticization of decay led some people to criticize the picturesque as socially irresponsible. If the English gentry preserved the picturesque on their estates, they would fail to improve their tenants' lives, thereby contradicting the values of moral uplift and material progress that were at least as influential as the aesthetic valuation of ruins. Let us note, if only in passing, that one solution in the nineteenth century (as well as today, as we just saw) was to improve peasant dwellings while disguising the results under a carefully constructed picturesque exterior (Kemp 1990, 103–6).

Seeking ruins, then, can be part of a realist project, one that is often tragic in its import; but aestheticized decay can also afford comic relief, as it were. Dirt at Colonial Williamsburg holds both possibilities, but, we would argue, in this museum its tragic implications often give way to the comic. Despite President Longsworth's assertion that in the portrayal of Williamsburg's "warts," creating a socially inclusive history is more important than leaving the grass unmown, we have found that reference to the latter is often substituted for discussion of the former in the museum's presentation of itself to the public.

For example, animal droppings are purposefully left on the streets, and staff members are taught to view them as icons of authenticity, meant to bolster Colonial Williamsburg's mimetic credibility. During an orientation session for new employees, a group of recruits were sent out into the Historic Area and asked "to tell us the one thing you learned on the town tour today." One of the first to respond remarked sarcastically that "I never knew the visitors thought the bird sounds were electronic." Another quickly chimed in, "I learned why they leave the horse manure on the street—to have authentic smells." The lesson of this training session was that visitors have to be protected form a tendency to view the site as artificial, as a historical Disneyland, and coached to recognize the residues of authenticity that they might, to their detriment, overlook.

Thus tours at Colonial Williamsburg often begin by calling attention to animal droppings. On walking tours, interpreters[7] sometimes walk backward while talking to their charges, and as they begin this maneuver they often ask visitors to warn them if they are in danger of stepping in shit. Indeed, on one tour that we took, references to shit were a prominent leitmotif structuring the entire performance. At the outset, a young boy was chosen to lead the tour, a task carrying a special onus, as the interpreter explained: "You have a very important job. Being the lowest [i.e., youngest] member of this group . . . we're gonna keep your nose very close to the pavement, so in case we walk past horse stuff, you tell us to move to the left or the right. You keep us out of that stuff."

As the tour progressed, the boy was chided for not shouting his warnings loud enough and commended when he performed his duties vigorously. As the tour was led down the steps leading to the print shop, which lies in a ravine below street level, the interpreter announced that "there's no horse poop down here. Hopefully no horse poop." In the shop itself, he dwelt humorously in the eighteenth-century use of uric acid in printing: "that's what we use to clean the type with. It takes the ink off. So watch what you get on yourself." And at the close of the tour, the interpreter disbanded his group with yet another humorous remark concerning the necessity to watch out for horse droppings.

As we already heard, Charlie Gibson described Duke of Gloucester Street as being "two feet deep . . . back in colonial times." Back in colonial times, but not today: Colonial Williamsburg interpreters frequently acknowledge to visitors that the city's paved streets are not authentic. Moreover, the existence of pavement and other modern conveniences is often attributed to visitor needs and expectations. Such admission of guilt serve, we think, to bolster the museum's claims to overall authenticity, for the confession of minor inaccuracies is also a statement about the purity of the institution's aims, which, nonetheless, must be compromised to satisfy the mass public.

The theme of deep mud is not confined to outdoor tours, as the following excerpt from a tour of the Raleigh Tavern shows: "Slaves have recently cleaned the floor, and they have to do it at least once a day. Because in the eighteenth century, the streets and sidewalks are about a foot deep, okay?—of assorted things besides mud. Which would be tracked in. I'll let you use your imagination [audience laughter]. You've walked up and down the street enough to know that."

In this passage, as in the references to animal droppings presented earlier, mention of dirt serves to bolster authenticity. But it serves other rhetorical functions as well. First, it intersects with a narrative of progress that is commonly articulated at Colonial Williamsburg. Despite the museum's stated aim to understand the past on its own terms, the eighteenth century is often presented to visitors as a more primitive version of our own world, a version beyond which we are glad to have progressed. The fantasy of the streets "two feet deep" will perhaps startle people acquainted with "premodern" settings, where most people do not walk around in shit, despite the lack of American-style plumbing. Indeed, eighteenth-century sources, cited in training documents by museum historians, do not confirm the image of streets "two feet deep." A 1722 traveler described what is today the Duke of Gloucester Street as "a pleasant, long dry walk." A 1770 traveler spoke of "the street deep with . . . white sand" (quoted Brinkley 1991, 3; Brinkley 1990, 9). In view of such sources, Colonial Williamsburg's muddy realism would seem to parody the past rather than present it as it seemed "from the native's point of view."

In addition to the presentism of progress, attention to shit often serves to create the trappings of a "friendly" relationship between interpreters and their audiences. This sort of rapport is considered crucial at Colonial Williamsburg and, more generally, in most "public contact" work in American institutions dealing with a mass clientele. For example, when interpreters ask their audience to warn them of the presence of shit, they are allowing their charges to join in the work of guiding the tour, thereby replacing a potentially authoritarian relationship (between guide and guest) with one that is, apparently, cooperative and egalitarian. More generally, constantly poking fun at the "unsanitary" conditions of the past is used by interpreters not only to get a laugh from their audiences; at the same time, it brings audience and interpreter together as members of an enlightened community who can look down at the foibles of more primitive others. In sum, shit may be "designed" to testify to authenticity, but in the daily life of the museum, it is used most often as a prop in a late-twentieth-century comedy of manners whose subject is what Jules Henry might have called "para-intimacy." Bathroom humor is, to borrow from Henry, one of those "tried and true skills that ring bells 100 percent of the time in the endless American game of interpersonal pinball" (1963, 148).

From Literal to Metaphorical Dirt

We have suggested above a parallel between the way dirt gets incorporated into the aesthetic of Colonial Williamsburg and the way ruin and decay become the picturesque in the Western aesthetic tradition. Just as the picturesque began as an apt vehicle for critique but became more likely comedy than tragedy, so "dirt" at Colonial Williamsburg loses its critical function as it reinforces preconceived notions about a primitive past. This is apparent in the examples of literal dirt presented earlier, but it is even more poignantly so in the case of the metaphorical dirt of social history.

We saw an example of this at the Courthouse during the summer of 1991. The Courthouse is Colonial Williamsburg's latest attempt at reconstruction with an eye toward social history. The Courthouse, it is said, is crucial for the story Colonial Williamsburg tells because it acted as "a sort of community that brought together all levels of Tidewater society. Democracy started here" (Olmert 1991, 9). It is shoddily furnished to reflect a society not eager to dip too deeply into the public purse. For example, the jury's chairs were meticulously mismatched in construction and then used for several months before being placed in the Courthouse in order to give them a patina of scruffiness. With regard to the life portrayed inside the building, administrative cases are argued by "character interpreters." The cases are meant, so one of the planners observed, to reflect not *LA Law* but the Department of Motor Vehicles—and it is hoped that "in these tedious, repetitive administrative hearings . . . the real bread and cheese of the eighteenth century can be tasted" (Olmert 1991, 11).

Unfortunately, tedium does not sell easily at a tourist attraction. To bring democratic life to the site in the peak visitation season, supplementary character interpreters were hired to act as a kind of hoi poloi attracted to the goings-on at the Courthouse. These characters portray riffraff—a Hogarth print come to life. There is the fat, drunken fool teetering on his spindle shanks. There is the bawdy wench with the broad, loud voice who can't keep from hitching up her skirts to reveal a sloppy ankle. There is the sharp-faced Irish jack-of-all-trades who holds up the latest advance in the dentist's trade—an ingenious little pliers guaranteed not to smash the offending molar or leave the splintered roots stuck in your inflamed jaw. He asks for volunteers for a demonstration. There is a dingy mother and her wide-eyed child, the woman plucking a chicken while a rooster peeks out of a basket at her feet. Ask her about her birds and she'll tell you about the pleasures of cockfighting or the best way to dispatch a hen without getting blood all over the place. The characters at the Courthouse may or may not be accurate representatives of eighteenth-century individuals, but as an ensemble, they are an exaggeration: the essence of the picturesque. Let us note that such picturesque or comedic roles are played at Colonial Williamsburg by characters representing "the lower and middling sorts." Founding Fathers and colonial elites are not ordinarily so parodied. This, we might add, is an extension of a more pervasive logic, in which "dirt" stands for democracy, the people, and "cleanliness" for exclusivism, the upper classes.

Throughout the summer, these low-brow characters attracted a crowd who laughed out loud or groaned at their antics. But, in the end, these performances, meant to put life on Colonial Williamsburg's streets, may have put an unilluminating distance between the audience and the eighteenth century by primitivizing the past. Managers in the foundation recognize that much of their audience comes to Williamsburg with a firm faith in the narrative of progress. From this perspective, a dirty past is also a primitive past. It is unsanitary and barbaric, like the dentist's pliers, because "they didn't know what we know," as one visitor put it. Although a picturesque past may be temporarily more lively, and for that reason fun to observe, the upshot is that one learns mainly to appreciate the good things that we have today.

The audience, it seems, enjoys believing that the past was dirty or crude or primitive. Colonial Williamsburg is an attraction, and there is considerable pressure on its "frontline" staff—those who deal with the public on a daily basis—to cater to what are seen as its audience's expectations. So it is not just part-time employees who camp it up for an appreciative crowd, but long-term employees as well. For example, an interpreter at the Harness Shop (where, among other things, they tan leather) might tell visitors that the best leather for the finest gloves and shoes was made from dog skin, hence the expression "putting on the dog." This elicits the shocked chuckle or the appreciative groan from an audience accustomed to the "civilized" treatment of its pets.

Such jokes are an embarrassment to management. A constant problem, several managers were quick to tell us, is to keep frontline staff from making fun of the eighteenth century—making jokes which, like "putting on the dog," often cast a barbaric light on pretensions of the eighteenth-century elite. One of the managers characterized the work of monitoring such jokes as like "pulling weeds" because no matter how diligent they are, the stories keep cropping up. He elaborated a list of such jokes, which usually take the form of an etymology, and in most of the cases—"big-wig" is another example—involve a humorous presentation of upper-class fashions and foibles.

In general, managers claim that such jokes are popular among frontline employees because, in the world of public contact, to get a laugh makes workers feel appreciated by their audience. Making fun of the eighteenth century, like using horse manure as a prop for scatological humor, is the quick, if dirty, road to audience rapport. But managers also admitted that there are other more egregious reasons for the popularity of these jokes, for to poke fun at eighteenth-century elites can also be a way to poke fun at the pretensions of an upper-middle-class twentieth-century audience. Managers know that frontline employees can tire of the constant public friendliness that their job requires; to "let off steam," they sometimes covertly tweak their visitors' noses.

Our conversations with and observations of the craftspeople and interpreters at work confirm this. "Putting on the dog" is a typical example because it depends as much, if not more, on the twentieth-century middle-class overvaluation of pets as it does on the eighteenth-century undervaluation of them. We found that the jokes which poke fun at the eighteenth century inevitably were meant to cause some visitor discomfort, even, ultimately, by calling critical attention to the very narrative of progress that making fun of the eighteenth century often ended up reinforcing. Thus, for example, the craftspeople told us a perhaps apocryphal story about a blacksmith's frustration with an endless series of stupid visitors who couldn't believe that the blacksmiths at the Anderson Forge produced, "like a factory," thousands upon thousands of nails. When yet another visitor remarked, "I didn't know they had nails back then," the blacksmith replied, "yeah, and I guess the Romans screwed Jesus to the cross." As they story is recounted, the visitor complained to Colonial Williamsburg's management and the blacksmith was fired.

This vignette casts an ironic light on the management's obsession with pulling out interpretive weeds, for it raises the possibility that the management's urge to avoid historiographical anachronism stems as much out of an urge to avoid controversy as it does an urge to promote accuracy. We can only intimate a larger argument here, but a critical history might well employ analogies that are not only discomforting but, in some senses, inherently anachronistic. How, for example, can one teach the history of eighteenth-century slavery to a contemporary American audience without some discussion of twentieth-century racism? When Colonial Williamsburg avoids (because it caters to visitor comfort or because it adheres to a naive objectivism) poking fun at either the eighteenth or the twentieth century, it replaces critique with quiescence. Thus many managers (and frontline employees) told us, when they explained what history can teach, that people in the past had much the same desires, foibles, and strengths as we do today. In this perspective, "history," as Hayden White puts it, is a confirmation of the "plausible" (1987, passim). The past recreated is merely an affirmation of the inevitability or naturalness of the present and the universality of human nature. It is a comforting, not a critical, history.

Resistance to Regimented Ruin

Management's obsession with the weeds of interpretation reflects, also, the inherent ironies of the corporate production of dirt and decay, for this involves regimenting Colonial Williamsburg's workforce, especially its craftspeople. Over the years, craftspeople at Colonial Williamsburg have perfected their hand skills to such a degree that they can manufacture objects more finely crafted than the objects routinely produced for sale by their eighteenth-century counterparts. A good example of this is the "fantasy rifle" that craftsworkers told us about—a hand-produced gun so accurate as a weapon that it was no longer an "accurate" replica of its eighteenth-century prototype. With the advent of social history at Colonial Williamsburg, craftspeople have been cajoled into making purposely shoddy or less-than-masterful artifacts. They have also been encouraged to emphasize the factory-like quality of eighteenth-century craftwork. Lately, with the need for corporate downsizing brought on by the economic recession, managers are forcing craftspeople to spend less time working their trades and more time interpreting. This move toward cost-efficiency has been justified as a way of "deskilling" craftspeople to levels more accurately reflecting life in the eighteenth century.

Given this, we might conclude that the craftspeople's propensity for the cutting joke reflects their discomfort with and resistance to regimentation. Not only does the corporation insist that they don a uniformly friendly aspect in dealing with visitors, but attending to those visitors takes them away from the highly valued practice of their craft. Most craftspeople we talked to asserted that if you only wanted to make things and didn't like talking to people, you wouldn't last long at Colonial Williamsburg. But they also talked fondly of an earlier era in Colonial Williamsburg's history when they spent a lot more of their time out of the public eye producing reproductions for Colonial Williamsburg's exhibits and for its wealthy patrons.

Craftspeople we talked with were generally angered by deskilling. They portrayed it less as an honest move toward greater accuracy—a dirtier truth—and more as the typically cynical manipulation of workers by "executoids" out of touch with the desires of their public and the needs of their employees for dignity. As a result, the management's urge to produce a more accurate past met with increasingly vocal resistance from its craftspeople, who employed another Colonial Williamsburg agenda—the need for "preservation"—to defend themselves against some of the repercussions of producing a messier and therefore more accurate past. From their perspective, their work as craftsmen—particularly in "dying" trades—was crucial to the preservation of the bodies of knowledge that comprise those trades. Thus their disgruntlement with "deskilling" may also explain their propensity to poke fun at eighteenth-century elites and at twentieth-century visitors: though they may be forced to practice their trades on management's terms, they can at least covertly ridicule their class betters, of either century.

Conclusion

Most everyone who works at Colonial Williamsburg, from the professional historian to the middle-level manager to the frontline employee, agrees that the museum is too clean to be an authentic portrayal of the past. Likewise, the critics of Colonial Williamsburg find the place too clean, and even its more ardent supporters—those who love, for example, its neat gardens, its shady, quiet streets, its aura of tidy comfort—recognize that it is not the "real past" that they enjoy, but a kind of would-that-it-were world, into which they can temporarily escape a decaying present.

Dirt, therefore, is truth in both the popular and professional imagination. Dirt is truth, by and large, for two reasons. Dirt is a symbol for that part of history which is unpleasant—conflict, class divisions, poverty in the midst of plenty, and even the exploited classes themselves: slaves, itinerants, the "lower orders" in general. Dirt is also a symbol for the primitive, and a dirty past implies a cleaner present. That is, dirt is the material through which a narrative of progress becomes experientially real.

It sometimes seems that dirt as manifestation of progress is the popular attribution, while dirt as critique is the professional attribution at Colonial Williamsburg. Architectural historians want to build shacks on the neat-lawned landscape of Williamsburg's suburban streets, partly to call attention to America's acceptance as natural of zoning regulations that often serve no other purpose than to segregate and insulate. "Foodways" interpreters who delight in arranging tableaux in which the meat is served with "the heads still on," because our forebears "wanted to know what they were eating," or who enjoy plucking a chicken on the public square, are calling attention to an analogous insulation in modern life. Meanwhile, the visitor who chuckles at the oft-repeated phrase that the Duke of Gloucester Street was "a mile long, a hundred feet wide, and two feet deep" appreciates the fact that the world he or she inhabits is more convenient, cleaner, better while enjoying a mild nostalgia for a simpler past.

This, at least, is how managers and professional historians would like to portray things—especially to us, their intellectual audience. They constantly assert that the public, or alternatively, the frontline, resists the true story they try to tell—either because of misconceptions about the past, or poor taste; or because they are paying customers, or because they are humans with inevitable needs for safety and comfort.

But at another level, because professionals can blame the public for a too clean history, they can maintain, despite their own keen awareness of their museum's inaccuracies, a certain faith in the progress of historical knowledge. This faith, we have intimated, is reinforced because it is never seriously put to the test at Colonial Williamsburg. There, the dominant view of the historiographical endeavor is one of increasing accuracy and detail, with the first versions of the restoration being a kind of map or sketch for the present Williamsburg. Dirt "fills in the gaps" of previous images of Williamsburg, making the whole more accurate, just as would the addition of shadow or color make a fine drawing more real. Dirt, a quantity, replaces dirt, a choice between competing interpretations of the past. Not surprisingly, then, when the professionals monitor the message their site is conveying and find it less than satisfying, they tend to blame it on an insufficiency: the place is not dirty enough. And, of course, it can never be dirty enough because, alas, the public would not accept it.

In the end, Colonial Williamsburg tells the story of progress, even as it only partially ruins but keeps largely intact what has become an ideal image of our past from which Americans have and continue to model their houses, their interior decorating, their neighborhoods—in brief, their notion of what a community should be (cf. Wallace 1986, 154). The public or, alternatively, the worker is blamed for inaccuracy, and management pats itself on the back for a job well done. They can defend themselves against the highbrow charge that they are too clean by pointing the finger of blame at their inferiors. At the same time, this posture allows them to avoid questioning the possibility of historiographical progress. If the restorations' deficiencies can be blamed on the public's whims, then the idea that deeper dirt is profounder truth need never be reconsidered.

Notes

1. This chapter was written for a January 1992 conference, The Culture of Ruins, sponsored by the Center for Cultural Studies in collaboration with the board of studies in anthropology of the University of California, Santa Cruz. Although we had never, before the conference, considered Colonial Williamsburg in comparison to "ruins," we found that particular comparative perspective intriguing, and we present the results of our thinking on the matter in the present chapter.

2. Mimetic accuracy is a primary goal but not the only goal. The museum's motto is "that the future may learn from the past." In keeping with this, mimesis is to serve a larger educational and moral mission: the inculcation of American principles and values. Moreover, mimetic realism is not the only epistemology that museum historians draw on, for, since the rise of social history and its entrance into museums in the 1970s, historical relativism has become an influential outlook at Colonial Williamsburg. However, we would argue that relativism is an encompassed epistemology and that belief in mimesis remains hegemonic; see Gable, Handler, and Lawson 1992.

3. This quotation is taken from the foundation newspaper, the *Colonial Williamsburg News*, "'Lookin' 'Round,'" March 29, 1966, 3; other articles from the newspaper include "Magazine to Inaugurate Many Activities in June," May 1962, 1; "Poll Shows 99.6% Approval of New Scenes Along Duke of Gloucester," October 17, 1962, 3; "Oxen Reappearing on Duke of Gloucester, Haul Wood to Shops and Buildings," August 1963, 1, 4; "'Life-on-the-Scenes' Addition Keeps Crows Out—Visitors' Cameras Busy," October 15, 1963, 4; "Nine Sheep Graze in Historical Area As Life-on-the-Scenes Program Grows," June 21, 1966, 1; "More on the Scene," April 4, 1967, 4; "Straw Bee Hives Adding New Dimension to Life-on-the-Scenes," September 7, 1967, 1.

4. Letter from James Warnke, September 3, 1981; response from Peter A. G. Brown, September 11, 1981; Colonial Williamsburg Foundation Archives, letters of commendation.

5. During the past fifteen years, Colonial Williamsburg's curators have been involved in a sustained scholarly effort to improve realism by decreasing the elegance of the museum's interiors. They have argued that the first generation of curators and architects were influenced by "Colonial Revival" high style and that faithfulness to the eighteenth century requires a "leaner look." For the insider's view, see Gilliam and Leviner 1992; for a critical assessment, see Gable, Handler, and Lawson 1992.

6. The program was taped and transcribed by the authors.

7. "Interpreter" is the term currently used at Colonial Williamsburg, and many other museums, for people who have also been called "guides," "docents," or "hosts," and "hostesses."

References

Bordewich, Fergus M. 1988. "Revising Colonial America." *Atlantic*, December, 26–32.

Brinkley, M. Kent. 1990. "Trees on 'the Duke.'" *Colonial Williamsburg Interpreter* 11(2): 9–10.

———. 1991. "The Lay of the Land." *Colonial Williamsburg Interpreter* 12(2): 1–5.

Cotter, John. 1970. "Exhibit Review: Colonial Williamsburg." *Technology and Culture* 11: 417–27.

CW [Colonial Williamsburg]. 1951. *The Official Guidebook of Colonial Williamsburg.* Williamsburg: Colonial Williamsburg Foundation.

Gable, Eric, Richard Handler, and Anna Lawson. 1992. "On the Uses of Relativism: Fact, Conjecture, and Black and White Histories at Colonial Williamsburg." *American Ethnologist* 19(4): 791–805.

Gilliam, Jan Kirsten, and Betty Crowe Leviner. 1992. *Furnishing Williamsburg's Historic Buildings.* Charlottesville: University Press of Virginia.

Henry, Jules. 1963. *Culture against Man.* New York: Random House.

Huxtable, Ada Louise. 1992. "Inventing American Reality." *New York Review of Books*, December 3, 24–29.

Kemp, Wolfgang. 1990. "Images of Decay: Photography in the Picturesque Tradition." Translated by Joyce Rheuban. *October* 54: 102–33 [originally 1978].

Kopper, Philip. 1986. *Colonial Williamsburg.* New York: Abrams.

Kundera, Milan. 1984. *The Unbearable Lightness of Being.* Translated by Michael Henry Heim. New York: Harper & Row.

Olmert, Michael. 1985. "The New, No-Frills Williamsburg." *Historic Preservation*, October, 27–33.

———. 1991. "The Court Is Now in Session." *Colonial Williamsburg* 13(4): 8–15.

Schlereth, Thomas. 1978. "It Wasn't That Simple." *Museum News* 56(1): 36–44.

———. 1984. "Causing Conflict, Doing Violence." *Museum News* 63: 45–52.

Van West, Carroll, and Mary Hoffschwelle. 1984. "'Slumbering on Its Old Foundations': Interpretation at Colonial Williamsburg." *South Atlantic Quarterly* 83(2): 157–75.

Wallace, Michael. 1986. "Visiting the Past: History Museums in the United States." In *Presenting the Past: Essays on History and the Public*, edited by S. P. Benson, S. B. Brier, and R. Rosenzweig, 137–61. Philadelphia: Temple University Press.

White, Hayden. 1987. *The Content of the Form: Narrative Discourse and Historical Representation.* Baltimore: Johns Hopkins University Press.

Whitehill, Walter Muir. 1966. "'Promoted to Glory . . .' The Origin of Preservation in the United States." In *With Heritage So Rich*, edited by A. Rains et al., 35–44. New York: Random House.

Targeting Heritage: The Abuse of Symbolic Sites in Modern Conflicts

11

JONATHAN GOLDEN

If you want to humble an empire it makes sense to maim its cathedrals. They are symbols of its faith and when they crumble and burn it tells us we are not so powerful and we are not safe.

NANCY GIBBS (2001)

Not marble, not the gilded monuments of princes, shall outlive this pow'rful rhyme.

WILLIAM SHAKESPEARE, SONNET 55

IN MODERN CONFLICTS BETWEEN ethnic, religious, and cultural groups, buildings and monuments with historic and religious value sometimes become the target of violent attacks. Places and monuments regarded as sacred are particularly effective as targets precisely because they embody a whole set of beliefs and ideals. Such acts, therefore, are often contrived and perceived as attacks on ideology, aesthetics, and identity. In formulating a collective reaction, there is often a tendency to condemn such acts as irrational acts of senseless violence. Understandably, attacks on symbols imbued with great meaning often draw a highly emotive response, yet when these acts are relegated to the level of the irrational, we can lose valuable lessons. Just as the founding of temples and monuments is infused with meaning, their destruction is also symbolically charged.

In this chapter, we will examine briefly three incidents of violent conflict involving the destruction of sacred buildings and monuments in an attempt to understand the way that heritage and claims to it play into modern ethno-political and religious conflicts. In no way does this discussion presume to offer a comprehensive picture for any of these attacks; rather, the intent is to examine the similarities and differences between them in the hopes of expanding our perspective on this phenomenon.

Sacred Buildings and Monuments as Targets

Babri Masjid (Mosque), Ayodhya, India

The Babri Masjid (mosque) was first established at Ayodhya during the sixteenth century by Zahir-ud-din Muhammad Babar, founder of the Mughal dynasty in India. A site of Muslim worship for several centuries, Babri Masjid became an arena for the conflict between Muslims and Hindus in the nineteenth century as tensions between these two groups increased; incidents of religious violence at the site were recorded as early as 1853. Although conflict surrounding the mosque is clearly a part of the ongoing antagonism between Hindus and Muslims, more specifically it is a dispute over historical claims to the site: some Hindus maintain that Muslims usurped the site traditionally recognized as the birthplace of Rama, the seventh avatar of god Vishnu and one of the most revered Hindu deities. Hindu hard-liners generally argue that Babar destroyed a Hindu temple at this site in order to make way for the mosque and therefore it is their duty to correct this historical injustice (Mehta 1994).

In 1949, in the aftermath of partition, conflict surrounding the mosque became increasingly intense after attempts were made to appropriate the building by introducing idols of Lord Rama and ultimately both groups filed civil suits. That same year the mosque was proclaimed a disputed area and the gates were locked while the matter went to court.

The site remained dormant for several decades, until 1984 when Hindus from various groups formed a committee, headed by BJP leader Lal Krishna Advani, to "liberate" the birthplace of Lord Rama and dedicate a temple in his honor. With the unshackling of the doors in 1986 and a ruling granting access to the site for Hindus, the controversy was reignited. Archaeologists were brought into the conflict to substantiate claims for primary occupation at the site (Sharma 2001; Lal 2001), but archaeological research produced contradictory evidence and some of the archaeologists themselves may have succumbed to partisan beliefs (Bernbeck and Pollock 1996).

For several decades, there has been a growing trend in India toward Hindu nationalism, or what is called *Hindutva*, "a movement towards building an essentially Hindu society in India where people of all faiths could live, but only by respecting the wishes of the majority community" (Rao and Reddy 2000, 139). For instance, the Bharatiya Janata Party (BJP) campaign aimed to create a "homogeneous Hindu nation by denying the pluralistic traditions in Indian society, by negating the Other (essentially Muslims)" (Rao and Reddy 2000, 140). At the time, many feared that the BJP campaign was designed to lay the foundations for the oppression of the Muslim minority and the BJP did little to allay these concerns when their leaders began to call for the "liberation" of the mosque from the hands of Muslims. On December 6, 1992, the Babri Masjid became the target of such Hindu extremism.

The planning and execution of the attack involved members from several Hindu hard-liner groups including the Vishwa Hindu Parishad (VHP) as well as the BJP, though current Prime Minister Atal Behari Vajpayee of the BJP has since publicly distanced himself from the incident. The campaign began as a holy chariot pilgrimage *(Rath yatra)* covering over one thousand miles and ending at a site adjacent to the mosque where a new Hindu Rama temple was to be built and dedicated. In the words of the BJP the *kar sevaks* (i.e., public servants) would be "performing prayers with shovels and bricks" (Mehta 1994, 178).

On arriving at the site, the marchers turned to mob and the mosque was under attack, as their shovels—accompanied by sledgehammers—became weapons of destruction. Local authorities did little to stop the mob and within thirty-six hours the mosque had been razed to the ground and swept away with barely a trace; immediately a makeshift Rama temple was raised in its place. The BJP justified the attack by claiming that this was merely a correction of the "historical wrong" perpetrated centuries ago when the Mughals destroyed an earlier Rama temple. Bernbeck and Pollock (1996) have suggested there is some irony in the fact that many of these Muslims are not descendents of the Mughals, but rather *dalits*, the low-caste Hindus who converted to Islam. Indeed, this is one of the very reasons for this hostility, for the VHP-led Hindu right has long considered the mass conversion of these Hindus to Islam as deeply insulting. They then threatened to target other prominent mosques, citing similar claims. In their view, they were taking the law into their own hands in the service of a higher purpose.

Bamiyan Buddhas, Afghanistan

The second case study involves a pair of giant Buddha statues carved into the cliffs overlooking Bamiyan in Afghanistan. Believed to date to the sixth–seventh century A.D., the statues were targeted in what was described by the assailants as an Islamic campaign against idolatry. The Taliban leader, Mullah Mohammed Omar, issued an edict ordering the destruction of all statues, saying, "these idols have been gods of the infidels," thereby rescinding a previous agreement with UNESCO and the international community that halted earlier threats of destruction by the Taliban.

In a highly publicized event during the spring of 2001, Taliban militia used explosives to obliterate the colossal Buddhas. At the time, Greek ambassador to

Pakistan, Dmitri Loundas, was quoted as saying "the decision to destroy Afghanistan's pre-Islamic heritage may have been a response to the isolation felt by the Taliban since the imposition of sanctions against them in January 2001" (Associated Press 2001). These sanctions were imposed as a result of their refusal to surrender Osama bin Laden, who was already wanted for the attack on the USS *Cole* in October 2000.

As forewarnings of the attack gained immediate and extensive media coverage, local groups such as the Society for the Preservation of Afghanistan's Cultural Heritage were joined by international groups such as UNESCO in issuing pleas to stop the destruction. Initially, the Taliban contrived a hostage situation, pledging that the destruction could be averted if money for food could be contributed to help the plight of the Afghan people. With more than just a trace of irony money is now being raised in the West to reconstruct the Buddhas (Tripath 2002). A narrow version of Islam as espoused by the Taliban inspired the attack, and the Shiite minority living in the Bamiyan region is generally unsympathetic to the Taliban and did not support the attack. Discussing the Bamiyan attacks, Meskell (2002) invoked the term *negative heritage* in describing "a conflictual site that becomes the repository of negative memory in the collective imaginary." According to her, "For the Taliban, the Buddhist statues represented a site of negative memory, one that required jettisoning from the nation's construction of contemporary identity and the act of erasure was a political statement about religious difference and international exclusion" (Meskell 2002, 561).

Joseph's Tomb, Nablus

The third case study involves conflict over a site in the West Bank town of Nablus, commonly known as Joseph's Tomb, although the identification of the structure as the resting place of the biblical patriarch is far from certain. This case is not unlike the battle over Babri Masjid, but in this case Jews and Muslims put forth competing heritage claims. This case differs because members of both groups share some common beliefs concerning the significance of the site.

The modern city of Nablus, one of the largest in the West Bank, is home to some 75,000 Palestinians. The Jewish presence is represented by the settlement of Elon Moreh and claims to heritage sites in the city's immediate vicinity include Tell Balata, which is now generally recognized as the biblical city of Shechem, and the Nablus tomb. The tell, bearing the name (Hebrew *ballut*) for a tree mentioned in the Bible, was first identified as ancient Shechem in 1903 and sporadic excavations were carried out there in the years that followed. An American team led by G. E. Wright excavated at the site from 1956 to 1962, with the results published in *Shechem: Biography of a Biblical City* (Wright 1965). Wright (1965) generally stressed the importance of Shechem not so much for its archaeological value, but rather for the multiple allusions to the site in various portions of the Bible (Steen 2002).

According to the biblical tradition, the patriarch Joseph was buried somewhere in the vicinity of the Shechem (see below). By the 1860s, a limestone structure in the town had come to be regarded by many Jews and Muslims as the location of the tomb. Muslims also recognize Joseph as a prophet; thus the site is referred to in Arabic as Qabr en-Nebi Yousif, that is, "Tomb of Prophet Joseph." Some Palestinians maintain that the site actually houses the remains of a Muslim sheikh named Yousif buried there two centuries ago (Benvenisti 2000).

None of these claims are substantiated by archaeological evidence. Relevant historical evidence is provided by the Madaba Map, which indicates the presence of the site, although the edifice depicted on the map does not appear to resemble a tomb (Piccirillo and Alliata 1999, 65). The map, which dates to the sixth century A.D., is generally regarded as a reliable geographical reference, especially since references in the map to other contemporary sites are for the most part accurate. The map is based on information from Eusebius, pushing the tradition even further back by several centuries. This suggests that there was some building in the area recognized as the tomb, but to this author's knowledge, there have been no archaeological investigations at the tomb site.

Prior to 1967, when Israel took control of Nablus, Muslims worshiped at the site. The history of Jewish worship at the tomb prior to this time is vague, but in the ensuing decade Jews visited the site with increasing frequency. In 1975 Muslims were prohibited from worshiping at the site and in 1992 a Torah scroll was installed and the niche facing Mecca covered (Philps 2001); the site also came to be used as a Jewish school (*yeshiva*). In accordance with the Oslo agreements, the Israelis withdrew from Nablus in 1995, though Jews continued to worship at the site under limited protection of the Israel Defense Forces (IDF). Control of the site was contested and it was the scene of sporadic conflict for several years to follow.

Tensions at the site flared in October 2000 when the IDF abandoned the site. On October 7 the tomb came under attack (Cohen 2000). Hebrew texts found inside the structure were burned and the prayer niche reopened. It was reported that Palestinian men attacked the shrine with pick axes and crowbars, setting portions of the structure aflame, and finally, raising a Palestinian flag. The incident received considerable press in the region and made international headlines as well (CNN and BBC covered the episode).

At the time, some Palestinians were quoted in the press stating that the tomb was destroyed in order to preclude the Israelis' return. "The people are happy that the Zionists are out of here," said Anwar al Masri, a uniformed policeman who was quoted at the scene. He was unequivocal in explaining the mob's goals: "They want to remove every single thing that would give [the Israelis] an excuse to come back" (Cohen 2000). As in the case of Babri Masjid, the term "liberation" was invoked to describe these actions. The dispute is by no means resolved, but as of October 2002, Israeli Defense Minister Binyamin Ben Eliezer reinstated the ban on Jewish pilgrimage to the site.

Understanding the role of the tomb in the context of the current conflict is a difficult task. Biblical references to the site, however, may provide some insight. Whether explicitly stated or not, the potential implications of a few of these references with regard to nationalism and territoriality cannot be overlooked. According to Genesis (12:6–7), it is at Shechem that Abraham learned that his descendants would inherit the Promised Land (Canaan). Shechem is mentioned again in the books of Chronicles, Kings, and Joshua. The story of the patriarch's burial is told in Joshua. Joseph was on his deathbed in Egypt when he requested that his brothers bury him in his homeland, and on his death Joseph's bones were brought to Shechem (Joshua 24:32). One could argue that this site has particular significance for the Zionist narrative, not only because this is where the Promised Land was first promised, but also because of the themes of repatriation and renewal that it embodies; after a period of exile in Egypt, this is where the Israelites would renew their covenant with God.

Interpreting the Attacks

Clearly there are important differences between these three incidents. One interpretation of the Nablus tomb attack is that it was used as a weapon of the weak, perpetrated as an act of defiance by a group that is subordinated. At Babri Masjid the incident could be explained, at least in part, as a weapon of those in power used for further weakening the resolve of the weak. The Nablus and Ayodhya incidents both involved what Hayden (2002) refers to as "shared shrines," where two or more opposing groups assert claims to the same monument. The struggle, therefore, can be viewed as a battle for both physical and symbolic space. Of course, it must be kept in mind that each event occurred within a specific cultural context with unique historical circumstances.

The motivation for the Bamiyan attacks is less clear. No doubt, the Taliban were driven by their religious belief that there is no place for idolatry on such a grand scale in what they consider Muslim land. A topic discussed in virtually all chapters of this volume is the way that archaeology is used as a means for constructing and presenting the past. Conversely, we observe here several instances where ancient and historical remains were abused, also as a way of presenting the past, or some abridged version of it.

The attack on the colossal Buddhas was part of a broader campaign that included the destruction of antiquities in the Afghanistan Museum led by the Taliban minister of information and culture, Qadratullah Jamal. Not satisfied with destroying what was on display, he extended the attack to objects held at the Afghanistan Culture Ministry's storage facility. In addition to the religious reasons cited for the violent campaigns, it also appears that the Taliban intended this attack as an opportunity to gain a large audience and draw attention to their movement. As stated earlier, the attacks were announced in advance, giving the media ample time to prepare for coverage of the event.

What is common to all three incidents is that in each case the primary target of violence was not a population, fortress, or arsenal, not a strategic point in a strict military sense, but rather they were attacks primarily aimed at monuments and places of worship—symbolic targets. Perry and Burnham (2001, 3), the president and chairman of World Monuments Watch, respectively, assert, "Weapons of mass destruction are not always aimed at battleships or military installations but at cultural icons that bind and inspire communities around the world . . . our landmarks, the Mostar Bridge, the Bamiyan Buddhas and the World Trade Center—have become prized targets for terrorists because they are what defines the cultures, ideals and achievements of the people who created them, who use them, who live with them." These attacks should probably be viewed as contiguous with more direct efforts to eradicate a people's presence through attacks on human targets. We therefore need to search for additional conceptual tools in order to comprehend the significance of these types of incidents.

Multiple meanings are attached to such attacks, just as there are multiple meanings attached to the targets themselves. Attacks on holy sites and monuments can be seen as attempts to undermine the credibility of the ideals that the targets embody. The destruction itself is a performance—the act is the weapon—both a fearful attack on an undefended "sitting duck," and a fearless challenge to the power and credibility of another's primacy. The Bamiyan Buddhas represent a specific form known as the Vairocana Buddha (believed to encompass the entire universe), and in their stupendous scale, this immensity—the larger of the two is thought to have been the world's largest—is made literal. Joseph's Tomb embodies an important Zionist theme: the return from exile to one's homeland. In their assault on the tomb, the Palestinian attackers boldly expressed their challenge to the credibility of Israeli claims to the site.

As we learned from the attacks of September 11, just as the standing monument captures our imagination, its destruction creates an enshrined space in the collective memory and it assumes the role of martyr. For now, the view of Lower Manhattan is immediately recognized for the glaring void once occupied by the Twin Towers. And while the group responsible for the destruction uses the attack as a rallying point, it is often the victimized group that musters even greater group cohesion as identities solidify as part of the collective response.

Conflict Theory and Political Violence

Each case discussed here involves the struggle between groups that have labeled each other as "the Other" and the attacks are the violent manifestations of one group's goal to undermine the other at the same time reinforcing the battle lines. The specific social and political context is essential to understanding the full meaning of such attacks.

Defining political violence and terror is a complex issue and deciding where to draw the line between the two can sometimes be difficult. Certain cases are generally perceived as "black and white," but in others there is inevitably some gray area. Political violence has been defined by Ted Honderich (1976) as "a considerable or destroying use of force against persons or things directed to a change in the policies, system, government and have also directed to a change in the lives of individuals within society." He construes this issue as the "politicization of ethnic identity," which arises when an "ethnic group perceives its position as being threatened in some vital respect and consciously reacts" (Honderich 1976, 242). Attacks on symbolic places usually involve an effort to advance one's cause and claims by undermining and discrediting those of the adversary. Meibar (1982) asserts that in active conflicts one objective is to induce change. One such "act of inducement" is "the strategy of significant elimination, the objective being the elimination of the other actor's credibility" (Meibar 1982, 65).

Rationalism and Terror

Another problem concerns the question of where these attacks fit within our general conceptual framework and system of rationale. A common reaction to such attacks, for instance, is to denounce them as senseless acts of violence. If we construe the temple or the monument as an inanimate object incapable of antagonism, an affront on it can be represented as an act of base barbarism.

It is sometimes easier for the group targeted to see the perpetrators as emanating from some primordial darkness (Aho 1994). The alternative is to recognize them as rational actors with interests that are neither illegitimate nor unreasonable, but simply in competition with those of the victim. The latter, however, is considerably more complicated.

Cultural rifts are widened when we imagine the enemy as irrational because the differences seem intractable, as if there is no common, fundamental moral ground to which both groups can appeal. It is difficult to accept that such acts and their perpetrators come out of a historical context with motives that they perceive as justified. An argument can be made that these acts are completely rational, and the idea of conflict as potentially positive and creative is an important component of contemporary conflict theory. One criterion for determining if an action is rational is whether it makes optimal use of the available means in order to achieve a certain goal (Popper 1963). From this perspective, the decision to use violence when it seems to be the most effective tool in certain circumstances can be viewed as completely rational. As defined by Simmel (1968), conflict is not the absence of social order, but represents a different form of social order. Conflict, for instance, can be useful for addressing social inequalities, while for Marxists conflict between socioeconomic groups is inevitable, necessary, and potentially quite positive.

Without promoting moral *hyper*relativism or condoning these acts of violence, little is gained by dismissing violent destruction as completely irrational or evil with no attempt at deeper analysis. We must, for example, raise the question: When a group resorts to violence with the objective of advancing their own interests, to what degree is the language of rationality useful? There is an inherent paradox when we invoke the language of rationality because such language carries implicit statements about universal standards, the root of efforts to protect heritage and human rights. Yet the act itself suggests that these standards are not universal, and appeals to such abstract notions tend to lose their meaning in the broader context where groups with competing ideologies seek to achieve what is in their view some higher justice. Archaeology involves the creation of meanings for the present from remains of the past, but again, these meanings are not universal. Again, understanding the way meanings vary and the significance of archaeology for contemporary social relations is a central theme of this volume (see Baram and Rowan, this volume).

Creating Identities: The Construction of the Enemy

It is not merely that these forms of conflict tend to fall along social, ethnic, and religious lines, but rather, they are a very part of those very identities. According to Woehrle and Coy (2000, 2), "People create conflict as part of their search for meaning, as part of their definition of themselves and of the groups to which they belong, and to achieve what they need to survive and develop. Conflict is thus part of the construction of our social reality."

The process by which people categorize themselves is based largely on their perceived relationship with other people and the world in general, and which has meaning within a specific context. A person's awareness and understanding of their membership in a social group also involves a certain emotional investment that is attached to that membership. Membership, of course, can be defined in a number of ways.

Social groups are often defined by their spatial configurations. In many cases, a group's relative geographic isolation and claims to territory are the "root and symbol of their existence" (Agnew 2000, 4). Honderich (1976, 245) explains that ethnic conflict may be aimed at control of the region inhabited by a group, especially in those cases where the region is ethnically homogeneous and has a historical tradition to which to relate. One strategic aspect of an attack may be the goal of complete homogeneity. In selecting ancient and historic landmarks as targets, homogeneity can be symbolically achieved not only in space, but in time as well, for the underlying message is: you are not here now and, in fact, you never were.

Hayden (2002, 217), discussing conflict in South Asia and the Balkans, argues that dominant groups often adopt "principles that exclude minorities from legitimacy." Noting the influence of religious nationalism in these conflicts, Hayden (2002, 217) argues that "minority religions themselves are seen as illegitimate, and therefore *symbols of their very presence* may not be tolerated" and discusses ways that shrines have been used as symbols of dominance in both regions. Symbolic sites such as in Nablus, Bamiyan, and Ayodhya became caught up in struggles for identity as well as power and dominance, thereby assuming the meanings that ultimately provoked their destruction. Similarly, Abu El-Haj (1998) has examined the ways in which some parts of the past are assumed as part of the national heritage while others are classified as part of a national past belonging to someone else.

Where religion constitutes a significant part of ethnic identity, religious institutions can become a driving force behind the identity and can be used as instruments for resistance against other groups. Virtually any constellation of these social identities, religious-ethnic-regional, is possible, and the conflict itself can engender or heighten divisiveness. The Babri Masjid incident in India had the effect of accelerating the process of identity creation. According to Mehta (1994, 182), "the mosque episode raised anew the whole issue of Indian identity. In the old secular climate, people tended to think of themselves as Indians first; in the new climate they were starting to think of themselves as Hindus and Muslims or Sikhs first."

Delineating the boundaries of ethnic identity within the context of the Israeli–Palestinian conflict is especially complicated. Palestinians are commonly represented as Muslims, but some 6–8 percent of the Palestinian population is Christian. At the same time, the Jewish population of Israel, ethnically speaking, comprises groups from such disparate ethno-regions as Eastern and Western Europeans, Northern and Eastern Africans, and "native" Middle Easterners. And while these differences are sometimes the source of conflict within Israel, to many outsiders, particularly their enemies, there is little reason to draw such distinctions. There are a great many Israeli citizens of Arab descent, including Bedouin and Druze, as well as those that identify themselves as Palestinians. This, of course, raises a number of important questions about nationalism and ethnicity that are beyond the scope of this chapter.

But while the incident at Nablus involved the battle over a religious site, the raising of the Palestinian flag also demonstrates the nationalist overtones of this act. Inherent in this problem is the tendency for identities to be oversimplified. When constructing an image of the enemy we often attempt to demonize the Other by focusing on a handful of features perceived as especially negative and then exaggerating them. In this way, the inherent contradictions and inconsistencies that inevitably arise when attempting to maintain these types of divisions can be more easily dispensed with.

The "Historicization" of Conflict

Yet another dimension to this problem concerns the historical value that is frequently attached to these sites. Histories of group relations can, of course, have a profound influence on the emergence and later escalation of conflicts (Woehrle and Coy 2000). The attack on a site with historical value achieves two things simultaneously: (1) eradication of the other group's historical presence and hence claims to the area and (2) creation of a historical context, giving the air of age-old blood feuds to conflicts only a few generations old.

During the process of creating histories, time is often manipulated. Typically, a few outstanding events, normally ordered as a developmental progression, are emphasized and a stylized version of the past emerges (Aho 1994). Thus sacred places and heritage sites that somehow represent key events—real or imagined—become landmarks not only in space, but in time as well. Shrinking the symbolic distance between these temporal landmarks can therefore be an effective means of drawing links between past and present, thereby reinforcing nationalist claims. This often seems to be especially true of the southern Levant for several reasons. Steen (2002, 3) for instance, argues that the "proximity of so many ancient sites on the landscape is part of what makes it so easy to slide between narratives of the past and present." A number of scholars (Silberman 1982; Zerubavel 1995; Abu El-Haj 1998; Baram 2000) have discussed the role of archaeology in the creation of the modern Israeli identity, pointing to the link between the modern state and ancient Israel that has been cultivated via large, government-sponsored excavation projects (also see Bauman, this volume). Furthermore, these types of narratives have been employed in order to bolster Israel's claims to land. Here we may wish to apply Kus's (1989) notion of ascending and descending anachronisms, where time is deliberately manipulated by pushing events back further in time or bringing them forward in order to connect them with the present. Applying this idea to the Ayodhya situation, Bernbeck and Pollock (1996) argue, for instance, that the destruction of Babri Masjid was conceived by some as a legitimate response to Muslim crimes of five hundred years ago. Employing this concept to the Nablus case suggests that it could be in Israel's interest to push time back in order to demonstrate through archaeology that Jews occupied the region first, while at the same time trying to shrink time in order to expurgate centuries of Islamic rule wedged between the Jewish exile and the Zionist return. Indeed, present Israeli law, which protects only sites dated to pre-1700 A.D., reveals a structure of valuation that serves to privilege the ancient biblical past over the more recent past (Baram 2000; Benvenisti 2000; Steen 2002). In selecting specific symbols as part of the process of identity creation, invariably there is also an attempt to make the connection between the symbol and the people it represents appear entirely natural—a goal well served by the use of a heritage site. Therefore, where identities based on ethnicity, geography, and religion are concerned, mosque and monument make highly effective targets.

Archaeological Responsibilities

The attacks on monuments discussed here may be construed as the manifestation of group conflict where the monument plays a central role in the formation of identity. We must not forget, however, that group identity can in many cases be a positive thing. The formation of identity—both that of the Other and that of one's self—tends to encourage diversity, which can, in the best cases, advance engagement and participation in community and government and is generally part of the human way of social adaptation. In the past decade alone we have seen a profound increase in the interest that peoples throughout the world have had in their own distinctive cultural identities. Sadly, the construction of identity seems to also entail the construction of barriers between peoples and it is the differences that tend to be emphasized. The active recognition of these differences often manifests in ethnic conflict, conflict that has gained a much greater capacity to mobilize than before.

Ancient and historical buildings and monuments often play a vital part in the formation and communication of cultural identities, and when conflicts over identity result in the destruction of these sites, archaeologists may actually find themselves faced with a quandary. On the one hand, archaeologists must often play the role of guardian of the past and are thereby naturally concerned with preserving and protecting ancient and historical remains. At the same time, archaeologists have for several decades now been calling for and, to varying extents, practicing an archaeology that shares many if not all of the theoretical concerns developed by cultural anthropology. As anthropologists then, we must also seek to understand the rationale—the specific histories and the sensitivities—which in-form terrorist attacks, rather than simply condemning them as irrational. Fortunately, these two positions are not mutually exclusive.

Both government and nongovernment organizations at both the international and local level have made attempts to deal with this issue in various ways, usually condemning and criminalizing attacks on holy sites and taking measures aimed at protecting these places.

At the Convention for the Protection of Cultural Property in the Event of Armed Conflict at The Hague on May 14, 1954, the concept of "cultural property" was defined (see Magness-Gardiner, this volume). The World Heritage Committee maintains several criteria by which they, in conjunction with the International Council on Monuments and Sites, and according to the UNESCO World Heritage Convention in 1972, judge whether a site has what they consider "outstanding universal value." The problem of attacks on sites and monuments is thereby framed as an affront on "world heritage," a notion that on the one hand purports to defend diversity, while on the other implies the existence of some shared and tangible world culture (Cleere 2001). According to UNESCO a "heritage crime" is defined as any act that means "damage to the cultural heritage of all mankind, since each people makes its own contribution to the culture of the world" (UNESCO 2000, 1).

Such resolutions and legislation are admirable goals, but it is not entirely clear how well these goals are achieved in all cases. Meskell (2002) has recently pointed out some of the flaws in the concept of world heritage altogether, arguing that while the notion of a shared world heritage may be desirable to some, it would be unwise to assume this sentiment is universal. According to Meskell (2002, 569), "The very concept of world heritage privileges an idea originating in the West and requires an attitude toward material culture that is also distinctly European in origin. The fact that world heritage is underpinned by the globalization of Western values has ultimately prompted challenges, resistance, and misunderstandings."

It is reasonable therefore to question whether such laws actually function as deterrents when the perpetrators of "heritage crimes" refuse in most cases to recognize as legitimate any part of that culture including both its monuments and its laws. It can also be difficult to invest faith in the ability of international organizations alone, without the input of the peoples directly involved in the conflicts, to provide effective and enforceable solutions. One alternative to the so-called universal laws is the use of local agreements that provide incentives for all interested parties. For example, the Mitchell Report, based on an American-led inquiry into Israeli–Palestinian violence completed in the spring of 2001, recommended that "the PA and [government of Israel] should consider a joint undertaking to preserve and protect holy places sacred to the traditions of Muslims, Jews, and Christians" (http://usinfo.state.gov/regional/nea/mitchell.htm).

The notion of world heritage also raises questions about the emergence of what many have called a "global culture." Though discussions of globalization often focus on commercialism and economic development, the notion of world heritage—and the motivation to defend it—must also be seen as part of this broader process (Meskell 2002). In fact, violent attacks on symbols, particularly attacks on modern cultural symbols such as the World Trade Center and McDonald's restaurants outside the United States, bespeak the underside of globalization: there are many who feel disenfranchised by and excluded from this process, and many who perceive themselves as victims of it may actively resist (Barber 2001).

But even in more localized conflicts, it is possible to detect a growing tension between the increasing incidence of "forced encounters" and the expression of difference. Thus more than ever it is important that cultures attempt to at least communicate if not share their values and aesthetics. Perhaps this can be one way of fostering greater respect and appreciation for each other's symbols. We must also seek to encourage people to develop more constructive means of expressing identity. Can the notion of identity itself provide a path toward alternative, less destructive means of expression? All of the cultures involved in the conflicts discussed here have produced awesome and enduring works of art and architecture and to be sure there are more positive and lasting identities associated with being the creator of something meaningful and beautiful rather than its destroyer.

Extremism in any form can be insidious and often seems to have a way of bringing about its own undoing. Extremism, for instance, often tests the parameters of cultural configurations as some may seek to downplay the divisions between peoples, at the same time distancing themselves from those representing the extremes of their own cultural tradition. In the wake of the September 11 attacks, for instance, countless letters and editorial and opinion pieces by Muslim scholars and religious leaders denied that these actions were a part of true Islam. "Destroying the sacred art of a noble and deeply spiritual tradition," explained Abdul Aziz Said (2001, AE7), is "an action that does not qualify as Islamic." If these extremist acts are intended to make a statement about the power of perpetrator, one may question their effectiveness, for just as the attack may cause some within that ethnic or religious group to condemn and to distance themselves from it, it often results in greater cohesion among members of the victimized group.

Ethnic and religious conflicts frequently entail socioeconomic struggle as well (or, in some cases, above all). Acute economic despair, however, can also weaken the appeal of extremist movements when they feed on people's misery as a source of support for their cause, but fail to deliver any tangible, positive results. Although violent attacks on monuments may offer immediate gratification for some, they rarely accomplish much in terms of improving the conditions that breed discontent in the first place. In India, concerns among voters that the BJP offered lit-

tle more than religious rhetoric on a single issue while ignoring the problems of unemployment, poverty, and hunger, forced the party to shift its position and seek a broader platform through the forming of coalitions (Rao and Reddy 2001).

It is also worthwhile to examine how the collective reactions to such events are constructed and what meanings lay behind them. Clinging to etiological myths about the emergence of Western civilization from savage society (Carter 1996) requires a steady flow of barbarian bad guys and axes of evil. The media is in part culpable when it comes to creating and managing images of the enemy with the chanting of catch phrases such as the faceless enemy and the face of evil, terms that deny the attackers' humanity. Within this perspective, the event is construed as a failure of civilization to restrain some vestiges of a savage past and enemies of modern, Western society are portrayed as "irrational monsters." But as offensive as these acts may be to the sensibilities of many, we must recognize that understanding them, even if not sympathetically, is still relevant to the comprehension of the full range of human social behavior and attitudes. Indeed, if we are to ever prevent these types of attacks from occurring, we would do well to study and comprehend the ones that have already taken place.

Monuments and holy places serve as important focal points for people who share the same religious beliefs, but there is a point where clinging to them can spiral downward into dogmatism. In some instances both the faithful worshiper and the archaeologist are faced with the decision of what is more important: preserving the past or peace in the present? At the same time, violence aimed at symbols rather than people also presents the uncomfortable dilemma of choosing between two evils. For we may ask, is not the loss of a temple or monument, with no one in it, preferable to destruction of human life? A number of social critics have also pointed out that the destruction of the Buddhas received considerably more attention than the everyday poverty and public health issues that afflict Afghanistan.

Conclusion

As we have seen, there are a number of ways to examine problems surrounding the abuse of heritage sites. A number of scholars, for instance, have focused on the problem of religious violence (Juergensmeyer 2003; Kepel 1999; Rapoport and Alexander 1982). Juergensmeyer (2003, 161) argues that "extremism in religion has led to violence at the same time that violent conflicts cry out for validation." In the cases of Bamiyan and Ayodhya, if not Nablus as well, the attackers espoused ideologies in which the attacks were seen as divinely sanctioned. But the utility of religious explanation is limited when we consider that more moderate members of all these religious generally do not endorse this form of violence. This attitude, for instance, is reflected in a statement issued by the Islamic Research Council at the Al Ahzar University in Cairo, a group considered to be one of the highest authorities on the interpretation of Islamic Law, shortly after the September 11 attacks, stating, "Islam provides clear rules and ethical norms that forbid . . . the destruction of property that is not being used in the hostilities" (*Al Hayat*, November 5, 2001). As we have seen, however, in some cases, buildings are often perceived as representing part of the hostilities.

Eradication of the Other is often a primary aim of attacks on symbols and monuments. The perpetrators of the Babri Masjid attack were clear in their beliefs, while those attacking the Nablus tomb could claim both a literal and a symbolic victory in the campaign to end Israeli occupation. The Taliban, having consolidated control of Afghanistan, made clear their intent to eradicate from Islamic lands elements that were viewed as anti-Islamic.

But as a means of solidifying identity, such acts can serve as the rallying point for both the victimizers and victimized. In addition, as with all symbols, the meanings that a landmark embodies are mutable. The meaning and value attached to a symbol is mutable, changing over time, and within a certain frame of time the symbol can mean different things to different people. Thus, the Eiffel Tower, which met with resistance at first has become a national symbol for France, and the Berlin Wall, long a symbol of division, in its destruction was more or less instantly transformed into a symbol of freedom and opportunity, if but for a brief moment of hope. The Twin Towers, disparaged by many as lacking in character at first, became in time an international symbol for many, and in their absence now represent a range of meanings—both negative and positive. As we also learn from this example, the problem becomes even more complex when symbols carry conflicting meanings for different peoples, for the opulence and wealth evident in the Twin Towers was a sign of American pride for some, American arrogance for others. In some cases, one group's monument to triumph is another's symbol of oppression. Western history has provided numerous examples where one of the crowning moments in a revolution was the destruction of the monument to the deposed king. No doubt there was an element of this behind the attack on the Nablus tomb, where Palestinians, in addition to the religious significance ascribed to the tomb, also came to view it as a symbol of Israeli occupation.

Faced with this complex dilemma, what can the archaeologist do? The first option is to be responsible in considering the broader implications of their work. Archaeologists play a vital role in the construction of meanings attached to ancient and historical sites (Hodder 1986; Shanks and Tilley 1987; Meskell 1998). And in recent years archaeologists have become more cognizant of the fact that what they say about the past can have an effect on the future. According to Bernbeck

and Pollock (1996), "The past plays a legitimating role for present groups (or would-be groups) by allowing them to trace their roots into earlier times." Similarly, Steen (2002, 1) asserts that "the narratives that archaeologists produce draw on nationalist narrative themes from outside of academic archaeology and also that archaeological narratives then feed back into a wider cultural world."

Responsible archaeologists, therefore, must attempt to present the results of their research in as neutral a manner as possible. As Abu El-Haj (1998) recommends, archaeologists should try to shift the focus of their research away from that which is centered on nationalist narratives. But as long as archaeological discourse continues to revolve around nationalist narratives, heritage sites are potential targets of negative attention and are thereby placed at risk.

Archaeologists can also contribute in a more productive way, not only by shifting away from the nationalist narratives but also by exposing the weaknesses in religious and nationalist claims that are based on tenuous evidence. Archaeological narratives undoubtedly have the power to reinforce dominant ideologies and the national myths that hold together modern nations. Perhaps archaeologists, particularly those working in areas that are politically volatile, can work instead toward producing archaeological narratives that challenge the dominant ideologies and national myths rather than support them—perhaps this can be one way to help diffuse tensions rather than fuel them (Schmidt and Patterson 1995).

It is not too farfetched to suggest, for instance, that serious archaeological investigation of the Nablus tomb could reveal a date for the structure going back but a few centuries, thereby altogether obviating at least the portion of the controversy that is focused on biblical claims. In yet another way, archaeologists can contribute to an understanding of this problem by exposing the insidious nature of "who was here first" cycles, for archaeologists regularly observe—with the assumed detachment of scientific inquiry—the decline of civilizations, and can therefore bear witness to the fact that no structure, great or small, pedestrian or pious, will last forever. Archaeologists generally celebrate the remains of the past, yet archaeology is in many ways the science of what does not remain. Although accepting the impermanence of things is in itself insufficient as a solution to attacks on heritage sites, this notion can be liberating in the sense that it may pave the way for more tempered claims to the past. Archaeologists can demonstrate that over the course of time any number of different peoples have lived in a region and that any building may have had multiple lives with varying meanings (Mostafavi and Leatherbarrow 1993); in this way archaeologists can sometimes help neutralize certain claims to heritage sites. And just as archaeologists can attest to the inevitable demise of all buildings and monuments in time, they can also testify that time and again, great monuments and sacred places are rebuilt and rededicated.

Acknowledgments

I would like to thank Yorke Rowan and Uzi Baram, the editors of this volume, for reading multiple drafts of this chapter; their insights and direction have proven invaluable. I would also like to express gratitude to Khaled Nashef for providing information about the Nablus tomb. Danielle Steen was also helpful in sorting out some of the issues, while Martin Kodis and Deborah Ben-David provided assistance with the initial spoken presentation. Of course, the author alone assumes full responsibility for any errors.

References

Abu El-Haj, Nadia. 1998. "Translating Truths: Nationalism, the Practice of Archaeology, and the Remaking of Past and Present in Contemporary Jerusalem." *American Ethnologist* 25(2): 166–88.

Abu-Nimer, Mohamed. 2001. *Reconciliation, Justice and Coexistence.* Lanham, Md.: Lexington.

Agnew, John. 2000. "The Geopolitical Context of Ethnopolitical Conflicts." In *Reconcilable Differences*, edited by S. Byrne and C. Irvin, 3–22. West Hartford: Kuvarian.

Aho, James A. 1994. *This Thing of Darkness: A Sociology of the Enemy.* Seattle: University of Washington Press.

Associated Press. 2001. "U.N. Pleads with Taliban Not to Destroy Buddha Statues." *New York Times*, March 3, A3.

Baram, Uzi. 2000. "Entangled Objects from the Palestinian Past: Archaeological Perspectives for the Ottoman Period, 1500–1900." In *Historical Archaeology of the Ottoman Empire: Breaking New Ground*, edited by U. Baram and L. Carroll, 137–60. New York: Kluwer/Plenum.

Barber, Benjamin. 2001. *Jihad vs. McWorld.* New York: Ballantine.

Baudrillard, Jean. 1993. *The Transparency of Evil: Essays on the Extreme Phenomena.* Translated by J. Benedict. London: Verso.

Benvenisti, Meron. 2000. *Sacred Landscape: The Buried History of the Holy Land since 1948.* Berkeley: University of California Press.

Bernbeck, Reinherd, and Pollock, Susan. 1996. "Ayodhya, Archaeology, and Identity." *Current Anthropology* 37 (Supplement): 138–42.

Binder, Leonard. 1999. "Introduction: The International Dimensions of Ethnic Conflict in the Middle East." In *Ethnic Conflict and International Politics in the Middle East*, edited by L. Binder, 1–40. Gainesville: University Press of Florida.

Carter, Simon. 1996. "Making Violence Useful." In *Defining Violence*, edited by H. Bradby, 125–39. Aldershot, U.K.: Avebury.

Cleere, H. 2001. "The Uneasy Bedfellows: Universality and Cultural Heritage." In *Destruction and Conservation of Cultural Property*, edited by R. Layton, P. Stone, J. Thomas, 24–31. New York: Routledge.

Cohen, Richard. 2000. "Joseph's Tomb." *Washington Post*, October 10.

Emadi, Hafizullah. 2001. *Politics of the Dispossessed: Superpowers and Developments in Middle East.* Westport, Conn.: Praeger.

Gibbs, Nancy. 2001. "If You Want to Humble an Empire." *Time,* September 14.

Hahn, Thich Nhat. 1974. *Zen Keys.* New York: Doubleday.

Hayden, Robert. 2000. "Muslims as 'Others' in Serbian and Croatian Politics." In *Neighbors at War: Anthropological Perspectives on Yugoslav Ethnicity, Culture, and History,* edited by J. Halpern and D. Kideckel, 116–24. University Park: Penn State University Press.

———. 2002. "Antagonistic Tolerance: Competitive Sharing of Religious Sites in South Asia and the Balkans." *Current Anthropology* 43(2): 205–31.

Hodder, Ian. 1986. *Reading the Past: Current Approaches to Interpretation in Archaeology.* Cambridge: Cambridge University Press.

Honderich, Ted. 1976. *Political Violence.* Ithaca: Cornell University Press.

Horowitz, Donald. 1985. *Ethnic Groups in Conflict.* Berkeley: University of California Press.

ICOMOS [International Council on Monuments and Sites]. 1954. *Convention for the Protection of Cultural Property in the Event of Armed Conflict.* www.icomos.org/hague.

Islamic Research Council. 2001. *Al Hayat,* November 5.

Jabri, Vivienne. 1996. *Discourses on Violence: Conflict Analysis Reconsidered.* Manchester: Manchester University Press.

Jeong, Ho-Won. 2000. "Peace Building in Identity Driven Ethnopolitical Conflicts." In *Reconcilable Differences,* edited by S. Byrne and C. Irvin, 115–26. West Hartford: Kuvarian.

Juergensmeyer, Mark. 2003. *Terror in the Mind of God: The Global Rise of Religious Violence.* 3rd ed. Berkeley: University of California Press.

Kepel, Gilles. 1999. "Toward a Social Analysis of Islamist Movements." In *Ethnic Conflict and International Politics in the Middle East,* edited by L. Binder, 181–206. Gainesville: University Press of Florida.

Kus, Susan. 1989. "Time Is on My Side." Paper presented at the Wenner-Gren Foundation symposium, Critical Approaches in Archeology: Material Life, Meaning, and Power, Cascais, Portugal, March 17–25.

Lal, B. 2001. "A Note on the Excavations at Ayodhya with reference to the Mandir-Masjid Issue." In *Destruction and Conservation of Cultural Property,* edited by R. Layton, P. Stone, J. Thomas, 117–26. New York: Routledge.

Mehta, Ved. 1994. *Rajiv Gandhi and Rama's Kingdom.* New Haven: Yale University Press.

Meibar, Basheer. 1982. *Political Culture, Foreign Policy, and Conflict: the Palestine Area Conflict System.* Westport, Conn.: Greenwood.

Meskell, Lynn. 2002. "Negative Heritage and Past Mastering in Archaeology." *Anthropological Quarterly,* 557–74.

Mostafavi, Mohsen, and Leatherbarrow, David. 1993. *On Weathering: The Life of Buildings in Time.* Cambridge: MIT Press.

Perry, Marilyn, and Burnham, Bonnie. 2001. "A Critical Mission: the World Monuments Watch." In "World Monuments Watch: 100 Most Endangered Sites" *2002,* 3–4.

Philps, Alan. 2001. "The Day the Dream Died." *Telegraph,* February 3. Online edition.

Piccirillo, Michele, and Alliata, Eugenio, eds. 1999. "The Madaba Map Centenary, 1897–1997: Travelling through the Byzantine Umayyad Period." Proceedings of the international conference held in Amman, April 7–9, 1997.

Popper, Karl. 1963. *Conjectures and Refutations: The Growth of Scientific Knowledge.* London: Routledge & Kegan Paul.

Rao, N., and Reddy, R. 2001. "Ayodhya, The Print Media and Communalism." In *Destruction and Conservation of Cultural Property,* edited by R. Layton, P. Stone, J. Thomas, 139–56. New York: Routledge.

Rapoport, David, and Alexander, Yonah, eds. 1982. *The Morality of Terrorism: Religious and Secular Justifications.* New York: Pergamon.

———. 2001. "Robbing the Archaeological Cradle." *Natural History* 110: 44–54.

Said, Abdul Aziz. 2001. "How Islamic Are the Taliban?" *Philadelphia Inquirer,* March 11, AE7.

Schmidt, P., and Patterson, T., eds. 1995. *Making Alternative Histories: The Practice of Archaeology and History in Non-Western Settings.* Santa Fe, N.M.: School of American Research Press.

Shanks, Michael, and Tilley, Christopher. 1987. *Re-constructing Archaeology: Theory and Practice.* Cambridge: Cambridge University Press.

Sharma, R. 2001. "The Ayodhya Issue." In *Destruction and Conservation of Cultural Property,* edited by R. Layton, P. Stone, J. Thomas, 127–39. New York: Routledge.

Silberman, Neil Asher. 1982. *Digging for God and Country: Exploration, Archeology, and the Secret Struggle for the Holy Land.* New York: Knopf.

Simmel, Georg. 1968. *The Conflict in Modern Culture, and Other Essays.* Translated by K. Peter Etzkorn. New York: Teachers College Press.

Steen, Danielle. 2002. "Nation Building and Archaeological Narratives in the West Bank." *Stanford Journal of Archaeology* 1: 1–13.

Tambiah, Stanley. 1996. *Leveling Crowds: Ethnonationalist Conflicts and Collective Violence in South Asia.* Berkeley: University of California Press.

Tripath, Salil. 2002. "A Movement Aims to Bring the Buddhas Back." *Wall Street Journal,* February 21.

UNESCO. 2000. "Convention Concerning the Protection of the World Cultural and Natural Heritage, Paris, November 16, 1972." *US/ICOMOS Scientific Journal–International Cultural Heritage Conventions* 2: 19–36.

Wiengrod, Alex. 1993. "Shadow Games: Ethnic Conflict and Political Exchange in Israel." In *The Territorial Management of Ethnic Conflict,* edited by J. Coakley, 190–220. London: Frank Cass.

Woehrle, Lynne, and Coy, Patrick. 2000. "Introduction: Collective Identities and the Development of Conflict Analysis." In *Social Conflicts and Collective Identities,* edited by L. Woehrle and P. Coy, 1–15. Lanham, Md.: Rowman & Littlefield.

Wright, G. E. *Shechem: The Biography of a Biblical City.* New York: McGraw Hill.

Zerubavel, Yael. 1995. *Recovered Roots: Collective Memory and the Making of Israeli National Tradition.* Chicago: University of Chicago Press.

REPRESENTING THE PAST   V

Tourism, the Ideology of Design, and the Nationalized Past in Zippori/Sepphoris, an Israeli National Park

12

JOEL BAUMAN

Beyond its economic value as a tool for regional development, tourism is also an effective and direct means of explaining Israel's affairs.

GIDEON PATT (QUOTED IN ROMAN 1990, 3)

It is here, in the public space, that the deed of ownership of the land of Israel is inscribed and displayed. Practices of inscription and display of this kind have been going on since the beginning of the Zionist movement, by the settlement enterprise itself, on maps, through archaeological excavation, by planting trees and designing new landscapes, and by the obliteration of settlements, vistas, and names. [These practices] have always consisted of a whole economy of memory and forgetfulness.

ARIELLA AZOULAY (1993, 185)

Palestine is no more of this work-day world. It is sacred to Poetry and tradition—it is dream-land.

MARK TWAIN (1966, 442)

SITUATED ON A MAJESTIC HILLTOP in the Galilee, less than a mile northwest of Nazareth, Zippori, known in antiquity as Sepphoris, is a popular Israeli national park. The site occupies an important place in Jewish and Christian traditions. Containing physical remains from many historical epochs, Sepphoris is identified as the birthplace of Mary, and the home of her parents, Anne and Joachim. It was also the seat of the Jewish rabbinical court, the Sanhedrin, where

Rabbi Yehuda Hanassi, leader of the second-century A.D. Jewish community, codified the Jewish oral tradition into the Mishna. The national park is located inside Zippori, an Israeli moshav (agricultural cooperative settlement) that is, increasingly, a popular resort and bedroom community for nearby urban developments, such as Upper Nazareth. The park and moshav occupy an area that until 1948 was known as Saffouriye, a large Palestinian village whose former residents established one of the largest neighborhoods in nearby Nazareth. (Even in this brief description, one can sense how place-names in Israel are overtly political acts; see Cohen and Kliot 1992; Boyarin 1992; Khalidi 1992.)

Although archaeological excavations of Sepphoris were initiated by the University of Michigan in 1931, its popularity has grown since the late 1980s and particularly in the 1990s. Recent excavations have been led by teams from Duke University, the Hebrew University of Jerusalem, Tel Aviv University, the University of Washington, and the University of South Florida. Especially since the development of the site as a national park, the archaeology of Sepphoris has been featured widely in both popular and academic media and has produced a traveling exhibit. As the provincial capital of Roman era Galilee, Sepphoris has offered significant insight into the cultural milieu in which Jesus lived and where Christianity first developed. At the park, in addition to viewing an impressive array of mosaics, visitors can stroll through landscaped forests, descend into the aqueduct system, enter reconstructed (and air-conditioned) Roman villas, see virtual reality reconstructions and play educational games at computer stations, watch videos, and enjoy *Zippori/Sepphoris Live*, a living theater production (commissioned by Zippori National Park) re-creating daily life in Galilee during the third century A.D. The presentation of such overwhelming physical evidence of cohabitation by Jews, Romans/pagans, and early Christians suggests to visitors that the material, spiritual, and cultural wealth of the city resulted from such pluralistic traditions.

The following study examines the creation and operation of Zippori as a national park to illustrate the larger, and often fragmented and conflicted, process of constructing an Israeli heritage and vision of place. On-site observations were made between 1992 and 1995, with shorter follow-up visits through September 2000. Through extensive interviews, I describe the presuppositions and intentions of Israelis who design and manufacture such landscapes and sites of collective memory.

Clearly the development of heritage sites is related to broader currents in Israeli society. During the period of my study, historic peace accords were signed and Prime Minister Itzhak Rabin was assassinated. This was also the advent of the suicide bombing campaigns. Israel was trying to assimilate an influx of over a million immigrants from the former Soviet Republics and the economy underwent drastic changes as it moved from centralized control toward a more free market

economy. The intensification of consumerism and materialism is now a conspicuous marker of contemporary Israeli society (Melman 1992). This phase in Israeli history is also marked by escalated violence in the internal secular and
religious civil conflicts, as well as with the Palestinians in the occupied territories.
At the same time, agreements with Jordan and the Palestinian Authority have redefined and continue to realign ambiguous geopolitical boundaries.

After presenting conversations with the people responsible for planning and development in the Israel National Parks Authority (INPA), the primary organization
responsible for developing the important historical and natural sites in Israel, I will
also present observations about the responses of visitors to Zippori. The confused
policies of those organizations charged with creating an imagined national identity
through archaeological sites and national parks (in particular the INPA) are a symbol of the broader Israeli identity crisis. An ethnography of the development and
design of an Israeli national park illustrates how tourism exacerbates this crisis.

This chapter aims to document and understand some of the competing interests and memories associated with the site of Zippori/Sepphoris, to clarify the relationship between public history and national identity in Israel, and to explore
how different fields of power articulate with representations of the past and how
specific representations become dominant. As an example of a "contested monument" (Kuklick 1991) among several imagined communities (Anderson 1991),
the tenuous invention of territorial and historical legitimacy was, and continues
to be, available for examination at Zippori National Park.

Historical representations, particularly through archaeological remains, are
culturally central to modern nation-states (Popular Memory Group 1982; Hobsbawm 1990; Anderson 1991; Newcomb 1979). Following Wright (1985, 24), I
consider the "heritage industry" to be a collection of social practices that attempt
to conscript the past in service to the state and nation. In Israel this is a deeply
contentious and conflicted process. Ensuring a hegemonic relationship to the past
is particularly difficult in Israel because it is a society composed of settlers and
immigrants with disparate cultural heritages in addition to an already heteroge-
neous indigenous population. Identifying a shared heritage is a specific practice by
which certain groups in modern states attempt to construct and reconstruct national identities. In Israel, constituting an identity and a shared collective existence
through the heritage industry occurs between two separate poles: the struggle over
the exact historical and cultural content of the "Jewishness" of the Israeli state
and the struggle with the presence of Palestinians—within the borders of modern society as citizens and with the presence of their remains within the landscapes
of ruins and memories. These two dialogues are expressed in particularly explicit
terms in Israeli national parks, which are among the institutions where versions of
history and heritage are selected, institutionalized, displayed, and popularized.

After more than a hundred years of Zionist settlement and colonization, and fifty years of statehood, which attractions, which historic sites and landscapes are restored, and which are ignored? Which groups are celebrated and which are excluded? What do visitors actually do at the national parks? In other words, how are the ideologies of nationalism related to the tourism and heritage industries and vice versa? In studying the manufacture of a touristic heritage park, I hope to focus attention on professional ideologies of design and the vision of Israeli nationhood they attempt to communicate, and how these ideas might be received, interpreted, and used.

Tourism and the Israel National Parks Authority

During the past decade, Israel's per capita income from tourism ranked eleventh highest in the world. Whereas revenue from tourism in 1993 was an estimated $2.5 billion, it reached an apogee of approximately $4.3 billion in 2000 (Israel Bureau of Statistics 1993, 2000). The potential economic benefits of tourism were a consistent theme in the government's efforts to mobilize support for the peace process. In 1994–1995, a record 2 million foreign tourists visited Israel, and a record number of Israelis also vacationed within its borders. In fact, the year 1994–1995 was officially designated as the Tourism of Peace Year. More recently, tourism continues to be one of Israel's largest industries despite the collapse of foreign tourism following the advent of the al-Aqsa intifada in September 2000.

The tourism and heritage industries, and the national parks within them, are part of a larger constellation of knowledge building practices and identity making technologies. A national park is one of the sites where collective memory is socially produced and distributed. While it can be a site through which agents constitute themselves as subjects, a park is, at the same time, a specific technology of power through which state agencies attempt to "create, control, and classify citizens" (Ferguson and Gupta 1992, 11). Therefore, national parks play a role in the production and extension of changing and competing ideologies in Israeli society.

In response to the long-standing traditions of Christian European mass tourism, during the early stages of Zionist state formation, an alternative space for "internal tourism for local Jewish residents" was created (Katz 1985; Berkowitz 1997). The belief in Jewish settlement as a return from exile to the homeland was a dominant motif throughout much of modern Israeli history. As early as 1916, David Ben-Gurion and Y. Ben-Zvi conclude in their book *Eretz Israel in the Past and the Present*, "The denationalization of Eretz Israel resulted in a state of affairs where the country lay in ruins and desolation. And the land waits for the Jewish people to come and repair and restore its old home."

Established in 1953, the Department for the Improvement or Repair of the Landscape and Historical Sites institutionalized this ideological connection between the land, state building, and memory. It was founded by Teddy Kollek, at the time the director of Prime Minister Ben-Gurion's office and later longtime mayor of Jerusalem. Yigael Yadin, who became a preeminent archaeologist as the excavator of Masada, and who served as army general chief of staff and later the defense minister, was its first director. Its sense of mission is revealed in the thirty-year summary report: "historic sites in Israel have existed for thousands of years; beauty was here since the six days of creation; but *until statehood* they were unavailable and inaccessible" (Yanni 1988, 1, emphasis mine). Its mission was to make visible the Jewish homeland in Palestine. In 1963, the work of the department was further professionalized when it was reorganized as the Israel National Parks Authority (INPA). In 1998, the INPA was merged with the Israel Nature Reserves Authority to make a "stronger and more efficient entity" whose mission is mandated to "develop, protect and promote Israel's natural, historical, and recreational sites." Tellingly, one of the newest market segments is ecotourism, and the redemption motif is being repackaged to meet this current consumer demand by suggesting that Zionism equates to redemption of the environment.

The belief in Jewish settlement as a return and even liberation of the land allowed the inequalities among different Jewish ethnic and social groups to be denied, and the presence of Palestinians to be ignored and forgotten. In addition to making claims about Israeli Jewish identity and citizenship, Israeli national parks and heritage sites are a significant force among the multitude of practices and structures involved in the process of both physical and symbolic displacement of Palestinians in Israel: from actual physical expropriation of land, to symbolic conquest during walking hikes, to excavating under them and removing the layers of their history, to planting trees to obscure remains of their villages, towns, and history. Designed to make the Jewish homeland visible, souvenir markets, *tiyulim* or walking tours, and other, more concrete "mechanisms of landscape transformation" have continued to be a significant feature of Israeli culture (Raz-Krakotzkin 1993; Cohen and Kliot 1992; Bar-Gal 1993; Shenhav-Keller 1993, Boyarin 1992a; Falah 1991; Benvenisti 2000).

But Israeli society is not static. Policies once used to create an almost monolithic symbolic landscape no longer operate so freely. Not only do the political realities of the peace process create limitations and opportunities on the ground; the demands of foreign tourism and significant changes in the leisure practices of Israeli society created enormous pressure for a greater diversity of touristic experiences. Sightseeing or pedagogic tourism as a touristic experience has declined somewhat while the experience categorized as vacationing increased significantly. Vacationers are mainly interested in "good tourism services and varied recreational opportunities, such as sports facilities, restaurants, discotheques, festivals, cultural events, and shops" (Roman 1990, 103; Littman 1994; Katz 1992). Despite this intense market pressure, archaeological, historic, and nature sites appear to remain high national priorities. The result is a crisis in the management of the heritage industry and its role in negotiating between the foreign and the internal Israeli tourism spaces and desires.

This crisis in historical representation, and the privileging of leisure/tourism services over historical sites, reflect the fragmentation and decline of the dominant Zionist narrative, the emergence of new (middle) classes, the effects of the peace process on the physical and ideological boundaries of the state, and the strengthening of the position of Palestinian citizens of Israel (Weingrod 1993, 307; Azoulay 1993; Rabinowitz 1993). These fundamental social processes are reflected in the negotiated design and multiple interpretations of the cultural meanings of historically oriented national parks, and Zippori/Sepphoris in particular.

Throughout the 1990s, heritage industry professionals expressed their concern that the historical landscape of Israel was being deformed by the desires for and requirements of capital investment for the perceived increases in foreign tourism, especially related to the millennium (Maranz 1993). Archaeological development was also used as a solution for massive unemployment among recent Russian and Ethiopian immigrants (Yudelman 1994). Some heritage professionals contended that there was too little debate over which built environments and which histories and cultures were to be preserved and presented. Furthermore, the interests, philosophies, and practices of tourism specialists clash with those of archaeologists. "Designers are a seductive threat to archaeologists," warns Neil Silberman, a scholar and former Israel Antiquities Authority archaeologist (Maranz 1993, 27), "to have the historical landscape of Israel transformed into Disneyworld would be a tragic loss. Tourism threatens the role of archaeology in modern society."

The legislative mandate of the INPA is to provide for the educational and recreational needs of Israeli citizens by developing sites with historical, archaeological, natural, and national values. Because it depended on entrance fees for 95 percent of its budget, the INPA was not able to effectively develop new sites. However, in the wake of the 1992 elections, Prime Minister Rabin's government rerouted investment from settlements in the occupied territories, and made reducing unemployment and increasing tourism national priorities. Improvement of tourist sites and infrastructure was heavily funded as public works projects within green line Israel. As a result, the INPA development budget increased tenfold and precipitated a crisis. The INPA is mandated to preserve and develop the heritage sites important to the nation and people of Israel. However, the new funding, distributed by the Israel Government Tourism Company, was specifically earmarked for sites of interest and relevance to the burgeoning tourism industry. Hence, the INPA had to emphasize tourism services and experiences. This tension resulted in an ongoing negotiation over the design, development, and interpretation of these sites and their histories.

Zippori National Park: A Case Study

The preeminent product of this process is Zippori National Park. The park sits on a hilltop in the Galilee region northwest of Nazareth, an area of rolling hills that is verdant and filled with abundant olive groves, fruit orchards, and agricultural fields. Because of its rich and varied history, the spectacular natural setting, and the exceptional beauty and quantity of its excavated mosaics, Zippori was established in 1993 as a national park.

Zippori/Sepphoris contains within it artifacts and ruins ranging in time from the second century B.C. through the Roman and Byzantine periods, the early Arab periods, the Ottoman period, and up to the present. In Christian tradition it is recognized as the home of Joachim and Anne, the parents of Mary, mother of Jesus. A historic Catholic monastery commemorates them. A fortress built during the Crusader period still dominates the hill. It was from here that the Crusader knights set out to battle with Salah ah Din at the Battle of Hittin in 1187. Saffouriye, the Arab village on this site, retained the name of the Crusaders, le Saphorie. In the eighteenth century, Safouriye was one of the strongholds of the local potentate Zahir al-Umar al-Zaydani. During the later Ottoman period, the fortress building was transformed into a school for girls of the village known as Saffouriye. The only mention of the Palestinian village is a short paragraph in the informational brochure that reads:

> During the Arab revolt (1936–39) and the War of Independence, Safouriye became the center of Arab guerrilla gangs fighting against the surrounding Jewish villages. The guerrilla fighters used the castle as their headquarters and their commander, Mahmud Saffouri, controlled the entire region, until it was conquered in the Dekel campaign. Moshav Zippori was founded in 1949.

Moshav Zippori "renews the ancient Hebrew name of the place."

The park particularly celebrates the Roman/Classical period. During the Roman period, Zippori was one of the centers of the Sanhedrin, the governing body and tribunal of the Jewish nation after the destruction of the Temple in 70 A.D. It is the site where, during the second century A.D., one of the most important sages, Rabbi Yehuda Hanassi, compiled and codified the Mishna, the Jewish oral tradition.

On a typical tour, visitors walk the streets of the excavated market complex, descend into the aqueduct, and climb to the top of the Ottoman era (but labeled as Crusader era) fortress to enjoy the spectacular view. They then enter the recon-structed Roman villa to see its striking and unique mosaic floor. It depicts a typ-ical Roman scene, a Dionysian bacchanal, but is crowned with a unique portrait of a woman. This mosaic has become renowned as the Mona Lisa of the Galilee.

Visitors then follow a path through a pleasant and appealing cactus garden, where on the left is a sign that reads Moslem Cemetery. The park's strategically planted pine forest, however, prevents many visitors from noticing that they are walking among the remains of the Muslim Palestinian town of Saffouriye, once one of the largest towns in the entire Galilee. Saffouriye ceased to exist physically as a Palestinian village when Israeli forces forcefully expelled families who did not flee. A significant percentage of the original inhabitants founded and settled a neighborhood of nearby Nazareth. From this neighborhood, the hilltop site of Zippori/Sepphoris/Saffouriye is clearly visible.

After 1949, this area became an Israeli moshav. What we are not told in any brochure is that immigrants from Bulgaria, Romania, and Turkey were pressured to settle there. This moshav's history, the struggles of the settlers to make ends meet despite protracted economic crises, like the history of Saffouriye, is not pre-sented at the national park.

In trying to erase Saffouriye and ignore the unsuccessful moshav, the develop-ment of Zippori National Park illuminates the larger process of constructing an Israeli national heritage. Like many sites in Israel, Zippori contains physical re-mains that represent many significant periods of history. Therefore, the selection of what to represent should give clues to imperatives of what certain social groups feel is important to a sense of identity and history. Analyzing the development of this site clarifies why certain choices are made and how some historic events and people are excluded and why.

To explore the assumptions and presuppositions held by the professionals in-volved in historic preservation and restoration, I interviewed archaeologists, archi-tects, curators, managers, and exhibit designers (the names below are pseudonyms). These discussions illuminate the models and values that are used in actualizing specific visions of the past and help to reveal the institutional context of historic preservation and heritage planning in Israel. I will then provide an as-sessment of the site interpretation, explain what the message is supposed to be, and present preliminary evaluations of how the visitors perceived the site.

"I Am the Public": Social Distinctions and the Ideology of Design

Sarah Hagan, a young Israeli woman in her late thirties, is responsible for the de-sign of new national parks and the expansion and reinterpretation of established parks. Although educated and trained as a landscape architect, she is, in effect, not only the chief architect but also the primary strategic planner for the INPA. Her description of the development and design process makes clear distinctions between recreational parks and archaeological sites and the kinds of people for whom they are appropriate. Recreation parks are seen as serving the needs of ethnic classes, usually lower and less educated, and not deemed to be interested in history and culture. Proper use of parks is enforced through fencing off large areas and collecting an entrance fee. Until recently, use of parks by these groups for picnic and grilling activities was deemed incompatible with the contemplation of the historical remains of the site. For archaeological parks, Sarah believes that decisions on what to exhibit, to restore or ignore, are made objectively and scientifically, based on the material revealed through archaeology. There is no agenda to portray a certain historical or cultural representation of Israel, Jewish or otherwise, she claims. She is convinced that at national parks there are no explicit or implicit messages other than "this is what the ground here has seen. This is what happened on this ground."

Regarding archaeological parks, she admits, however, that the Parks Authority wants to emphasize and to familiarize the public with certain things that are "important to us":

> In regards to archaeological parks, we want to emphasize and to familiarize the public with things that are important to us. But to us is not something other than different than the public, because when I try to judge what's important, *I am myself the Public* . . . and through whose eyes I look during a committee meeting. When I ask what will we exhibit to the public, I am none other than the public. I don't differ from the public/audience. Especially, because I didn't have a background in the historical or archaeological sciences. (Emphasis mine)

She then offers Zippori as an example.

> At Zippori, it might have happened that the excavators would've decided that what was most important to show at Zippori is just the structures of the Jewish quarter just to show the Jewish period. And would not even deal with the Roman Byzantine period. And one can say that the Jewish period is not the most interesting to the public because the remains are not attractive; the craftsmanship was poor. But that's not the situation. There is no way that the archaeologists and certainly not us, the development people, are disconnected from the types of things that will captivate the public. One of the first questions in developing a site is, What is its quality through the lenses of the visitor?

At one point, her self-described lack of formal archaeological training allows Sarah to consider herself part of the general public. Her authority for planning

history is derived from being of the public, from a shared deficiency of disciplinary knowledge. Her authority to design historical scenes is derived from a knowledge of certain aesthetic judgments that allows her to make decisions in the name
of the public, which will then be captivated.

When I ask about her distinction between recreational and historic parks, she
appears to recognize that there is a problem in furnishing strictly historic sites for
public consumption. She is very anxious to include "some green, a river . . . things
that will soften or ameliorate the visit, help the mostly urban-based visitors recre-
ate and recover from the mass amounts of dry information at antiquities sites."
There was resistance to this design philosophy because the story, the history of a
site, is recognized as its highlight and developers are not allowed to incorporate
recreational features to lessen the force of facts. Sarah, however, is intent on incorporating more recreational features into historic sites because usually there is "so
much to see and take in at once, that you really need a break." Despite her conviction that they know what the public wants (it wants historic parks, and a particular kind of history at that), Sarah acknowledges that it might be too boring.
Perhaps this is evidence that the information offered for the "education of con-
sent" may not be compelling enough. This is recognition of how intensive and
heavy handed the attempt of the state is to produce and convey specific messages.
The INPA believes there is a decline in site use, and that Israelis only visit sites
once, perhaps as school trips, during one of the educational trips with the army, or
with their families. Then there is nothing left to see. Few sites are continuously excavated and most have no active interpretation. This suggests a failure of the past
to endear the public to these sites. It suggests, furthermore, that the INPA may actually be disconnected from broad sections of the public, particularly groups who
are not of the same socioeconomic categories as the professionals in the INPA.

According to Sarah, her responsibility is to

> give people an opportunity to come into contact with the culture of this country
> (ha'aretz hazo). Not just the stories that happened in the land of Israel (ha'aretz) but
> also what is the background, the environment in which they happened. This is a
> new approach. A hurried visitor may not get it, but we, as planners, need to pre-
> sent it to complete the picture.
>
> In exhibiting we try to show all the spectrum of life, but there are places where
> we have to choose . . . Hellenistic, Roman, Ottoman. . . . What we choose to ex-
> hibit is according to *what's most dramatic, or what is more complete*. Sometimes we exhibit
> what's not complete and on this the archaeologists have major input, but they un-
> derstand what to exhibit. We are partners. (Emphasis added)

Although the narrative interpretation of the site is left to the education department, Sarah believes that the message of the site can be obtained through the

architecture and the landscape experience. She perceives decisions on what is exhibited or ignored are made impartially and are based on the material available. She reveals this in her evaluation of whether or not there are any explicit or implicit messages at national parks:

> I don't think that someone who comes to [our parks] gets a message "*This* is Israel." The opposite, because we have so many historical archaeological sites maybe one gets the message "*all this* is Israel" (*zot hi Yisrael*), but not of Israel today, but in the sense of history: Crusaders, Romans, pagans. . . . This ground (*adama*) has seen so much, I would say that the message is maybe, This is what the ground here has seen. This is what happened on this ground.

Sarah presents the territory of the Israeli state as an envelope or container of historical events. The way this container has been made through agencies like the INPA (or colonial history, wars, and occupation) is, of course, obscured. Sarah avoids use of the loaded phrase Eretz Israel (Land of Israel) in its political Zionist connotation to discuss the INPA. She creates a new vocabulary substituting the more disinterested sounding "ground" (*adama* or *ha'aretz*) which is more ambiguous, less loaded as a term. She, and perhaps the visitor, is convinced of the neutrality of the state's representations and practices. While Sarah recognizes that perhaps some implied interpretation may take place, where someone might insist that 'this [land] is ours," she considers this "only an unrepresentative extreme."

She continues explaining her mission in designing heritage sites: "'I live here, and I want to see everything that happened on this ground and to show it to my children, the story of this place.' I think that it's important that people know what happened in the surroundings in which they live today. . . But not in the sense of 'this is ours. This is Israeli' like the fans with the yellow scarves of [the soccer team] Betar Jerusalem. Not in this context, but in the context of 'the game of soccer.'"

Sarah attributes nationalistic interpretations and uses of national parks to the same people who are fans of the popular Betar Jerusalem soccer team. This is an explicit marker of class and ethnic divisions in Israel. These are the same disinterested or hurried groups the INPA believes are not interested in their historic parks, and for whom recreational parks are developed. That one should be cultured to appreciate historic sites like Zippori is communicated through such practices as naming the Dionysus mosaic Mona Lisa. This connotes high culture and secularism. The institutionalization of distinctive tourism practices and spaces, whereby national heritage is segregated into cultural and recreational segments, suggests the class-based predisposition of designers to imagine appropriate citizens/customers for whom a certain form of national heritage is produced.

Despite the above distinctions, Sarah is convinced of the pluralistic character of Israel and of INPA decision making. Sarah is convinced that the state is representing "history as is." The relationship of Israel to the past is transparent and available to be seen by everyone. As an Israeli, she wants to know everything that happened here. This image of modern Israeli identity is being projected on an ancient national history that is made to appear pluralistic and somehow multicultural.

National Parks and Jewish Redemption

In 1993 I met frequently with Leonard Levine, an American-born-and-trained architect in his mid-fifties, who designed many of the largest restoration projects in the national parks. At Zippori, he created the Roman villa that houses the Mona Lisa mosaic. The "villa" is actually a cement and stucco structure that protects the mosaic floors—essentially a museum gallery building. It was designed both to be "reminiscent" of the original Roman villa built on the original foundation and to resemble an incomplete ruin, despite being a thoroughly modern, air-conditioned building.

Leonard affirmed some of the same assumptions as Sarah. Despite Sarah's very clear view of INPA goals and vision in planning, Leonard appears to be as mystified by the process as he is about what the message is supposed to be. During one meeting in his office he was working on something and moving nervously from table to table and from design to design. His ruminations were almost stream of consciousness. His description of the decision-making process is as illuminating in its noninformation as it is entertaining:

> The entire decision-making apparatus and the entire design was based on some guy who woke up in the morning and fell off the bed on left side instead of the right side and ran into an interplanetary, uh, uh, uh, meteorite that crashed through the ceiling and that was the motivating factor for design work. Are you familiar with the stories Kurt Vonnegut writes? Well, in my opinion, here, design decisions are made by some bizarre force clearly irrelevant to what's really happening or necessary.

This from an educated professional architect who has been working in the field for decades and knows all the people involved. He believes reflexivity is totally lacking regarding what an antiquities site is or should be. What is presented there is an innate reality and logic to excavations; as if they are not products of the assumptions and interpretations of archaeologists and the agencies that fund them.

In deciding how to develop a site, he explains, "You're receiving whatever history has bequeathed to you." Again, authority is granted by the remains with no prefigured outcome. Like Sarah, he acknowledges that the most impressive items in any one site may not be Jewish and thus the INPA, he affirms, is not interested in developing Jewish sites per se. To prove this, he lists a range of sites with which he has been involved. He describes at length all the Jewish attributes of several sites that are not being developed. "Jewish here means that national and cultural content, not necessarily the religious content," he clarifies. He concedes that perhaps the Jewish factor was heightened in sites on the Golan Heights (Syrian territory occupied by Israel since 1967). These sites were not developed in a sentimental search for Jewish roots, but are a result of hard-nosed politics as tactical moves for negotiations with Syria.

For Zippori, he explains that it could be developed into a site with significant Talmudic connections, "yet what are we doing?" he exclaims, "developing the mosaic floors that have nothing to do with the whole story. The Jewish section of site is no interest to anyone. The Middle Ages building is used for the view. There are picnic areas, but there is no Jewish identity. No Jewish angle."

Leonard notes that sites are aimed at foreign tourists and the projects provide employment, particularly to the recent wave of immigrants from the former Soviet Union. This is a determining factor in choosing which site to develop.

> Lately enormous amounts of money have been made available for development of tourist sites, particularly in the last three years. Because of the Russian immigration. The easiest way to find employment for them is to create public works, and the most obvious public works are archaeological excavations, large-scale excavations.

In addition to being a resource for symbols of collective identity and a reason for being in this land, developing national parks are apparently practical solutions for feeding as well as educating the new citizens and new working classes.

In deciding which sites to develop for this purpose, Leonard continues,

> There is no straightforward relationship between the projects that are chosen and their importance, but that they provide immediate employment. They put people to work. Now, that's very Jewish, if you want to talk about Jewish. They're not interested in the Arab sector at all. Ha! That's very clear. Replace Arab workers with Russian workers. Employment for Jews. It's a Jewish country.

Leonard concludes his thoughts by stating unequivocally, "I really can't see a consistent pattern in site selection."

And that, perhaps, is the pattern—to obscure and conceal the selective nature of these sites. The state remains a neutral party responsible for developing these naturally and logically occurring sites with no ideological weight. It also suggests to me a lack of culpability. The ad hoc process of decision making and the fact that what is presented is only what is available through excavations allow these people to deny any ulterior motives for exhibiting specific stories. Their authority derives from the ground itself, not the state.

According to Leonard, the history and landscape of Israel are being designed and produced primarily because of an awareness of the potential capital investment by foreign visitors, political brinkmanship, particularly in the Golan, and as a solution to the massive unemployment, particularly among the new, mostly Russian immigrants.

Israel continues to be a site of an ongoing and increasingly violent struggle to define the cultural content, the sets of meaningful and worthwhile guidelines for people's lives as citizens of the nation. One of the most contentious issues is the combination of territory and religion. It is not surprising then that the state might now attempt to produce sites that, even if they include a high religious content, like Zippori, may be interpreted as nationalistic yet tolerant, where religious extremism gave way to pragmatic political decisions in order to survive.

After a hiatus of several months, I again met with Leonard. The first thing he said was, "I've been doing a little checking since we talked. My friends tell me I'm wrong. *I guess there is an emphasis on things Jewish*" (emphasis added). Belatedly realizing the emphasis on things Jewish, Leonard illustrates how the nature of this Jewishness, a perpetually contested identity, appears to be undergoing significant transformation. The contested nature of this identity is clearly evident at the end of our discussion. After describing the large amounts of funding available for the development of sites with impressive architectural remains "but with very little Jewish content," he describes how he points out to people the contrast between the decadent, depraved Romans and the morally upstanding Jews of the time.

The following excerpt appears as an allegory. It recapitulates the master narrative of Jewish redemption of the land. It helps explain why the state, the Jewish nation, is spending many millions on these "non-Jewish" sites. However grand and complex they are, it is due to the perseverance of the Jewish people, and their restoration to the land, that allows them to now lay claim to their grandeur by a sort of sympathetic history. This kind of site symbolizes a secular state at the same time as it symbolizes the triumph of Jewish history.

Leonard explains,

> and here's the irony, that all of the cultural content that stood behind all these magnificent buildings disappeared and is gone. And is wiped out forever. All we have is the empty shell, like a seashell where the creature has died. And yet here *we* are! The Jews who, we, our, foundations although they were not physical, like this, were actually much stronger and enabled the Jewish people to survive. *And now here we are!* Actually using these buildings, sort of come back down out of the hills to

take possession from them, you know, from the . . . you know, that sort of thing is very interesting to me.

This astonishing statement conveys his sense of feeling part of a collective national redemption, allowing Leonard, via a moral authority, to lay claim to the material remains of another past and from an unnamed people.

This educated professional experiences an intersubjective identity, which he tries to communicate and perhaps to elicit through his design of historic sites. Through these heritage sites, the Jews of two thousand years ago become us. A clear sense of identity in relation to specific narratives at specific places is produced. This, I believe, illustrates in an individual what Boyarin (1992a) suggests for an Israeli identity as primarily territorially grounded and only marginally spiritual. For Leonard, Jewish is not religious Judaism but a cultural and moral content of identity. That cultural or moral content, furthermore, is being expressed or practiced through landscapes and objects. Neither of the two planners is willing to concede any overt attempts to produce specifically Jewish national sites. Their work is presented as a neutral historical presentation engineered to represent interesting, dramatic, and impressive history. The INPA is attempting to overtly produce sites representative of a cosmopolitan message that is seen to be a product of a value-free neutral scientific process. This theme is overlaid on supposedly neutral remains. On the other hand, that these sites can be manipulated and rendered interesting to different visiting groups, whether Israelis or tourists, is ignored. Sarah did not express a sense of Jewish revenge, only of presenting what happened. Although only interested in what is interesting, dramatic, or impressive, this is deemed so, because we are here to resuscitate it and we are a certain group creating a certain sense of belonging.

Sarah claims to create sites through presenting excavated materials without embellishment, but she invests them with class distinctions. Leonard, also working with available remains, tries to invest them with a sense of Jewish redemption. Leonard expresses a strong feeling of inclusion and participation in a national redemption that allows him, via a moral authority, to lay claim to the material remains of another past. Sarah and Leonard personify individual negotiations of the discourse, the practice, and the process of Israeli, Jewish identities becoming grounded in the territory of the state of Israel, rather than in the cultures of Diaspora Judaism (Boyarin 1992b; Paine 1992).

Another Zippori

Joseph Hoshia, a thirty-six-year-old recent immigrant from the United States who lives in a nearby modern-orthodox, religious settlement, is the on-site project manager contracted by the INPA. Interestingly, he also heads a private fund-raising organization for the development of the Galilee. Because he is responsible for the management of daily operations he has great responsibility for site interpretation and interacts extensively with Sarah and Leonard. He expresses yet another philosophy of developing historic sites.

While Sarah attempts to create sites by strictly presenting only available remains and Leonard, while also stressing available remains, tries to invest them with a sense of Jewish redemption, for Joseph the site is a medium to be created through which a meaningful message is transmitted. His philosophy of historic restoration is that regardless of the relative abundance or lack of physical remains, their presence or absence can be overcome by presenting a vision or story that overtly speaks to the material and spiritual condition of people today.

He insists that the fundamental message conveyed through the park is that two cultures (Jewish and non-Jewish, secular and orthodox) coexisted in an atmosphere of tolerance, and that while extremists and zealots revolted and brought about the destruction of their country, the enlightened people of Sepphoris lived in peace with the Romans. In Joseph's eyes, the people here "laid the foundation to answer the question of how are Jews going to survive. Rabbi Hanassi will be presented as a political genius, as opposed to the Zealots over at Masada and Gamla who chose death over letting Torah survive."

While the INPA markets the mosaics as the symbol of Zippori (and of national and secular state history) through its advertising, souvenirs, and presentation of finds, for Joseph the symbol of the park is Yehuda Hanassi. Hanassi was the president of the Sanhedrin, of the Jewish community that campaigned against fighting the Romans. "Mosaics and columns are nice, but so what? The history of people is in the context and the content. These may be only stories without material remains, but we present them in their physical context." This he sees as being doubly powerful. Regardless of the physical remains, "the soul of Zippori National Park are the stories of what happened."

Joseph intends to convey this message via a comprehensive educational program designed to enrich the experience of the visitor. This means a highly mobilized recruitment of school-age groups to visit, providing guides during weekends to interpret the site to the general public. During holidays this is expanded to living history theatrical demonstrations replete with Hebrew- and English-speaking, period-dressed actors revivifying the Zippori of Talmudic times.

Tourists, the Past, and the Hegemony of the Jewish Present

Most often, the reconstruction of ancient Zippori celebrates a liberal and open city where "non-Jews of all classes lived in the various quarters. And where there

were synagogues and markets, sages, simple folk, city councilors, pagans, kabbal-
ists, Jewish-Christians, heretics, old established families and new immigrants from
the Diaspora" (Hershman 1989, 14). The central feature of the site, a Roman
villa with pagan mosaic and beautiful likeness of a woman, is presented as having
belonged to "an affluent Jew with a liberal outlook" (Hershman 1989, 14). This
interpretation tells us much about the issues and images in and of Israeli society
at the time, which continue today. The pluralistic ideology is being legitimized by
being grounded in Israeli history and territory at places like Zippori, and expresses
the ongoing definition of the cultural content of Israeliness and Jewishness. For
all its attack on Zionist hegemony, advocates of this new ideology do not acknowledge the role of the Jewish peasants whose taxes provided basis for the
wealth of Zippori (Maranz 1993, 18), and they refrain from acknowledging the
memories of the Palestinians, the Saffouriyen villagers who lived on the site until
1948.

Based on interviews conducted at Zippori National Park, it appears the responses of Israeli visitors more or less emulate the expectations and suppositions
of the INPA planners. Asked to rate the most important aspects of the site, visitors overwhelmingly chose the specifically non-Jewish features of the site: the mosaics, the Roman villa, and the Ottoman fortress, respectively. However, when
commenting about what they learned at the site, a majority included some variation of "we learned of a new Jewish City"; "we learned that Zippori was a large
Jewish settlement with a mixed population"; "we learned of the importance of the
place in Jewish history."

These seemingly contradictory interpretations reflect the continued dominance of one of Zionism's root narratives: "A way to be Jewish without having to
have Judaism provide the *content* of Jewishness, while paradoxically invoking history, descent, and heritage as the bases of its legitimacy" (Dominguez 1990, 87).

Those items with the least Jewish but "high culture" features were rated highest, thereby allowing them to be appropriated as Israeli in a context of an important Jewish place. Visitors can feel closer to the history and the Land without
identifying with religious Judaism. Asked if being at Zippori made the visitor feel
a stronger bond to Judaism, one respondent actually crossed out the word Judaism,
wrote in "history of Eretz Yisrael" (Land of Israel) and then proceeded to agree
strongly. Indicating a powerful Zionistic process of "territorial socialization" (Bar-
Gal 1993, 422), the sensation that they have discovered a new and Jewish city, and
thereby feel closer to the land suggests that Israeli visitors, and some foreign Jewish
tourists, are inscribing the site with secular and nationalist Jewish associations.

However, there were also oppositional or contrarian readings of the site. Some
complained they "learned more about Romans and Greeks than about Jews" and felt
no identification with the site. At least two respondents felt that Zippori provided a

particularly bad message of capitulation. One of them compared the people of Zippori to the present day Peace Now movement. Additionally, a modern-orthodox group's leader said that they were disgusted by the pagan mosaic and would not view it. This, despite the park's interpretation of the mosaic as that of the wealthy and pluralistic Rabbi Yehuda Hanassi.

When this interpretation is related to social groups, hegemony does not seem to extend itself to visitor identifications with a united Israeli collective. Visitors were asked to identify which social groups they thought would benefit the most by visiting the site. The top three groups selected were, respectively, new immigrants, Jewish tourists from abroad, and secular Israelis. The groups for whom a visit to the site was thought to be least beneficial were non-Jewish tourists, Orthodox Jewish Israelis, and, last, Arabs (meaning Palestinian citizens of Israel). One particularly outspoken respondent indicated Arabs as the first and most important group to bring to this site, "so they can be shown that it's ours and not theirs." Such responses reveal the fractures and tensions latent in the nature of Jewish Israeli citizenship and its relationship to Palestinian citizens of Israel.

The Palestinian Presence:
"A discomfort . . . a little bit . . ."

To the designers and archaeologists of Israeli parks, the Palestinian issue occurs at a different level of discourse and experience than the Israeli question of Jewish identity. The dialogue with this other interlocutor about the existential condition of who really is local and native to this land takes place on the level of the visible landscape.

The presentation of history at Zippori is not detailed at all beyond the Roman and Byzantine periods. Perhaps the Crusader period is mentioned but the whole modern history of the site is silenced and ignored. How is this gap in historical continuity obtained? Who is aware of this gap, of this empty yet very dense history?

In observing and traversing the land(scape) they live in, Israelis confront the existence of the Palestinian people and of the ruins of their existence. If, as Sarah believes, all available evidence is presented as it exists, how are the remains that convey the confusion and reality of the "multivocality" and "multilocality" (Rodman 1992) of the land, dealt with? How do planners and visitors get ideologically, and physically, around the Palestinian presence? At Zippori, I once observed a particularly conscientious guide, just before descending into the Cactus Garden and field of rubble, tell her group that the town of Saffouriye had existed here. What had been a fairly lively group suddenly grew silent. There was a collective shuffling of feet, and then, without any more questions or comments, the group moved on. What makes it possible to decide that a comment about the hostility of the Saffouriyens to the Zionists, a sign for the Muslim cemetery, and piles of rubble are sufficient as the proper references to local and Palestinian history? What is the meaning of the collective shuffling of feet? Clearly the development and interpretation of this heritage site in Israel continues to preserve a certain distribution of power (Khalidi 1992; Baram 2002).

I asked Leonard about the relationship of Zippori to the town of Nazareth and if there is any reason for the Arab residents to visit Zippori.

> Well, yes. The building we're restoring now used to be the elementary school of the Arab village that was destroyed in 1948. And there's a lot of Arabs that come there you can just tell, I can't understand the language, but you get these old folks who are obviously telling their grandchildren "they went to school there and before the Jews came and tore the place down, this is the place we used to live."
>
> It's really a kind of a very ambivalent reason for a lot of Arabs to come and visit the place now. And uh, uh, they have a picnic area, they [INPA] put up this picnic area, a lot of discussion occurred as to whether to put this picnic area within the fence, where you have to pay money, or outside the fence, where you don't have to pay money. And the reasoning was if we didn't put it beyond the fence where you had to pay money, then the Arabs will have picnics there, and they'll be there all the time, the Arabs from Nazareth.
>
> And it was, ah, it was a discussion, there were some people that said in the discussion I heard "I mean, what the hell do you want?! I mean they live there too, this area is for the public, they're part of the public." There were other people who said, "yeah, but it's not good for the site."

He continues: "It wasn't something that there was a consensus on, on the other hand there was an obvious . . . a discomfort . . . a little bit. This site was not for the Arabs. It was for the Jews and the tourists. Tourists maybe first of all and Jews maybe second of all."

The allegory of Leonard's triumph of Jewish morality as giving license to reconstruct Roman remains can be transposed to the military authority of the conquering Israelis to deconstruct the remains of the Palestinians.

Keeping in mind the earlier remonstrations that they use only what's given by the ground, the following excerpt from an interview with the chief Israeli archaeologist at Zippori is as disorienting and revealing as it is disheartening. I asked about the relationship of the park to Nazareth and to try to verify the location of the village. After asking if there were any plans to refer to it, the answer was (and was not) surprising. "Look, this is a problematic question. A difficult question because the village is destroyed and it doesn't actually exist. There are only ruins."

> It was destroyed; it started during the war but ended later. But it's destroyed it doesn't exist. Look, in ancient history it has no meaning it's not important. In

modern history it's a political issue, one of interpretation. In ancient history there was no Zippori on the map as an historical Arab settlement. Thus, naturally, there is no such development, but if there were to be some drastic political change and suddenly Arabs also will want to show their roots, and the state of Israel will decide that in every place where an Arab village stood, will be built a monument. I don't see this happening, but in purely theoretically speaking, then it might happen. But there is no interest in doing so, in the INPA or the government—this is too much. We have enough problems without this. Without going to this, you understand?

"So it doesn't appear to me to be an issue," and he concludes, "I certainly don't think that we need to bring up this problem."

The existence of Palestinian ruins and people within the social and imagined landscapes of Israeli identity and citizenship is a problem for the Israeli Zionist state. Zippori's seemingly progressive message of pluralism, where secular and orthodox/fundamentalist can live together, is belied because this dialogue is internal to Jewish Israeli discourse and refers to relations with foreign and secular groups. Palestinians are still excluded. In fact, Zippori the park continues the process of destroying the village by excluding its citizens from the picnic area. Indeed, in 1993, the park hosted a celebration of the forty-fifth anniversary of the "liberation" of Zippori. It is a continuing history of expropriation that is inscribed onto the landscape. That this remains an important problem to the Saffouriyens is evidenced by the riots throughout the Galilee and around Zippori during Land Day in 1997 and the violent outbreaks in Nazareth led by the Saffouriyen neighborhoods in 2000 (Arnold 2000). During the al-Aqsa intifada, to date, at least twelve Israeli Palestinians have been killed in Nazareth.

The development and design of Israeli national parks illustrates that not all citizens have equal access to the means of commemoration and that communities of interest control commemorative practices (Simon 1993, 86). The discourses and practices of the heritage industry partake of some basic cultural and social processes in Israel; the most conspicuous being the struggle between religious and secular Jewish citizens, between market economy reformers and socialist and welfare state adherents, and between histories of Palestinian and Jewish citizens of Israel. The making of a heritage site, Zippori for example, suggests that although wedded to state power, modern Jewish nationalism is conflicted and in crisis, both influencing and being influenced by the competing tendencies of tourism and other identity-making practices. Despite the emergence of a new ideology of pluralism, a market-oriented economy, and new middle classes, the Zionist ideology (of the return and redemption of the land, the unification of Jewish difference, and the correlated denial of Palestinian rights) continues to be used by certain groups to dominate the memories, spaces, and identities of others.

The interpretations of archaeological sites are more than mere narrative practices. In addition to entering the field of ideological and physical struggle over collective memories, the way such sites are designed, accessed, and used also reinforces the "spatial legitimization of class difference" (Munt 1994, 19; Harvey 1996). The development of Zippori/Sepphoris National Park illustrates how cultural and historical identities become embedded in specific places through practices that are political and economic as well as semiotic and discursive.

Acknowledgments

I am indebted to Jonathan Boyarin who provided the inspiration for this work, particularly in Boyarin 1992a, where he seeks to sketch "the possible receptions of ruins or traces of Palestinian life in Contemporary Israel," and the grant support of the Lady Davis Foundation and the National Foundation for Jewish Culture. Finally, this chapter would not be possible without the friendly and consistent encouragement of Yorke Rowan and without the ardent and unwavering support of Uzi Baram.

References

Anderson, Benedict. 1991. *Imagined Communities.* London: Verso.

Anderson, Kay, and Fay Gale, eds. 1992. *Inventing Places: Studies in Cultural Geography.* Melbourne: Longman Cheshire.

Arnold, Shimon. 2000. "Fear and Loathing in the Galilee." *Jerusalem Post,* November 13, A1.

Aronoff, Myron J. 1986. *The Frailty of Authority.* New Brunswick, N.J.: Transaction.

Azoulay, Ariella. 1993. "With Open Doors: Museums of History and the Israeli Public Space." *Theory and Criticism: An Israeli Forum* 2(4): 182–83. Jerusalem: Van Leer Institute.

Baram, Uzi. 2002. "The Development of Historical Archaeology in Israel: An Overview and Prospects." *Historical Archaeology* 36(4): 12–29.

Bar-Gal, Yehoshua. 1993. "Boundaries as a Topic in Geographic Education: The Case of Israel." *Political Geography* 12(5): 421–35.

Ben-Ari, Eliyahu, and Yoram Bilu, eds. 1997. *Grasping Land: Space and Place in Contemporary Israeli Discourse and Experience.* Albany: SUNY Press.

Ben-Gurion, David, and Itzhak Ben-Zvi. [1916] 1979. *Eretz Israel in the Past and in the Present.* Translated by David Niv. Jerusalem: Yad Yitshak Ben-Tsevi Institute.

Benvenisti, Meron. 2000. *Sacred Landscape.* Berkeley: University of California Press.

Berkowitz, Michael. 1997. *Western Jewry and the Zionist Project, 1914–1933.* Cambridge: Cambridge University Press.

Bishara, Azmi. 1992. "Between Place and Space." *Studio* 37: 6–10. In Hebrew.

Bommes, Michael, and Patrick Wright. 1982. "Charms of Residence: The Public and the Past." In *Making Histories: Studies in History Writing and Politics,* edited by R. Johnson, G. Mclennan, B. Schwarz, D. Sutton, 251–302. Minneapolis: University of Minnesota Press.

Boyarin, Jonathan. 1992a. "Ruins, Mounting toward Jerusalem." *Studio* 37: 10–12. In Hebrew.

———. 1992b. *Storm from Paradise: The Politics of Jewish Memory*. Minneapolis: University of Minnesota Press.

Bourdieu, Pierre. 1984. *Distinction: A Social Critique of the Judgment of Taste*. Translated by Richard Nice. Cambridge: Harvard University Press.

Brow, James. 1990. "Notes on Community, Hegemony, and Uses of the Past." *Anthropological Quarterly* 63(1): 1–6.

Brunner, E., and P. Gorfain. 1984. "Dialogic Narration and the Paradoxes of Masada." In *Text, Play, and Story*, edited by E. Brunner, 57–79. Washington, D.C.: American Ethnological Association.

Cohen, S. B., and N. Kliot. 1992. "Place Names in Israel's Ideological Struggle over the Administered Territories." *Annals of the Association of American Geographers* 82(4): 652–80.

Dominguez, Virginia. 1989. *People as Subject, People as Object: Selfhood and Peoplehood in Contemporary Israel*. Madison: University of Wisconsin Press.

———. 1990. "The Politics of Heritage." In *Nationalist Ideologies and the Production of National Cultures*, edited by R. G. Fox. Washington: American Anthropological Association.

Falah, G. 1991. "Israeli Judaization Policy in Galilee." *Journal of Palestine Studies* 20(4): 69–85.

Ferguson, J., and A. Gupta. 1992. "Space, Identity, and the Politics of Difference." *Cultural Anthropology* 7(1): 1–18.

Foster, R. J. 1991. "Making National Cultures in the Global Ecumene." *Annual Review of Anthropology* 20: 235–60.

Fox, Roger G., ed. 1990. *Nationalist Ideologies and the Production of National Cultures*. Washington: American Anthropological Association.

Friedman, Jonathan. 1992. "The Past in the Future: History and the Politics of Identity." *American Anthropologist* 94(4): 837–59.

Harvey, David. 1989. *The Condition Of Postmodernity: An Enquiry into the Origins Of Cultural Change*. Cambridge, Mass.: Blackwell.

———. 1996. *Justice, Nature, and the Geography of Difference*. Cambridge, Mass: Blackwell.

Hershman, Deborah. 1989. "An Epic Mosaic." *Eretz* 5(1): 14–18.

Hobsbawm, Eric J. 1990. *Nations and Nationalism since 1780: Programme, Myth, Reality*. New York: Cambridge University Press.

Hobsbawm, Eric J., and Terrence Ranger, eds. 1983. *The Invention of Tradition*. Cambridge: Cambridge University Press.

Johnson R., with G. Mclennan, B. Schwarz, D. Sutton, eds. 1982. *Making Histories: Studies in History Writing and Politics*. Minneapolis: University of Minnesota Press.

Katriel, Tamar. 1990. "Tower and Stockade: Dialogic Narration in Israeli Settlement Ethos." *Quarterly Journal of Speech* 76(4): 359–80.

———. 1997. "Remaking Place: Cultural Production in Israeli Pioneer Museums." In *Grasping Land: Space and Place in Contemporary Israeli Discourse and Experience*, edited by E. Ben-Ari and Yoram Bilu, 147–75. Albany: SUNY Press.

Katz, Elihu, et al. 1992. *Leisure in Israel, 1970–1990*. Jerusalem: Guttman Center for Applied Social Research. In Hebrew.

Katz, Saul. 1985. "The Israeli Teacher-Guide: The Emergence and Perpetuation of a Role." *Annals of Tourism Research* 22(12): 49–72.

Khalidi, Walid. 1992. *All That Remains.* Washington, D.C.: Institute for Palestine Studies.

Kimmerling, Baruch. 1992. "Sociology, Ideology and Nation Building: The Palestinians and Their Meaning in Israeli Society." *American Sociological Review* 57(4): 446–60.

Kuklick, Helga. 1991. "Contested Monuments: The Politics of Archaeology in Southern Africa." In *Colonial Situations: Essays on the Contextualization of Ethnographic Knowledge,* edited by G. Stocking, 135–69. Madison: University of Wisconsin Press.

Layton, Robert. 1989. *Who Needs the Past?* London: Unwin Hyman.

Liebman, C., and E. Don-Yehiya. 1983. *Civil Religion in Israel.* Berkeley: University of California Press.

Littman, L. 1994. "The New Israeli Leisure Industry." *New Aliyon* 15(1): 4–7.

Maranz, Felice. 1993. "Lost in the Ruins." *Jerusalem Report,* July 15, 16–18.

Melman, Yossi. 1992. *The New Israelis: An Intimate Portrait of a Changing People.* New York: Birch Lane.

Meyers, Eric, with Ehud Netzer and C. Meyers. 1992. *Sepphoris.* Winona Lake, Ind.: Eisenbrauns.

Munt, Ian. 1994. "The 'Other' Postmodern Tourism: Culture, Travel, and the New Middle Classes." *Theory, Culture & Society* 11: 101–23.

Nash, Denison. 1981. "Tourism as an Anthropological Subject." *Current Anthropology* 22(5): 461–81.

Newcomb, Robert M. 1979. *Planning the Past: Historical Landscape Resources and Recreation.* Kent, U.K.: Dawson Archon.

Nora, Pierre. 1989. "Between Memory and History: Les Lieux De Memoire." *Representations* 26: 7–25.

O'Brien, Jay, and William Roseberry, eds. 1991. *Golden Ages, Dark Ages: Imagining the Past in Anthropology and History.* Berkeley: University of California Press.

Paine, Robert. 1992. "Jewish Ontologies of Time and Political Legitimation in Israel." In *The Politics of Time,* edited by H. Rutz. American Ethnological Society Monograph, no. 4. Washington, D.C.: American Anthropological Society.

Popular Memory Group. 1982. "Popular Memory: Theory, Politics, Method." In *Making Histories: Studies in History Writing and Politics,* edited by R. Johnson, G. Mclennan, B. Schwarz, D. Sutton, 205–51. Minneapolis: University of Minnesota Press.

Rabinowitz, Daniel. 1993. Oriental Nostalgia: "The Transformation of the Palestinians into 'Israeli Arabs.'" *Theory and Criticism* 4: 179–80.

Raz-Krakotzkin, A. 1993. "Exile within Sovereignty: Toward a Critique of the 'Negation of Exile' in Israeli Culture." *Theory and Criticism* 4: 184.

Rodman, M. 1992. "Empowering Place: Multilocality and Multivocality." *American Anthropologist* 94(3): 640–56.

Roman, Yadin. 1990. "The Birth of an Industry: The Development of Tourism in Israel." *Eretz* 5(3).

Rutz, H., ed. 1992. *The Politics of Time.* American Ethnological Society Monograph, no. 4. Washington, D.C.: American Anthropological Society.

Said, Edward. 1992. *The Question of Palestine.* New York: Vintage.

Sharon, M. ed. 1988. *Pillars of Smoke and Fire: The Holy Land in History and Thought.* Johannesburg: Southern.

Shenhav-Keller, S. 1993. "The Israeli Souvenir: Its Text and Context." *Annals of Tourism Research* (20): 182–96.

Silberman, Neil A. 1989. *Between Past and Present: Archeology, Ideology, and Nationalism in the Modern Middle East.* New York: Doubleday.

———. 1997. "Structuring the Past: Israelis, Palestinians, and the Symbolic Authority of Archaeological Monuments." In *The Archaeology of Israel: Constructing the Past, Interpreting the Present,* edited by N. A. Silberman and D. Small, 62–81. Sheffield: Sheffield University Press.

Simon, Roger. 1993. "Forms of Insurgency in the Production of Popular Memories: The Columbus Quincentenary and the Pedagogy of Counter-Commemoration." *Cultural Studies* 7(1): 73–87.

State of Israel. 1993. *Statistical Abstract of Israel.* Jerusalem: Central Bureau of Statistics.

———. 2000. *Statistical Abstract of Israel.* Jerusalem: Central Bureau of Statistics.

Trigger, Bruce G. 1984. "Alternative Archaeologies: Nationalist, Colonialist, Imperialist." *Man* 19(1): 355–70.

Twain, Mark. [1869] 1966. *The Innocents Abroad, or the New Pilgrims Progress Being Some Account of the Steamship Quaker City's Pleasure Excursion to Europe and the Holy Land; With Descriptions of Countries, Nations, Incidents and Adventures, As They Appeared to the Author.* New York: Signet.

Watson, G. L., and J. P. Kopachevsky. 1994. "Interpretations of Tourism as Commodity." *Annals of Tourism Research* 21(3): 643–60.

Weingrod, A. 1993. "Changing Israeli Landscapes: Buildings and the Uses of the Past." *Cultural Anthropology* 8(3): 370–87.

Williams, Raymond. 1977. *Marxism and Literature.* Oxford: Oxford University Press.

Wright, Patrick. 1985. *On Living in an Old Country: The National Past in Contemporary Britain.* London: Verso.

Yanni, Ya'acov. 1988. Israel National Parks Authority Annual Report. Tel Aviv.

Yerushalmi, Yosef. 1989. *Zakhor: Jewish Memory and Jewish History.* New York: Schocken.

Yudelman, Michal. 1994. *Jerusalem Post International Edition,* February 26, A11.

The Roads to Ruins: Accessing Islamic Heritage in Jordan

13

ERIN ADDISON

RACTICAL EDITING DECISIONS about cultural heritage conservation are inevitable: it is a simple fact that for a wide variety of reasons not everything can be conserved. In best-case scenarios these decisions are based on policy that considers local, global, and scholarly values along with the inevitable financial and logistical concerns. In southwest Asia heritage conservation is especially fraught with political implications. Joel Bauman (this volume) helped to illuminate the politics of national identity in the physical and ideological construction of archaeological parks in Israel/Palestine. The present chapter will address the politics of heritage conservation in another part of the "Holy Land," the Hashemite Kingdom of Jordan.

A relatively small country carved out by the Sykes-Picot Agreement and territorial mandates of the post–World War I era, Jordan has few natural resources, little industry, and one of the highest birthrates in the world. Since its inception as a nation-state, Jordan has also accepted refugees, especially Palestinians, after each major conflagration that displaced them—in 1948, 1967, and again when the Palestinians were expelled from Kuwait following the Gulf War. The economic burden of its growing population places increasing strain on the government and infrastructure—a burden which King Hussein and his son King 'Abdullah have sought to lighten significantly through foreign aid. Jordan is among the highest per capita recipients of U.S. foreign aid. Under the circumstances tourism seems an obvious possibility for economic development.

Jordan is enormously rich in archaeological sites, boasting visually powerful remains from more than ten thousand years of vigorous human construction projects. While enormously valuable to the researcher, this historical record is perhaps more significant to Jordan, qua nation-state, as a tourist attraction. There

is a mutual relationship between foreign aid and the tourist market: Jordan's economic development is commonly thought to depend heavily on the success of its
tourist industry. The success of the tourist trade thus brings money into Jordan
directly, in the form of tourism dollars per se, and indirectly, as foreign assistance
for tourism development and for other projects predicated on economic growth
resulting from tourism.

It is thus in the interests of the state to shape in positive ways the impressions
of tourists, who come to Jordan overwhelmingly to visit archaeological and biblical sites. The richest tourist market is of course the West, construed by Jordanians
as primarily "Christians," who were expected to come in droves to the Holy Land
in celebration of the millennium. In the effort to convey an image of Jordanian
society as peaceful, inclusive, and westernized, the conservation of material remains in Jordan is increasingly pressed into diplomatic and economic service.
These interests are served at least in part by obscuring Jordan's dramatic Islamic
remains and emphasizing the Christian past.

Marking Jordan's Past

As noted, there is more to cultural heritage in Jordan than Islamic and Christian
remains. Apart from world-famous Petra and the Decapolis city of Jerash, there are
copious Roman, Byzantine, and prehistoric sites, and a less well-known body of
Mameluke, Ottoman, and Jewish remains. Much of the argument following could
be applied as easily to these sites (excepting Petra and Jerash) as to the early Islamic
sites under discussion. While Jerash figures in the New Testament as Gerasa and
features several elegant Byzantine churches with mosaic floors, it is most often
billed as "the Decapolis city of Jerash." We will not here consider it a specifically
Christian site in the same way we will sites where the only or central structure of
interest is a church, though it is listed as a Christian holy site in *The Holy Sites of Jordan* (130–31). There is also a tiny mosque on the antiquities site at Jerash, probably from the Umayyad period,[1] but it is overgrown and unmarked, and it is not
mentioned in the interpretive center. What makes Jordan's early Islamic remains a
particularly pointed example of cultural "editing" is, first, that Jordan is 98 percent
Muslim; second, the early Islamic remains in Jordan constitute one of the richest
early records of Islam anywhere—the only comparable body of remains is in Syria,
which has long been less accessible to researchers and tourists alike. While it is unacceptable scholarly practice to privilege one period of history over another, it is ar-
guable that unique bodies of remains might be conserved with special vigor and
attention. The reverse principle seems to be at work in Jordan.

It is important to keep in mind that by and large the struggles to be delineated
in this chapter are not scholarly ones—they are political struggles aimed primarily

toward shaping Jordan into an economically viable nation-state, or at least a palatable vector of foreign aid to maintain the Hashemite regime. Thus a significant site is a site that draws tourists. Within the context of this chapter, sites will be viewed not through the lenses of historiography or anthropology, for example, but the way a tourist encounters them, and the way they are viewed by those who package them for market. In identifying the Christian or Islamic significance of a site we will follow the text of *The Holy Sites of Jordan* (henceforth *HSJ*), a glossy coffee-table book financed by USAID (*HSJ* I) and produced largely under the patronage of Hashemite Prince Ghazi bin Mohammed, since these are the commonly held traditions about the holy sites. *HSJ* is also displayed prominently for sale at every tourist facility and hotel bookshop. The English spellings of site names used in this chapter will follow those used most often on road signs, where the latter exist.

For the sake of conciseness we will use as a measure of government policy the development of signs and road access to sites. While there is foreign development aid, private development, and scholarly research money involved in other aspects of site development, signs and access are predominantly Jordanian government inputs, and therefore reflect Jordanian policy more accurately. Signs and roads are inputs provided by the government to encourage access to sites—they are the sine qua non of tourist infrastructure, and as such they indicate the value of a site as perceived by the state.

Classification of Signs and Roads

Since the preparations for the Arab economic summit convened in 'Amman in October 1995, enormous progress has been made toward providing internationally interpretable road signs throughout Jordan. In 1995 signs of any kind were scarce, and usually in Arabic only. Over the intervening years a system of road signs has been established and most signs, especially on the major thoroughfares, are written in both Arabic and English. Many signs now have nontext icons meant to be interpretable internationally. There are three basic categories of signs: (1) traffic signs—white writing on blue background, black writing and illustrations on white background, or white writing on red background; (2) pilgrimage signs—white writing on green background; and (3) tourist signs—cream writing on brown background.

In addition to the often whimsical depictions of traffic dangers (e.g., a car bouncing down a rocky hill into water, two cars colliding with rays of damage radiating around them, etc.) and the international signs for food, lodging, petrol, and coffee, "icons" have been developed for some tourist and pilgrimage sites. Signs for Petra, for example, sport a drawing of the world-famous *khazneh*. The Dead Sea signs show a swimmer. Islamic pilgrimage sites, of which there are thirty-eight in Jordan, bear a symbol made up of a crescent, minaret, and dome (figure 13.1).

Figure 13.1.   Crescent, minaret, and dome compose the nontext icon for Islamic holy sites (*magamat*). Photo by Erin Addison.

Before 1995 there was no systematic attempt to distinguish signs for tourist attractions from any other signs. In many cases the old blue and white signs from the period prior to 1995 are still in place. These signs, present as traces of an earlier way of thinking about the sites they demarcate, afford some curious insights into the logic of the new system.

Because of the expense and effort required to construct physical communications, road quality is a concrete measure of the perceived value of access to a site. In the following discussion road quality is evaluated in terms of the width and number of lanes, quality of pavement, elevation above the surrounding terrain, the presence of reinforced culverts and safety features such as raised guard strips, reflectors, and fog lines, and whether or not curves are banked. Classification is as follows: (1) first class—two or more lanes divided by median or painted lines; well-paved and maintained; raised; fog lines, reflectors, guardrails, and/or raised guard strips; banked curves; reinforced culverts, bridges; (2) second class—two-car width or two lanes separated by painted lines; raised; paved and reasonably well-maintained; reinforced culverts/bridges; occasional reflectors, fog lines, guardrails where necessary; (3) third class—one lane, poorly maintained paved or graded gravel, not raised; (4) fourth class—gravel or dirt track formed by truck traffic; little or no constructed drainage or passage through wadi beds (i.e., few or no culverts or bridges, tendency for track to wash out); and (5) "off-road"—no track at all, or a track so damaged that a four-wheel drive vehicle is mandatory.

It is not possible within the scope of this chapter to give a detailed discussion of all the major and minor roadways in Jordan, so we will focus on the roads most used by tourists (see figure 13.1). Most tourists come to Jordan on one- to three-night stays as part of packages that include Israel/Palestine, and they stay in 'Amman, the Petra area, or 'Aqaba. European tourists sometimes come directly to 'Aqaba and are more likely to overnight at Wadi Rum or the Dead Sea, but the latter are by far secondary to 'Amman, 'Aqaba, and Petra. The most popularly visited sites in Jordan are Petra and Jerash, making the road to Jerash and 'Ajlun an important secondary tourist road. The Madaba area is another important tourist attraction found just west of the Desert Highway, and access to Madaba is a heavily traveled first-class road. We will therefore be considering the Desert Highway from 'Amman to 'Aqaba, the Madaba Road, and the 'Amman-Jerash and Jerash-'Ajlun Roads (map 13.1). The first three of these are the roads with the heaviest general traffic as well.

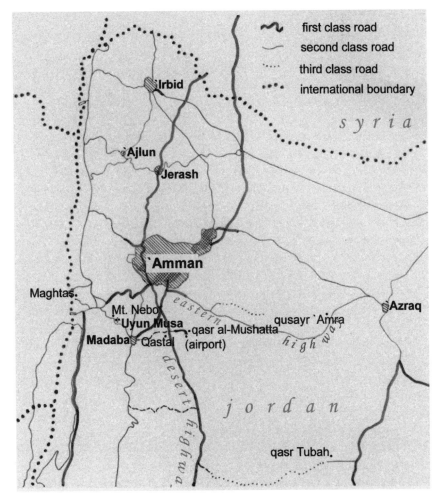

Map 13.1.   Map of sites discussed.

Signs

Of the roads outlined above the Desert Highway is far and away the most heavily traveled, a conduit for commercial traffic from Turkey and Syria to Saudi Arabia, as well as the primary connection between Jordan's most economically important and populous cities—Irbid, 'Amman, and the port city of 'Aqaba. From 'Amman one must travel the Desert Highway to reach the airport or any of the other main roads to be considered here. Its importance as a main artery for local and international traffic is evident from the fact that it is signed continuously along its entire length, some five hundred kilometers, by privately owned businesses, even along extensive stretches of highway with no population or cross traffic. The King's Highway and Eastern Highway are much less densely signed, except in the area between 'Amman and Madaba. By way of contrast the Desert Highway has in some places as many as twenty-two *private sector* signs per kilometer, whereas the Jafr Road—250 kilometers of first-class highway—sports not a single private sector sign.

Traveling southbound on the Desert Highway between 'Amman and Qatrana there are eighteen brown tourist signs, including signs for such attractions as the Queen 'Alia International Airport and a Little League stadium, Petra, and the Dead Sea, among others. Of the eighteen, there are six for Christian sites, none for Islamic sites. Qasr al-'Amman, Deir al-Kahf, Qastal, and al-Mushatta—all significant, visually impressive Islamic sites on or within a few kilometers of the highway—are unsigned. There is no sign to direct the traveler even to the turnoff for Qusayr 'Amra, one of only two UNESCO World Heritage sites in Jordan (along with Petra).

On the northbound side there are four brown tourist signs. Three signal Christian sites and one directs the northbound traveler to the turnoff for Qusayr 'Amra, only twenty kilometers south of 'Amman. It remains unclear why the single sign for this UNESCO site is placed on the northbound side when the vast majority of travelers would more logically be heading southbound onto the "Desert Castle Loop" from 'Amman, rather than departing from the northbound exit on the long drive back from Petra or 'Aqaba. This question is underscored by the fact that density of private-sector signs is much heavier on the southbound side than the northbound: a business that has to pay for its sign places it where it will be most visible. Interestingly, five of the old blue signs remain on this section of highway. Three are for Islamic sites (one for Khan az-Zabib and two for Qasr at-Tubah), two are for Umm ar-Rasas, a Christian site. Only the Umm ar-Rasas signs have been replaced with new brown iconic signs.

Between 'Amman and Jerash there are seventeen brown tourist signs, none for either specifically Christian or specifically Islamic sites. Once one turns onto the Jerash Road, however, there are twenty-eight signs between the turnoff and 'Ajlun.

Seven signs indicate Christian sites, and six direct the traveler to Salah ad-Din's fortress at 'Ajlun. It is worth pausing to consider these more closely. The seven "Christian" signs represent four different sites (Our Lady of the Mountain, Mar Elias, St. George's Church, and the Byzantine Icon Shop). Only Mar Elias is of even marginal historical interest (see below); the other three are very recent structures—two are specifically pilgrimage sites and the Byzantine Icon Shop is a private business! Even Mar Elias is a pilgrimage site. Yet there are also three important Islamic pilgrimage sites in the same area—one is actually on the way to Mar Elias—as well as a historically significant Mameluke mosque in 'Ajlun itself, but not a single sign of any kind is apparent on any of the roads in question. Green iconic signs for Islamic holy sites appear only on ancillary, third-class roads.

On the Madaba Road and within Madaba on the four main traffic circles there are seventeen signs, eleven for Christian sites and none for Islamic sites. In Madaba as in 'Ajlun there are signs for Christian sites over an hour away (e.g., Mukawir), when there are considerably more significant and impressive Islamic sites (Qastal, Mushatta) within fifteen minutes—but no signs. Madaba visitors center is noted here as a Christian site, since there is not a single reference to Islam in the "information center," which concentrates overwhelmingly on the historic Christian community at Madaba. One of the old photos on display depicts a mosque, but there is no identifying information about it—not even a name. It is also intriguing that one of the very few display objects at the center is a large, striking Umayyad period jar—again with no identifying information offered. The attendant said that it came from Umm ar-Rasas.

While this totting-up of road signs may seem tedious, it provides a quantifiable indicator of government inputs into tourist sites. On these main arteries there are eighty-four brown tourist signs: twenty-seven direct the traveler to nine specifically Christian historical and pilgrimage sites; nine point to two Islamic historical sites. In the immediate vicinity of these same roads (less than twenty kilometers from the main road), however, there are three monumental early Islamic sites (Qasr 'Amman, Qasr al-Mushatta, Qasr al-Qastal), several more historically important and visually interesting sites (e.g., Umm al-Walid), and thirteen Islamic holy sites[2] that are unsigned. There is also some indication that Islamic sites which were once signed are no longer to be so.

It might be tempting to think this is all just absent-minded until we begin to examine in detail the placement and distribution of signs in relation to the quality and significance of the sites they denote. This is a delicate matter, but for our purposes sheer visual power is useful as a measure—for indeed it is spectacle, a visual "wow," that attracts tourists. It is, for example, well-known among archaeologists and conservationists in Jordan that the presence of mosaics on a site elicits unusually rapid response and support from the Department of Antiquities. At

Qastal there was an appropriate example: when the oldest standing minaret in the world (Addison 2000, 489) was badly vandalized in the summer of 1998, it took six weeks of pleading to get a security person (*haris*) assigned to the site. Vandalism continues all around the site and the *haris* is rarely in evidence. When, however, spectacular mosaics were discovered nearby in February 2000, a *haris* was appointed within twenty-four hours and the land was purchased by the Ministry of Tourism within a few months. Thus the power of the "wow factor." Let us compare the signs devoted to two extremely powerful Islamic sites—Qusayr 'Amra and Qastal—to two Christian sites with less "wow."

Both Islamic sites have been recognized by Western-identified organizations as worthy of note: Qusayr 'Amra as a UNESCO World Heritage site, both 'Amra and Qastal by Museum With No Frontiers (MWNF), a cultural tourism concern promoted by the European Commission. Qusayr 'Amra is a triple-vaulted Umayyad period reception hall and bathhouse with notable mosaics and world-famous frescoed walls. In 1999 a small visitors center was added to the complex and fitted with excellent reconstructions of the frescoes and the structure itself, as well as scholarly text in English, French, and Arabic. Qastal is a less polished site, but over forty rooms of the seventy-square-meter palace have been cleared since 1998, several notable mosaics exposed, and the site contains the oldest extant minaret in the world (Addison 2000, 489). Four hundred meters northwest of the minaret are mosaics that rival any in southwest Asia (Addison 2001, 1). In 2002 a visiting official from the United Nations Development Program said of the site, "Once you're inside it, it's completely fantastic."

As mentioned earlier, the signing for 'Amra is oddly placed on the major thoroughfares. The Eastern Highway actually departs from deep inside the industrial outskirts of 'Amman, at the *midan sharq al-'awsat*. This traffic circle is difficult even for most Jordanians to find if they don't use the artery regularly, yet placed there is a brown tourist sign—in English—for Qusayr 'Amra. The easier way to access the Eastern Highway is to exit the Desert Highway at the Madaba interchange, but head east toward Yadoudah until one intersects the highway. One might expect a sign for 'Amra at this Desert Highway exit, where there are signs for Madaba and Mount Nebo in both directions. The single sign for 'Amra noted above is, however, at the next exit traveling north, the Na'ur exit which leads (after half an hour or more) to *midan sharq al-'awsat*. Even on the Yadoudah road it is necessary to travel through ten kilometers of depressed urban sprawl and heavy traffic before encountering a sign for Qusayr 'Amra just at the exit for the Eastern Highway. In short, unless one already knows, it is hard to find and the signs are likely to hinder rather than help.

Qastal is actually *on* the frontage road for the Desert Highway, visible from the highway, three kilometers north of the airport exit (twenty-five kilometers south of 'Amman). There are no signs whatsoever for Qastal.

In contrast to the visitors center at 'Amra, the Madaba visitors center is not associated with any historic site. No text beyond the simplest labeling of the photographs is available for the few exhibits offered. At the Yadoudah/Madaba road and for the fifteen southbound kilometers preceding it there are signs—seven brown tourist signs as well as blue directional signs—for Madaba and Christian sites in Madaba. In the fifteen kilometers of first-class road between the highway and the town, there are seven more—three of them for the Madaba visitors center. It is virtually impossible *not* to find it, even if one is not looking for it.

Mar Elias, near 'Ajlun, is the site of a small Byzantine church. The remains consist of foundation courses and some badly damaged, naive tricolor mosaics. There has recently, however, been an effort by the Department of Antiquities to create a more significant site there by constructing a large, semicircular stone terrace and seating to showcase the beautiful view to the north, as well as cutting new blocks to rebuild walls and steps. Interestingly, the holy place devoted to Saint *(mar)* Elias by Arab pilgrims—both Christian and Muslim—is located elsewhere, to the south near the village of Mahas, but there are no signs for that site located on first- or second-class roads. The third-class road leading to the northern Mar Elias site, however, has been repaved and there are three well-placed signs on the important Jerash-'Ajlun road and leading from 'Ajlun to the site itself.

It is hard to find the logic for this sign distribution: on the roads carrying the most tourist traffic in Jordan there is one sign for one Islamic site, Qusayr 'Amra, and none for Qastal, though both are recognized as noteworthy by prestigious international organizations. For the Madaba visitors center and Mar Elias, largely "fabricated" sites, that is, with no historic remains or very little, respectively, there are six brown tourist signs, judiciously placed. Neither the Madaba visitors center (nor any other Christian site in or around Madaba) nor Mar Elias has been recognized by UNESCO or MWNF. There is evidently a heuristic at work here other than pure touristic value (the previously mentioned "wow factor").

It is worth remarking too on the iconography of the new brown sign system. Not every site has been assigned an "icon," a symbol representing specifically that site and no other. The only Islamic site that has an icon is Qusayr 'Amra and the icon is, appropriately, a triple-vaulted building. The icon for 'Amman is a Roman amphitheater, though a recent multimillion-dollar project has restored the dramatic palace of Caliph Yazid II on the acropolis, next to the antiquities museum. For Madaba and Umm ar-Rasas the icons are recognizably cruciform mosaic patterns. For Mount Nebo the icon is actually a cross—the image represents the large cross-*cum*-sculpture that stands in the church courtyard. While there are recognizably Christian forms placed frequently on the major highways, no brown tourist signs carry a recognizably Muslim symbol (figure 13.2).

**brown tourist signs with icons
(clockwise from above):
to Mount Nebo
to `Amman
to Madaba
to Umm ar-Rasas**

Figure 13.2.   Brown tourist signs for Mount Nebo, 'Amman, Madaba, and Umm ar-Rasas with their respective icons. Photo by Erin Addison.

This theme is continued with the signs for holy sites, or "pilgrimage signs." While signs for Mar Elias, Our Lady of the Mountain, and other Christian holy sites are frequently seen on the heavily traveled roads under discussion, not a single sign for any of the thirty-eight Muslim holy sites is visible on these highways.

It is not that the sites are unsigned. Every one of the Islamic holy sites, even in the most remote villages, is signed; but the signs are never visible from the heavily traveled tourist roads we are considering. Let us consider Mount Nebo, known to most Arabic speakers as *siyagha*. Nebo is a holy site to both Christians and Muslims, to whom it is *maqam nabi allah musa*, "The Holy Site of the Prophet of God Moses." According to tradition Mount Nebo is the site of Moses' death. Though there is another site so claimed on the west side of the Jordan River near Ariha/ Jericho, Mount Nebo is one of the best-known and most-visited sites in Jordan, and except for Petra the most heavily signed, as well: on the Desert Highway, Jerash Road, Madaba Road, Maghtas Road, and the Rawda-Madaba Road there are an impressive eighteen brown tourist signs for Mount Nebo.

The top of Mount Siyagha is now dominated by a Franciscan church and monastery, and since 1933 the Franciscans have pursued archaeological research there. In the forecourt of the church there is a huge twentieth-century metal cross visible for miles around. The site is walled and gated, and there is no trace of Islamic heritage evident.

It is odd that there is no indication that this is a Muslim holy site; also that there is no sign for 'Uyun Musa, another holy site that lies on a tiny, steep third-class road halfway down the hill crowned by the church. This road dips down through the wadi that creates the falls at 'Uyun Musa, turns into a fourth-class road, and then dead-ends at some small farms after another kilometer. There is no longer any sign at all for 'Uyun Musa, though there was one at least as recently as 1996. At the top of the hill on the return to the main road, however, there is a pilgrimage sign for *maqam nabi allah musa* (Mount Nebo) facing downhill, away from the main road. The sign is firmly placed—it was intended to be where it is, however inexplicably. In the three hours I spent hiking around 'Uyun Musa in the spring of 2002, the only person I encountered was a Bedouin woman collecting water at the springs. No cars used the road.

On the opposite side of the Madaba-Nebo Road another third-class track takes off to the northwest to Khirbet Mukhayyet, a small Byzantine church with a brilliant mosaic floor. The track quickly deteriorates, and for a third of each year it is difficult to make it to the church without four-wheel drive. The road dead-ends at the church. On the return to the main road, however, there is another pilgrimage sign for *maqam nabi allah musa*—again facing away from the main road. The signs for the Muslim holy site seem deliberately positioned so that they are invisible to the normal flow of traffic to and from the site.

As if this weren't peculiar enough, a comparison of the old blue and white signs with the new brown tourist signs offers us another piece of information to consider. There are no longer any references to *siyagha*, the traditional Arabic name for the site, on government signs, though there is one restaurant whose sign refers to it. Approaching Mount Nebo from the Jordan Valley the road takes a sharp turn, and there is a new brown sign for "Madaba" and "Nebo," with *jabal nibu* provided in Arabic—"Mount Nebo." Just after the new sign, however, there remains an old blue and white sign that reads, in Arabic, *maqam nabi musa*, and below that in English, "Mount Nebo" (figure 13.3). This indicates that until very recently the old Muslim name was used at least in Arabic. This is no longer so. Now all of the eighteen brown signs use the Christianized name for the site *even in Arabic*.

It is unavoidable that the impression forming in the tourist's mind is that of a landscape heavy with Christian history and virtually void of Islamic remains. The roadsides, busy with signs for Christian sites and showcases for the presence of Christians on the landscape, remain silent about the huge and varied Islamic remains.

Figure 13.3.   Old blue tourist signs for Mount Nebo. The Arabic script identifies the site as *maqam nabi Musa*—"the holy place of the prophet Moses," indicating its status as a Muslim holy site. Photo by Erin Addison.

Road Access

At this point let us turn from the major thoroughfares to consider sites where considerable resources have been invested in road access. The three sites to be considered are Qasr at-Tubah and Qasr al-Mushatta, both monumental Islamic sites, and Maghtas, traditionally claimed by some as the scene of Jesus' baptism.

One of the more acute problems for the Jordanian tourist industry is competition with holy land tourism to Israel. At conference after conference discussion turns to the question of how to get tourists to come to Jordan not as a day trip (literally) or a weekend "add-on," but as a primary destination. Thus it is no surprise that just before the anticipated deluge of millennium tourism, "the sites of John the Baptist were rediscovered by His Royal Highness Prince Ghazi bin Mohammed and the Franciscan Archaeologist of Mount Nebo" (*HSJ* 103). In *The Holy Sites of Jordan* Father Michele Piccarillo writes further, "plans are being developed to renovate this sacred site," and "a new project for the protection and renovation of this holy site is invisaged" (103). Bethabara, as the baptism site is called in *HSJ*, is now the fifth site where Jesus is claimed to have been baptized—the other four are in Israel and the West Bank. The site is now more commonly referred to as Maghtas, or simply as the Baptism Site.

Visitors to the site are given a guided tour through a carefully groomed and framed series of cisterns, simple tricolor geometric mosaic fragments, a few foundation courses for an otherwise vanished church, and some reconstructed arches intended to represent another tiny church site. By far the most conspicuous structure is a brand-new, polished marble terrace surrounding immersion pools complete with handrails for the unsteady. This intervention no doubt anticipated droves of Christian pilgrims who might want to be baptized/immersed at the "historic" site. That the grandiose historical claims for this site are rather inflated is irrelevant—from a scholarly perspective the same is true for most of the traditional holy sites. There was, in fact, a Byzantine church at Maghtas and there were, in fact, cisterns (though it is difficult to demonstrate that they were immersion pools). What is so striking about Maghtas is that there is so little there at all, even compared to sites like Mar Elias and Lot's Cave, another Byzantine church site and a pilgrimage site shared by Muslims and Christians alike.

What makes Maghtas interesting for our purposes is that a JD400,000 (US$560,000) road was constructed to connect Maghtas to Mount Nebo for the purposes of pilgrimage tourism (*Jordan Times* 1999). The "Maghtas Road," as it is commonly called, winds over ten stark, scenic kilometers through the barren hills overlooking the Dead Sea and Jordan Valley, connecting to the Jerusalem Road just east of the turnoff to the border town of South Shouneh. Except for the gas station at this intersection, the good (second-class) Maghtas Road does not serve a single business or community. It is strictly a tourist road.

Compare the Maghtas Road to what is known to a very few people in Jordan as *tariq an-nifayat al-khatirah*—"the Hazardous Waste Road." The Hazardous Waste Road is a second-class road of even better quality than the Maghtas Road, and departs from what is arguably the best road in Jordan—the nearly deserted Jafr Road. There are no signs at all at the turn (figure 13.4). After fourteen kilometers one encounters a large, well-built, unmarked installation which is the new hazardous waste plant under construction at Wadi Ghadaf. The paved road continues for 1.3 kilometers before ending at the east edge of the wadi bed, where the plant wall turns south. A very rough track continues west on the other side of the wadi. If one turns back, then, toward the Jafr Road, one might—if the light is right and you're looking for it—see on the north side of the road, close to the ground, a tiny (10 x 30 inches), rusted, blue-and-white sign that reads "Qasr Tubah." There is no structure visible, however, and apparently no road (figure 13.5).

Qasr at-Tubah is indeed four kilometers northeast of the sign. There is in fact a track that begins just beyond the area disturbed for the HAZMAT road construction. A four-wheel drive vehicle is necessary to negotiate it. Following the east edge of the wadi the palace is impossible to miss: a gigantic, vaulted structure built of slender mud brick, standing in splendid isolation. Qasr at-Tubah is internationally known and revered by the local Bedouin as a landmark and source of pride. It is also melting away, literally, out of neglect, and badly in need of conservation.

Figure 13.4.   Intersection of Jafr Road and the "Hazardous Waste Road," 70 kilometers south of 'Azraq. Photo by Erin Addison.

There is, it may be recalled, another way to get to Qasr at-Tubah. On the Desert Highway there remain two of the old blue and white signs, one facing northbound, one southbound, which read in Arabic and in English:

Qasr Tuba
an Umayyad Palace 67 km
Department of Antiquities

A fourth-class road then departs to the east. Within a few kilometers it diminishes to a faint dirt track. At the eighth kilometer the track forks, and there is a small white sign with black Arabic lettering which reads

tariq makab al-nifayat al-khatirah
("hazardous waste dump road")

and points to the southerly fork. The hazardous waste management apparently felt that the track was ambiguous enough to post a sign. There is, however, no sign at all for Qasr at-Tubah. While documenting this article in May 2002, I was approached at this fork by two truckloads of soldiers who expressed their concern about my

Figure 13.5.   Old blue-and-white sign for Qasr at-Tubah on *tariq an-nifayat al-khatirah*. Photo by Erin Addison.

continuing down the track in my rental car. They assured me that it was not possible to get to Tubah from there, and that I should turn back; but an adventurous and skilled driver with six or eight hours to spare, someone who already knows where the road is going and where Tubah is, can in fact get there on this track. After sixty-six kilometers one crosses Wadi Ghadaf from the west and meets the west end of the Hazardous Waste Road, and the little rusted blue and white sign for Qasr at-Tubah.

There are visually powerful historic remains at Tubah in a striking scenic context. There is a good road already in place to access it, if the four-kilometer track were merely regraded from the HAZMAT plant. Yet there is not one sign on the Eastern Highway or the Jafr Road to indicate that the Islamic site is there. It seems unlikely that many tourists will negotiate the sixty-six-kilometer track from the Desert Highway, and it would seem that those in charge of such matters have tacitly agreed on this point, since the old blue and white signs have never been replaced with brown tourist signs to alert the adventurous.

A final example is Qasr al-Mushatta, less than thirty kilometers from 'Amman and adjacent to the Queen 'Alia International Airport. Qasr al-Mushatta is another MWNF site, another eighth-century Umayyad palace with soaring vaults and an impressive surrounding wall buttressed by turrets. Within the walls is also an unfinished mosque cleared and partially reconstructed in the 1960s. What remains of Mushatta's famous facade (most of which presently resides in a museum in Berlin) is ornately carved into diamond and rosette patterns. A colonnade of gray marble columns leads into a cloverleaf reception hall, and huge pieces of carved marble lintel lie lined up along the entryway.

Until at least 1998 Mushatta was accessible from the airport ring road itself. At the intersection of the freeway exit and the ring road there was a brown and white tourist sign pointing the way clearly. The sign has since been removed. The intersection has been re-signed, and Mushatta is not included on it.

There has long been another route to Mushatta as well. Until 2000 it was a small, third-class road which departed from the industrial area of North Qastal, passed Mushatta and ended when it intersected with the airport ring road. In 2000–2001 this road was refurbished into a 7.5-kilometer first-class road to serve the new customs installation for the airport. Where the old road climbed up a hill and made a sharp turn to the south to pass Mushatta, the new road actually ends at the *qasr* parking lot. At the time of writing the site was so neglected that this parking lot had for many months been used as a storage lot for heavy construction equipment. Traffic from the customs road here makes a right turn into the first security gate for the airport.

Every sign for the *qasr* that was once visible on either the airport road or from the old road is gone. It's hard to miss the *qasr* itself, but unless one gets out and walks up to the front entrance of the building, there is nothing to identify it. Clear and efficient new signs guide traffic to the new customs road: there is a sign and arrow at every turn from the Desert Highway to the security gate, five coming southbound and two northbound. There is, however, not a single sign for Qasr al-Mushatta.

One might dismiss the whole matter by reasoning that these sites are too inaccessible to warrant the expense of road access and signs, but this is hardly the case with Mushatta. It is only ten kilometers from the exit on the Desert Highway to the *qasr* itself. Overall it is less than thirty kilometers from 'Amman. Like Qastal, it is an easy stop on any bus tour to Madaba, Petra, or 'Aqaba. There is a fine new road and government signposts with plenty of room for additional signs (elsewhere different ministries share signposts). The road leads directly to the parking area at the *qasr*. But there isn't a sign in all Jordan that hints at its existence.

Conclusion

What emerges from this survey goes beyond policy that favors devoting resources to Christian sites over Islamic sites because the former are what tourists want to see. That would be troubling enough but understandable. More disturbing is the evident concomitant policy by which Islamic heritage—history, religion, pilgrimage and Muslims themselves—are deliberately obscured from Western visitors who use the signs in English *and* from Arabic-language tourists. Islamic pilgrimage signs are distributed and oriented away from first- and second-class roads. Those responsible fail to sign important and visually spectacular Islamic heritage sites—even Qusayr 'Amra, chosen as a World Heritage site. Names for sites such as Siyagha have been shifted away from the traditional Arabic designations in favor of the use of Western Christian epithets even in Arabic. Visitors are steered away from Muslim Jordanians as much as possible, as evidenced in the construction of the Maghtas Road and the shift of the Mar Elias pilgrimage stop from the site near 'Amman, actually used by both Muslims and Christians, to an isolated site in the north.

In a bizarre final twist to this story, the very Westerners who are supposedly being courted appear to disagree with the Jordanian government on the matter of what is worth conserving *even in the interests of tourism*. UNESCO has protected only Petra and Qusayr 'Amra, an Islamic site. When the EuroMed partnership inaugurated the exhibition trail for Museum With No Frontiers, it chose to showcase the fabulous palaces of the Umayyad dynasty. 'Amra, Qastal, Mushatta, Tubah, 'Amman, Deir al-Kahf, and Umm al-Walid were all selected as primary sites for the catalogue; of Maghtas, Mount Nebo, Mukawir, Mar Elias, Madaba visitors center, Our Lady of the Mountain, St. George's Church, the Byzantine Icon Shop—none. UNESCO is recognized as one of the premiere arbiters of international cultural heritage management. EuroMed is specifically a promoter of cultural tourism, linking Europe with twelve southern and eastern Mediterranean countries. It seems odd that their preferences are so signally ignored.

It is in this disjuncture that we see why it is important for Jordan to promote a particular tourism that distances the state from things Islamic and from the particular fragrance of danger they seem to carry. In September 2002, the *Jordan Times* announced that "a JD6 million (US$8.4 million) joint government-USAID project" will augment the tourist infrastructure at Maghtas (Dajani 2002, 1). The same article reports that in the first eight months of 2002, 31,368 visitors toured Maghtas, a decrease from 2001. If even 50,000 tourists pay admission fees of JD5 each in 2002, the Ministry of Tourism will bring in JD250,000 (US$350,000) over the course of a year—a pittance compared to the millions the United States will hand out in aid for tourism *development*. Ultimately the educated opinions of organizations such as UNESCO or MWNF matter as little as the less rarified tastes of the Christian tourists: cultural heritage management policy is being shaped by the big money that passes from state to state in the context of global politics.

As Baram and Rowan point out so forcefully in the introduction to this volume, "the bundle of processes involved in globalization is weakening the nation-state and subsuming nationalism." Baram and Rowan continue by saying that an examination of the global context presents a shift in cultural heritage management: whereas "twentieth-century states employed archaeology for fostering national identity," Jordan began to do the opposite precisely in anticipation of the dawning twenty-first. The preparations for the eagerly awaited influx of millennium-minded Christian tourists appear to turn on a policy deliberately *effacing* Jordan's own national identity and in particular its Islamic heritage.

Due to worldwide economic recession and perceived terrorist threats, the flood of millennium tourists never materialized. The second Palestinian intifada and events of September 11, 2001, have subsequently decimated the tourist trade in Jordan, even though Jordan continues at the time of this writing to be a stable and easy place to travel. It thus becomes ever more important for the Jordanian state to identify itself with the interests of the United States and to sustain the sense that tourism development is a worthwhile investment of foreign aid. Subtly, then, tourism serves as a barometer of perceived stability in "the Middle East," and any Euramerican *perception* of Jordan as Muslim-identified, militant, or hazardous is costly on many levels. Since it is not the dollars they spend per se but the sense of economic possibility that they represent, tourists must be courted into a landscape as free as possible of any hint of threat or discomfort. As countries worldwide scramble to identify themselves with American interests, the Hashemite regime in particular has worked overtime to configure itself as a secular, Western-identified state.

Notes

1. The Umayyad caliphate was the first political dynasty of Islam, based in Damascus from A.D. 661 to 750. The Umayyad caliphs reigned over the expansion of the Islamic empire from a primarily Arabian phenomenon to a world power stretching from India to Spain and France to sub-Saharan Africa. The Marwanids, particularly, were also enthusiastic builders of monumental structures including, for example, the Dome of the Rock in Jerusalem. Over 80 percent of the surviving remains of the Umayyad period are located in Jordan and Syria. See, inter alia, Hodgeson (1974, 187–279).

2. In the 'Ajlun area are Maqam Shurhabil bin Husnah, Maqam Ikrimah bin Abi Jahl, Maqam Nebi Allah Hud; around 'Amman are Maqam Nebi Allah Khidr Elias, Maqam Abd al-Rahman bin Auf, Maqam Nebi Allah Shu'ayb, Maqam Bilal bin Rabah, Deir al-Kahf (a.k.a. Cave of the Seven Sleepers), and Gadur; near Madaba are Siyagha (Maqam Nebi Allah Musa), 'Uyun Musa, Maqam Nebi Allah Yahya (Mukawir), and Maqam Abu Dharr al-Ghifari.

References

Addison, Erin. 2000. "The Mosque at al-Qastal: Report from al-Qastal Conservation and Development Project, 1999–2000." *Annual of the Department of Antiquities of Jordan* 44: 477–91.

———. 2001. "Qastal, 1998–2001." *ACOR Newsletter,* Spring 2001, 1–4.

Dajani, Dalya. 2002. "Baptism Site Continues to See Expansion." *Jordan Times Online,* September 9, 2002. Accessed September 9, 2002.

Hodgeson, Marshall. 1974. *The Venture of Islam.* Chicago.

"Jordan, Israel Tourism Leaders to Meet." 1999. *Jordan Times Online,* September 8, 1999. Accessed September 15, 2002.

Mohammed, Ghazi bin. 1996. *The Holy Sites of Jordan.* Amman.

Repackaging the Pilgrimage: Visiting the Holy Land in Orlando

14

YORKE ROWAN

ACRED TO JEWISH, Christian, and Muslim communities, the Holy Land has long captured the imagination of artists, travelers, statesmen, warriors, pilgrims, traders, and tourists. An iconic landscape in the Western eye, it is a place where the ancient is conceptualized as familiar, personal, and benign while the modern is constructed as foreign, exotic, and dangerous. For many who look to the Holy Land as blessed territory, it not only is history but evokes connections to a spiritual heritage. And for those who consider that landscape sacred, the value of that heritage is measured not by critical proofs of historical accuracy but by the power of the symbols found in the Holy Land.

In the "Holy Land," the vaguely defined region generally limited in modern experience to Israel, Palestine, and Jordan, the presentation of the past has a long history. As a number of scholars have discussed, archaeology was integral to nationalistic interests during the early years in Israel's history. However, as some argue (e.g., Baram and Rowan, this volume; Silberman 1997), the state of Israel's interest in archaeology can no longer be adequately summed up as a solely nationalistic one. Instead, the importance of tourism has expanded considerably during the past few decades, consciously targeted for specific, primarily Christian and Jewish, audiences for economic purposes.

Modern political realities, however, persistently intrude on the tourism industry. There are many Americans who find the distance, cost, or potential danger of a visit to the Holy Land prohibitive, and increasingly dangerous in the current political situation. One solution to this problem is to create a site for heritage consumption (and perhaps in the future, potential pilgrimage) closer to home, far from political turmoil and at much lower expense for the visitor. Just such an alternative to foreign travel is now available in a new theme park called the Holy Land Experience (henceforth, HLE) in Orlando, Florida.

Critics might interpret such efforts as just another cynical endeavor to substitute authentic experience with a version of history that is sanitized, inaccurate, and largely entertainment for profit. Yet there is a long tradition and appetite for the place of the Holy Land in the American consciousness, manifest in a variety of ways. These have included various forms of visual imagery and representations, such as models of various Holy Land sites, naming of towns with biblical names (Davison 1977), and the popularity of innumerable traveler's accounts (Goell and Katz-Hyman 1977; Handy 1977; Klatzer 1997). However, there is an implicit problem of authenticity when promoting such a venture.

The "heritage industry" has been variously described as, for example, a crusade (see Lowenthal 1998), a commodity (Ebron 2000), or applied (or public) history (Glassberg 2001; Shackel 2000). Until recently, the concept of heritage was generally treated as a set of problems to be solved, and there was relatively limited interest in examining the nature of heritage as a cultural process. More recently, heritage has moved away from the practice (training people for specific skills) to one increasingly inclusive of theory and ideas.

This chapter explores the attraction such a site holds for visitors, and whether the ideal of authenticity so central to heritage tourism is a useful standard or is irrelevant in this context. I would like to focus on the demonstrable continuity such a creation displays with other places in American history and suggest some ways to understand what might attract visitors to the site, and how this attraction relates to archaeology and the past.

The substantial blurring between museums and other venues for popular tourism that incorporate perspectives on the past has been the topic for debate among academics and professionals. Increasing competition among institutions offering authentic experiences to cultural tourists means that institutions such as museums no longer claim exclusive authority as providers of historically related experiences, but represent simply an early form of institutional commodification of culture (Prentice 2001). The notion of authenticity is a problem inherent to museums as well, for whatever they select for subject matter, museums utilize objects, subject them to interpretation, and present them as information. However, the removal of objects to museums and interpretation limit that authenticity, for the objects become media and are no longer in their context (Prentice 2001).

Background

The Holy Land Experience, opened on February 5, 2001, is a $16 million self-described "living biblical museum" located on fifteen acres about five miles southwest of Orlando. It is focused on a time period between 1450 B.C. and A.D. 70. At this biblically based theme park, costumed employees sell "Camel Coolers" to the thirsty, perform dramatic enactments for the pilgrims, and provide a place for quiet contemplation of the grace of God. Music written exclusively for the project is piped in, and multimedia presentations are used to dramatize selected important biblical events. The periods that the park attempts to encompass range from the time of Moses (c. 1450 B.C.) and the Exodus to Jesus' teachings and eventual crucifixion.

Marvin Rosenthal is the founder of HLE, and president and CEO of Zion's Hope, a nonprofit evangelical Christian ministry. According to their promotional literature, the purpose of Zion's Hope is "to share the message of the Bible accurately in its historical and *cultural context*" (emphasis mine). Rosenthal, the author of books such as *The Pre-Wrath Rapture of the Church* (1990) and *Not without Design* (1980), attended the Philadelphia College of Bible and Dallas Theological Seminary, and was ordained into the ministry in 1968.

According to the website and promotional literature for HLE, its purpose is to

1. Create a wholesome, family oriented, and educational facility where Christians can come to be encouraged and reinforced in their faith . . .
2. create a "total immersion" experience that offers historical proof of the Bible and dynamically demonstrates that the Bible is God's Word to man . . .
3. lovingly share the message of the grace of God for sinful men, as demonstrated in the death, burial, and resurrection of His Son.

The overtly Christian, evangelical mission of the HLE is fostered throughout the theme park, providing facsimile structures and reenactments of Christ on the cross, singers in traditional biblical garb, a film, and special admission rates for groups or annual membership. There is a cafeteria with piped-in music, shopping opportunities, a model of the Old City of Jerusalem, and entertainment, with additional special events on schedules listed on the HLE website.

In contrast to the far larger Disney parks, HLE is modest in size and aspiration, with no rides, parades, or games. Within the park, the Holy Land Experience consists of approximately six buildings, plus replicas of the Dead Sea Scrolls cave and Calvary's Garden Tomb. An additional structure, built in a fourth-century Byzantine style according to the HLE literature, is The Scriptorium: Center for Biblical Antiquities.

The Experience

Guests arrive by driving through a Roman-arch replica entrance, based on arches from Jerash (ancient Gerasa) in central Jordan.

Entrance to the park is through turnstiles placed within the arched city gate modeled on the (Ottoman) Bab el-Khalil, or Jaffa Gate of the Old City of

Jerusalem, replete with guards in Roman dress. Just inside the gate, a small court-yard centered on a faux well, a few tables, and a cart with souvenir items for sale forms the Jerusalem Street Market. The "street" continues slightly to the left, but directly ahead of the visitor is an entrance to the first and most upscale shop, the Methusaleh Mosaic store, which connects inside to another shop, the Old Scroll Shop. A diverse selection of merchandise is available, including souvenirs (refrigerator magnets, T-shirts, etc.), stones from the Holy Land, jewelry, videos, Dead Sea scroll items, and a variety of books, from cookbooks to religious materials. A striking amount of Judaica is available in the gift shops, such as hannukias, mezuzot, and seder plates.

Passing through either the shops or the Jerusalem Street Market, the passage then opens onto the path where a number of choices are available to the visitor. To the right, the Wilderness Tabernacle provides a shaded area modeled after a Bedouin tent where visitors sit, awaiting a twenty-five-minute multimedia presentation, *The Old Testament Ritual of Worship*. Inside, visitors are seated on bleacher-style seats, where the presentation includes two actors dressed as Levitical priests, reenacting the rites of the ancient priesthood against a backdrop of stars (photo 14.1). This includes a cutaway view of what is termed the "sacred Ark of the Covenant."

After viewing the presentation of the Old Testament ritual of worship in the Wilderness Tabernacle, the visitor exits into the Plaza of the Nations, an open stone courtyard expanse surrounded by thirty Roman columns and dominated by the Temple of the Great King. Within the courtyard leading up to the Temple of the Great King, concerts and biblical drama reconstructions are staged on the steps. To the left of the plaza is the main entrance, centered directly in front of and framing the temple. Visitors are shepherded into an area outside of the temple to wait for the next showing of a video entitled *The Seed of Promise*. Although visitors are free to choose their own plan of action, they are also ushered along from one venue to the next in a carefully conceived plan that exposes them to the optimal amount of religious content and greatest number of shopping opportunities.

The six-story gleaming Temple of the Great King, based on an assumed facade of the Herodian temple, a "one-half scale representation of the holy Jerusalem Temple that stood on hallowed Mount Moriah in the first century A.D." is touted as "God's home on earth. It was the same place where Abraham, nearly two millennia before Christ was born, was to offer his son Isaac as a sacrifice. King Solomon also built the very first Temple on the same site. And in the time of Jesus, the priests would gather on the steps and sing Psalms of Ascent to the Lord."

Inside of the Temple of the Great King is the Theater of Life, where the movie *The Seed of Promise* is shown to visitors. According to Zion's Hope, the film "powerfully communicates God's master plan for redeeming mankind." The film opens in A.D. 70 as the Romans use a battering ram to crash through the temple doors

Photo 14.1.   Postcard for sale at Holy Land Experience depicting a scene from a performance in the Wilderness Tabernacle.

while "the priests hold unwaveringly to the belief that their sacrifices will save them from destruction." Alternating with the images of the battering ram are images of a stake being driven through the hand of Jesus, giving the impression that these events occurred simultaneously as viewed on the big screen. At the end of the film, dry ice is piped into the auditorium below the seats to simulate the effect that the viewers are in heaven meeting the creator, mirroring the images in the film. The effect on the audience was profound; many in the audience were tearful, many were praying. After the film the path leads visitors from the temple to Calvary's Garden Tomb.

To the left, Calvary's Garden Tomb (photo 14.2) is found down the Via Dolorosa Path leading past the imitations of a Roman road, an olive press, and indigenous plants and trees of the Holy Land toward the Garden Tomb. In the brochure, the opportunity to spend "some time resting, praying, or reflecting in the Garden" is offered, with periodic dramas enacted by actors in traditional biblical garb—cowl and sandals—depicting the message of the gospel in word and music. On the website of the HLE, Calvary's Garden Tomb is promoted as "an authentic replication of the actual tomb of Jesus in Jerusalem" (Holy Land Experience 2001), presumably based on the tomb outside of Jerusalem's Old City that many Protestants regard as the site of Christ's entombment. However, the Church of the Holy Sepulchre is widely regarded in the Catholic and Orthodox churches as the site of Christ's crucifixion, burial, and resurrection. Choosing one or the other for replication at HLE is a religious decision based on historical precedents and preferences. The more barren, unembellished tomb cut into stone may appeal to Protestant preferences by avoiding any reference to the Catholic and Orthodox churches, and avoiding the ritual- and symbol-laden hierarchies those churches represent.

Photo 14.2.   Calvary's Garden Tomb, Holy Land Experience. Photo by Morag Kersel.

Visitors can meet their more basic needs by turning right: food and beverages are the next stop on the logical progression through the theme park. Adjacent to the courtyard of the Plaza of the Nations is the Oasis Palms Café (photo 14.3), an Arabian-themed cafeteria-style (buffeteria) restaurant where patrons sit among Bedouin rugs, traditional agricultural implements of the Near East, and music with an Arabic flavor. Along with time-honored American fare exoticized with biblical names such as Goliath burgers, Jaffa hot dogs and fries, or chicken sandwiches and Coca-Cola, patrons may order Jaffa felafel, Israeli salad, or hummus and pita from a wall menu in the shape of Torah scrolls.

The final building, where the Jerusalem Model A.D. 66 is housed, is the Shofar Auditorium. Inside is the model of the Old City of Jerusalem, touted as the largest indoor model of Jerusalem in the world, requiring over a year to construct. Periodically throughout the day, a detailed presentation is provided including a discussion of the development of the city and Jesus' movements during the last week of his life until his crucifixion. Extensive shopping opportunities are also available within the building.

Two exhibits remained unfinished at the time of our visit, the Qumran Dead Sea Caves and the Scriptorium, although the structures for each appeared to be completed externally. According to our guide, David Rosenthal, son of the president of Zion's Hope and founder of HLE, the Scriptorium will house "one of the finest private collections of biblical artifacts in the world including cuneiform, scrolls, codices, manuscripts, and Bibles." Rosenthal told us that a Michigan collector (whom he did not identify) donated a large portion of the HLE collection. The concept behind the Scriptorium, according to Rosenthal, will be to present the various authentic forms of the Bible through time.

Photo 14.3.   Oasis Palms Café.

The structure representing the Qumran Dead Sea Caves, created using forced perspective, appears to be complete on the exterior but was not quite finished during our visit. Rosenthal alluded to future plans for park expansion, including reproductions of Capernaum and other aspects of the Sea of Galilee region. It will come as little surprise if additional shopping opportunities and food venues accompany any new exhibit spaces. Finally, HLE is exited through the same entrance gate, channeling visitors back through the Jerusalem Street Market, the two nearby shops, and a final opportunity for any last-minute shopping.

Representing the Other in the Holy Land

The linkage between Americans and the Holy Land was established from the earliest days in North America. According to Ben-Arieh, until the eighteenth century Jerusalem was viewed by Christians as important as the city of God, but not for its physical or geographical characteristics (1997, 27). For the Puritans, the North American land was conceptualized as sacred, and their entry into it divine; early settlers also projected the Holy Land onto the geography of America, naming over a thousand places with biblical names (Greenberg 1991). With the rapid growth of Protestantism in the late nineteenth and early twentieth centuries, many Americans shared similar experiences growing up to those of Edward Robinson, when biblical scenes were not only experienced in Sunday school but at home, in school, and often on a daily basis (Handy 1977, 37). As children grew up, biblical place-names were heard and read, and reinforced on the landscape of America as well. Robinson's travel writings thus tapped into an awareness of biblical scenes and stories held in common for many Americans.

In the nineteenth century, a new form of Christian pilgrimage literature, inclusive of millenarian views, grew with the expanding travel accounts by Protestants. During this period, emphasis on the physical land and geography supplanted that of the earlier metaphysical ideals of the Holy Land. Examining evidence from Robert E. M. Bain's prints in the large, predominantly photographic volume *Earthly Footsteps of the Man of Galilee* (1894), John Davis (1992) argues that when the inhabitants of the Holy Land didn't measure up to scripturally derived American expectations, Americans were happy to appropriate the role of the chosen people. As Davis argues, these early examples of American Holy Land depictions confronted a dilemma—the people inhabiting that land. Davis contends that Bain's photographs of sacred locales, following Christ's footsteps in chronological and geographical order, either eliminated indigenous people or diminished them through ridicule or scorn. For similar reasons, the re-creation and replication of Palestine in North America allowed participants to focus on sacred geography without the intrusive presence of the Jewish and Muslim inhabitants.

One common thread throughout the many images of the Holy Land was the desire to represent biblical narratives as well as the landscape that formed an important facet of American social and historical identities. That identity, a specifically Protestant one, often ignored the indigenous peoples. Despite the large increase in travel to the Holy Land after the Civil War, pilgrimage remained restricted to the few. Although there was an expansion in travel through time, problems of distance, cost, and logistics continued to limit potential visitors. There were alternatives, however, such as the scholarly writings of the biblical geographer and father of biblical archaeology, Edward Robinson, and the many inspired by him who created a burgeoning Holy Land travel literature, particularly after the Ottoman authorities lifted the ban on the establishment of Protestant missions (Ben-Arieh 1997, 27–28). Travelers and pilgrims to the Holy Land during the nineteenth century were shocked when their expectations were poorly met by the Holy Land reality, most famously remarked by Mark Twain and Herman Melville (Davison 1977, 13). Coupled with this realization and the limited successes of missionary efforts in the Holy Land (Handy 1977, 38–39), the possibility for expanding the idea of the sacred land within North America could be elaborated. Two such examples are exemplified by replicas such as Palestine Park at the Chautauqua Institution and the St. Louis World's Fair of 1904.

The Chautauqua Movement and Palestine Park

The Chautauqua movement was a religious and educational enterprise, originally opening as a Sunday school institute in New York in 1874, initiated by John Vincent, essayist for the book *Earthly Footsteps* in which Bain's photographs appeared (Vincent 1971, 16). Sermons were few and no services were held; the concept was based on the thoughtful study of the Bible, nature, and science as part of teaching sacred geography. In the early years this included exhibitions of panoramic paintings, stereo photographs of Palestine, complemented by lectures on the early aspects of life in the Holy Land, to instruction in Aramaic, Hebrew, and Arabic (Davis 1992, 257).

Within a few years of opening, Chautauqua was successful, and it was not long afterward that a local resident, W. W. Wythe, opened a landscaped park known as Palestine Park (Davis 1992, 257). It was a 170-foot scale model of the central most religiously relevant portions of the Holy Land, using Chautauqua Lake as the Mediterranean. Based on the popularity of the area, Palestine Park underwent several reconstructions, with the addition of cast-metal cities and growing to 350 feet. The outdoor geographic model was used as a teaching instrument, with lectures around the diminutive mountains and the Sea of Galilee. The nature of this enterprise—re-creating the Holy Land in North America—was envisioned as a long-term project with sacred underpinnings to the pedagogy: "The old model of Palestine will by that time have been repaired. Returning merchant-ships from the Levant will have brought quantities of rock, earth, and timber from Syria itself; these will be transferred to Chautauqua, become a part of our own model of Palestine, and people may tread the sacred soil without crossing the sea" (Vincent 1971, 235).

Davis (1992) argues that Palestine Park represented American desires to dwell in the "real" Holy Land. Visitors to Palestine Park often donned Oriental costumes, including Reverend Ostrander, who spoke daily before a model of the Jewish Tabernacle of the Wilderness while wearing the "miter, robe, and breastplate of the high priest" (Davis 1992, 264, fig. 16) similar to performances by employees (photo 14.4) and the multimedia presentation of the Wilderness Tabernacle of HLE.

Another regular, known for delivering lectures in Arab garb, climbed atop a re-creation of a Jerusalem dwelling to sound the call to prayer like a muezzin, indicative of the desire for people to move from the role of the chosen race in the New World to that of the Old World (Davis 1992). Unlike the Chautauquan conflation of Jewish and Islamic culture, ancient and present time, represented by an amalgamation of Middle Eastern Bible people, the HLE is more specifically aimed at framing the Jewish people as the antecedents to Christians, not as contemporaries.

Photo 14.4.   Employee of the Holy Land Experience dressed as a levitical priest and blowing a shofar. Photo by Morag Kersel.

St. Louis World's Fair of 1904

A predecessor to HLE, the big hit of the St. Louis World's Fair of 1904 (the Louisiana Purchase Exposition), was the extensive area called the "Pike," a commercial endeavor over a mile long with concessions and amusements that included a reproduction of the Holy City with twenty-two streets and three hundred buildings, covering eleven acres (Davis 1992, 266). The St. Louis World's Fair was twice the size of the Chicago Fair, and included the largest anthropological exhibit of any world's fair. Representations of the Church of the Holy Sepulchre, the Western (Wailing) Wall, and the Dome of the Rock surrounded 1,000 people imported from Jaffa for the event. Although on a grander scale and including the active participation of foreign peoples, its goals were to provide a similar experience to Palestine Park—all aspects of the St. Louis Jerusalem were tightly controlled, just as Palestine Park provided a safe place, sanctified by the overt religious intent. Similar to HLE, the St. Louis version focused on representing Jerusalem, but more inclusive of symbolically critical structures than created for HLE.

Gilbert (1994) suggests that world's fairs, as the destinations of modern pilgrimages, fit within the long history of sacred travel in Western society. Like earlier forms of pilgrimages to ancient holy places, where sacred fragments of bone, water, or wood could confer authenticity on the traveler's experience, souvenirs from fairs also conferred a modern form of experiential authenticity, despite the mass production of souvenirs (Gilbert 1994, 23).

Representations and Commodification of the Holy Land

For MacCannell (1973, 1976), tourists are alienated people seeking authenticity as a form of fulfillment. Greater interest in heritage as a perceived more natural, nonmodern, or pristine time may be viewed as one component of this desire to find authenticity. Authenticity, however, is a fluid concept. In some respects, the tourist's desire for authentic experience is a modern embodiment of the religious pilgrim, a ritual process forming or reaffirming a collective consciousness (Graburn 1989). As heritage undergoes a process of commodification, niche tourism reflects different meanings attached to what the individual believes to be an appropriate use of leisure time. The search for an authentic experience is less crucial to understand the motivation of tourism according to Turner and Turner (1978), who also view tourism travel similar to a pilgrimage by representing a period of liminality for participants, where daily life and the structured organization of society is suspended during the antistructural aspects of the ritual process (Turner 1969).

Although at many heritage sites a reconstruction offers the opportunity to step back in time and experience what life was really like, there must always be a selective portrayal of events and histories that are tailored to reflect the tastes of the modern visitor. At a site such as the HLE, the creators recognize the limits on authenticity, set as it is far from the actual Middle East and based on replication. (Indeed, David Rosenthal at HLE noted several times the great expense and concerted effort necessary to replicate structures such as the entrance gate or the caves in which the Dead Sea scrolls were found.) At the same time, the experience is less contingent on exact replication of events, reconstruction of buildings, or portrayals of personages. Instead, the emphasis is on promotion of biblical narratives for education and spiritual edification of visitors. In this way, the specific desire to promote something similar to a religious pilgrimage is overt, not covertly arising out of alienation. Nevertheless, particular events and narratives must be and are chosen with a particular goal in mind, that of eliciting a religious experience or education. This follows in a tradition of American interest in the Holy Land without the obtrusive realities of the current affairs; people, their political aspirations, and their very place in the land of the Bible are removed.

How might authenticity be conferred? Prentice (2001, 12) suggests a variety of associations may be used to impart authenticity. Museums, for example, evoke authenticity through original artifacts from the past; association with a location, as memorial museums often do, may also commemorate events through proximity to where something important occurred, or is thought to have occurred (Prentice 2001, 7–8). How might the authentic be evoked in the absence of typical key elements, or even direct experience? Although a venue such as HLE cannot offer claims to nationalism given the diverse background of Americans, authenticity may be conferred through establishing what Prentice termed the "offer of origins" (Prentice 2001, 19). Just as English (Hewison 1991), Irish (Costa, this volume), or African (Ebron 2000) identity is marketed to tourists, so this idea may be extended to include those common origins people seek or recognize, defined beyond national borders. Authenticity may be promoted through shared spiritual origins, by tapping into beliefs centered on mutual religious origins. In this particular respect, HLE may be seen as analogous to study tours, one for Protestant believers, who wish for betterment and enrichment by gaining insights and a reaffirmation of faith enhanced by experiential encounters. Yet there can be little doubt that HLE represents what Prentice termed "constructed authenticity," the offer of an experience otherwise unobtainable through other means.

HLE represents an additional installment in the unfolding and changing perception of the Holy Land as a key metaphor for aspirations to Protestant dominion over a land regarded sacred. Out of necessity, that perspective is also aimed at a specific audience, much less general than earlier symbolic representations of the Holy Land such as those exemplified by Palestine Park at Chautauqua and the St. Louis World's Fair. Moreover, it encourages the extension of a continued transnational postimperial era attachment to the biblical past, to which the United States was an enthusiastic latecomer.

This is obviously a significant difference from the use of archaeological images, finds, and heritage for nation-states to claim ancient glories as their own. Instead, there is a subcultural aspiration to highlight Jesus' path in the Holy Land. Yet there are some similarities. Christianity, of course, considers the sacred nature of the land primarily based on Jesus' central role after descending in the form of a man, and his return from that land. If the divine presence is considered to dwell in the land of Palestine and Israel, the periods when the nascent Jewish and Christian faiths ripened are the periods of specific interest to the HLE enterprise, as they are to much of the Western world (Ben-Arieh 1991, 10). For Christian evangelicals, Israel as Zion is predicated on an understanding of that land as sacred, spiritual territory, one that in some way must be restored for redemption. This is not a recent Christian perspective but one established for centuries; the land of Christ's incarnation and redemption, the nativity, Christ's childhood, preaching, resurrection, and ascension all occurred on the landscape regardless of whether later associations are historically authentic or not (Werblowsky 1997, 12). Nevertheless, this seems to be a particularly Protestant vision; Rome as the particular focal nexus for pilgrimage retains centrality for many Catholics (Klatzker 1991, 69–70).

Although there are clear drawbacks to planning to create a representation of the Holy Land in Orlando (cost, lack of clear authenticity, lack of sacred landscape), there are benefits as well. Control over what is represented and how it is presented is perhaps the most obvious mitigating factor. In this way, choices underscore the facets of the mythical Holy Land that Christians, particularly those open to the evangelical message of Zion's Hope, consider central to representing the land of the Bible such as Christ's tomb, the temple, and the holy city of Jerusalem. Equally emblematic are those many elements that are left out, such as Masada, the Church of the Holy Sepulchre, or the Dome of the Rock, and a host of other sites with emotive value to others, but not viewed as central to Jesus' path. Obviously, all aspects of the biblical narrative and landscape cannot possibly be represented. Nevertheless, there are similarities with other depictions and visual images of the Holy Land dating back to the nineteenth century that suggest historical continuity in motivation. This allows participants, in particular believers, to validate and elevate their sense of placement in history.

HLE is a decidedly and unabashedly Christian version of the Holy Land; Judaism is virtually nonexistent except in its role as the essential roots of Christianity, and as a purchasing opportunity. Islam, of course, is absent. Virtually no mention of Jewish inhabitants is made during the public presentation of the model of Jerusalem. It is also interesting to note that nowhere at the HLE is there any discussion of archaeology, despite Rosenthal's focus on accurate replication and rendering of structures and use of objects (such as the authentic forms of the Bible to be displayed in the Scriptorium) to establish authenticity. Everything that is replicated or fabricated derives from biblical, rather than archaeological, sources. Calvary's Garden Tomb, apparently named and modeled after the Garden Tomb near the Damascus Gate outside of Jerusalem's Old City, is promoted as the actual tomb of Jesus without inclination to offer proof, nor is a rationale offered as to why this particular tomb is more likely than that of the Church of the Holy Sepulchre, the latter also traditionally considered the place of Jesus' entombment and his resurrection to Catholic and Orthodox believers.

The solution at Chautauqua was different because it was participatory, obviating the need for indigenous peoples or actors. The desire to modify space to a surrogate Holy Land, playing a role as both an instructional device and part of the spiritual and physical lives of the Chautauquans, is nevertheless quite similar to HLE.

This is not to suggest that the creators of the HLE are solely manipulating visitors for profit; their interest in bringing the Bible to visitors is repeatedly stated and seems earnest.[1] Nor is this necessarily a completely inaccurate depiction of the current Old City of Jerusalem, where at least two of the four main gates leading into the Old City also confront the visitor with a vast array of souvenirs, food and drink, and religious paraphernalia—primarily Christian and Jewish. In the city of Jerusalem, one is treated to a booming sound and light show at the Tower of David Museum utilizing an array of models, reconstructions, and electronic visual aids including film. Multimedia are increasingly incorporated at other sites with historical content in Jerusalem and Israel, and a model of ancient Jerusalem is a popular tourist destination. In fact one visitor to the Holy Land Experience suggested that it is was better than the real thing, not as "smelly" as butcher's alley (*suq el-lahham*) in Jerusalem's Old City—and much less crowded. This sentiment is apparently common, and was echoed by Senator J. R. Burton at the dedication ceremony of the Jerusalem Exhibition at the St. Louis World's Fair, when he noted more than once that a visit to the exhibit would be superior to visiting the real Jerusalem (Rubin 2000, 67).

Similarly, the more technologically advanced HLE provides a transformative experience, albeit brief. By fetishizing the Holy Land and despite the blatantly replicated aspects, HLE is able to exploit a sentiment somewhat similar to what John K. Wright (1966) termed *geopiety*, such that participants are able to maintain not only an attachment to a geographic area, but a perceived spiritual and cultural superiority. The overt marketing, even by a nonprofit venture, is simply the next logical step that many other ventures tapping into heritage employ.

It would be unsurprising to find what is sometimes known as the heritage industry, especially those in charge of museums and historical sites, disdainful of such places as the HLE. There is, of course, no claim of authenticity around the chosen plot of land, the buildings, or the performers and sales people hired by the organization. Rubin underscores four typical American characteristics reflected in the Jerusalem Exhibition at St. Louis (Rubin 2000, 68), three of which remain major factors at the HLE nearly one hundred years later. First, similar to the model at the St. Louis Exposition, which was claimed to be the largest of its kind, the Scriptorium at HLE is claimed to house "the world's largest indoor model of first-century Jerusalem" (Holy Land Experience 2003). Second, the emphasis on a live experience, a "virtual visit," is a trend shared not just with the World's Fair at St. Louis and HLE, but also Williamsburg, Virginia, and other similar historically themed sites. Third, the central role Holy Scripture and the Holy Land play as a theme throughout American culture, particularly among Protestants. Only the profit motive, a primary goal in American society (Rubin 2000, 68), is not clearly a fundamental goal of HLE, although marketing of goods is clearly intended to generate substantial revenue.

In some sense, this then is the most purely commercialized form of commodifying the past, the next logical step in promoting versions of the past where mass cultural tourism and pilgrimage intersect. Visitors wishing to become closer to the biblical narrative are only one additional step removed from authenticity, that of proximity, than those who actually walk in one of the various putative Garden Tombs in Jerusalem or along the Via Dolorosa. I would argue that the distance from the authentic place located within Israel/Palestine is not of vital concern to visitors attracted to the HLE, because people are interested in constructing authentic relationships with a particular retelling of the past, and that past assists them in the construction or reaffirmation in a sense of identity. As David Lowenthal (1996, 128) points out, "heritage passes on exclusive myths of origin and continuance, endowing a select group with prestige and common purpose." Creating that constructed experience of shared spiritual identity is only enhanced through use of authenticating elements such as ancient texts and agricultural implements, not dependent on them.

The Holy Land Experience condenses various experiences into one place. As a tourist venue containing models, performances, multimedia displays, and, of course, shopping, it represents a theme park destination. As a site for religious observation, biblical education, and spiritual edification, aspects of pilgrimage are evoked. And finally, as a model of a foreign place considered sacred by its creators and visitors, the site maintains the continuity of tradition Americans feel for a religious setting.

Visitors to HLE occupy a particular subset of the tourism industry, one that does not fit neatly within the larger realm of international tourism. Superficially, visiting HLE has more in common with family vacations to Disney World, but perhaps with similar motivations to those fueling visits to battlefield sites or art museums. At the same time, the religious impetus parallels the one that stimulated travel and pilgrimage to the Middle East. But HLE provides the opportunity to evoke religious sentiments while avoiding costly travel, inconvenient political realities, and face-to-face encounters with people of differing cultural backgrounds.

If, over time, the HLE exhibits the power to motivate visitors as active participants in pilgrimages, additional layers of semantic complexity will be involved through the ritual process as a form of group creation and affirmation. Nevertheless, the commercial strategy will undoubtedly remain, underscoring the contradictory aspect to the self-conscious production of solidarity through the avowed evangelical and spiritual mission.

A major focal point for current cultural analyses centers on investigative approaches to studying global and local processes. HLE represents a different permutation of what Benedict Anderson (1991) termed "long-distance nationalism," in this case a nationalism with continuity to American perceptions of what is sacred in the Holy Land. This commodification of the past fits well into the process of globalization, where time and place are deemphasized in favor of reconstructing a past and place regardless of earlier political or natural boundaries. People seeking to anchor themselves in an identity through the HLE are cultivating relationships through communities, despite their separation from the physical place being replicated. Even if they are not located in the Middle East, places may arouse great passion; like many people, those that HLE is trying to reach and draw in are those living in that small place between the future we envision and that past many wish to recapture. In this way, HLE performs a similar role as many archaeologies from around the world, by providing material correlates for stories and myths of identity and belonging. It is here, perhaps, that archaeologists should examine how easily a gulf may form between an academic perception of how the public should understand the past and how easily the past may become decontextualized and dehistoricized in favor of simplified, profitable renditions of the past divorced from any scholarly influence.

Note

1. Although Zion's Hope, Inc., is a nonprofit ministry, a recent ruling granted a tax exemption for the sanctuary and administration building but not the theme park (*New York Times*, November 23, 2001).

Acknowledgments

The author would like to thank Uzi Baram, Morag Kersel, and Stephen Shoemaker for their constructive comments on this chapter. David Rosenthal kindly provided a guided tour of the park, for which the author expresses his appreciation.

References

Anderson, Benedict. 1991. *Imagined Communities: Reflections on the Origin and Spread of Nationalism.* New York: Verso.

Baram, Uzi. n.d. "National Identity, History, and Heritage: Perspectives on Tourism and Archaeology in Israel." Manuscript in possession of author.

Ben-Arieh, Yehoshua. 1991. "Holy Land Views in Nineteenth-Century Western Travel Literature." In *With Eyes toward Zion—III,* edited by M. Davis and Y. Ben-Arieh, 10–29. New York: Praeger.

———. 1997. "Jerusalem Travel Literature as Historical Source and Cultural Phenomenon." In *Jerusalem in the Mind of the Western World, 1800–1948,* edited by Y. Ben-Arieh and M. Davis, 25–46. Westport, Conn.: Praeger.

Davis, John. 1992. "Holy Land, Holy People? Photography, Semitic Wannabes, and Chautauqua's Palestine Park." *Prospects, An Annual of American Cultural Studies* 17: 241–71.

Davison, Roderic H. 1977. "The Search for Sources." In *With Eyes toward Zion,* edited by M. Davis, 88–99. New York: Arno.

Ebron, Paula. 2000. "Tourists as Pilgrims: Commercial Fashioning of Transatlantic Politics." *American Ethnologist* 26(4): 910–32.

Gilbert, James. 1994. "World's Fairs as Historical Events." In *Fair Representations,* edited by R. Rydell and N. Guinn, 14–27. Amsterdam: Amsterdam University Press.

Glassberg, David. 2001. *Sense of History: The Place of the Past in American Life.* Amherst: University of Massachusetts Press.

Goell, Yohai, and Martha B. Katz-Hyman. 1977. "Americans in the Holy Land, 1850–1900: A Select Bibliography." In *With Eyes toward Zion,* edited by M. Davis, 100–125. New York: Arno.

Goulding, Christina. 2000. "The Commodification of the Past, Postmodern Pastiche, and the Search for Authentic Experiences at Contemporary Heritage Attractions." *European Journal of Marketing* 34(7): 835–53.

Graburn, N. 1989. "Tourism: The Sacred Journey." In *Hosts and Guests: The Anthropology of Tourism,* edited by V. Smith, 21–36. Philadelphia: University of Pennsylvania Press.

Greenberg, Gershon. 1991. "America—Holy Land and Religious Studies: On Expressing a Sacred Reality." In *With Eyes toward Zion—III,* edited by M. Davis and Y. Ben-Arieh, 50–62. New York: Praeger.

Handy, Robert T. 1977. "Sources for Understanding American Christian Attitudes toward the Holy Land, 1800–1950." In *With Eyes toward Zion,* edited by M. Davis, 34–56. New York: Arno.

Hewison, R. 1991. *The Heritage Industry: Britain in a Climate of Decline.* London: Methuen.

Holy Land Experience. 2001. Press information. www.theholylandexperience.com/press/construction.html. Accessed October 2001.

———. 2003. The Holy Land Experience Fact Sheet. www.theholylandexperience.com/press/facts.html. Accessed June 17, 2003.

Klatzer, David. 1991. "American Christian Travelers to the Holy Land, 1821–1939." In *With Eyes toward Zion—III,* edited by M. Davis and Y. Ben-Arieh, 63–76. New York: Praeger.

———. 1997. "Sacred Journeys: Jerusalem in the Eyes of American Travelers before 1948." In *Jerusalem in the Mind of the Western World, 1800–1948,* edited by Y. Ben-Arieh and M. Davis, 47–58. Westport, Conn.: Praeger.

Lowenthal, David. 1996. *Possessed by the Past: The Heritage Crusade and the Spoils of History.* New York: Free Press.

———. 1998. *The Heritage Crusade and the Spoils of History.* Cambridge: University of Cambridge Press.

MacCannell, Dean. 1973. "Staged Authenticity: Arrangements of Social Space in Tourist Settings." *American Journal of Sociology* 79(3): 589–603.

———. 1976. *The Tourist: A New Theory of the Leisure Class.* London: Macmillan.

Prentice, Richard. 2001. "Experiential Cultural Tourism: Museums and the Marketing of the New Romanticism of Evoked Authenticity." *Museum Management and Curatorship* 19(1): 5–26.

Rubin, Rehav. 2000. "When Jerusalem Was Built in St. Louis: A Large Scale Model of Jerusalem in the Louisiana Purchase Exposition 1904." *Palestine Exploration Quarterly* 132: 59–70.

Shackel, Paul A. 2000. *Archaeology and Created Memory: Public History in a National Park.* New York: Kluwer Academic/Plenum.

Silberman, Neil A. 1997. "Structuring the Past: Israelis, Palestinians, and the Symbolic Authority of Archaeological Monuments." In *The Archaeology of Israel: Constructing the Past, Interpreting the Present,* edited by N. A. Silberman and D. Small, 62–81. Sheffield: Sheffield Academic Press.

Tuan, Yi-Fu. 1975. "Geopiety: A Theme in Man's Attachment to Nature and to Place." In *Geographies of the Mind: Essays in Historical Geosophy,* edited by D. Lowenthal and M. J. Bowden, 11–39. New York: Oxford University Press.

Turner, V. 1969. *The Ritual Process: Structure and Anti-structure.* Chicago: Aldine.

Turner, Victor, and Edith Turner. 1978. *Image and Pilgrimage in Christian Culture.* New York: Columbia.

Vincent, John H. [1885] 1971. *The Chautauqua Movement.* New York: Books for Libraries.

Vogel, Lester I. 1991. *To See a Promised Land.* University Park: Pennsylvania State University Press.

Werblowsky, R. J. Zwi. 1997. "The Meaning of Jerusalem to Jews, Christians, and Muslims." In *Jerusalem in the Mind of the Western World, 1800–1948,* edited by Y. Ben-Arieh and M. Davis, 7–21. Westport, Conn.: Praeger.

Wright, John K. 1966. "Notes on Early American Geopiety." In *Human Nature in Geography,* edited by J. K. Wright, 250–85. Cambridge: Harvard University Press.

ARCHAEOLOGISTS AND THE
MARKETING OF HERITAGE

VI

Is the Medium the Message? The Art of Interpreting Archaeology in U.S. National Parks   15

BARBARA J. LITTLE

ARCHAEOLOGICAL COMMUNICATION WITH and for the public is a booming enterprise. Marketing our discipline has never been seen as quite so important, as public support is perceived as being tied to the very survival of the archaeological resource base (e.g., SAA 1990; Smith and Ehrenhard 1991). The number of publications devoted to reaching the public has increased over the past decade (e.g., Jameson 1997; Little 2002; McManamon 1991; Stone and Molyneaux 1994; Stone and MacKenzie 1994; Smardz and Smith 2000), and the topic can now support the relatively new journal *Public Archaeology.*

Archaeologists have always borrowed from other disciplines, and now the art of interpretation is coming into the spotlight as archaeologists look for proven ways to engage the general public in places outside of the classroom. Archaeologists and interpreters undoubtedly will find themselves working more closely together at many heritage sites.

Interpreters are sensitive to the often expressed belief that theirs is an art which anyone who can speak or write can do. There is an ongoing discussion in the National Association for Interpretation (NAI) about the merits of certification and the professionalization of the discipline (e.g., Basman 1997; Blodgett 2000; LaPage 1998). Archaeologists, also plagued by a persistent idea that anyone with an interest in artifacts and a shovel can call him or herself an archaeologist, should be empathetic. Archeologists working with interpreters have to be prepared to learn enough to understand their colleagues' approaches, decisions, and motivations and, possibly, to become proficient in another profession.

One goal for this chapter is to discuss the generally accepted approach to interpretation within the National Park Service based on the influential work of Freeman Tilden (1977) and how that affects the choice of messages and the ways in which those messages are conveyed to visitors. A by-product of this effort is to provide resources to archaeologists who are interested in public outreach and interpretation (see especially the tables and appendix). Archaeologists may find it hard to understand why there are difficulties in connecting what we think the public should learn or appreciate and what interpreters think the public is likely to come away with from any interpretive experience. The rules of interpretation will affect the message that is conveyed to the public. Some current ideas about the best interpretation are, perhaps inadvertently, geared to the rules of media that privilege emotion over nearly any other desired result (Mathis 2002). I summarize Tilden's principles and contrast the interpretation of particulars and universals to suggest some ways that archaeologists might adapt the best principles of interpretation toward archaeological messages. I use the site of Jamestown, Virginia, as an illustration of the maturing of interpretation as a discipline as it seeks to create effective, inclusive interpretation, particularly at places that carry some chauvinistic, historical baggage.

Ground Shifts in the National Park Service

In the 1930s the National Park Service (NPS) underwent a fundamental ground shift with the addition of forty-four historic areas to a system mainly comprised of natural and scenic areas and the passage of the Historic Sites Act of 1935. One of the results of that legislation was to firmly establish the role of the service in education. It directed the secretary of the interior to develop "an educational program and service for the purpose of making available to the public facts and information pertaining to American historic and archeological sites, buildings, properties of national significance" (An Act to Provide for the Preservation of Historic American Sites, Buildings, Objects, and Antiquities of National Significance, and for Other Purposes, 49 Stat. 666, August 21, 1935).

A second ground shift is illustrated by the following two quotations concerning the purpose of such educational programs called for in the 1935 statute. Verne E. Chatelain, the first chief historian of the NPS, had the goal in mind of teaching the foundations of citizenship. In a 1935 presentation to the American Planning and Civic Association, he stated (as quoted in Mackintosh 1986):

> The conception which underlies the whole policy of the National Park Service in connection with [historical and archeological] sites is that of using the uniquely graphic qualities which inhere in any area where stirring and significant events have taken place to drive home to the visitor the meaning of those events showing not only their importance in themselves but their integral relationship to the whole history of American development. In other words, the task is to breathe the breath of life into American history for those to whom it has been a dull recital of meaningless facts—to recreate for the average citizen something of the color, the pageantry, and the dignity of our national past.

Dwight Pitcaithley, the current chief historian, also writes with citizenship in mind, but with a broader and more complex perception of the relationship between citizenship and history. He writes (as quoted in Diamant 2000, 40–41):

> Our goal is to offer a window into the historical richness of the National Park System and the opportunity it presents for understanding who we are, where we have been and how we as a society might approach the future. This collection of special places also allows us to examine our past—the contested along with the comfortable, the complex along with the simple, the controversial along with the inspirational.

This move toward historical inclusion represents another major ground shift, as social conscience is recognized as meaningful and appropriate in NPS public engagement. As Rolf Diamant (2000, 41) observes, "The national parks have become, in effect, a living part of our democracy contributing in many ways to the stability and continuity of civil society."

In 1937 a National Park Service booklet introduced historical areas in the eastern United States. The following is part of what the public was expected to find meaningful at Jamestown, which came under NPS jurisdiction when Colonial was proclaimed a national monument by President Herbert Hoover in 1930 (NPS 1937):

> Few historical shrines in America are of more interest than Jamestown Island. . . . At Jamestown Island on May 13, 1607, 13 years before the landing of the Pilgrims at Plymouth Rock, the English made their first permanent settlement in America. There in 1612 tobacco was first successfully raised by an Englishman. There the first legislative assembly in America was held in 1619, and in the same year negro [sic] slaves were introduced into an English colony for the first time.
>
> Under the direction of a trained staff, the National Park Service is conducting an extensive program of archeological and historical research on the island. Numerous brick foundations have been uncovered and antique pottery, glassware, ironware, and other interesting artifacts have been found, some of which are on display in the museum.

Contrast the varied assumptions that underlie such a statement with more recently stated themes. Jamestown is part of a larger park unit whose purpose is stated in the Jamestown long-range (i.e., 5–10 year) interpretive plan (NPS 2000, 6): "Colonial National Historical Park exists to preserve and interpret historic resources, landscapes and artifacts associated with the American colonial period from 1607 to 1781, at Jamestown, Yorktown and related sites, and to provide for a scenic highway connecting those sites for the benefit and enjoyment of the people." One cannot help but be struck by the breadth of the park's interpretive theme

1, which encourages a global view and multiple perspectives. This theme states (NPS 2000, 14): "The history and resources of Jamestown, Green Spring, Williamsburg, and Yorktown represent the cultural, military, political, social, economic, and diplomatic forces that changed English, other Europeans, Africans, and First Americans, in the thirteen colonies, into citizens of an independent United States."

The second parkwide theme, which highlights a different sort of significance (NPS 2000, 15), reads: "The resources of Jamestown, Williamsburg, and Yorktown were the subject of some of the earliest national preservation efforts." Box 15.1 lists the current primary and secondary themes specific to Jamestown.

The creation of parks and the choice of what messages to present to the public are an important part of building a sense of national identity. The way parks are interpreted "shape public history and public memory" (Diamant 2000, 32). In contrast to parks designated for their natural resources, cultural or historic

---

Box 15.1. Jamestown Themes (NPS 2000, 15–17)

Primary Themes

1. "As the first permanent English settlement in North America, Jamestown and its people experience many changes and adaptations often through experimentation that left a legacy of laws, language, and customs that were beneficial as well as tragic depending upon one's race."

   "This theme . . . is the interpretive expression of Jamestown's significance. . . . Under this theme, interpretation will explore the transfer as well as the clash of cultures, the creation and survival of a New World definition of communities, economies, and governments, and even the transformation of the landscapes and the exploitation of natural resources."

2. "Jamestown's people, native, immigrant, and enslaved, reflected diverse national and cultural traditions that influenced the emerging New World society."

3. "Jamestown experienced significant periods of development and decline as it physically and functionally evolved."

Secondary Themes

1. "The history of Jamestown reflects the many different ways that humans have interacted with the natural world."

2. "Jamestown, located on the James River, possessed strategic value during military conflicts from seventeenth to the nineteeth centuries."

3. "During the twentieth century, some of the most innovative methods and applications of the science of historical archeology were developed and applied in the exploring and rediscovery of Jamestown."

parks need active interpretation if the public is to understand their significance, as few historic sites can be appreciated without explanation (Mackintosh 1986). The ways in which the messages are chosen and conveyed are the interpreter's domain. The authors (NPS 2000, 29) of the most recent Jamestown interpretive plan express this widespread challenge: "Jamestown shares a basic problem with nearly every other historical site—most visitors struggle with context and relevance. They do not understand how a particular historical event or place fits into the bigger picture. Significance is fuzzy. Relevance to contemporary life is little considered, or worse, dismissed as nonexistent. Who cares? So what?"

The so-what challenge is met in various ways, according to agency principles, planning, and training. In the next section I introduce basic NPS approaches to interpretation. In the final section I offer some thoughts about the intersection between approaches to interpretation and the messages that may be conveyed through them.

Interpretation in the National Park Service

There have been many changes in interpretation in NPS since its establishment, but one constant over the past four decades is the influence of Freeman Tilden through his 1957 book, *Interpreting Our Heritage.* In a recent biographical piece, Robyn Dochterman (2002, 18) observes that "Tilden is widely revered as a teacher, mentor, and philosopher." Tilden was a well-known writer who started his career as a journalist at the turn of the twentieth century. He met Newton Drury, director of the National Park Service, in the 1940s and began consulting and writing for the NPS. Travels that he undertook to write *The National Parks: What They Mean to You and Me* (Tilden 1951) left Tilden impressed with the parks but unimpressed with the state of interpretation. As a result he convinced Director Conrad Wirth to fund a study of interpretation. Tilden undertook a "reappraisal of the basic principles which underlie the program of natural and historical interpretation in the National Park System" (Dochterman 2002, 24–25).

Tilden performed something like a writer's ethnography to see what general principles of effective interpretation he might discern. He traveled widely through the parks and took on roles as both interpreter and visitor. Tilden (1977, 36) writes of his experience in the parks that led to his principles:

> My experience is that the groups of people who seek out interpretation in the areas of the National Park System are wonderfully well-mannered and pathetically eager for guidance toward the larger aspects of things that lead toward wisdom and toward the consolations that come from a sense of living in a natural world and a historic continuity that "makes sense." And as a participant in such groups I have so many times had my enthusiasm wilted by an interlocutor who mistook information for interpretation—who became a poor instructor when he could have been an inspiring guide.

He also expresses his impatience with subject-matter experts. According to Tilden, the abhorrence of artistic form is what makes specialists bad interpreters (1977, 30): "To the specialist the use of metaphor is calamitous, and simile as almost an obscenity. Analogy may be employed, but only for the purpose of further perplexing a student." Clearly he believes in the effectiveness of such writers' tools and understands interpretation as an art form. Appreciation is a key factor. Tilden (1977, 90) writes of love as the priceless ingredient: "If you love the thing you interpret, and love the people who come to enjoy it, you need commit nothing to memory." He is particularly concerned with reverence for the many aspects of beauty. He (1977, 110) lists four: (1) scenic or landscape; (2) beauty of adventures of the mind: revelation of order of nature; (3) beauty of the artifact: inspiration to create beautiful things; and (4) beauty of human conduct or behavior. This fourth aspect of beauty clearly is more in keeping with Chatelain's concept of the pageantry and dignity of America's past than with a current understanding that interpretations of history need to confront the difficult and controversial.

Tilden's six principles of interpretation (box 15.2) are widely used and regarded as fundamental and fixed by many interpreters in the NPS and in other settings. The NAI definition of interpretation blends several of Tilden's points: "Interpretation is a communication process that forges emotional and intellectual connections between the interests of the audience and the inherent meanings in the resource." NPS interpretation rests squarely on Tilden's principles.

Tilden (1977, 38) summarizes one of the main purposes of interpretation by quoting an NPS administrative manual: "Through interpretation, understanding; through understanding, appreciation; through appreciation, protection." This focus on protection as the outcome of good interpretation persists within the NPS. In the current agency Management Policies (NPS 2001a, 73–77), the introductory paragraph to the chapter on interpretation and education states,

> Through interpretive and educational programs, the National Park Service will instill in park visitors an understanding, appreciation, and enjoyment of the significance of parks and their resources. Interpretive and educational programs will encourage the development of a personal stewardship ethic, and broaden public support for preserving park resources.

The NPS interpretive development program trains interpreters to use Tilden's principles to promote resource protection. The training program consists of modules numbered similarly to typical college courses. Module 101, "Fulfilling the NPS Mission: the Process of Interpretation," is the cornerstone module of the curriculum. The purpose of the module states that "every decision an interpreter makes for any interpretive effort must be based on the fundamental philosophies contained within this module." Therefore I describe its contents at some length.

Box 15.2. Interpretation According to Tilden (1977, 8–9)

Definition of Interpretation
"An educational activity which aims to reveal meanings and relationships through the use of original objects, by firsthand experience, and by illustrative media, rather than simply to communicate factual information" (8).

Concepts of Interpretation
"Interpretation is the revelation of a larger truth that lies behind any statement of fact" (8).
"Interpretation should capitalize mere curiosity for the enrichment of the human mind and spirit" (8).

The Principles of Interpretation
1. Any interpretation that does not somehow relate what is being displayed or described to something within the personality or experience of the visitor will be sterile (9).
2. Information, as such, is not interpretation. Interpretation is revelation based upon information. But they are entirely different things. However, all interpretation includes information (9).
3. Interpretation is an art, which combines many arts, whether the materials presented are scientific, historical or architectural. Any art is in some degree teachable (9).
4. The chief aim of interpretation is not instruction but provocation (9).
5. Interpretation should aim to present a whole rather than a part, and must address itself to the whole man rather than any phase (9).
6. Interpretation addressed to children (say, up to the age of twelve) should not be a dilution of the presentation to adults, but should follow a fundamentally different approach. To be at its best it will require a separate program (9).

The first of three components, "Why We Do Interpretation: Meeting the NPS Mission," establishes the foundation for Module 101 and provides a set of ground rules for interpreters to establish their own interpretive philosophy and explore ways in which interpretation contributes to resource protection and stewardship. The module clearly states that public recognition and support of their resource stewardship opportunities is the larger role of interpretation.

Module 101's second component, "What Is Interpretation: Tangibles, Intangibles, and Universal Concepts," describes the relationship between the resource and the audience and how interpretation, by presenting broadly relevant meaning, facilitates the connection of the two. The tangible/intangible linkages and universal concepts model addresses the "so what" of interpretation by describing the content of interpretive products: relevance and provocation, information, and technique. This model is suggested as a useful way to get at the "meanings" of the resource. Box 15.3 provides this component's core ideas, which are drawn from Tilden's principles. The linkages can be thought of as the important hooks for grabbing an audience described by authors such as Mitch Allen (2002) in his advice for writing and by Heather Hembrey (2001) in her advice about website design.

Box 15.3. Core Ideas of Module 101 Component: "What Is Interpretation: Tangibles, Intangibles, and Universal Concepts"

Linking Tangible Resources to Intangible Resources and Meanings

1. All parks have tangible resources, like physical features, buildings, artifacts, etc.
2. All parks have intangible resources, like past events, people, systems, ideas, values, etc.
3. All effective interpretation can be described as linking tangible resources to intangible resources in order to reveal meanings.
4. Some intangible anecdotes, events, people, and easily understood concepts can be used in a tangible way.
5. Tangible/intangible linkages provide varying degrees of relevance for the audience.

Universal Concepts

1. Universal concepts provide the greatest degree of relevance and meaning to the greatest number of people.
2. Universal concepts are intangible resources that almost everyone can relate to. They might also be described as universal intangibles.
3. Not all people will agree on the meaning of or share the same perspective towards a universal concept, but all people will relate to the concept in some significant way
4. Universal concepts make meanings accessible and the resource relevant to a widely diverse audience.
5. The implications of and techniques for presenting universal concepts (universal concepts don't necessarily have to be explained to be experienced or understood) will differ from resource to resource. However, all interpretation seeks to place the visitor in relationship with broad meanings.
6. Tangible/intangible/universal concepts can be captured and illustrated well by the theme of the interpretive product. The cohesive development of a relevant idea or ideas within an interpretive effort of any kind is enhanced by making links between tangibles, intangibles and universals. Example: The rocks (tangible) of Yosemite tell many stories of beauty, danger, and mystery (intangible).

The third component, "How Interpretation Works: The Interpretive Equation," introduces the interpreter to the five basic elements of the interpretive process through the use of a formula known as the "interpretive equation." This shorthand method reminds the interpreter of basic concepts that relate to all interpretive activities. Box 15.4 outlines the elements of the interpretive equation.

The NPS "compelling stories" idea, developed in the mid-1990s, is part of what the interpretive program calls the "Interpretive (R)evolution." The introduction to the compelling stories workbook (NPS n.d.) states in part:

> The Compelling Story concept . . . is an opportunity for interpreters to further embrace Freeman Tilden's Principles of Interpretation, and to apply them in innovative, thought provoking ways. The stories we tell and the resources we manage and protect, must be placed in a context of broader meaning and significance. When we interpret well, our audiences become participants, not spectators, and the resources we interpret become theirs. When we do our job well, visitors develop a deeper commitment to the stewardship of our national treasures.

The eight guidelines for measuring the effect of compelling stories are listed in box 15.5. Box 15.6 lists two "think exercises" that are an important part of the workbook and illustrate some of the directions that NPS interpretation is taking. Within Module 101, as part of skill development concerning universal concepts, interpreters are given an assignment that seems shockingly ambitious to any anthropologist. Each "learner should create a list of universal concepts and then study each item on the list and determine what it means in the context of human history and culture versus what it means in the context of Nature. What are the differences? What are the similarities? Will the conclusions allow for more fully integrated universal concepts in interpretive products?"

Tilden (1977, 91) wrote, "There is the challenge! To put your visitor in possession of at least one disturbing idea that may grow into a fruitful interest." In at least one sense, that single idea is currently promoted as stewardship of at-risk resources. The hook to capture interest is the emotion and empathy tied to a "universal." What does this mean for the interpretation of archaeology?

Story, Plot, and the Universe

Archaeology interpreted for the public is not simple translation. The methods and goals of interpreters affect what is considered important enough to convey to the public. The choice of message will be affected by current interpretive principles and by an interpreter's understanding of the craft. The choice of the story to tell will be affected by assessment of its universal concepts and ties to the conservation message.

Box 15.4. The Interpretive Equation

(KR + KA) × AT = IO (Knowledge of the Resource + Knowledge of the Audience) × Appropriate Techniques = Interpretive Opportunities

Knowledge of the resource, such as a particular archaeological site, cultural landscape or ecosystem, is needed if the interpreter is to identify compelling stories.

Knowledge of the audience includes understanding of the visitors' rights and the continuum of awareness of stewardship. The ultimate goal of interpretation is to provide opportunities for visitors to forge compelling linkages with the resources so that they develop an active stewardship ethic.

Visitors' Bill of Rights

Whether visiting a park on-site or off, visitors have a right to

1. have their privacy and independence respected
2. retain and express their own values
3. be treated with courtesy and consideration
4. receive accurate and balanced information

Visitor Continuum

Visitors generally fall into a continuum in one of the following five categories, any of which may lead to increasing awareness of the relationships between tangible resources and their intangible and universal values:

1. recreation/"trophy hunting"
2. nostalgia/refuge/isolation
3. information/knowledge
4. connections/linkages
5. stewardship/patrons

The interpreter's job is to ensure that visitors have a positive experience at any of these levels and to help visitors reach a deeper and richer level of understanding if possible. No matter where the visitors are on the continuum, the interpreter should strive to give them something of value to take home.

Appropriate techniques include (1) informational and orientation program, (2) interpretive programs, (3) curriculum-based educational programs, and (4) interpretive media. These are delivered through a variety of personal and nonpersonal tools.

Through personal services, staff interact with visitors such as at visitor centers and other contact points, and through talks, illustrated programs, conducted activities, demonstrations, performing arts, junior ranger programs, special events, and educational programs.

Non-personal services do not require the presence of staff and include printed media, exhibits, waysides, web pages, AV presentations, and radio information systems.

Box 15.5. Guidelines for Measuring the Effect of Compelling Stories (NPS n.d., 5)

Does the story move the visitor?
Do visitors care more about the resource because of the story?
Are visitors moved to some action that supports the stewardship of the resource?
Is the story emblematic? Does it represent some larger concept or meaning?
How does it connect to that larger meaning?
Can visitors clearly understand the connection?
Does the compelling story touch on a universal concept that is relevant to the visitor?
Is the story at its very core something that people care about?

What is important enough to study? to commemorate? to interpret? The ways in which archaeologists prioritize archaeological research and elevate certain time periods or resources into the category of "things worth studying" are clearly related to judgments about what is interesting enough or important enough to interpret. But the answers may differ widely, based on the respondent's training (as well as all other aspects of social context). Acts of commemoration, whether through park making and interpretation in the public sphere or through scholarly legitimization in the academic sphere, must somehow come to terms with the wider social, political, and economic context in which they are performed.

In marketing heritage, importance both in the interpretive sphere and in the academic sphere intersect with the economic sphere, where it matters what is appealing enough and organized enough for tourism. In that sphere, the visitor must be attracted and visitor characteristics identified. Are they casual or dedicated? School groups, families, individuals? What do they expect? In NPS interpretation, for example, the issue of whether provocation (Tilden's fourth principle) should be aimed at the casual visitor or the well-informed enthusiast is a constant dilemma (Mackintosh 1986). Many heritage sites have an economic interest in the bottom line and judge that paid admissions reflect how interpretive choices are received by the public.

Much heritage marketing is place based, but often the place is well-known for just part of its history. Consider that Jamestown could be presented simply as a place where the English established their first permanent settlement in the Americas. Interpretation is more complete, however, and satisfies more visitors, when it includes Powhatan and other Native Americans, Africans, and other Europeans along with the English. The NPS Untold Stories project focuses on filling in some of the stories that have not been told traditionally in national parks (e.g., NPS 2001b). One good research tool to fill in "knowledge of the resource" (box 15.4) is the NPS revised thematic framework for history and prehistory (NPS 1996).

The framework suggests a structure for researching inclusive and appropriately complex histories. It should help to foster discussion of the fundamental social and economic structures related to a place. Using the new framework can encourage interdisciplinary dialogue between interpretive and resource professionals. The framework is one of the tools available to help interpreters develop stories about people, place, and time. Using it increases the opportunity to tell integrated, compelling stories that enrich visitor experiences. Holistic stories may be used to connect significant events and activities in one place with those in other parks, thereby enriching visitor experience of a region.

The thematic framework is a useful companion to the compelling stories workbook. An interpreter can use the thematic framework as a conceptual tool to identify themes, make tangible-intangible links, apply Freeman Tilden's principles of interpretation, and get to the "knowledge of the resources," which is the first part of the interpretive equation. The larger implications and research possibilities of a place or site can then emerge more readily and produce better answers to the question "so what?" Appealing to—or even believing in—universal emotional hooks can lead to ahistorical and noncritical interpretation. The universal presents a challenge for archaeology and other types of history. It is difficult to suggest cause and effect within social and historical context if the focus is on people living their everyday lives; visitors are likely to walk away with the message that all lives are the same. Why would historical conditions and ethnographic facts matter if the point is simply the universal love for children or our common humanity with those past and future? The challenge is to link the local and the global in both time and space.

There is a pervasive trend in the broader media business that I offer as a caution in connection with the focus on compelling stories. In the early 1980s there was a change in the movie industry as power shifted from directors to producers. This shift resulted in the creation of the "high concept" (i.e., one-line ideas or situations). The overwhelming importance of high concept started at Paramount and rapidly took over the industry. Novelist David Morrell writes (2002, 42), "The purpose of high concept is to reduce a story to its simplest level and then to make sure that this simple reduction has some punch to it." He continues, "one trouble with this approach is that many great plots are too complicated to be reduced to a couple of words" and notes that the high concept eventually corrupted the book business as well as the movie industry. His (2002, 43) grievance may be enlightening for interpreters caught in the bind of telling catchy stories about complex events: "It's hard enough to invent an interesting, meaningful plot without being forced to choose one that can be summarized in a compelling sentence."

Morrell (2002, 44) uses E. M. Forster's distinction between a story and a plot in his attempt to counter reliance on high concept. A story is a series of events. The audience for a story asks, "and then? and then?" as a story demands only curiosity. A plot is based on causality and demands intelligence and memory, as the audience asks, "why?"

The story that tugs on universal emotions doesn't need a "why" or a historically based explanation of conflict or controversy. Even in the presentation of sites of struggle, the acknowledgment of universal experiences of pain, struggle, and sorrow serve the positive purpose of heightening empathy but may not offer any insight into the lessons that such history could offer. The "compelling story" idea is not necessarily restricted to "story" in the sense that Forster and Morrell use it, but the danger is there if it is approached formulaically. Interpreting the "why" demands more scholarly and artistic responsibility. The skill to suggest cause and effect also requires an ability to suggest that explanations might be incomplete or under constant reexamination and revision.

Tilden's principles were not written with diversity and inclusiveness in mind; nor were they written in an era that embraced difficult history. They were written to clarify what makes a particular art effective and they do not preclude any sort of content. In other words, nothing I write here should be taken to suggest that interpreters should abandon Tilden's principles or the methods derived from them. I don't suggest doing away with stories but want to see some of the stories reconceptualized as plot so that the visitor's intellect is as explicitly engaged as the emotions. What would Tilden say? It is worth remembering that in his discussion of the fifth principle (1977, 45–46), he warns the interpreter not to underestimate any visitor's intelligence.

The story–plot contrast is reminiscent of some of the theory wars in archaeology. Processually trained archaeologists may find some irony in discovering that the universal is not very useful in interpreting archaeological sites and ancient history unless interpretation focuses on method and preservation. It turns out that archaeologists need to know more than we thought we needed to. John Terrell (1990) makes some interesting observations about storytelling and prehistory as he emphasizes that story does not equal bad science and indeed structures what archaeologists tell. Referencing Hayden White, he worries that much of history is unwritten because nothing "happens" in the sense that we expect it to given the narrative structure we expect and use. Plot, therefore, may be necessary if many of the insights archaeologists gain are to be turned into stories of recognizable, and perhaps popular, form.

I have written elsewhere about compelling reasons for storytelling (Little 2000) and there is somewhat of a movement in historical archaeology surrounding storytelling (e.g., Praetzellis 1998). Archaeology has often suffered from searching only for what archaeologists thought they could definitively find: Witness the tightly drawn ecosystem models of the 1970s. Archaeology, along with many other scientific disciplines, is now reincorporating humanism, reuniting seemingly opposite approaches to knowledge. Good interpretation will also serve to prompt further analysis in that it demands certain information we are usually ill prepared to answer. If we want characters—and it is exceedingly difficult to weave a plot without them—we need to know more about people because artifacts make poor protagonists. If we want richly described scenes, then we need good environmental reconstructions and detailed architectural and artifactual information (Little 2000).

Closing Thoughts

I suggest that those who work at the intersection of archaeology and public must be aware of the public search for a useable past and be explicit about their role in creating and promoting such a past. James Green (2000) writes about "movement history" that is an activist history for social justice. He describes a public history that is useful in contemporary struggles as people call on the past for instruction and inspiration.

Some archaeological versions of such public engagement have focused on revealing methods so that the public might better judge the versions of the past offered to them (e.g., Leone et al. 1987; Potter 1994). This attention to the ways in which histories are made is widely applicable to archaeological interpretation because it focuses on shared methods and in that sense tends toward the universal. Currently, it is easy to sell conservation or preservation as a message of universal importance. Generally it is seen as a universal good by archaeologists. It is also an easy sell to interpreters to talk to the public about archaeological methods. The visible, field component of archaeology is still unusual enough to attract visitors for that reason alone.

Such interpretive focus can be balanced with attention to the historical particulars of a place. There are a growing number of community-based archaeological projects (e.g., Derry and Malloy 2003; Shackel and Chambers 2004). These tend more toward activist public history in Green's sense, as communities are impatient to get beyond method into the details and lessons of their own pasts. Archaeologists who work in publicly accessible places are in a good position to work closely with interpreters to broaden the usefulness of knowledge about the past.

Box 15.6. Sample "Think Exercises" from the NPS Compelling Stories Workbook

Think Exercise (NPS n.d., 5)

Think of a story or "set" of information that you interpret. Then reexamine Tilden's principles listed in box 15.2 [numbers 2, 4–5] and consider the following questions:

1. What is the *revelation* we seek for park visitors?
2. What thoughts or actions do we hope to *provoke*?
3. What *whole* are we trying to communicate to visitors?
4. Why do we, as an agency, believe interpretation is important? What do we wish to accomplish?"

Think Exercise (NPS n.d., 12)

Identifying the universal: can you link any of your significant resources and interpretive themes to

Conflict between people or cultures
Conflict between people and natural systems
Internal conflicts within individuals with broader implications
Resolution of conflict
Nonresolution of conflict
Consequences of action
Consequences of in-action
Commitment to universals
   Courage
   Politics
   Religion
   Race
   Violence
   Family
   Sacrifice
   Love
   Hate
Other universal conditions you may suggest

Appendix 15.1: Online Resources from the National Park Service

NPS Interpretive Development Program Website. www.nps.gov/idp/interp/index.htm. See particularly "Effective Interpretation of Archeological Resources: The Archeology-Interpreter Shared Competency Course of Study" www.nps.gov/idp/interp/440/module.htm. Supporting materials are available at the Archeology and Ethnography Program's distance learning website: www.cr.nps.gov/aad/tools/distlearn.htm.

National Park Service Museum Management Program. *2001 Museum Handbook*, pt. 3, chap. 7, "Using Museum Collections in Exhibits." www.cr.nps.gov/museum/publications/handbook.html.

National Park Service Harpers Ferry Center Interpretive Media Institute. 2001. "Criteria for Selecting Exhibit Topics and Themes." www.nps.gov/hfc/pdf/imi/exhibit_topics.pdf.

———. 2001. "Criteria for Evaluating Exhibit Concepts." www.nps.gov/hfc/pdf/imi/exhibit_concepts.pdf.

National Park Service Harpers Ferry Center. 2001. "Media Design Standards: A Checklist for Evaluating the Effectiveness of Interpretive Media" (by Betsy Ehrlich). www.nps.gov/hfc/pdf/imi/design_standards_checklist.pdf.

Thomson, Ron, and Marilyn Harper. 2000. *Telling the Stories: Planning Effective Interpretive Programs for Properties Listed in the National Register of Historic Places*. National Park Service. National Register of Historic Places. National Register Bulletin. www.cr.nps.gov/nr/publications/bulletins/interp.

Acknowledgments

Many thanks to the editors of this volume for inviting me to contribute, thus forcing me to organize my thoughts and observations in a hopefully useful way. Thanks as well to Paul Shackel for his helpful comments. The opinions expressed here are those of the author and do not necessarily reflect any official position of the National Park Service.

References

Allen, Mitch. 2002. "Reaching the Hidden Audience: Ten Rules for the Archaeological Writer." In *Public Benefits of Archaeology*, edited by Barbara J. Little, 244–51. Gainesville: University Press of Florida.

Basman, Cem M. 1997. "On Defining Professionalism." *Legacy* 8(6). www.interpnet.com/interpnet/issues/defin_prof.htm. Accessed June 17, 2003.

Blodgett, Sarah D. 2000. "A Certifiable Improvement." *Legacy* 11(4). www.interpnet.com/interpnet/issues/certifiable.htm. Accessed June 17, 2003.

Derry, Linda, and Maureen Malloy, eds. 2003. *Archaeologists and Local Communities: Partners in Exploring the Past*. Washington, D.C.: Society for American Archaeology.

Diamant, Rolf. 2000. "From Management to Stewardship: The Making and Remaking of the U.S. National Park System." *George Wright Forum* 17(2): 31–45.

Dochterman, Robyn. 2002. "Freeman Tilden: The Writer-Wanderer Who Showed Us the Way." *Legacy* 13(3): 16–25.

Green, James. 2000. *Taking History to Heart: The Power of the Past in Building Social Movements.* Amherst: University of Massachusetts Press.

Hembrey, Heather A. E. 2001. "Hooks, Layers, and Other Techniques to Help Archaeologists Design Effective Websites." *SAA Archaeological Record,* September, 29–31.

Jameson, J. H., Jr., ed. 1997. *Presenting Archaeology to the Public: Digging for Truths.* Walnut Creek, Calif.: AltaMira Press.

LaPage, Will. 1998. "The Power of Professionalism." *Legacy* 9(3). www.interpnet.com/interpnet/issues/power_profession.htm. Accessed June 17, 2003.

Leone, Mark P., Parker B. Potter, Jr., and Paul A. Shackel. 1987. "Toward a Critical Archaeology." *Current Anthropology* 28(3): 283–302.

Little, Barbara J. 2000. "Compelling Images through Storytelling: Comment on Imaginary, But by No Means Unimaginable: Storytelling, Science, and Historical Archaeology." *Historical Archaeology* 34(2): 10–13.

Little, Barbara J., ed. 2002. *The Public Benefits of Archaeology.* Gainesville: University Press of Florida.

Mackintosh, Barry. 1986. *Interpretation in the National Park Service: A Historical Perspective.* Washington, D.C.: National Park Service, History Division. www.cr.nps.gov/history/online_books/mackintosh2. Accessed June 17, 2003.

Mathis, Mark. 2002. *Feeding the Media Beast: An Easy Recipe for Great Publicity.* West Lafayette, Ind.: Purdue University Press.

McManamon, Francis P. 1991. "The Many Publics for Archaeology." *American Antiquity* 56(1): 121–30.

Morrell, David. 2002. *Lessons from a Lifetime of Writing: A Novelist Looks at His Craft.* Cincinnati: Writers Digest Books.

National Park Service. n.d. *Achieving Excellence in Interpretation: Compelling Stories.* Washington, D.C.: Division of Interpretation.

———. 1937. *Glimpses of Historical Areas East of the Mississippi River Administered by the National Park Service.* Washington, D.C.: Government Printing Office. www.cr.nps.gov/history/online_books/glimpses3/index.htm. Accessed June 17, 2003.

———. 1996. *Revised Thematic Framework.* Washington, D.C.: NPS History Division. www.cr.nps.gov/history/hisnps/NPSThinking/revthem.htm. Accessed June 17, 2003.

———. 2000. *Jamestown Long-Range Interpretive Plan.* On file at Colonial National Historical Park, Jamestown, Virginia.

———. 2001a. *Management Policies.* Washington, D.C. www.nps.gov/policy/mp/policies.pdf. Accessed June 17, 2003.

———. 2001b. *National Park Service Community Report.* Washington, D.C. www.nps.gov/community. Accessed June 17, 2003.

Potter, Parker B., Jr. 1994. *Public Archaeology in Annapolis: A Critical Approach to History in Maryland's Ancient City.* Washington, D.C.: Smithsonian Institution Press.

Praetzellis, Mary, ed. 1998. "Archaeologists as Storytellers." *Historical Archaeology* 32(1).

(SAA) Society for American Archaeology. 1990. *Save the Past for the Future: Actions for the 90s.* Washington, D.C.: Society for American Archaeology. Final Report Taos Working Conference on Preventing Archaeological Looting and Vandalism.

Shackel, Paul A., and Erve Chambers, eds. 2004. *Places in Mind: Archaeology as Applied Anthropology.* New York: Routledge.

Smardz, K., and S. J. Smith, eds. 2000. *The Archaeological Education Handbook: Sharing the Past with Kids.* Walnut Creek, Calif.: AltaMira Press.

Smith, George S., and John E. Ehrenhard, eds. 1991. *Protecting the Past.* Boca Raton, Fla.: CRC Press.

Stone, Peter, and R. MacKenzie, eds. 1994. *The Excluded Past: Archaeology in Education.* London: Routledge.

Stone, Peter, and B. L. Molyneaux, eds. 1994. *The Presented Past: Heritage, Museums, and Education.* London: Routledge.

Terrell, John. 1990. "Storytelling and Prehistory." *Archaeological Method and Theory* 2:1–29. Tucson: University of Arizona Press.

Tilden, Freeman. 1951. *The National Parks: What They Mean to You and Me.* New York: Knopf.

———. [1957] 1977. *Interpreting Our Heritage.* 3d ed. Chapel Hill: University of North Carolina Press.

———. 1986. *The National Parks: The Classic Book on the National Parks, National Monuments, and Historic Sites.* New York: Knopf. Revised and updated edition of Tilden's 1951 volume.

Engaging with Heritage Issues: The Role of the World Archaeological Congress

16

JOAN M. GERO

SINCE THE IMMEDIATE OBJECTS of archaeological study are not human beings—but rather material remains—archaeology has been thought, by its practitioners and by others, to lack a critical perspective in the modern world. Archaeology is perceived as a curiously apolitical, "head-in-the-sand" endeavor with little relevance to contemporary social and political life. In this chapter I argue that archaeology has undertaken its own critical trajectory parallel to the critical perspectives that have developed in other areas of anthropology, and that this perspective motivates and is most visible in the World Archaeological Congress.

From the start, archaeology developed out of parallel industrial and capitalist roots as anthropology, in North America and elsewhere. In the second half of the 1800s, archaeology emerged from the very same sand pits and limestone quarries, railroad beds, and factory foundations that displaced anthropology's first objects of study: "primitive" human groups. Archaeology's twentieth-century development has also, like anthropology, witnessed an increasingly exclusionary trajectory of professionalization, representing ever less diversity in the voices that speak for the past, an increased sidelining of the descendant groups whose ancestors and antecedents are of interest to archaeologists, and a greater convergence on single interpretative stances.

At the same time, the international arrangements of archaeology have allowed, encouraged, and even ensured the dominant nations exclusive rights to mine the pasts of poorer and less influential countries and, of course, to tell the stories of these nations in generalized, rationalized, scientized terms. Many of the oldest and most splendid sites are located in the poorest countries in the world and are considered "world patrimony." They are studied and reconstructed in nonnative languages and nonnative imaginations, put forward as repositories of knowledge about MAN (in genderal), while access to knowledge about these sites is controlled—at least in part—by the agendas, funding agencies, and cultural institutions of hegemonic regions such as the United States and western Europe . . . locking out other interpretive voices. In fact, the modern global distribution of archaeological research maps global power. Archaeology underwrites, reasserts, and reinforces the present-day world order, and it is little wonder that many First Nations people on this continent, as well as indigenous peoples on other continents, feel little affinity for the goals and methods of archaeology.

Meanwhile, it has been commonplace for practicing archaeologists in industrialized centers to oppose the unseemly "insertion" of politics into archaeology. Self-approving, normative, unself-reflective, the archaeological community often employs research models that distance it from knowledge production and erase context, including the very perspective that defines the relationship between subjects and objects. Thus archaeologists can maintain that archaeology has nothing to do with politics, politics should be left out of archaeology, and archaeology pursues facts about the past. Yet archaeological organizations retain heavy lobbying contingents in political centers and involve few minorities and indigenous voices in interpretations of the past. The cover of an issue of the *Society for American Archaeology Bulletin* featured a photo of the executive head of SAA standing with Bruce Babbitt, one-time secretary of the U.S. Department of the Interior! The politics of the past may be invisible to those whose day-to-day lives revolve around them, but they form the very foundation for unequal access to resources, as well as unequal awareness of, and control over, one's heritage.

Formation of the World Archaeological Congress

An international forum for archaeological research was first organized in 1931 with the founding of the International Union of Pre- and Proto-Historic Sciences (IUPPS). The practice of archaeology was largely restricted (at the time) to Europe and to other small pockets of the developed world, and the IUPPS was— and continued to be—run by and for Western European intellectuals. All but one of its conferences has been held in a major European city, and they are organized around European perceptions of worldwide archaeology; Europeans dominate its policy-making bodies. Although the IUPPS was the only organization with an international responsibility for archaeology, other organizations like the Pan-African Congress and the International Congress of Americanists arose with time to compensate for the IUPPS geographic bias.

It is not surprising, then, that IUPPS planned its Eleventh International Congress for Southhampton, United Kingdom, to take place in September 1986. But it was quite a sensation when the local labor-dominated city government of Southampton announced, late in 1985, that it would withhold promised financial support for IUPPS unless the IUPPS disallowed South African and Namibian delegates to participate. Against a backdrop of growing violence in South Africa, and in light of the U.N. cultural and academic bans against Botha's apartheid regime, local Southampton conference organizers upheld the city's decision to ban South African participants from the event. They argued that the entire conference would collapse financially if they didn't go along with the city ruling. Also, they insisted, this was a moral issue, and it was time for archaeology to recognize its potential for contributing to change in the present. IUPPS responded with outrage, framing the issue in terms of academic freedom: "the conference had to be open to all bona fide archaeologists and related scientists with no distinction of race, country or philosophical persuasion" (Clark 1989, 214). The Society for American Archaeology executive committee issued a December 1985 statement to all its members that "the SAA upheld, and will continue to uphold, the principles of freedom of research and the freedom of scholars from all nations to meet and exchange ideas" (cited in Hodder 1986, 113–14).

In January 1986, after negotiations had made it clear that no middle ground would be accepted, the IUPPS secretary-general and its international executive committee met in Paris and disavowed the Southampton conference. Most of the IUPPS British Committee resigned further involvement in the congress, and the media had a heyday. Outraged headlines (not only in *Science* and the *Times Literary Supplement* but also in *Newsweek*) pitched the battle between academic freedom and the free practice of science on one hand, and apartheid politics on the other. All but a handful of North American archaeologists withdrew papers and canceled their participation, but there was a flood of support from the Eastern European bloc, Africa, India, and South America.

The North American boycott of the Southampton conference cannot be seen as a simple litmus test of righteous positions. Some North Americans who defied the boycott and went to Southampton were substantially ignorant of the events that had transpired between the city of Southampton and IUPPS, or they were aware but figured that it just didn't matter that much one way or the other . . . while other North Americans attended precisely because they embraced the strong-minded political agenda represented by the Southampton City Council. By the same token, reasons for *not* attending WAC-1 ranged widely, including an informed indignation on the part of some North American archaeologists who had worked in South Africa and recognized that their excluded South African colleagues were among the most active and vociferous opponents to the apartheid regime. Other North Americans pointed to allegedly arbitrary and inconsistent criteria in banning South Africans but not participants from other countries whose politics were also thought abhorrent. Others said that banning archaeologists, as opposed to athletes, simply lacked the clout to make this a meaningful action. Anger, rancor, confusion, and dismay were all apparent.

Still, the national secretary of the Congress, Peter Ucko, insisted on moving ahead with a newly reorganized meeting under the name the World Archaeological Congress (WAC), no longer linked with the IUPPS. From its inception, WAC emphasized its differences from its antecedent institution. It insisted on recognizing that science, far from being politically neutral, constitutes a value system linked to dominant social interests, and the idea of science "being open to all" is ultimately a belief about the way the world should be, rather than how it is. WAC made clear statements that the discipline of archaeology had long served state interests in shoring up nationalist identities and asserting territorial domains. At the same time, WAC put itself forward as a forum not merely for professional archaeologists and allied scientists, but for everyone interested in the past, with native people from underdeveloped countries specifically encouraged to attend, their travel supported by high registration fees from those who could afford it. (A particularly controversial action taken by WAC was to retain the registration fees of withdrawn attendees, specifically to fund attendance by people who could otherwise not afford to come.)

Since 1986, WAC has constituted itself as a uniquely representative nonprofit organization of worldwide archaeology that recognizes the historical and social role, as well as the political context, of archaeology, and the need to make archaeological studies relevant to the wider community. It especially seeks to debate and refute institutionalized views that serve the interests of a privileged few to the detriment of disenfranchised others. WAC explicitly values diversity against institutionalized mechanisms that marginalize the cultural heritage of indigenous peoples, minorities, and the poor.

A central function of WAC is to hold a major international conference every four years—in 1990 in Barquisimeto, Venezuela; in 1994 in New Delhi, India; and—coming full circle from the first divisive congress—in 1999 in Cape Town, South Africa. The fifth WAC Congress was held in Washington, D.C., in 2003. In years between major congresses, WAC has sponsored regional thematic "Inter-Congresses": in 1989 in Vermillion, South Dakota: "Archaeological ethics and the treatment of the dead"; in 1993 in Mombasa, Kenya: "Urban origins in Africa"; in 1998 in Brac, Croatia: "The destruction and restoration of cultural heritage"; in 2000 in Olavarría, Argentina: "Theory in South America"; in 2001 in New Zealand: "Indigenous issues and archaeology"; and in 2001 in Curaçao in the Caribbean: "African Diaspora."

The agenda of the World Archaeological Congress continues to grow. Working without any permanent funds and with no full-time staff, WAC solicits funds on a project-to-project basis. Since WAC was conceived in part because many less advantaged colleagues, indigenous caretakers of sites, and concerned groups from around the world were being excluded from international debate, for either personal or institutional/financial reasons, WAC has funded approximately one-third of the attendance at the major conferences out of solicited funds and other inscription fees. It has supported the training of colleagues from less developed parts of the world with tutorial programs and museum training. Resolutions passed by the WAC executive draw attention to local archaeological communities trying to protect archaeological sites, or indigenous groups protecting sacred sites from industrial encroachment or tourism development. WAC was recently approached by the World Commission on Dams (WCD) to create a panel of experts for collaboration, working toward the WCD Year 2000 Report regarding the effect of dams and reservoirs on different cultural heritage sites around the world. WAC is working on resolutions to address issues of tourism, heritage, and illicit traffic in prehistoric artifacts. WAC communications include its newsletters and the World Archaeological bulletins, as well as the fifty-volume list in the One World Archeology series, published by Routledge and based on the proceedings of the first four World Archaeological Congresses, which yield royalties to help representatives attend congresses. In addition, a recently launched journal called *Public Archaeology* has its editorial board composed almost entirely of past WAC executive officers.

Whither WAC? What Comes Out of Having More Voices?

The World Archaeological Congress was founded with the primary goal of bringing together a plurality and democracy of viewpoints about the human past. WAC represents the only fully international forum of practicing archaeologists; it meets in order to promote the exchange of information about archaeological research across national and theoretical and political and wealth divides. WAC's other explicit aims are

- to encourage professional training and public education for disadvantaged nations, groups, and communities
- to empower and contribute to the betterment of indigenous groups and First Nations peoples
- to contribute to the conservation of heritage sites, sacred sites, and endangered archaeological resources that are threatened by looting, vandalism, urban growth, tourism, development, or war

The emergence of WAC has established and legitimated, and in turn been supported and legitimated by, a new kind of archaeology—or archaeologies—sometimes called "value-committed archaeologies" (Preucel and Hodder 1996, 526–27) or what I have termed engaged archaeology. The call for the reconstitution of archaeology in terms of value commitment emerged immediately after the first WAC conference (Shanks and Tilley 1987), and since that time, value-committed archaeology has taken many forms. All share an admission that archaeology carries in it a source of empowerment, not only in the generalized sense, as a means of knowledge production about the past, but more specifically as a means to grant time depth and legitimation to individuals, groups, or nations.

This turn toward admitting values in archaeology—the acceptance that political commitment and ethical judgment *count* in archaeology and constitute an important *focus* of inquiry—these programs carry serious consequences. Epistemic implications include—and we have started to see—an abandoning of the rationalized, disembodied, homogenizing systems of knowledge that archaeology has regularly imposed onto the intimate living traditions of ancestors and sacredness, meaningful history, and oral stories of peoples on the margins of state-level societies. Pluralistic perspectives, multiple voices, divergent interpretations can be accommodated, and the once hierarchical voice of the project director can, will, and is learning to lay out newly complex, interactive, and parallel courses of investigation at single sites.

At the same time, indigenous and non-Western groups are being encouraged and sometimes required to participate from their own perspectives rather than being spoken for through a paternalistic or universalistic science (Preucel and Hodder 1996, 527). In the United States, the Native American Graves Protection and Repatriation Act (NAGPRA) has forced American Indian groups to engage with archaeologists, learn federal process, and perform "legalese" speech acts to repossess the skeletal remains and sacred objects of ancient burials. But interaction is taking place, accords are being struck, and native voices are empowered to be involved in archaeological research. Community-based archaeology projects incorporate local knowledge, history, education, and work schedules into research agendas. Indeed, the very objectives of archaeological research are now being set by local communities, as value-committed archaeologists put themselves at the service of endangered ethnic minorities.

Thus WAC maintains a primary commitment to be inclusive, and its congresses have enjoyed the participation of up to sixty-seven different nations, rich and poor, hegemonic and underdeveloped, in dialog with one another. Not only do delegates come from different continents and nations but they represent different positions in relation to capital consolidations and heritage professionals. They also bring startling different assumptions and perspectives about heritage: one archaeologist's "cultural resource" to be rationally managed is another archaeologist's "sacred dreaming place" to be kept secret at all costs. The isolation of curated artifacts in perfectly balanced, temperature- and humidity-controlled environments for optimal storage and preservation may be discussed at WAC congresses, but it will be in contrast to another ideal: a respectful and spirit-preserving environment where venerated objects must be ritually handled with appropriate incantations (and sometimes smoke) to renew them at regular intervals. Rather than converge and recommend—or impose—single practices on all communities that strive for "heritage," WAC seeks to recognize and support different systems of meaning that underlie the preservation of historical and social significance.

WAC Values Multivocality

Honoring some heritages over others and managing the terms in which heritage will be honored in the end perpetuates an unequal access to the past, as well as an unequal awareness of, and control over, one's heritage. But WAC's consistent rejection to privileging a single dominant interpretive ideology is more than "merely" a political stance, although it is that. The narrowing and generalizing of interpretations also suggests that a cultural past once existed that was a monolithic, noncontested, and homogeneous set of understandings and ideas, a reified idea of culture, that is inconsistent with many views of how people actually experience social life. We suspect that modern conflicts over whose heritage is to dominate, and the constant reordering of monuments to be restored and rededicated in the public memory, are not restricted to contemporary times. Rather, the competition for the inscribing of historic meanings is a regular feature of cultural life, and it is rare for multiple, sometimes competitive, discourses to be simultaneously honored. Yet at WAC multivocality is valued and welcomed because it is the fabric of the social experience that archaeologists are appointed to reconstruct and convey.

The World Archaeological Congress anticipates that this multivocality is the archaeology of the future. The discipline of archaeology is no longer the exclusive province of white European upper-class men, and there is no going back to a pre-WAC era of exclusionary, hierarchical, and scientized knowledge that marginalizes the voices from the peripheries. The question of "who controls the past?" is no longer a conundrum because it must be generally conceded that there are many pasts and they will be known differently from many views.

Although the WAC forum provides an excellent opportunity to forefront issues and craft policy against the exploitation of heritage sites, sacred landscapes, and endangered archaeological materials, at the same time WAC's potentially powerful position is mitigated against by the very plurality of its constituency: for every voice there is a counter-voice, and past examples of political positions applied in the context of WAC actions have proven predictably divisive. Indeed, this is the virtue and the plague of valuing many perspectives.

References

Clark, J. D. 1989. Review of Ucko's "Academic Freedom and Apartheid." *American Antiquity* 54: 213–16.

Hodder, Ian. 1986. "Politics and Ideology in the World Archaeological Congress, 1986." *Archaeological Review from Cambridge* 5: 113–19.

Preucel, Robert, and Ian Hodder. 1996. "Representations and Anti-representations." In *Contemporary Archaeology in Theory,* edited by Robert Preucel and Ian Hodder, 519–30. London: Blackwell.

Shanks, Michael, and Christopher Tilley. 1987. *Reconstructing Archaeology.* Cambridge: Cambridge University Press.

Making the Past Profitable in an Age of Globalization and National Ownership: Contradictions and Considerations

17

PHILIP L. KOHL

ARCHAEOLOGISTS TODAY ARE INCREASINGLY aware of the political and eco-nomic implications of their work. The chapters presented in this volume exemplify this self-awareness and implicitly or explicitly recognize the growing economic force of tourism throughout the world. Most of the chapters are not so concerned with what archaeologists directly do, but with how archaeo-logical sites and materials are marketed, how the past is commodified for financial gain either on the part of private entrepreneurs and/or, more typically, states that have become dependent on tourism. The phenomenon itself is not new, but, as Baram and Rowan convincingly argue, the scale at which it occurs and its eco-nomic consequences are profoundly more significant in an age of increasing glob-alization, including relatively easy travel to exotic sites. Archaeologists almost inevitably become embroiled in this qualitatively distinct form of marketing her-itage and, as such, they have every right to study it.

Nor is there any question that they will continue to do so. This volume con-stitutes one of the first systematic efforts to analyze this new global marketing of the past; it will not be the last. A subfield of inquiry is defining itself that ad-dresses a series of questions manifest in the chapters collected here: Who owns the past? Whose past is included, whose excluded in representations of the past? Who benefits from and who may be adversely affected by archaeological tourism? What constitutes "authentic" portrayals of the past or, perhaps more profoundly, is "au-thenticity" a desirable and realizable goal? If so, how does one achieve it? Is there something inherently wrong or morally suspect with profiting from the past? If not, why or how should one be critical of its commodification? Reading this rich, diverse collection of articles leads to the realization that the answers to these ques-tions are not always—one is even tempted to say typically—straightforward.

There are several claimants to those Parthenon Marbles, as there are to Priam's Treasure and numerous contested archaeological remains. Ethnic, national, and world claims do not often coincide, and state borders, which are themselves impermanent, never perfectly delimit one nation's past from another's.

These brief comments will consider some of these questions in relation to specific examples presented here, and they will attempt to explore some of the contradictions and ambiguities that emerge in answering them. First, however, a question of methods must be addressed. If a new subfield of scholarship concerned with marketing heritage is defining itself, then that study must develop rigorous standards for conducting its research. This same issue arises for any new field of inquiry, including, I would argue, archaeology's multifaceted relationship with nationalism and nationalist politics. What constitutes solid fieldwork and convincing documentation and what is more superficial? Participant observation clearly represents one viable approach, as many of the articles here relate the experiences of the contributors' participation on tourist excursions from Stonehenge and Newgrange to Zippori and the Holy Land Experience in Orlando, Florida. But how often should one visit? How representative is a specific tour guide's presentation? Does one always recognize the unusually effective or, conversely, hapless park ranger interpreting America's heritage? Undoubtedly, innovative, highly specific methods will be forged, as nicely illustrated here by E. Addison's attention to the quality of roads and road signs in Jordan that privilege non-Islamic over Islamic remains. How does one evaluate the publications of national departments of tourism or explicitly international journals and media, such as *Mundo Maya* and *Archaeology?* What sources are available or should one consult to assess the economic significance of tourism? Presumably, such sources, including even their availability, differ from one country to another. The point is not to criticize any specific study but to insist that new fields of scholarly inquiry must recognize the need for establishing procedures and criteria for doing their work and set and abide by them.

The chapters collected here address diverse, albeit related, issues. Let us turn first to the question of authenticity: something to strive for in one's reconstruction of the past or an elusive, unattainable will-of-the-wisp? The quest for authenticity (and/or its total absence) can assume ludicrous, even perversely humorous dimensions, as is seen here in the attempts to dirty the streets of Colonial Williamsburg or to simulate the Holy Land in Orlando, Florida, a park not coincidentally proximate to the equally make-believe world of Walt Disney. A closely related issue concerns multivocality, or multiple versions and interpretations of a given past. Are these always desirable, as J. Gero insists, or should one exercise some caution as to which competing versions are acceptable and which are not? If the latter, what are the criteria for acceptance or rejection? And how does "authenticity" or its absence relate to these multiple perspectives on the past?

One of the fascinations with the Holy Land Experience in Orlando is its total lack of authenticity. Presumably, the vast majority of visitors know that they are not experiencing the real Holy Land and are not at all bothered by it. As Y. Rowan makes clear, many visitors not only enjoy the vicarious, constructed experience, but find it spiritually edifying as well. Why not let them spend their dollars to enrich their souls? There is a reason for dismay, I believe. Only one peculiarly Protestant vision of the Holy Land is presented; the ongoing conflict, contested terrain, and even the smells of contemporary Jerusalem are excluded in this highly selected and sanitized experience. Ultimately, I find objectionable the way visitors are politically manipulated by the creators of this theme park. Lack of authenticity is dangerous in this instance in that it plays into and fosters the hardly tolerant beliefs of Christian fundamentalism, now a potent and dangerous force in American politics.

How about deliberately dirtying those streets of reconstructed eighteenth-century Williamsburg for the sake of being more authentic? Gable and Handler object to "primitivizing the past" and creating a history of Williamsburg that is comfortable, not critical. It has been years since I visited Williamsburg, and my vague recollection is that I experienced the earlier hygienic version. For this reason perhaps I feel some sympathy for the planners who have tried to revivify the smells, sounds, and shit of the colonial experience. Undoubtedly they could do a better job, including possibly presenting more perspectives and voices on this experience. A too critical perspective, however, seems unfair; the planners are sort of damned if they try or damned if they don't. The quest for authenticity is not the problem, but rather its simplification.

The state-of-the-art Mashantucket Pequot Museum and Research Center near Mystic, Connecticut (lavishly financed by casino earnings), deliberately tries to juxtapose indigenous Pequot perspectives alongside "scientific" archaeological reconstructions; there is at least one exhibit that highlights alternative and equally plausible interpretations of the same archaeological evidence. These multiple windows on the Pequot past unquestionably enrich visitors' appreciation of prehistoric and early historic life in northeastern Connecticut. Should multiple perspectives always be encouraged or should some be resisted? How and who decides the latter? J. Gero's assessment strikes me as too inclusive and unqualified. Some voices need not be heard because they are simply so preposterous. There must be some degree of plausibility and/or cultural meaning (a trickier issue) for a perspective to be presented or accorded credibility with an exhibit. Giving equal time to every group just does not make sense. More seriously, some perspectives or "readings" of the past are simply dangerous and should be contested. Some archaeologists interpret Late Bronze fortified sites in the trans-Ural region of southern Russia as evidence for the homeland of the Aryans; such an interpretation is not equivalent to viewing

Stonehenge as a place to celebrate Druidic ceremonies. The latter is innocuous; the former—given the rise of neo-Nazi nationalist movements in contemporary Russia—is not.

J. Golden addresses a similar point when he discusses what archaeologists should do when confronted with dangerously contested visions of the past. Archaeologists could unequivocally document that the Nablus tomb is neither what the Israeli settlers nor the Palestinians claim. It is good to debunk scientifically the Shroud of Turin, but it would be much better—given the political violence that envelops life in Nablus—to disprove the biblical origins of Joseph's Tomb. I also agree with his general recommendation for archaeologists to document the impermanence of the past and to stress that many different peoples at different times have occupied the same region. It is necessary to add, however, that archaeological discoveries and political agendas or policies can and should be disassociated from one another. It is not unimportant that a Hindu temple was not found beneath the Babri Masjid, but, even if such a temple had been found, it would not justify the destruction of the mosque. It is also true that one needs to understand empathetically irrational acts of destruction, such as the demolition of the Buddhas at Bamiyan, but one can do this at the same time as one condemns the destruction of this unique site of world historical significance. Yes, the appalling poverty and even in some cases the starvation of Afghan peoples are more pressing and deserving of condemnation than the destruction of these statues. That admitted, one still should condemn the horrible state decision to destroy an invaluable part of its own national heritage.

The very fact that the world did nothing to stop the Taliban from executing its iconoclastic fury symbolically underscores the fact that we still live in a world of nation-states and that nearly always nations are allowed to do what they want with the remains found within their borders. The articles collected here eloquently illustrate the transnational forces of consumption and marketing that may override narrowly defined national concerns. Increasing globalization is an undeniable fact of life in the twenty-first century, but it is premature to view this commercialization of the past as overtaking or rendering obsolete states' manipulation of the past for nationalist purposes. Both phenomena exist and complement each other; neither is opposed to or replaces the other. Thus all the international conventions for protecting cultural property, which are so nicely summarized by B. Magness-Gardiner, are predicated on agreements among or between nation-states. Even the mighty United States can only impose import restrictions on materials coming from individual countries with which it has reached a special agreement. T. Arden shows clearly how the marketing of Maya remains, which are distributed across several states, is an international business, reaping profits for all engaged in it, save the Maya themselves. Yet she too writes that "all the countries of the Maya area maintain national control of archaeological properties" and that "almost all of the advertisements have a nationalistic aspect." The highly productive and sensitively structured Lower Mekong Archaeological Project (LOMAP) still seeks the "cradle of Khmer civilization" safely within the borders of Cambodia, despite the obvious reality that these remains extend over the border into neighboring Vietnam. Apparently it is still too early to build an international project in Southeast Asia that would unite the search for prehistoric and early historic archaeological materials that inconveniently, though quite typically, are distributed beyond the borders of individual states.

Has the practice of archaeology in Israel become less nationalistic and more attuned to global market interests as the state strives to profit from the lucrative and very large business of archaeological tourism? Or has the national archaeological discourse simply become more inclusive to incorporate beautiful Roman and Byzantine, though not yet Ottoman and Palestinian, remains? J. Bauman begins his striking and, to me at least, depressing and sobering study of the creation of the Israeli National Park at Zippori/Sepphoris by citing the Israeli minister of tourism: "Beyond its economic value as a tool for regional development, tourism is also an effective and direct means of explaining Israel's affairs." Such candor acknowledges both the growing economic *and* continuing political importance of tourism for the Israeli state. The former does not replace the latter, but each feeds on and reinforces the other. The incredible profitability of tourism in Israel, which is cited by Bauman as reaching its apogee of $4.3 billion in 2000, is clearly tied to political events, this high-water mark being reached prior to the outbreak of the second intifada at the end of September 2000. Such a linkage, of course, is not unique to Israel, but true worldwide. I remember once making the mistake of trying to organize a tourist excursion to visit archaeological sites in Armenia and Georgia in the early 1990s, when the Armenians were fighting the Azeris over Nagorno-Karabagh and the Georgians were descending into the chaos of a very crippling civil war. There were no takers. Political realities also condition how inclusive or exclusive the practice of archaeology or the discourse concerning archaeological remains will be. I would imagine that there is no official movement today to acknowledge the remains of the Palestinian village of Saffouriye into this national park.

Assuming that we do not descend into a world war or world recession, tourism will continue to grow exponentially, even after September 11 and the continuous threat of global terrorism. Hence the enduring value of the studies collected in this volume. How do we as archaeologists assess the incredibly important and ever increasing economic force of tourism? With disdain, envy, or some other reaction based on our superior knowledge and authority? Are tourists to be dismissed as "alienated people seeking authenticity" or is that too cynical a view? Personally, when I visit a new place, which I always like to do, I do so quite consciously as a tourist, having done my homework by reading the requisite guidebooks, learning the essential foreign phrases, and snapping innumerable photos of places I have never seen before. I do not feel alienated or inferior by so doing, but rather believe I am continuing to educate myself by having these firsthand experiences. Many chapters, such as T. Arden's revealing study of the marketing of things Mayan, make the very important point that often the people who benefit economically from tourism are not the descendants of the people whose remains are visited. Does this have to be the case? Or to put it more crudely, is there anything inherently wrong or morally suspect about making a profit from guiding tourists around archaeological sites?

A similar question is raised at the end of J. James's convincing analysis of the contradictions inherent in the search to recover "authentic" German heritage: "All of this does not mean that restoring landmarks and celebrating heritage are necessarily pernicious activities." Such activities, which need not be intrinsically suspect or terrible, nevertheless should be critically scrutinized in terms of what or whom they include and exclude. In this fascinating case, the quest to preserve the romantically imagined unspoiled German remains from the former GDR is potentially at odds with the official rhetoric of the newly united German nation, whose citizens are supposedly united by civic, not ethnic, principles.

Let me conclude these remarks by turning once again to the sad example of Afghanistan—a desperately poor and still quite lawless multiethnic country. If one accepts—as I do—that Afghanistan should continue to exist—as it has for over 250 years—as a political entity or state, then it needs to foster a common national identity and to develop economically in a way that promotes internal order and union. The development of its national archaeology and the promotion of archaeological tourism have important roles to play in this process. If feasible, I would even favor the construction of two new colossal Buddha statues at Bamiyan. Such statues should resemble as faithfully as possible the destroyed originals, but they would necessarily be inauthentic, not the real thing. So be it. If correctly done, they would still be built in their proper setting tucked away against the cliff faces of that fabulously beautiful valley in the central Hindu Kush where they were first carved. The state should benefit from their construction, but so should the much maligned and discriminated against Hazara villagers who continue to reside in that valley. Decent roads would have to be built to bring intrepid tourists to these monuments, but they existed before and can be built again. Everyone benefits. No losers, just winners.

The picture I am envisioning, of course, is idyllic, a best-case scenario unlikely to emerge in the immediate future as Afghanistan once more drops off the world's media radar screen. But I hope it happens, and the point I am trying to make here is that "marketing heritage" is not necessarily a suspect activity. The context and the manner in which it is pursued are all-important. Yorke Rowan and Uzi Baram deserve great credit for this pioneering collection of articles devoted to a theme of such mushrooming economic and political significance.

Index

Page numbers set in *italics* refer to figures.

About the Contributors

Erin Addison earned her Ph.D. at UC Santa Barbara studying the apocalyptic literature and social movements in the Hellenistic world. During eight years of teaching her research shifted from textual to material culture, and in 1994 she began moving her work to Jordan. From 1998 to 2002 Addison codirected the Qastal Conservation and Development Project at Qastal, Jordan. She is presently an MLA candidate at the School of Landscape Architecture, University of Arizona, Tucson, where she studies xeriscape design. Her current research focuses on monumental public landscapes as emblems of cultural and political identity.

Traci Ardren is assistant professor of anthropology at the University of Miami. She recently completed five years as codirector of the Pakbeh Regional Economy Program, an archaeological project centered at the ancient Maya trading city of Chunchucmil, Yucatán, Mexico. In addition to writing about descendant communities and archaeological ethics, she has researched gender, iconography, architecture, and other forms of symbolic representation in the ancient world.

Uzi Baram is an associate professor of anthropology at New College of Florida. His research interests focus on the period that the Ottoman Empire ruled over Palestine. Among his publications, Baram is coeditor of *A Historical Archaeology of the Ottoman Empire: Breaking New Ground* (2000). While Ottoman remains are visible throughout the eastern Mediterranean, they are either ignored or mislabeled; the silencing of the Ottoman period propelled his concern for the presentations of the past.

Joel Bauman, after receiving a BA from the University of Denver, worked for the National Park Service at Glen Canyon and on Ellis Island. Bauman received an MA in anthropology from the New School for Social Research and began his studies of Zippori as a doctoral student. His work was funded by the Lady Davis Foundation at the Hebrew University of Jerusalem and by the National Foundation for Jewish Culture while a visiting doctoral student at Haifa University. Bauman has served as assistant director of the Jewish National Fund Overseas Education Programs and currently serves as dean of admissions and financial aid at New College of Florida.

Kelli Ann Costa received her Ph.D. from the University of Massachusetts in 1998. Much of her work has taken place in Europe, particularly Austria and Ireland. This chapter represents the beginning of her research in Ireland on the marketing and management of ancient "tourism appropriate" sites. Questions that she finds most compelling regarding these ideas concern the creation of tourist landscapes and the archaeological imagination. Her recently published work includes *The Brokered Image* (2001). She is editor of the *Journal of the Society for the Anthropology of Europe* and coeditor (with Robert Paynter) of the forthcoming *Anthropology Comes All the Way Home: Papers in Honor of John W. Cole*. She teaches in the Anthropology Department at Franklin Pierce College in Rindge, New Hampshire.

Eric Gable teaches at Mary Washington College. In addition to studying the production and consumption of public history in the United States, he has done anthropological research on political and religious change in rural Guinea-Bissau and in upland Sulawesi. He is the author, with Richard Handler, of *The New History in an Old Museum* (1997).

Amy Gazin-Schwartz began her archaeological career in Britain, working on prehistoric Roman and Norse sites. She has a particular interest in popular ideas about archaeological features, which she explored in her Ph.D. dissertation on archaeology and folklore in Scotland, as well as several articles. Currently she is beginning research on rural settlement in highland Scotland. She is assistant professor of anthropology at Assumption College, Worcester, Massachusetts.

Joan M. Gero teaches anthropology at American University in Washington, D.C. She focuses her field research on gender and power issues in prehistory, especially in the Andean regions of Argentina and Peru, and has directed excavations at early administrative centers as well as at domestic household complexes in the Andes. She writes about the origins of state-level society, feminist interpretations of prehistory, and the sociopolitics of archaeological practice, and is interested in the epistemology of archaeological knowledge, especially in Paleoindian studies. Her publications include the popular book *Engendering Archaeology: Women and Prehistory* (with Margaret Conkey). Presently Joan Gero serves as senior North American representative to the World Archaeological Congress and as academic secretary for the Fifth World Archaeological Congress (June 2003).

Jonathan Golden (Ph.D., University of Pennsylvania) teaches anthropology at Drew University and Fairleigh Dickinson University. Golden specializes in the study of both ancient and modern cultures of the Middle East. He is currently preparing two books: *Handbooks on Ancient Civilizations: Ancient Israel*, part of a reference-style series, and *Dawn of the Metal Age*, a study of early socioeconomic systems in the southern Levant. He has participated in numerous excavations in the Middle East, Europe, and the United States. Golden lives in Philadelphia and New Jersey.

P. Bion Griffin is professor of anthropology and associate dean, College of Social Sciences, University of Hawaii at Manoa. He has conducted archaeological and ethnographic research in Southeast Asia since 1972. He did research among the Agta foragers of the Philippines and managed a research program with Universitas Pattimura in Ambon, Maluku, Indonesia, in 1994. Subsequently he became codirector of the East-West Center/University of Hawaii/Royal University of Fine Arts Program in the Archaeology, Anthropology, Art History and Architecture of the Kingdom of Cambodia. In 2002–2004 he is codirector of the Naga Research Group's Eastern Cambodia Archaeological Survey.

Richard Handler is professor of anthropology at the University of Virginia. He is the author of *Nationalism and the Politics of Culture in Quebec* (1988) and, with Eric Gable, of *The New History in an Old Museum: Creating the Past at Colonial Williamsburg* (1997). He is the editor of *History of Anthropology* and is completing a book of essays on anthropology, cultural studies, and cultural criticism.

Jason James is a visiting assistant professor at Lafayette College for the academic year 2003–2004. He recently spent two years as a Mellon Fellow in the Humanities at Barnard College, where he wrote and taught on issues of commemoration, nationalism, and postsocialist Europe. He received his Ph.D. in cultural anthropology from the University of California, San Diego. His research focuses on remembrance, belonging, citizenship, and social change. The manuscript he is currently writing addresses these issues in the context of debates over heritage preservation and urban renewal a small city in Eastern Germany.

Morag Kersel is a Ph.D. research student at the University of Cambridge. She is studying the illicit trade in antiquities, collecting, and antiquities markets. She has worked extensively as an archaeologist in Israel, Jordan, Egypt, Greece, Canada, and the United States and participated in historic preservation projects, including design review, architectural survey, and preservation planning in the United States, England, and West Africa. Her ongoing research interests include cultural property protection, international issues in historic preservation, heritage tourism, and the archaeology of the Levant.

Philip L. Kohl is a professor of anthropology at Wellesley College and a Bronze Age prehistorian who has conducted fieldwork in Iran, Afghanistan, Central Asia, and the Caucasus. He has studied third-millennium B.C. patterns of exchange and interconnections throughout western Asia and is the author of *Central Asia: Palaeolithic Beginnings to the Iron Age* (1983). He coedited a volume entitled *Nationalism, Politics, and the Practice of Archaeology* (1995) and is the author of numerous articles discussing the relationship between nationalism and archaeology, including most recently a coauthored article (with J. A. Perez Gollan) on "Religion, Politics, and Prehistory: Reassessing the Lingering Legacy of Oswald Menghin," *Current Anthropology* 43, no. 4 (2002).

Barbara J. Little (Ph.D. 1987, State University of New York at Buffalo) worked extensively with the Archaeology in Annapolis project, where she was involved with the public program, giving on-site tours. She taught at George Mason University and the University of Maryland at College Park before joining the U.S. National Park Service in 1992. Among her duties in the national Archeology and Ethnography program are public outreach and education, through both the Internet (www.cr.nps.gov/aad/) and interdisciplinary training to improve the public interpretation of archaeological sites in parks. She is the editor of *Public Benefits of Archaeology* (2002) and is particularly interested in the valuation and interpretation of archaeological places.

Bonnie Magness-Gardiner (Ph.D. 1987, University of Arizona) is senior cultural property analyst at the U.S. Department of State, Bureau of Educational and Cultural Affairs. Among her duties in the cultural property office are providing research, analysis, and technical advice on cultural heritage issues to the State Department. Prior to coming to the State Department, she worked as a program officer at the Library of Congress and the National Endowment for the Humanities, and taught archaeology at Bryn Mawr College.

Yorke Rowan (Ph.D., University of Texas at Austin) is a research associate in the Department of Anthropology at the National Museum of Natural History, Smithsonian Institution, and visiting assistant professor at the University of Notre Dame (2004–2005). He has participated in field and research projects in the Middle East, Europe, and the United States. He studies the fifth to fourth millennium B.C. in the southern Levant, with particular research interests in the rise of social complexity, material culture, and prehistoric symbolic systems.

Miriam T. Stark (B.A., University of Michigan; M.A., Ph.D., University of Arizona) teaches at the University of Hawaii. She has extensive experience in Southeast Asian and North American archaeology, and has published in both regions. Her current research focuses on early state formation in the Mekong delta. Stark has codirected the Lower Mekong

Archaeological Project in southern Cambodia since 1996. This interdisciplinary project has dual goals of research and training. Cambodian students from the Royal University of Fine Arts (Phnom Penh) receive advanced field training with the project to gain skills needed to become Cambodia's future heritage management specialists.

Steve Vinson is an Egyptologist and assistant professor of ancient history at the State University of New York College at New Paltz, where he has been on the faculty since 2000. He received his Ph.D. from the Johns Hopkins University in 1995. His interests include the social and economic history of ancient Egypt, especially of the New Kingdom and Graeco-Roman periods; he has worked extensively on the Nile River shipping industry. Current interests are Egyptian literature, especially Demotic literature, and the historiography of ancient Egypt. He is the author of *Egyptian Boats and Ships* (1994) and *The Nile Boatman at Work* (1998).